Contemporary
Educational
Administration

WILLIAM G. MONAHAN

West Virginia University

HERBERT R. HENGST

The University of Oklahoma

Contemporary Educational Administration

Macmillan Publishing Co., Inc.

New York

Collier Macmillan Publishers

London

Macmillan Publishing Co., Inc.
866 Third Avenue, New York, New York 10022

Collier Macmillan Canada, Inc.

Library of Congress Cataloging in Publication Data

Monahan, William G.
  Contemporary educational administration.

  Bibliography: p.
  Includes index.
  1. School management and organization.
I. Hengst, Herbert R.   II. Title.
LB2806.M59   371.2   81-8280
ISBN 0-02-381930-8   AACR2

Printing: 1 2 3 4 5 6 7 8   Year: 2 3 4 5 6 7 8 9

DEDICATION

To the late James G. Harlow

Friend, scholar, colleague
to whom both of us owe much for
administrative example and ideals

Preface

This book was undertaken in response to discussions with many practicing school administrators who indicated their belief that an introductory text ought to include content "closer" to contemporary reality. In pursuing that aim, we became increasingly fascinated with the total environment within which schools and their executives must function in the late twentieth century and began to think more and more of that reality in terms of the idea of the *context* of administration. This led us, in the final section, to some discussion of the notion of contextualism itself, and as we now view the entire work, it seems to us that contextualism has been its consistent format and pattern.

Because we have tried to remain aware of the importance of the contemporary, we really believe it would be accurate to refer to this text as a "practical" book, but not so in the familiar sense of a handbook of "do's" and "don'ts." We do believe it reflects the essential issues, concerns, and challenges that confront the administrative process, and we believe as well that it offers the basis for the knowledge requisite for potentially effective and informed execution.

The collaboration on this project brought two people together again who shared an office as young doctoral students at Michigan State University longer ago than public knowledge deserves to know nor history should politely note. Although we are different persons now, old habits of enthusiasm and the candor necessary to a cooperative endeavor, which were lessons learned then, have remained the strengths in our relationship. That is at once a tribute to our respect for each other and to that grand institution on the Red Cedar River that formed and shaped the *context* of our careers.

We have owed much to many during the period we have worked. The West Virginia Association of School Administrators was particularly helpful during early formulations of the project; Richard Phalunas, graduate student in Educational Administration at West Virginia University, was especially helpful in searching the literature in collective bargaining and other areas of statistical data; Dr. Keith Esch, Assistant Superintendent for Personnel Relations, Wichita, Kansas Schools, deserves special appreciation for his assistance with research in school personnel, which he has permitted us to incorporate. Dr. Michael Sexton, currently associated with the University of North Carolina, Fayetteville Graduate Center, provided significant contribution to Chapter 4 in its original draft. We are also indebted to a number of people who read appropriate parts of the manuscript and provided constructive suggestions; among these we offer special thanks to Dr. Thomas Gallaher, Associate Professor of Education at the University of Oklahoma, who provided useful comment on several chapters; to President Gordon Gee of West Virginia University for his critical appraisal of Chapter 4, "Education and the Judiciary"; and to Dr. Willard R. Lane, Professor of Educational Administration, University of Iowa, and a collaborator in a previous venture, for his overall critical and constructive reading of the manuscript. The judgment of our peers is always appreciated and represents the only ultimate authority in scholarship and we have depended heavily on it.

We also appreciate the permissions granted us by many publishers and corporate agencies to cite relevant material, and although we have acknowledged those contributions appropriately in the body of the text, such books as this would not be possible without the willingness to disseminate knowledge.

Finally, we express deep and sincere gratitude to Ms. Donna Moore, Secretary to the Dean, College of Human Resources and Education, at West Virginia University, and Ms. Robbie Hackler in the Center for Studies in Higher Education, University of Oklahoma, who both struggled with the copy, turned it into neatly typed pages, and surprisingly, made it all decipherable.

W. G. M.

H. R. H.

Contents

PART III
THE LEADERSHIP CONTEXT

PART I

The Educational Administration Milieu

Chapter 1

Introduction: The Environment of the Contemporary School Administrator

When all the rhetoric has fallen away, the fundamental functions of school administrators can be defined in terms of two conceptual and operational categories: leadership and management. These broad functions are intimately related, and the reasonably successful professional educational administrator must give consideration to both—probably in about equal measure.

The more enduring principles and ideals related to leadership deserve our attention primarily in terms of refinement and skills. The principles of management are more responsive to the variables of institutional equilibrium as well as to technological and sociocultural patterns as these evolve in systematic interaction. By systematic interaction, we mean simply that technological advance both generates and is frequently a consequence of responses to sociocultural phenomena. However, because social changes due to technology are more rapid than are changes in social institutions, conflicts arise.[1] And, as the social environment responds to new events and needs, institutional management experiences the challenge of adaptation.

By the 1970s, the culmination of events and conditions that arose in the 1950s and 1960s marked the beginning of a new era in educational administration. This has led irrevocably toward a decidedly different pattern of preparation not only in terms of technical competencies but also in terms of philosophy and risk and, therefore, of leadership. In the face of ongoing "visions and revisions," contemporary educational administration confronts a remarkable redefinition of its management environment.

[1]See, for example, Philip Hauser, "The Chaotic Society: Product of Social Morphological Revolution," *American Sociological Review*, Vol. 34, no. 1 (1969), 16–17.

THE MANAGEMENT ENVIRONMENT

It is with reference to this quite different environment of school administration and the postures appropriate to dealing with it that the first part of this text is aimed: the management context. And although educational leadership is influenced by the management environment, we have decided to consider the leadership issues as being more appropriate to the second half of this book. Despite the difficulties of treating *management* and *leadership* separately, we believe that it is important to characterize at the outset some critical aspects of the new environment with which any prospective contemporary school administrator must deal.

The Changed Environment of Educational Managers

Over the last ten years or so, in the field of public education, there is a striking recognition of events that have had almost revolutionary impact on the management of educational institutions. Not surprisingly, the conditions confronting school administrators in the 1970s were due largely to mandates that arose in the turbulent 1960s and that led to the cultural revolution of the 1970s. Implications for the educational administrator and for public education in general derive from the following, all of which owe their genesis to one or another of the events that came to a head between 1963 and 1969:

- Growing enthusiasm for the "open" classroom, which, by 1978, was a fading idea.
- A renewed yet different quality of emphasis on "career" education.
- A "full employment" advocacy and the Humphrey–Hawkins bill.
- The issue of escalating educational costs, run-away inflation, and the so-called taxpayers' revolt.
- The "test decline" syndrome and its consequent effects for an invigorated emphasis on basic skills.
- The "competency testing" and "3R" debate resulting in legislative mandates for secondary school graduation standards.
- Growing concern about a teacher surplus, itself the consequence of an attitude that blossomed during the 1960s concerning birth control, legalized abortion, and ideological convictions regarding an overpopulated globe. (As the 1980s began there were signs of approaching teacher shortages again.)
- The complexities associated with startling increases in violence and vandalism, terrorism, and senseless destruction of property.

- Increased litigation generally, ranging from liability to broad due process issues.
- A remarkably accelerated regulatory apparatus at both state and federal levels involving such wide-ranging concerns as

    Occupational health and safety, whether in the public or the private sector.

    Civil rights and "affirmative action," with added new emphases on rights for women and the handicapped.

    New demands for assessments of personnel in all manner of concerns.

    Stringent new directives regarding the use and conservation of energy.

- Massive problems associated with transportation related not only to school desegregation but also to simple personal movement from place to place and implications for the serious problems related to shortages of fossil fuels.
- Increasing concern about nutrition and the ever-growing popularity of "junk food."
- Striking expansion of collective bargaining by public employees not only with reference to teachers but including other sectors of public safety (e.g., fire and constabulary systems) that seemed only a few years ago to be a sacred trust.
- National concerns for welfare reform and the effects of that on school policies and procedures.
- Increased interest in and expenditures for staff development and in-service education of educational personnel.
- Continuing territorial disputes and further compartmentalization of the so-called administrative team, principals going one way, supervisors another, and central office staff still another.
- A consequent new interest and investment in conflict management and conflict resolution.
- The perennial problems of school consolidations, costs, poorly prepared teachers, loss of local control, overemphasis on athletics, equipment, tenure, "dirty books," and snow days.

However incomplete, this list does suggest at least some of the dimensions of the environment of the 1970s. Accordingly, let us examine some of these emerging issues in more detail.

CURRICULUM AND INSTRUCTIONAL ISSUES

While the problems of resource acquisition and allocation represent important administrative concerns in educational settings, the more fundamental aim of school managers is to see that resources are applied to the maintenance and improvement of instruction. Over the past ten years or so, the curriculum issues that confront all schools have continued to attract interest and study.

As a response to a variety of issues confronting secondary schools, it was proposed, by Terrel H. Bell, then commissioner of education, that a national conference be held in the spring of 1976. Attended by principals, district superintendents, state education agency chiefs, college and university personnel, federal officials, and teachers and students, some 780 persons met in Denver, Colorado for four days to consider ways in which secondary schools could best meet societal demands. Commissioner Bell began the conference by charging the participants to "dejuvenilize" the high schools.[2]

In defining that charge, a number of curricular-related conclusions emerged from the Denver conference. First, the student role clearly needed expansion; this meant that the secondary school students needed to be more responsible for and involved in the scholastic decisions that affected them. Second, there was recognition of the importance and utility of a more formal emphasis on "values education," that is, "that the 'hidden' values of a school or community be identified and examined to see if they will prepare our students to be citizens in 20th and 21st Century America."[3] Third, important aspects of curricula must focus on the particular rather than on the general, whereby, in social studies, for example, the school community is utilized as a learning laboratory.[4] Fourth, there must be greater emphasis on the arts and humanities; ". . . the school blends into an ever-expanding community, and the arts and the humanities compound into a vast segment of our culture."[5] And, fifth, there was recognition of the increased articulation between school and the "world of work," as manifested by emphasis on guidance and career opportunities, on breaking the patterns of perceived rejection and futility that characterize too many high schools, especially the predominantly black ones, and on job training and work study.

While this national conference confronted a variety of school and societal issues, the conference failed to consider the actual operational definitions of programs and activities within a typical high school curriculum that might be aimed at resolving these issues. The fundamental problem in curriculum theory has always concerned the translation of conditional knowledge into program design. That fundamental difficulty remains unchanged from the time that "curriculum" emerged as a recognized field for formal theoretical interest among educators. (It is not, therefore, dissimilar from *any* situation that requires translating theory into practice.)

[2]Terrel H. Bell, "Let's 'Dejuvenilize' Secondary Education," in *New Dimensions for Secondary Youth*, ed. John Chaffee, Jr. (Denver: U.S. Office of Education and Nat'l. Assn. of Secondary School Principals, 1976), pp. 8–10.
[3]Sheilah N. Thomas, "Values Education: Back to a Basic," in ibid., p. 39.
[4]Helen K. Masterson, "A New Approach to the Social Sciences," in ibid., p. 45.
[5]Alvin C. Eurich, "Arts and Humanities in School and Community," in ibid., p. 49.

Writing in the early 1930s, William Heard Kilpatrick laid down the basic model for curriculum reform:[6]

Our aims need to be clarified, appropriate content needs to be conceived, and the compelling reasons more firmly grasped; while all of us, including the many who hesitate, need to be surer of the road to take.

Being "surer of the road to take" is hindered by the numerous points of view that confront the curriculum designer. To be sure, the softest route is the traditional route—in large measure, precisely that kind of curriculum that Kilpatrick wanted to "remake" and that kind of curriculum that the participants in the Denver conference had in mind when they agreed to consider "new dimensions for educating youth." A point we sometimes forget, of course, is that the program of studies, together with the activities that constitute the student's scholastic life—the "curriculum," is always a temporal phenomenon and consequently requires continuous revision as the society it is designed to both reflect and advance makes always-changing demands upon it. The school (and those who are legally constituted to oversee it) struggles, within the constraints formally and routinely placed upon it, to remain as current as it can. Yet, because of these various constraints, school programming almost inevitably lags behind appropriate currency; indeed, considering the remarkable diversity of places and resource bases, value differences, traditions, and popular attitudes, no school can ever be very easily labeled as "right" in what its curriculum tries to accomplish.

For this reason, much of what comes to be known as "innovative" is really "imitative." It is also for this reason that there remains a strong similarity among curricula; in the United States, we really have a system of national public schools. This fact no longer derives from the historical bases of the early democratic conviction about the relationship of enlightened publics with enlightened government; it rests now on the highly developed professionalization of education personnel and on that profession's own subcultural values associated with the rewards of meeting together at state, regional, and national levels to discuss, debate, consider, and commit to relatively stabilized and rational courses of action.

This is not to say that there is not acute and responsive sensitivity to local sentiment or to the local adaptation of whatever is currently popular nationally; rather, our universal system of public schools has been a dramatic implement in the nationalization of the country, and that nationalized condition tends, in turn, to provide cues to the further development of school systems.

[6]William H. Kilpatrick, *Remaking the Curriculum* (New York: Newson, 1936), p. 13.

The Humanistic Movement in Curriculum

Almost from its beginnings, the American school concept has been characterized by an urge toward *humanistic* impulses. That urge has been generated primarily by two large and pervasive realities: first, the tendency for any massive institutionalization to *de*humanize and, second, the recognized authority of the school and its teachers over its students. To provide any kind of service to large numbers of persons simultaneously, simple logistics dictates that individuals are managed more easily as collectivities than as single entities. As a result, the educating professions have made a "credo" of the importance of individual differences despite their having to deal with individual likenesses. Recognition of the dehumanizing aspects of mass public education gave early and continuing legitimacy to *humane* considerations. The second reality—that of discipline—sanctions a broad spectrum of authoritarian behavior and has led to the belief of many that children must be treated with dignity.

This "humanistic movement" traces its origins at least to the 1300s and to those educators who favored study of the classics: grammar, rhetoric, poetry, and history. In an excellent educational history, R. Freeman Butts illuminates this perspective:[7]

From its beginning in the fourteenth century humanism was closely identified with *professional educators* and did *not* originate outside organized education as is so often asserted by European historians. Its prime purpose was to promote the study of the ancient classics in schools and universities, *not* to formulate a whole new Renaissance philosophy based on man and human nature in order to replace the medieval philosophy based on God and the spiritual world.

This "humanist" movement with a strong flavor of "basics" prevails even today. Despite a growing number of highly sophisticated psychologists, psychometricians, counselors, and teachers, an altogether quite modern educational "establishment" has, in Butts's words, "adumbrated such a corps of scientific diagnosticians and therapists as a part of the basic educational enterprise"[8] that "The most vociferous voices in favor of traditional educational values came from [those] who reaffirmed humanistic and intellectual positions." Moreover,[9]

New humanists of a variety of persuasions reflected a defensive reaction against progress of modern civilization and reasserted the role of the great intellectual literary and religious heritage of the West as the prime essential in educational content and method. Science, technology, and the social sciences were reviewed as diluters of the traditional values to be served by the humanities in the educational program.

[7]R. Freeman Butts, *The Education of the West* (New York: McGraw-Hill, 1973), p. 203.
[8]Ibid., p. 474.
[9]Ibid., p. 475.

A New Humanism?

If there is a "new" humanism in the development of curricula, is its synonym "values"? In 1977 the Association for Supervision and Curriculum Development (ASCD), the national educational organization that by its own charter speaks on curricular matters for the education professions, published a small volume titled *Curriculum Theory*.[10] Despite the absence of real theory, the book is useful for focusing more precisely on the broad issue of "humanism" as a curricular ethic.[11]

The foreword to *Curriculum Theory* suggests that the papers "challenge us to look at the real purpose of education, whether it is to maintain the social structure as it has existed or to improve the existing structure by providing an educational environment that maximizes human potential." The foreword to *Humanistic Education: Objectives and Assessment* asserts that this small set of statements assists in "beginning the task of humanizing schools." The foreword to the ASCD Yearbook suggests a return to the more traditional notion of humanistic studies by observing that the critical issues of the day demand of the schools "to provide training in analytical thinking."

What seems to us rather compelling about these several major statements about curriculum issues as presented in the twilight years of the 1970s is that "humanistic" education is at least three things: (1) the "basics," (2) a "learning experience," and (3) a "values education." And for any school administrator struggling with managerial and leadership responsibilities, these three views are somewhat at odds. On the one hand, humanistic education is indeed what it has pretty much always been: rhetoric, history, and basic communication skills.[12]

The second view holds that it is particularly humane to both allow and encourage school incumbents to do and behave pretty much as they are moved to do, intervening in that behavioral pattern at appropriate times to move students toward socially redeeming "learning." Knowing *how* to do that is quite another matter and probably accounts for the heavy intrusion of operant conditioning principles and procedures into the content of educational psychology over the past ten years.

The third view seems to emphasize the analysis of values and value-based concerns as the essence of humanistic education. This pattern has gained enough

---

[10]A. Molnar and J. Zahorik, eds., *Curriculum Theory* (Washington, D.C.: ASCD, 1977), 126 pp.

[11]See, for comparison, Robert Leeper, ed., *Humanistic Education: Objectives and Assessments: A Report of the ASCD Working Group on Humanistic Education* (Washington, D.C.: ASCD, 1978), 55 pp, and J. J. Jelinek, ed., *Improving the Human Condition*, ASCD 1978 Yearbook (Washington, D.C.: ASCD, 1978), 265 pp.

[12]Robert A. Ubbelohde, "A Neo-Conservative Approach to Curriculum," in Molnar and Zahorik, op. cit., pp. 28–29.

support and comment that it is often seen as a separate curricular entity: "values education."

In all three perspectives, humanistic education seems nevertheless to be a general response to the impending chaos of youthful barbarism. Schools have always served the larger purpose of civilizing the young, and in recent years there seems ample reason to conclude that there is more self-consciousness within scholastic professional concerns about our failures in this regard than in any other.

BEHAVIOR—CONTROL AND FUNCTION

If there is any single universal concern about public schools—especially of junior and senior high schools—it is the control and management of behavior, that is, "discipline."

This issue emerges again and again in polls, curbstone conferences, workshops, and community discussions. The consensus is that youth runs literally "amok" through the school years—undisciplined, irresponsible, insensitive, destructive, unmotivated, and inadequately skilled in even the fundamentals of learning. While this attitude has almost always been a favorite and predictable topic of discussion, today it holds a larger measure of truth than at any previous time in the history of American mass education.

The circumstances involved deserve our attention at this point for several reasons. First, just how prevalent *is* the issue of adolescent nonconformity? Second, if it is indeed a problem, how did it come about? Third, if "humanistic" education is a part of the general response to it, what other postures must be given consideration? Fourth, what is the proper and effective role of school administrators in dealing with it? And, while the last of these is our principal concern in the following discussion, that cannot be reasonably treated apart from the other three.

Adolescent Irresponsibility: Dimensions of the Problem

The first question for the typical potential school administrator is, quite simply, whether the dimensions of negative student behavior are substantially descriptive enough to constitute a problem deserving systematic attention.

Well, the answer to that is an emphatic "yes"—ask *any* school employee. And even discounting values and attitudes ranging from the most permissive to the most harsh, the consensus is impressive: Kids are insensitive, uncaring, irresponsible, cruel, and thoughtless nerds! Now, of course, not *all* of them—

not, maybe, even a substantial minority of them—and in some schools not very many at all. But, in general, *too* many of them. Consider only the data on vandalism of schools: in 1975, the Los Angeles and Chicago school systems each reported costs of $17 million for school vandalism and property damage; the yearly national costs, according to testimony presented before Senator Birch Bayh's Subcommittee to Investigate Juvenile Delinquence (1974) placed the annual national costs for vandalism to schools alone at $500 million.[13] Adding the cost of general vandalism to all other public facilities, the costs soar another $100 million. Yet it should be emphasized that there is little basis other than logic to presume that this damage is all credited to youth; on the contrary, it is obvious that much indiscriminate defacing of, or damage to, public property in general is not just a youth problem. Yet, equally obvious with reference to school vandalism, the culprits are predominantly youngsters.

Violence

The data on vandalism are only part of authoritative support for the concern that juvenile behavior is out of control. Consider that, between 1970 and 1973, there were more than 70,000 serious assaults on teachers and other school personnel, representing an increase of more than 75 percent over the previous ten years; at the same time assaults on other students increased by 85 percent, robberies by 36 percent, rapes and attempted rapes by 40 percent, and homicides by 18 percent. Between 1970 and 1973 (the period for reporting based on 757 school districts in the Senate subcommittee study), confiscation of weapons increased by 54 percent.

A more recent study, based on intensive and exhaustive case study and interview data from a clinical research analysis, provides some basis for understanding the nature of youth-related troubles.[14] Although the analyses were primarily within the urban setting, they surely relate to rural and suburban localities as well. The incidence is greater in urban environments only because those environments have the most compact enrollments—large junior and senior high schools—on relatively constrained sites. By the same token, these schools reflect, in the minds of the public, the most visible deterioration of the meta-societies in which they are immersed. Yet suburban junior and senior high schools also are experiencing a critical increase in vandalism and violence, as are rural schools, and the phenomenon is a growing problem in many elementary schools as well.

---

[13]See, for example, J. P. DeCecco and A. K. Richards, "Civil War in the High Schools," *Psychology Today*, Vol. 13, no. 9 (November 1975), p. 51.

[14]Patricia Ross, *Trouble in School* (New York: Avon Books, 1979).

The case study analysis of twelve troubled youths was confined to ninth graders and is as much an analysis of the school as it is of the youngsters:[15]

This is an account, too, of trouble in school. It is a detailed and systematic account of what the world of school is like for twelve youth "troublemakers," who never managed to stay within the school rules. It is a close-up portrait of what educators *seem* to be like—in a medium-sized junior high school—to these "tough kids" who are thought of as deviant, disturbed and delinquent.

What emerges most clearly from this study is the familiar conflict of expectations and cultural mores between school and home, and while that finding is not new, the intensity and scope of that conflict is dramatically more pathological today.

Why? And what can be done about it?

There is a variety of explanations for these kinds of problems, and there are particular ways in which school administrators can deal effectively with them. We will treat these issues in greater detail in Chapter 3. It is clear, however, that there is a firm and systematic relationship between and among issues and problems such as adolescent behavior, curriculum and instructional concerns, patterns of philosophical postures (such as increasing emphasis on, and interest in, "values clarification"), and the generalized attitudes and expectations of the schools' various publics as the costs supporting public education continue to escalate.

COMPETENCY STANDARDS

There is no better illustration of the relationship of these various phenomena than the contemporary excitement over what is now being referred to as competency standards and competency testing. There is little question that the present emphasis on competency assessment (which has resulted in legislative mandates in a number of states) is being fueled by a general public dissatisfaction with schools and schooling accompanied, either explicitly or implicitly, by a lack of confidence in schools management.

In the most recent Gallup poll of public attitudes toward schools, the top five problems ranked in order were discipline, use of drugs, lack of proper financial support, integration and busing (combined), and poor curriculum and poor standards.[16] The overall "rating" of the public schools was down in 1978 and

---

[15]Ibid., p. 6.

[16]George H. Gallup, "The 10th Annual Gallup Poll," *Phi Delta Kappan*, vol. 60, no. 1 (September 1978), 33–45.

this has been a trend since 1974. And while there are differences by regions, by race, and by some other demographic characteristics, the general conclusion is simply that there is an erosion of public confidence in public schools. In any case, it seems reasonable to conclude that people see adolescent behavior and academic performance as negatively correlated—both are bad, getting worse, and neither will improve, in the public view, unless some kinds of changes take place and quickly.

When asked what schools should be doing that they are not doing, respondents gave rather predictable responses: discipline should be stricter; teachers should be more effective; basics should be stressed; parental involvement should be increased; standards should be higher; health-related instruction should be expanded (mostly implying problems associated with alcohol and drug education); and career education should be emphasized.[17]

Whether directly or indirectly, the current lack of confidence in the quality and performance of public schools reflects a general perception of lack of competence. If one thinks of this idea of competence with a lowercase versus a capital "c," the issue comes somewhat more into perspective. For example, in this case, "competency," through a curious process of institutionalization, becomes "Competency," under its attendant "Competency-based Education" or "Competency Standards" or "Competency Certification" or "Competency-Testing."

Arthur Wise has given considerable attention to this process and sees it as something of a systems analytic pattern of organizational behavior. He has referred to the phenomenon on several occasions as "hyperrationalization." States Wise,[18]

I reject minimum competency testing primarily because it offers no credible theory of education; it is another fad. I distinguish between rationalization and hyperrationalization. Rationalization is sensible. You try to make sure the activities you engage in will get you the results that you have chosen are attainable given the activities and resources you have. Hyperrationalization is when you engage in apparent rationalization, but there is no basis for thinking that you are really improving the connection between activities and outcome.

Wise holds that "hyperrationalization" is at least partly a product of a kind of systems analytic progression of "historical sequence" that began with " 'accountability' [followed by] 'competency-based education' [and] we are currently caught-up in 'minimum competency testing.' "[19] He believes that next

[17]Ibid., p. 36.
[18]Arthur Wise, "Why Minimum Competency Testing Will Not Improve Education," *Educational Leadership*, Vol. 36, no. 8 (May 1979), 548.
[19]Ibid., p. 546.

in the sequence will be legislatively mandated statewide curricula. A chilling thought? It is already in the works in at least one state.

Wise's views are typically not shared by some (perhaps many) educators. Conservatives both within and without professional education see it as long overdue; some school principals and central office evaluation-type administrators see it as an opportunity "by which teachers and other support staff monitor the healthy development of students—socially, as well as intellectually."[20]

More important, it seems to us, the potential school administrator must attempt to see these various concerns in a holistic fashion. Because these kinds of concerns reflect a rather broad perception that schools are in deep, deep trouble, to that extent, we agree with Wise that the whole competency syndrome is decidedly faddish; but unlike some other fads in the long history of American mass education, this one seems to us to be flavored with panic.

Perhaps the most ambitious attempt to assess the status and prospects of the American public school system is the long-term study that John Goodlad is now completing. Goodlad's initial prediction is not optimistic: "my skepticism regarding many of our most popular beliefs about education . . . is such that I would more readily predict, from much of our effort, poorer rather than better schools for the future."[21]

Goodlad shares Arthur Wise's attitude regarding systems analytic postures at least in a generic sense:[22]

there is growing suspicion that the much touted supposed reforms of the sixties never occurred—they were for the most part, movements. On the other hand, there is all around us evidence to the effect that accountability by objectives, PPBS, Competency-based teacher education, and the like have dominated the scene for some time. Is it not time to consider seriously the proposition that this cult of efficiency has failed to make our schools more efficient? Is the time not overdue for seriously considering other ways of accounting for what goes on in the educational system and our schools?

Goodlad rejects the more popular *imitative* models of change that educational systems have tended to adopt—that cult of efficiency that presumes schools are no less "push-pull, click-click" than our typical technological assembly lines (and the competency testing attitude seems to us to be quite compatible with that ideology)—but, rather, speaks in behalf of a "school Zeitgeist"—a climate of professional dedication. And it is that kind of environment that administrators can be most instrumental in fostering; they cannot create it and they cannot "engineer it," but they can foster it. Goodlad places the primary burden of that effort on the principal—at least he assigns the most direct influence to that

[20]W. B. Newman, "Competency Testing: A Response to Arthur Wise," op. cit., p. 551.

[21]John Goodlad, "Can Our Schools Get Better?" *Phi Delta Kappan*, Vol. 60, no. 5 (January 1979), 342.

[22]Ibid., p. 343.

role.[23] But obviously, it is the central authoritative staff—the superintendent's office—that makes that leadership possible.

THE RISE OF FEMINISM, THE CENTRALIZATION OF AUTHORITY, AND THE EMANCIPATION OF THE HANDICAPPED

At least three more important pieces of the management environment deserve comment in this rather broad introduction. While we will have more to say specifically about these and other problem areas in the chapters that follow, the general "picture" is less than complete without comment about the emergent status of women and the expanding regulatory apparatus at both state and federal levels with which the school administrator must function in the remaining years of the twentieth century. And related to both of these phenomena is the new concern for the rights of handicapped persons.

The Women's Movement

A major contributor to changes in life in the twentieth century is that whole set of interests, ideas, and activities that is known as "the women's movement." Just as the decade of the 1960s reflected a cultural revolution among youth, those years also spawned a resurgency of a feminine emancipation. While it may be argued that this emancipation will not be realized fully—at least in a legal sense—unless and until the Equal Rights Amendment is ratified by the required number of states, the fact remains that, through education, social pressure, assaults on tradition, and laws and regulations, the feminist revolution has been accomplished.

As with any revolution, this one has not been waged without costs to the societal fabric that it set about to amend. Some of these social costs are not yet easily or fully determinable, but there is some, albeit still obscure, emerging recognition that aspects of the women's movement have been, and are, antagonistic to children. These aspects of the women's movement need to be differentiated quite clearly from the social evils of *sexism* itself.

Sexism is "the belief that one sex [male or female] is inherently superior to the other [and is manifested] in behaviors which restrict one sex from opportunities, activities, and privileges normally granted to the other sex."[24]

It was to this general attitude toward sexism that Barbara Jordan referred when, as a member of a special "Convocation on the State of Individual Free-

---

[23]Ibid., p. 346.

[24]J. Boyer, R. E. Waters, and F. M. Harris, "Justice, Society, and the Individual," in J. J. Jelinek, op. cit., p. 179.

dom," sponsored by the Center for the Study of Democratic Institutions, she observed,[25]

> One of the reasons why the Equal Rights Amendment to the Constitution is necessary is that the [Supreme] Court has been so uneven, inconsistent, and a little shallow in its efforts to address the rights of women as persons. . . . Women are not a minority. We are treated as a minority. But we are beginning to make the necessary transition, so that we can act as members of the majority, which we are.

The congruence of *sexism* and the general civil rights of Americans has been brought into sharp perspective in recent years. Moreover, to ensure that sex is an important dimension of civil rights, a variety of regulatory concerns has been brought to bear; while the most notable attempt to deal with this issue is, indeed, the Equal Rights Amendment, some hold that other rules and legislation render that amendment either unnecessary or merely as a strong social prescription.

One particularly frustrated associate superintendent for personnel relations in a large midwestern metropolitan school district put the issue well in a personal communication with one of the authors:[26]

> You certainly can no longer talk—much less think—in terms of trying to hire the "best-man-for-the-job"! That attitude as reflected in a cliche that has been as much a part of our language as the masculine use of "him," "his" and "he" in the pronouns of English grammar for a thousand years is not only any longer acceptable—it is anathema! Our problems increasingly have to do with trying to figure out *how*, much more than *who* to hire and we know that once someone is finally aboard it will almost take an "act of Congress" to get rid of them no matter how bad they may turn out to be. If it happens to be a woman and she also turns out to be incompetent by just about anyone's standards, and if she wants to be even a little troublesome, you're just about stuck with her. Curiously, in all such matters, the general effect on the larger and more noble purpose of influencing the positive aspects of children's lives, directly or indirectly, seems increasingly not only irrelevant but subversive—whose freedom and "opportunity-to-become" are we really concerned about in these matters? I wish someone of influence in this whole business of what's-best-for-whom would take kids into primary consideration just once!

Differentiation between "sexism" and "the women's movement" is a difficult one for school administrators to undertake, yet it does seem clear that those who have seen certain aspects of the "women's movement" as being antagonistic to children are at least partially correct.

Probably any emerging set of ideological attitudes will be accompanied by

[25]Barbara Jordan, "Discussion," *The Center Magazine,* Vol. 12, no. 2 (March–April 1979), 11.

[26]W. G. Monahan, "Problems and Practices of Personnel Directors in Large City Schools: A Survey," unpublished paper, College of Human Resources and Education, West Virginia University, Morgantown, 1978, 66 pp.

some social costs. When the Supreme Court declared the maintenance of "separate but equal schools" for blacks to be unconstitutional, there were significant "costs" for some black systems. Over the years, that decision has created real difficulty for some small black colleges and immediately jeopardized the jobs of many black schoolteachers who knew that cultural norms could not be erased by court decisions; given the choice between a black teacher and a white one, regardless of credentials, integration required the price of unemployment for many black teachers in the South. It was a price many were willing to pay at the time, but additional revisions and interpretations of civil rights regulations, over time, have helped to ameliorate these dislocations. Now it is not the predominantly black, "southern" states that face the most difficulty in these matters but, rather, the heavily black-populated "northern" cities where de facto segregation tended to prevail.

Yet all these issues do not change the fact that new attitudes and new patterns of cultural accommodation, especially with reference to the role of women in the world of work, have had curious effects on the status of children and that some of these effects have been decidedly negative.

To a large extent, it is this dimension of the women's movement wherein one must try to draw a distinction between what is "female" and what is "feminine." Among the more coherent essays we have read on this subject was by Henry Fairlie in a 1978 issue of the *New Republic:*[27]

> By *female,* I mean the biological, what is given by the gender . . .
> By *feminine,* I mean, not what is given, but what is acquired; what is cultivated . . . the feminine is the attributes and properties which, in differing ways in different cultures, women and men regard as necessary to establish, protect, and give expression to the female . . .
> By *womanly,* I mean the whole human being who is formed by play of the female and the feminine in matters that are otherwise common to us. . . . The womanly is indeed what we ought to mean by the person.

Fairlie goes on to suggest a further conflict between the "feminine" and the "female" that highlights the notion that aspects of the movement are antagonistic to children:[28]

It is my contention here that the feminine is today being made the enemy of the female and the womanly; that the crucial flow in the women's movement is its all-but-exclusive concern with feminineness; that the notion of what it can mean to be female and womanly is being narrowed and impoverished rather than widened and enriched; that the creation of the "female human being" . . . is farther off than ever; [and] that with all this, the

---

[27]Henry Fairlie, "The Real Life of Women," *New Republic,* Vol. 179, nos. 9–10. (August–September 1978), 17.
[28]Ibid., p. 19.

male and the manly, as distinct from the masculine, are being undone as well; and that as a result, a terrible desperation is creeping into relations between the sexes, clawing at them both.

This "clawing" is at the heart of the status of children—especially the younger ones. It is easy for the perceptive child to conclude that he or she is a liability in the relationship of an active and sometimes volatile male-female parental controversy. Also, the child is often seen by both parents as an impediment to self-determination, as a source of fundamental inconvenience and yet, curiously also, as a functional experimental variable in a life-style that can tolerate normatively presumed biological and cultural parental roles within a context of external career pursuits. Thus a child of such marriages is both wanted and yet resented.

The fundamental theoretical issue in this regard was thoroughly considered by the late Talcott Parsons; as an almost passing observation, he asserted,[29]

We believe sex to constitute in a developmental sense the most "primitive" of the differentiations of generic personality types. . . . These differential meanings become the major focus of orientation of the individual. . . . Motivationally it means the acceptance of the set of goals ascribed to one's own sex-role, and correspondingly renunciation of those ascribed to the other.

That was written long before there was any women's movement. The point is that, so far as children are concerned, the relationship between the sexes is joined irrevocably. "Marriage" may be defined in a variety of ways to be sure; yet when children are involved, a relationship between the sexes is clearly manifested whether "vows" are or are not spoken. In any case, in Parsons's view "a clearly differentiated system" has been executed, and it is as a consequence of dealing with this "differentiated" system that the child becomes a factor in the life-styles, ideologies, and self-interested values of its parents.

To that extent, some children are much more subject to dependence upon social institutions *other* than the nuclear family than are others. Such children, not atypically, find the schools as their "parents" since they are perceived at home as interlopers. Schools are not, more probably can ever truly be, equipped to fill this role. Children of such relationships, whether from impoverished and deteriorated family environments due to primitive economic conditions or libertarian insensitivity, become "wards" of the school, and ill-equipped to respond to these sociocultural mandates, schools tend merely to alienate further this surprisingly large number of children from the normative mainstream of cultural and civilizing indoctrination.

We will deal with these considerations with somewhat more deliberate atten-

---

[29]T. Parsons and R. F. Bales, *Family, Socialization and Interaction Process* (New York: Free Press, 1955), p. 387.

tion in following chapters; at this point, we want merely to emphasize that, again, schools have little choice but to confront expectations far beyond their original "charters" for dealing only with the intellectual development of youth. That whether resources are or are not available, schools must nevertheless cope with such exigencies as a consequence of their general societal functions as youth-serving agencies.

The Handicapped

A third area in which schools now confront revised responses has to do with the youthful handicapped.

"Special education" services are not new to the public schools. Yet, as a professional area of concern, special educators (and more explicitly, "exceptional students") are of rather recent origin. It was not until after World War II that special education really emerged as a particular area of instructional concern. In recent years and as a consequence of two major thrusts—the enactment of P.L. 94-142 (Education of All Handicapped) and the recognition by the educating professions to do something about handicapped students—"exceptional child" activities have proliferated.

It is true that early efforts emphasized the "trainable" and "educable" mentally retarded. Yet, long before P.L. 94-142 was enacted, many schools were developing programs for the learning disabled, the emotionally disturbed, the hyperactive, the academically talented (gifted), and the physically handicapped child. P.L. 94-142 has given both legitimacy and legal support for still more aggressive activity in these broad areas; too, it recognized that some schools have done little and must now do much. It should not be presumed on the basis of the fact that there was considerable activity in several areas of education for the handicapped that any really diverse and routinized programs for handicapped children were common; they were not. It has not been until the last five to ten years that programs of appropriate diversity have become available, and much of that is owing to the aggressive lobbying efforts of the parents of handicapped youngsters.

At the same time, there is reason to conclude that much of the thrust of energy and activity that has resulted in widespread programming in elementary and secondary schools for a whole variety of human services orientations—programs not only for the handicapped, but for remediation in basic skills for disadvantaged youngsters, work-study innovations, and still other special programs like Teacher Corps, Teacher Education Centers, and bi-lingual education programs—was being affected by the budget-cutting slow-downs of the Reagan administration as 1981 wore on into the summer. Many educational institutions and programs that had depended heavily on federal dollars for development and programming discovered rather quickly that Democratic congressional support was not forthcoming as sometimes promised and universally hoped. By mid-summer, it had become obvious that there was indeed a strong public reaction to which Washington politicos were responding and that the Reagan election was interpreted as a mandate to reduce federal participation in educational affairs at all levels. Moreover, the squeeze on spending was not only a federal one; the states had already experienced that mood and the Reagan administration merely reflected it at the national level and took advantage of it. It could be concluded that this swing in public sentiment began with the passage of California's Proposition 13 back in 1978, but in any case, since that time, the mood of the country seems clearly to be in favor of less spending for education; as of July, 1981, seventeen states have followed California's example and enacted provisions for limiting such spending, and there does seem to be something of a pattern to it. Chris Pipho states, "Although comparing states is difficult, the industrial states of the northeast appear hardest hit by legislated spending limits combined with inflation-driven cost increases, declining enrollments, and a recession-triggered drop in taxes."[30]

At least with reference to special education, certain provisions of P.L. 94-142 seem reasonably safe from the budget-cutting spree characteristic of the federal establishment since the Congress has written much of the provisions of this law and the powerful special education lobby is not going to see it tampered with without great opposition. Nevertheless, P.L. 94-142 is a special target of the Reagan administration because it is replete with many regulations and they are detailed, rigid, and complex and the Administration has already gone on record as intending to reduce federal enforcement of some handicapped education rights.[31]

SUMMARY

All these new responsibilities perhaps place a much more centralized authority on the American public school system than it has ever known. Certainly, this grants public schools a more important function as a major institutionalizing activity.

To some extent, schools are being asked to assume more and more of the functions once assigned informally to the family and to the church. Some believe not only that schools cannot meet these new expectations but that they are not

[30]Chris Pipho, "Rich States, Poor States," *Phi Delta Kappan,* Vol. 62, no. 10 (June 1981), p. 722.

[31]David G. Savage, "Washington Report," *Phi Delta Kappan,* Vol. 62, no. 10 (June 1981), p. 693.

appropriate institutions for doing so; still others believe that schools are the most capable of our institutions in this regard.

In any case, the challenges presented for school administrators are massive and sobering. How we perform is at least in no small measure a function of our understanding of what we can, and cannot, do and how well we can learn to do the best we can.

It is within that spirit that this book is offered. In the chapters that follow, we lay out the ''territory,'' the content required, and the postures demanded and provide a little advice for making the best of it all.

SUGGESTED REFERENCES

The Danforth and Ford Foundations. *The School and the Democratic Environment*. New York: Columbia University Press, 1970.

Dewey, John. *The Child and the Curriculum* and *The School and Society*. Chicago: University of Chicago Press, 1971. (*The Child* . . . was originally published in 1902; *The School and Society,* in 1900.)

Roe, William H., and Thelbert L. Drake. *The Principalship,* Second Edition. New York: Macmillan Publishing Co., 1980. See especially Chapters 15 and 16.

Ulich, Robert, ed. *Education and the Idea of Mankind*. Chicago: University of Chicago Press—Phoenix Books, 1964.

Weinberg, Richard A., and Frank H. Woods (eds.). *Observation of Pupils and Teachers in Mainstream and Special Education Settings: Alternative Strategies*. Minneapolis, Minnesota: University of Minnesota, 1975.

Weinstein, Gerald, and Mario D. Fantini (eds.). *Toward a Humanistic Education*. New York: Praeger Publishers, The Ford Foundation. 1970.

Chapter 2 ——————————————————————

Critical Dimensions of Education Management: Past and Present

THE HISTORICAL PERSPECTIVE

The organizational pattern by which rudimentary mass education was made available to Americans is a curious invention. Butts, for one, has observed that,[1]

The growing consensus in America that universal, free, and compulsory elementary education should be established in schools controlled and supported under public auspices was a remarkable and distinctive achievement. . . .

The significant thing is that in America both the Republicans (and the Democrats who succeeded them) and the Federalists (and the Whigs who succeeded *them*) in large part came to agree that popular, practical education was a good thing for them and for American Society.

A "good thing" indeed has characterized the idea of free public schools almost from the beginning of this nation. And yet certain key developments in the achievement of a mass public school system, as we have come to know it today, did not come about without controversy and opposition.

Education was made available to the masses by the "district system"; that is, public schools were organized as districted entities, under the generally decentralized jurisdiction of some existing political subdivision—county, township, city, or (much later as in the case of Hawaii) state-as-a-whole.

Early on, the New England town was the basic unit for managing the provision

---

[1] R. F. Butts, *The Education of the West* (New York: McGraw-Hill, 1973), pp. 402–403.

of education services. And because the New England states were the first to advocate extensive public education as well as to have had considerable experience with the new democratic attitudes being fomented in colonial America, the general pattern developed there was followed throughout the new country. Yet it was not until after Independence that education as a general public "right" came much more into its own.[2]

It is sometimes forgotten that schools, like any other societal institution, have evolved over a rather long period, during which their status and condition reflected the prevailing sentiments of the times. Early efforts to establish formal schooling in this country were not only generated from strong convictions about the close relationship between moral virtue and religious indoctrination but also from concerns still influenced by the view that scholasticism was to have primarily a classical focus. This latter notion held that educated people were schooled in Latin and Greek, were grounded in some mathematics, and were most heavily "bent" in knowledge of theological issues, since even the tradition of the top educational structures of Europe were oriented heavily toward the preparation of the clergy.

Beyond a doubt, early efforts to establish schools in colonial America were profoundly affected by the ideas of current theological discourse. That formal schooling should exist for any purpose other than for training for the clergy was unthinkable. Understandably, this attitude was a carry-over of the generally accepted colonial immigrants' notions of the purposes served by formal schooling. The facts of the cultural revolution and the emerging new political and social ethic that these adventurous colonists espoused had little immediate impact on their views about education. The general notion of what education was, and ought to be about, in eighteenth-century America is characterized as follows by Callahan:[3]

European education in the Seventeenth Century reflected the European class structure. The lowest level consisted of elementary schools in which the teaching was done in the vernacular, generally either German, French, or English. For the most part these schools were located in the towns and evidence suggests that few of them existed. Students, generally from the lower classes, attended for a few years, or until they had learned to read and write, and this constituted their formal education. Occasionally it happened that pupils from the middle class attended these schools for a few years prior to their entrance into a secondary school, but more often they received their early education from tutors as aid to the sons of the nobility.

[2]For background in this formative period, see Ellwood Cubberly, *Public School Administration* (Boston: Houghton Mifflin, 1929); N. Edwards and H. G. Richey, *The School in the American Social Order* (Boston: Houghton Mifflin, 1947); V. T. Thayer, *The Role of the School in American Society* (New York: Dodd, Mead, 1961); and W. O. Stanley et al., *Social Foundations of Education* (New York: Dryden Press, 1957), Chapter 8.

[3]Raymond Callahan, *An Introduction to Education in American Society,* 2nd ed. (New York: Knopf, 1960), p. 111.

Callahan's reference to the "sons of the nobility" is not a casual one. Whether of the nobility or lesser classes, the idea of education for females was unthinkable. Even for males from the lower classes, formal education of any kind was seldom given serious consideration.

This attitude toward education was relatively well entrenched even by those libertarians (by seventeenth-century standards) who chose to cast their lot in the New World. We know only a little about the character and ideals of those early Americans and very little about their deeper and private motives. However, we do know that, in the main, they were political and theological misfits (i.e., fundamentalist Christians who were disenchanted with contemporary standards of religious conviction in Europe), mostly poor, and typically disenfranchised at least to the extent that they were without property or potential prospect in the European society they endured. We know as well that they were either reasonably adventurous or without any reasonable prospects otherwise. We know also that many among these early Americans were criminals, ne'er-do-wells, and "last-chance" opportunists who welcomed even the remotest possibility of living out their lives in a place free from sheriff's authority or king's influence. Yet we know, as well, that a number of these early Americans were a hardy stock, enterprising, God-fearing, and oddly capable of seeing any future free with promise and hope. Thus, a majority of colonists also brought an enlightened attitude of freedom from tyranny with them, a strong sense of survival, fundamental skills to sustain that sense, and a basic faith in the possibility of building a new life within common law. It is undeniable that, for many years, that combination of virtues resulted in a stultifying Puritanism as the basis for societal management. Yet without that curious severity of attitude, it is questionable whether or not our present society could have evolved.

Gradually, the concept of "common good" gained dominance over religious fervor as the purpose of education. Nowhere is this conclusion more evident than in an excerpt from a pamphlet concerning the purposes of the newly established Harvard College, portions of which were published in London in 1643:[4]

After God had carried us safe to New England, and wee had builded our houses, provided necessaries for our livelihood, rear'd convenient places for God's worship, and settled, the Civill Government; one of the next things we longed for, and looked after was to advance Learning and perpetuate it to posterity, dreading to leave an illiterate ministry to churches, when our present Ministers shall lie in the Dust.

While this statement was clothed in apostolic rhetoric, the longing for advanced learning was characteristic of the concern among many for general schooling.

[4]E. P. Cubberley, *Readings in Public Education in the United States* (Boston: Houghton Mifflin, 1934), p. 13.

It was no accident, then, that in his Farewell Address to the republic in 1796, George Washington also recognized the future importance of this relationship: "Promote then, as an object of primary importance, institutions for the general diffusion of knowledge. In proportion as the structure of government gives force to public opinion it is essential that public opinion should be enlightened."

By the second decade of the nineteenth century, the youthful United States had achieved a measure of established international respect and some internal stability. Under Henry Clay's ambitious influence in behalf of internal improvements, the young nation set about the work of dealing with its own destiny.

The great French sociological scholar, Alexis de Tocqueville, visited the country in 1831 and came away impressed with its enormous potential. Andrew Jackson was elected president of the country in 1828, and, although some may have deplored this backwoodsman's having achieved the highest office in the land, his election established for all time not only that the common man could speak effectively with his ballot but that education for all was a vital necessity in the survival of the young republic.

Following 1830, educational activity proliferated:[5]

The period from 1830 to 1860 saw not only the establishment but also the expansion of the public school system. In the curriculum this expansion consisted of a more extensive training in the three "R's" but it included also such new subjects as geography, grammar, and history. In 1848, a graded system of instruction was introduced into the Boston Schools, and then spread rapidly all over the Country where the schools were of any size. The graded system required a large number of pupils and several teachers and this combination generally existed in the towns. In the rural areas grading was introduced much later. As the high schools increased in number the trend toward arranging a continuous program from the elementary schools through high school began. Finally, the State universities were connected with and extended out from the high schools and the famous American "ladder system" was a reality.

The "high school" was, however, not considered appropriate or necessary, or "public" in the sense of "free" schooling until late in the nineteenth century. The general consensus held that the "common school" was sufficient. Comment about "grammar schools" indicates that instruction in Latin, Greek, geography, and mathematics would be available only to a carefully selected few. Thomas Jefferson, generally regarded as a most innovative advocate of publicly supported education, agreed. While serving in the Virginia legislature in 1799, he introduced a bill to provide schools and said of his plan,[6]

These [common] schools to be under a visitor, who is annually to choose the boy of most genius whose parents are too poor to give them further education and to send him

[5]Callahan, op. cit., p. 130.
[6]Cited in F. M. Raubinger et al., *The Development of Secondary Education* (London: Colbek-Macmillan, 1969), p. 4.

forward to one of the grammar schools. . . . Of the boys sent in any one year, trial is to be made at the grammar schools one or two years; and the best genius of the whole selected . . . and the residue dismissed.

It is generally acknowledged that the first public high school was established in Boston in 1821 and that other similar high schools followed in other large cities. By the time of the American Civil War, enrollments were still small and admissions quite selective, however. Curricula remained fairly "classical," and it was not until after 1900 that secondary education began to move toward its present pattern and functions.[7]

The key event in the proliferation of secondary education, of course, was the 1872 landmark case decided in Kalamazoo, Michigan, in which the Michigan supreme court recognized the right of towns and communities to tax themselves for support of secondary schools. The significant implication of this decision was that high schools could serve anyone just as had been the pattern of the common schools.

The number of high schools grew rapidly during the last quarter of the nineteenth century due to the impetus of the Kalamazoo case. Understandably, as well, the general curriculum and purposes of the high schools began to change as suggested. By 1900, enrollment in public high schools was twice that of ten years earlier, yet 1890 is seen by some as perhaps the real beginning of the modern secondary school:[8]

in the development of secondary education, 1890 was a watershed. Much had been accomplished. The struggle to establish the common school was won. The legality of the public high school had been upheld. The academies, which had made great contributions . . . were yielding to the public high school.

Nonetheless, the majority of young people of high school age still did not attend school in 1910, though 1910 marked the appearance of the first junior high schools in California. During this period, too, recommendations for educational programs emerged that were to characterize the pattern of secondary education that prevailed until after World War II.[9]

The Influence of Colleges and Universities

"Higher education" as an idea was not easily distinguishable from "secondary education" until well into the nineteenth century as many of the highly

---

[7]Ibid., p. 5.
[8]Ibid., p. 10.
[9]G. R. Cressman and Harold W. Benda, *Public Education in America* (New York: Appleton-Century-Crofts, 1956), p. 36.

selective secondary schools provided programs and served youngsters approaching college age. Moreover, there were not many colleges in the mold of the contemporary institutions we know today. The earliest "normal" schools were little more than secondary schools (and many were of lesser quality). The secondary schools established in the larger cities between 1830 and 1860 almost all offered a curriculum in normal studies.[10] The first exclusively normal schools were established privately and the first public normal school was begun in Lexington, Massachusetts in 1827. By 1860 there were eleven publicly supported normal schools in eight states.[11]

Yet with the federal government's strong commitment to the need for more highly trained labor as manifested in passage of the Morrill Act of 1862, the American State University began the development that led to the professionalization of many occupations that had functioned previously primarily through guilds and apprenticeships. This was a major event in the history of American public education, and its impact has been greater than anyone can appreciate. As background, the Morrill Act was a "war measure" first proposed in 1859 to assist in the accelerated development of agriculture and mechanical arts. Yet its general thrust was comprehensive. Allan Nevins saw it as characterizing "a fundamental emotion that gave force to the principle that every child should have free opportunity for as complete an education as his tastes and abilities warranted."[12] But there was something else "American" about the Morrill Act that is sometimes overlooked—namely, the capacity of the act to reject the classical and elitist flavor of the major colleges and universities of the time, most of which were private, prudish, and pontifical.

While it required about a half century for the sentiment to find expression in law, the evolution of the idea of the "common man" in America had to move both the policies and philosophy of the young nation toward emphasis on the practical and the pragmatic. Alexis de Tocqueville saw this clearly during his American visit:[13]

permanent inequality of lot leads men to confine themselves to the proud and sterile search for abstract truths, whilst the institutions of democratic society tend to make them look only for the immediate practical applications of science. This tendency is natural and inevitable.

---

[10]The term "normal" was adapted from the French for "model" or "rule," the notion being that one should study model ways to teach.

[11]Butts, op. cit., p. 430.

[12]Allan Nevins, *The State Universities and Democracy* (Urbana: University of Illinois Press, 1962), p. 16.

[13]Alexis de Tocqueville, *Democracy in America,* N. P. Mayer and Max Lerner, eds., George Lawrence, trans. (New York: Harper & Row, 1966), p. 430.

Science and Religion—Resolving the Conflicts

It was this "inevitable tendency" that the Morrill Act helped to legislate. And while the act emphasized the applications of science toward the improvement of farming and the development of the engineering capacity necessary to accommodate and accelerate the nation's growing industrial potential, the equally important thrust toward a more pragmatic concern with the arts and humanities was also implied.

The general mood of the country concurred with this federal role, but the emphasis that would be placed on science and research nevertheless faced some tough battles. It must be remembered that the same attitude that characterized Americans as a practical and "down-to-earth" people also imbued them with a strong sense of religious fervor. The heritage of Calvinism and Puritanism remained strong, especially among those rural people for whom the Morrill Act was designed. To some extent, the conflict between science and religion was softened by events and ideas that gained some prominence in the early nineteenth century.

With reference to education generally, one such important distinction was accomplished by the work of Horace Mann (1796–1859). As secretary of the Massachusetts State Board of Education, his annual reports contained a number of forceful clarifications on the role and function of public, nonsectarian schooling. In his *Twelfth Annual Report* (1848), Mann provided a particular and detailed explanation as to how public education could serve the general ethic of moral and spiritual values without either dependence on or damage to any particular sectarian view. Much of Horace Mann's work was designed to convince people that public education in the United States was a "natural right" and required the support of public taxation for its survival. While the idea of a tax to support the schooling of someone else's child is so well established today as to be unquestionable otherwise, Mann's view was an innovation in the history of modern education, and in pursuing it, the question of the religious aspects of indoctrination were never far removed from the argument:[14]

The religious education which a child receives at school, is not imparted to him for the purpose of making him join this or that denomination when he arrives at years of discretion, but for the purpose of enabling him to judge for himself, according to the dictates of his own reason and conscience, what his religious obligations are, and whither they lead. But if a man is taxed to support a school, where religious doctrines are inculcated which he believes to be false, and which he believes that God condemns; then

---

[14]Lawrence A. Cremin, ed., *The Republic and the School: Horace Mann on the Education of Free Men, Classics in Education, No. 1* (New York: Bureau of Publications, Teachers College, Columbia University, 1959), p. 104.

he is excluded from the school by the divine law, at the same time that he is compelled to support it by the human law.

One intellectual who helped to defuse the conflict between scientific and religious experience in the latter half of the nineteenth century was John Fiske (1842–1901), an articulate spokesperson on the issue of "evolution." There is little doubt that Fiske's work, though appearing after the passage of the first Morrill Act in 1862, was instrumental in the acceleration of the scientific inquiry that characterized the work of the fledgling land grant universities between 1870–1900.

Of Science and Philosophical Discourse

Within the scientific community, the single most dramatic event of the period was the publication of Charles Darwin's *The Origin of the Species* (in 1859), followed by his equally revolutionary *Descent of Man* (in 1871). Although Darwin dominated science in his day, others had helped to pave the way and had made his work, if not possible, at least propitious. Many of these others were of a philosophical or political "bent," but their somewhat larger concerns with the strain between freedom and authority not only influenced the flavor of the American republic but helped to fashion all aspects of democratic institutions as well. In this regard, Franklin Parker has observed the following:[15]

The search for freedom is old; yet the modern application of freedom to education probably began with the philosophers of the French Revolution whose sharp minds were roused by Rene Descartes' (1596–1658) emphasis on intellect ("I think, therefore I am") and John Locke's (1792–1856) emphasis on empiricism ("The mind is a tabula rasa on which experience writes"). Secularism replaced religion, reason supplanted revelation, rationalism replaced dogma, and the rights of man replaced the rights of kings as "natural rights" because man was man and could build his own heaven on earth. The new Liberalism's anti-authoritarianism was spread by Voltaire (1694–1778), Denis Diderot (1713–1784), Etienne Condillaç (1715–1780), Jean Jacques Rousseau (1712–1778), and many others. In politics, the new freedom meant self-government; in economics via the Physiocrats it meant laissez-faire trade; in religion it meant freedom to worship or not, according to conscience; in education via Rousseau it meant the removal of institutional restraints and the substitution of emotion and feeling for authority.

Rousseau—this romantic rebel and vagabond, this man of personal grievance who could not long keep a job, exalted freedom over authority, impulse over discipline, feeling over convention, expression over repression, the individual over the mass. The church held: man's nature is corrupt but salvageable by God's grace. Locke implied:

---

[15]Franklin Parker, "Freedom and Authority: Background for the Great Debates in American Education," cited in W. G. Monahan, *Theoretical Dimensions of Educational Administration* (New York: Macmillan, 1975), pp. 315–316. Used with permission.

Man's nature is neutral and is shaped by experience and environment. Rousseau said: man's nature is good; corrupting evil lies in the effects of his institutions.

This alienated man without attachments, this father of the romantic movement, this moralist who gave his five illegitimate children to an orphanage, this stranger in the highly socialized Paris of his day, this "sickly genius" as Jacques Maritain (1882–1973) called him, was a powerful force in his own and the following centuries. His advance of freedom in the naturalism he yearned for echoes in our day and authoritarians are still shaken by the avalanche he unleashed.

The new double aim he gave education of child-centeredness and social reconstruction might have come about without him. It was part of French revolutionary thought: to counter religions and political authoritarianism, new generations must be educated to be free-thinking individuals who are critical of, and thus correctors of, their institutions. "The aim of education," wrote Condorcet, "is not to instill admiration for the existing political system but to create a critical attitude toward it."

To Americans just coming into national self-consciousness, the view of education as corrective of human institutions, particularly political institutions, had strong appeal. This appeal was voiced by Benjamin Rush (1745–1813) who believed this corrective view most suitable for the new American Republic. Samuel Knox (1756–1832) wrote, "The welfare of society depends on education based upon science instead of superstition and prejudice."

The Impact of the "Enlightenment"

The late eighteenth century and most of the nineteenth were characterized by an intellectual brilliance probably unrivalled in human history. While much of the commentary was abstract, it reflected an enlightenment that provided us with dramatic scientific, technological, and philosophical advances. Consider just a few of the scholarly "milestones" that have contributed to our present-day points of view:

Edmund Burke (1729–1797). In 1756, Edmund Burke published *A Vindication of Natural Society;* in 1770, *Thoughts on the Causes of the Present Discontents;* and in 1790, *Reflections on the Revolution in France.* Burke was fundamentally a philosophical conservative with a curious passion for individualism; he saw this concept sustained better in the traditional rather than the radical. Yet his comments about individual freedom were founded on a profound distrust of anything that seemed to him to be alien to the established social traditions, the better aspects of Christianity, and the idea of the beneficence of a "landed class."

Condorcet [Marquis de Condorcet (Marie Jean Antoine Nicholas Coritat) (1743–1794)]. Condorcet's major contribution was the *Outline of a Historical Picture of the Progress of the Human Mind,* published in 1795, a year after his death. Condorcet was included in that group of intellectuals known as the "philosophes.'' A French revolutionary, his primary passion was the release of the human mind from all the institutional and indoctrinational sorts of superstitions and guilts that traditional medievalism had imposed upon it. Condorcet saw the revolution as an opportunity for the person to become something more than what he was previously "programmed" to become otherwise.

Emile Durkheim (1858–1917). Followed closely by Karl Marx (1818–1883) and Georg Simmel (1858–1918) in Germany, by Herbert Spencer (1820–1903) in England, and by Auguste Comte (1798–1857)—the generally acknowledged "father" of sociology, who died the year before Durkheim was born in France— Durkheim was *the* recognized genius of the nineteenth century. His was an almost encyclopedic mind, and his major works are still studied by sociologists as much as those of any contemporary authority. More than any other writer, with the possible exception of Marx, his work is appropriate to students of educational history. Particularly influential in the context with which we are currently concerned are his *Division of Labor* (1893); *Moral Education,* published almost ten years after his death, in 1925 (and which is most familiar to educationists); and *Suicide* (1867). Durkheim was a "transitional" scholar whose work reflected the most notable cross-currents of what was germane to the broad issues of individualism and authority in the nineteenth century. Although he did not address the larger philosophical issues of man and politics as much as did some of his contemporaries, his contributions to rigorous scholarly methodology and his treatment of major implications of political and sociocultural process are classic. He was, and is, the dominant intellect of the period, and no educator's experience is complete without a firsthand acquaintance with Durkheim's works.

Karl Marx (1818–1883). More notable than most other intellectuals of the nineteenth century, Marx was probably far less a "Marxist" than almost any of those who later used his work for their own purposes. He was a brilliant and articulate "activist economist" and, though his best-known work was his *Manifesto of the Communist Party* (1848), it was far less than his best. Better by far were his *Critique of Political Economy* (1859) and his *The Class Struggle in France* (1850). Yet Marx, trained primarily in history, was an intellectual who understood and utilized history as a discipline for revolutionary thought.

There were many others—some less visible and renowned than those mentioned but whose work generally contributed to the structure of a new order in the affairs of men as these were gradually manifested throughout the nineteenth-century world and especially in the United States. These included the following:

Louis Bonald (1754–1840). Bonald, a leading philosopher in postrevolutionary France, advocated a "new order" of traditionalism.

François de Chateaubriand (1768–1848). Chateaubriand was a devout Roman Catholic and something of a romantic conservative who saw the passing of the medieval period as a loss of utopian existence for common folk given only that benevolent and just patrimonial rulers could be ascended. His *Genius of Christianity* (1802) is sometimes seen as the "last gasp" of compromise in the passing of an age. Yet its persuasiveness served as a source of balance in future events.

Friedrich Engels (1820–1895). Some consider Engels the real founder of scientific socialism. His work has been overshadowed by that of Marx and yet he was, some consider, the more brilliant and temperate of the two. His *The Origin of the Family, Private Property, and the State,* published in 1884, was the fundamental basis for (still is) a rationale of some views of socialism, including the rationale for the establishment of the American Socialist party.

There are many others, too many to detail; as examples: Fuestel de Coulonges (1830–1889), a historian; Sir Henry Maine (1822–1888), a jurist and historian; Georg Hegel (1770–1854), a philosopher whose views have significantly influenced modern events; Robert Michaels (1876–1936), an economist whose treatise on political parties combined an exquisite combination of sociological and economic analysis; *Pierre Leplay* (1806–1882), a mineralogist and engineer of sorts whose interests in the working class and their problems led to major sociological studies of lower-class conditions; *Ferdinand Tonnies* (1855–1936), a German whose work concerning the relationship of "community and society" gave significant terms, in the original, to our language of gregarious phenomena (*Gesellschaft und Gemeinschaft*). It was published in 1887 and remains a classic in sociological literature.

But, again for our purposes, no such listing would be complete without special mention of Alexis Charles Henri Maurice Clerel de Tocqueville (1805–1859); generally recognized as a French historian and sociologist, de Tocqueville had perhaps the most influence on American attitudes and thought, not only in this country but throughout the world. Tocqueville put together two statements that constituted a major empirical treatment: his *Democracy in America* (1840) and *The Old Regime and the French Revolution* (1856). Of this work Nisbet states,[16]

Tocqueville's *Democracy in America* is the first systematic and empirical study of the effects of political power on modern society. This work is much else also, but at bottom it is a study, and a remarkably dispassionate one, of the impact of democracy on the traditions, values, and social structures descended from medieval society. In his second major work, *The Old Regime and the French Revolution,* Tocqueville explored the

---

[16]Robert Nisbet, *The Sociological Tradition* (New York: Basic Books, 1966), p. 120.

sources of modern political power, with its twin aspects of centralization and bureaucratization. . . . And no one reading *Democracy in America* will have any difficulty in seeing, between the lines, the thesis of the later work. Both studies have to be understood in the light of Tocqueville's obsession with the revolution and its impact upon the social order.

The Strains Between Individual and Society

Just as Professor Parker has observed that the "search for freedom is old," the larger issue, as it began most clearly to be articulated, especially in the nineteenth century, concerned the strains between the drive for equality and the tendency toward a centralization of authority to compromise that drive. The conflicting views of centralized "justice" and individual freedom emerged as a major issue in modern civilization. How much freedom, how much equality? That is indeed the question. Robert Nisbet sees a sort of benevolent and just centralization as the best way out of the dilemma:[17]

All that has magnified equality of condition has necessarily tended to abolish or diminish the buffers to central power which are constituted by social classes, kindreds, guilds, and other groups whose virtual essence is hierarchy. As Tocqueville—and before him Burke—perceived some degree of inequality is the very condition of the social bond. Variations among individuals, in strength, intelligence, age, aspiration, ability, of whatever kind, and aptitude, will always tend toward the inequality of result. Only through operation of a single centralized structure of power that reaches all individuals in a community, that strives to obliterate all gradations of power, rank, and affluence, not of this power's own making, can these variations and this inequality be moderated.

Unquestionably, school systems enjoyed a relatively remarkable "local" authority to do almost as they pleased with the masses of youth that came (increasingly unwillingly) into their jurisdiction for some years before and after World War II, but this situation may now be seen as being reversed. Again, interestingly, this reversal is itself a product of the strains between the individual and political authority. On the one hand, there is a resurgence of the ideas, issues, and tentative solutions that characterized the "progressive education movement" of the 1930s, and on the other, there is an immensely expanded centralization of bureaucratic authority as manifested by a proliferated regulatory apparatus. We will return to this dimension of educational development. For the moment let us discuss briefly the developments at colleges and universities that contributed to the achievement of a public system of schools by about 1920.

[17]Robert Nisbet, *The Twilight of Authority* (New York: Oxford University Press, 1975), p. 209.

TOWARD AN EDUCATION PROFESSION

After the establishment of the land grant university system, the attention given to education at the postsecondary level grew rapidly. By 1820, only ten state universities had been chartered, and some of these existed for years without any students. (Although the University of Virginia was established in 1819, for example, there were so few students qualified to attend that classes did not begin until 1825.) These early state universities, as noted previously, were elitist and oriented toward classical education. Moreover, they suffered an indifferent concern and poor fiscal support from legislatures.

After 1865, with federal intervention, "chairs" in pedagogy sprang up in both state and land grant universities and normal schools proliferated and gained increased recognition. In large measure, this was a response to the fact that the idea of free, public elementary education was catching on and communities—especially the cities—were demanding more and more of their schools.

Recognition of the institutionalization of schools as an established enterprise, together with the professionalization of its personnel, is marked to some degree by the first convention, in 1867, of the National Teachers Association (now the National Education Association) and by the establishment of the U.S. Office of Education also in 1867 (known then as the Department of Education). In 1865, the National Association of School Superintendents was formed and merged with the NEA in 1870 known thereafter as the Department of Superintendence until 1937 when its name was changed to the American Association of School Administrators.

Yet even with these early efforts of professional education personnel to organize nationally, teaching and other education-related careers retained a rather low prestige until almost the middle of the twentieth century. Writing in 1929, William Bagley (1874–1946), who served in the Teachers College, Columbia University, from 1917 to 1940, made these observations:[18]

In reviewing the handicaps that have beset the development (of the advancement in the status of the teacher's calling) . . . something akin' to contempt, has found expression. . . . In the first place, until recently, the teaching personnel of our public schools have been transient and unstable. Twenty years ago, the average period of service of the public school teacher was not more than four years. The occupation was distinctly recognized in most communities as temporary, and those who . . . were compelled to make it a life work were naturally regarded with something akin to pity [and] . . . although

[18]William Bagley, "The Profession of Teaching in the United States," *School and Society*, Vol. 29 (January 1929). Reprinted in Wade Baskin, ed., *Classics in Education* (New York: Philosophical Theory, 1966), pp. 49–51.

every state maintained professional schools for teachers not one in four of those employed in the public schools was a product of such an institution. As short a time ago as 1916, Judd and Parker asserted in an official bulletin of the Bureau of Education that the United States gave less attention to the training of teachers than did any other civilized nation. With brief tenure and lack of training quite naturally went meager compensation, and in a country where occupations won public regard in direct proportion to the material rewards that they provided, this condition itself was a sufficient stigma to the teacher's calling.

The School Administrator

School administrators enjoyed a somewhat better status than that characterized by Professor Bagley. First, such persons were generally regarded less as "schoolmasters" and more as "businessmen." By the last quarter of the nineteenth century, most of the larger places had school superintendents. It became rather obvious to the school boards in the larger cities that they could no longer cope with the increasing day-to-day difficulties of overseeing an emerging system of "free" schools. According to Knezevich, "thirteen school systems established the city school superintendency between 1837 and 1850 (and Buffalo and Louisville are credited with the creation, in 1837, of the first superintendencies in public education)."[19]

By 1890, thirty-nine cities in twenty-six different states from east to west had established "superintendents." Significantly absent were cities in the southwest and the deep south, with the exception of Georgia and Louisiana—Savannah named a superintendent of schools in 1866 and Atlanta in 1871, New Orleans established the office as early as 1841. New York State led with four superintendencies, and Massachusetts, with a relatively strong public schools tradition, had three cities with such offices. The smallest city to establish such an office at the time was Los Angeles, which in 1853 had a population of only 1610.[20]

These early school administrators were, in the main, little more than "clerks" in their general managerial functions and were heavily loaded with the responsibility for program or "curriculum" oversight beyond that. To a large extent, these latter aspects of their responsibility evolved into school "principalships." The success of these early superintendents rested generally on their abilities to convince their "trustees" or "boards" that they could perform efficiently and provide reasonably adequate instruction at low cost.[21]

[19]Stephen J. Knezevich, *Administration of Public Education*, 3rd ed. (New York: Harper & Row, 1975), p. 341.

[20]These data are derived from Theodore Reller, "The Development of the City Superintendency," in a table cited by Knezevich, op. cit., p. 342.

[21]For a discussion of this expectation of the early superintendency, see W. R. Lane, R. G. Corwin, and W. G. Monahan, *Foundations of Educational Administration: A Behavioral Analysis* (New York: Macmillan, 1967), pp. 12–14, and Raymond Callahan, *Education and the Cult of Efficiency* (Chicago: University of Chicago Press, 1962), pp. 12–13.

To a large extent, the role of the early superintendent was fashioned from at least two important axes of concern: on the one hand, there was the simple expedient of growing need and demand for schooling in the cities; on the other hand, there was a frequently explicit mandate from school trustees to meet that set of goals as "cheaply" as possible. This point of view has to be understood in the context of the times, which was characterized by competing and sometimes conflicting values. Clearly, the great influx of foreigners to the cities demanded that something be done to help indoctrinate these new "Americans" into the values of a still young and emerging nation. At the same time, the idea that *every* young American regardless of circumstance was entitled to some kind of chance at a rudimentary education was much further advanced in the cities than elsewhere. Even though it may be presumed that some members of the boards of education did not support such a democratic notion of education, they had little choice but to try to deal with it. Still, the idea of public taxation for such "services" was a tender topic, and the boards were always conscious of having to walk the fence between ideology and costs.

Accordingly, between 1890 and 1920, school superintendencies tended to develop in terms of the prevalent philosophy of "scientific management" simply because, at that stage in their evolution, public schools could probably not have survived without viable attention to the ideas of prudent fiscal oversight. During this period, the most successful and upwardly mobile city school superintendents were those who could somehow demonstrate effective instruction at the smallest cost.[22]

Many of these early school managers were drawn from the Protestant ministry; all held a "tight-fisted" attitude toward fiscal resources, but most were convinced of the value and importance of education; only a few did not believe that public schools were indeed *the* democratizing institution that gave America its opportunity for greatness.

Regarding their explicit preparation as school administrators, little is truly known. It is clear that these men (they were almost without exception "male") read the available literature about public education because they wanted to or had to—they were familiar with much of the current educational theory and some were notably influential in the development of both curriculum and administrative innovations.[23] Yet it became increasingly apparent that some formal instruction with reference to this emerging role was badly required. Apart from the conventions some small numbers attended and workshop activities that were organized, however, little explicit formal instruction was available until well after 1900.

[22]Needless to say, efficiency of cost was much easier to demonstrate than was effectiveness of instruction; most boards of education understood the former and assumed the latter.

[23]A notable exception to the "maleness" of early superintendents was Chicago's Ella Flagg Young in the early 1900s. A student of John Dewey's, she collaborated with him on some of his writing, and of her, he is alleged to have said that she saw educational matters better than he.

Graduate Education and School Administration

Two eventualities helped to change this situation—one somewhat general, one quite explicit.

Attempts to establish the study of "Education" at universities arose when those institutions began to accept some responsibility for the training of public school personnel. The first bona fide efforts in this regard were initiated at Indiana University in 1852, at Iowa in 1855, at the University of Wisconsin in 1856, at Kentucky in 1881, and in Utah, North Dakota, South Dakota, and Wyoming—all state universities—by 1875. As the "normal school movement" proliferated in these states, most of the universities would just as soon have discontinued any interest in teacher education, and many did. But the rapid expansion of the development of common schools forced such universities to provide some service in these fields.[24]

Among the more interesting efforts to establish Education as a legitimate aspect of university programs were those in the University of Michigan at Ann Arbor between 1837 and 1879. As early as 1837, the first superintendent of public instruction in Michigan urged that programs for teachers be established at the young university. Not much happened. In 1848, a bill was introduced in the legislature in Michigan to establish a normal school branch at Ann Arbor; it failed in the Michigan House. In 1852, a normal school was established separately at Ypsilanti (now Eastern Michigan University), yet the university at Ann Arbor persisted in the presumption that it had a role to perform and an expertise to provide. The university continued to offer some courses and to express continual interest in pedagogy throughout the intervening years, and, finally, in 1879, a chair of the Science and Art of Teaching was authorized. Appointed to this professorship was William Payne who observed that, "As at present constituted, the normal schools are not fitted to dispense the professional education needed by head masters, principals, superintendents, or even first assistants in high schools."[25]

A seemingly unrelated historical event occurred with the establishment of the Johns Hopkins University, in 1876 at Baltimore, Maryland, and the forerunner of the university as we know it today. Patterned after the German institutions whereby research was a major emphasis, the idea of "graduate education" came into reality in the United States. Hopkins became *the* center for advanced study,

---

[24]This discussion draws heavily on Charles Judd, "The School of Education" in Raymond A. Kent ed., *Higher Education in America* (Boston: Ginn, 1930), pp. 160–162.

[25]W. H. Payne, *Contributions to the Science of Education*, cited in G. W. A. Luckey, "The Professional Training of Secondary Teachers in the United States," doctoral thesis, Faculty in Philosophy, Columbia University, New York, 1903, p. 113.

and it was here that a number of notable men, later dramatically associated with educational developments, became established.[26]

But the important thing for us to remember is that the *idea* of advanced, or graduate, education was now clearly established, and since school administrators were generally far beyond the average level of teachers, the opportunities opened up by the graduate school development also provided new and legitimate opportunities for further preparation for this still small group of educators. Following the Hopkins model (which established its "chair" in 1884 and awarded it to Hall), chairs, departments, or schools of pedagogy followed at New York University in 1890, Chicago in 1901, and Teachers College in 1889, which was incorporated with Columbia University in 1898.

In 1910, the first doctoral degree in education administration was awarded at Teachers College, Columbia University, and thereafter the establishment of school administration as a professional and legitimate career was clear. That singular event heralded a pattern of preparation that grew and matured. Some departures from this pattern have, at one or another time, challenged its general flavor or its methodological structure, but today there is no longer much to distinguish the doctorate in education from the more traditional doctor of philosophy degree, and few people try to draw distinctions.

The dimensions of the mass educational environment now confronting schools' management require the greatest breadth of knowledge and sophistication in our history. As that for a point of departure, we turn now to the more quantitative and qualitative aspects of the contemporary environment in educational management.

CONTEMPORARY CONCERNS

Between 1960 and 1970, two major related demographic trends have had, and continue to have, profound effects on the nature and management of public schools. The first was a shift in both population and occupations out of the central cities; the second was a dramatic slowing of population growth generally

---

[26]For example, John Dewey received his doctorate there in 1884. Equally important, Dewey studied there with G. Stanley Hall. Hall had enjoyed extremely broad preparation in theology, philosophy, and psychology at Williams, Harvard, Bonn, Berlin, and Leipzig; had been a student of William James, of Wundt, and of Trendelenburg; and was the founder of what is still known as the child study movement as a consequence of his publication, in 1883, of *The Contents of Children's Minds on Entering Schools*. He pursued his interests in these areas not only during the six years he was at Johns Hopkins but also during his thirty-year tenure thereafter as president of Clark University.

and a recognition of a rapidly approaching zero birth rate. While demographers differ somewhat as to timing, the zero birth rate is apparently approaching.[27]

Schools, Students, and Personnel

It is important with reference to demographic data to recognize the important difference between growth as measured by absolute numbers of children and declines as measured by the proportions of change that are occurring. These trends can sometimes be confusing because, in effect, we know that the potential secondary school student of 1990 has already been born and thus can project secondary enrollments using absolute figures. On the other hand, simply calculating the total number of students in schools in any particular year as compared with those in school in some subsequent year provides the most dramatic and clear representation of trends.

For example, enrollments in public schools in 1971 increased for the twenty-seventh straight year, reaching a high of 46.1 million. But in the five years after 1971, each year saw a slight decrease, and in the fall of 1977, total enrollment declined to 44.3 million. All these decreases have occurred at the elementary level simply because of the grade progression pattern of schooling. In other words, enrollments in grades 9 to 12 have continued to rise, peaking at 14.3 million in the fall of 1976.[28]

At the same time that overall enrollment has seen gradual decreases, other aspects of educational patterns—costs, teaching staff and other personnel, capital construction, interest on debts, salaries, and average cost per pupil—continue to rise (see Figure 2-1).

Quite clearly, with slight variations due to local conditions, the data in Figure 2-1 may be applied to most of America's 16,000 school districts. Also, clearly, the "culprit" in this curious scenario of "fewer pupils, more costs" is inflation! In 1978, the annualized inflation rate was hovering around 10 percent, and that pattern has been reasonably constant, give or take a percentage point or two, since 1973. But if there is any good news to be drawn from these facts, for the nation as a whole (and thus for most of its school systems), the ratio of teachers to pupils is down.

An increase in classroom teachers between 1971–72 and 1976–77 by 130,000

[27]Katherine Eisenberger, "New Population Trends Changing America," *The School Administrator*, Vol. 34, no. 7 (July–August 1977), 18.

[28]U.S. Department of Education, National Center for Education Statistics, *Statistics of Public Elementary and Secondary Day Schools, Fall, 1976*, and estimates of the National Center for Education Statistics, 1977, *The Digest* (Washington, D.C.: GPO, 1977), Chapter 2. The information in this and the discussions that follow are drawn from various documents from this source and is so acknowledged.

Figure 2-1. Selected Trends, Public Schools: 1971–72 to 1976–77

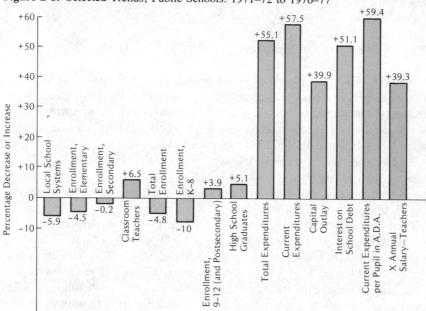

Adapted from U.S. Department of Education, National Center for Education Statistics, *Statistics of Public Elementary and Secondary Schools, Fall, 1976* (Washington, D.C.: GPO, 1978).

(for a total of 2,193,000 in the fall 1976) has resulted in a gross decrease in the pupil-teacher ratio from 22.3 to 1 to 20.2 to 1 during the full-year period involved. The *range* in the pupil-teacher ratio is more difficult to determine and, except for certain local conditions, probably would not mean very much. Yet that this ratio is experiencing a reduction is cause for encouragement.

School District Organization. Also of interest is the continued trend toward the elimination of inefficient and ineffective school districts. By 1976–77, for example, there were about 1000 fewer school districts and almost 3000 fewer elementary schools than in 1971–72, even though the number of secondary schools remained almost constant. While it surely must be true that some elementary schools in relatively large systems were closed due to population shifts, the elimination of most of the 1000 school systems was a consequence of the elimination of specifically ''elementary school districts.''

During this period of five years, twenty-nine different states eliminated one or more school districts. Nebraska led this group by eliminating 359 school districts, while Georgia, New Mexico and South Carolina each eliminated 1. During this same period, six states added school districts, Alaska leading by establishing 23 under a new reorganization plan designed to effect greater localized efficiency.

Deconsolidation. During this period too were several isolated instances of attempts to "deconsolidate" schools, especially secondary programs. There is, by way of clarification, an important distinction among school consolidations, district mergers, and school district eliminations, and it may be useful to clarify the distinctions among these terms before citing one of these "deconsolidation" efforts.

In the case of most school district reductions, the districts eliminated are those generally referred to as a "nonoperating districts," that is, districts that, in effect, do not "operate" schools; sometimes they are referred to as "sending districts" because, although these quasi-corporations have elected trustees or boards (and may or may not have an executive administrator), the children of a particular district are "sent" to other operating systems and pay to that district a tuition. Of the 359 school districts eliminated in Nebraska, for example, between 1972 and 1976, many were nonoperating, and the same is true of other of the twenty-eight states that eliminated districts. (Yet, latest data available as of the fall 1976, disclosed that there were still 325 nonoperating school districts in the country.)

School consolidations are a totally different idea and process. "Consolidations" merely put together two or more schools that are normally under the general jurisdiction of an existing and established school system. Typically, such consolidations involve "too small" secondary schools, and such rearrangements are pursued for the benefits of enriched curricula and greater fiscal efficiency.

Finally, in the case of district mergers, one established quasi-corporate entity reorganizes with another, usually contiguous, district. The primary motivation for such "mergers" has to do with revenue patterns; that is, the district to which another chooses to be attached has a favorable revenue base. State law on such matters varies of course, but in most cases some rational basis of relationship must exist—either contiguity or patterns of constitutional condition. In Kentucky, for example, the county is the constitutional school system and city or "independent" districts are allowed to exist, under law, simultaneously with the county district systems by statute. Consequently, in Kentucky (and in some other, mostly southern, states), the county is *not* an "intermediate" school system but an actual school district, and if an "independent" (typically a "city system") chooses to "merge" with the county, the latter has no real choice under the law except to accept and incorporate the other district. By the same token, in such mergers, the former independent district is simply giving over to the county all its capital outlay and its governance. In Oklahoma, on the other hand, state law merely requires that mergers of school districts must meet the initial requirement of contiguity (i.e., if any part of one district's boundaries "touches" another's, the *possibility* for merger is satisfied). The procedure then follows a kind of "advise-and-consent" pattern, based fundamentally on popular referendum. Accordingly, a district that seeks merger and can demonstrate a clear will of its patrons can be "annexed." One or the other of these two patterns with slight variation is typical throughout the country. Yet, in any of these circumstances, the issues are always heated and may even be accompanied by violence. The adage that "where children walk, sentiment follows closely" is never more apparent than where school district reorganization is concerned.

Deconsolidation. Some final comments with reference to school district organization are appropriate in connection with the idea of "deconsolidation." The motivation of some school patrons to restore schools that are lost through consolidation is generally active for some years after new patterns have been established. Unquestionably, there are also some who never accept the new arrangements and who have waged continuing efforts to reconstitute the older arrangements. In the great majority of cases concerning consolidations of small, localized secondary schools into larger and more effective units, once the reorganization has been accomplished, the opposition fades. In those cases where the new, larger unit achieves notable success in team sports, opposition fades even more quickly. One of the more interesting recent attempts at deconsolidation, in West Virginia, highlights the important role of state education agencies.

Clearly, the reorganization of school systems requires adherence to legitimately established procedures under law or regulation. In most cases, legislation provides guidelines that authorize the state board of education to act in an official capacity with reference to school reorganization issues, and these powers must be balanced against the traditional recognition of the important concept of local control. Although there may not be absolute authority assigned to the state by legislative statute to force the closing of schools for any reason, the State Department of Education in all states has the responsibility of "overseeing" schools. As a part of this responsibility, some states have the power to "accredit" schools and there is also the authority to withhold state financial aid. Thus, even though a state may not be able to close a school absolutely, there are other powerful sanctions that can be used to ensure conformity to mandates.

There is one notable recent attempt to deconsolidate schools. In Preston County, West Virginia, there was agreement to establish a reorganization that resulted in the consolidation of several high schools based on a special plan developed and submitted to the state board of education. These plans were required of all county systems by the state for the purpose of approving the allocation and utilization of a state-wide school construction bond issue. Known as "comprehensive facilities plans," each county board of education proposed a plan and had it considered by the State Department of Education. In the case of Preston County, a subsequent school board election resulted in a switch in the balance of power in favor of anticonsolidation forces and by votes of 3–2, the local board began a program designed to restore the previously closed high schools. This meant a repudiation of the original "comprehensive facilities plan," and to do this appropriately, the new majority on the board presented their case as an official "Revision" of the plan and submitted it to the state board for consideration.

On August 10, 1979, the State Board of Education, after hearing testimony from "experts" from both sides of the issue, voted to uphold the original plan calling for consolidation and, in effect, enjoined the current board majority from proceeding with its deconsolidation plan. A legal battle now looms.

The point, of course, is merely that the State Education Agency continues to emerge as a growing and powerful force in the determination of public school policy and condition. And while some such agencies are much stronger and more influential than others, *all* are relatively more vital than just ten years ago. We will deal with these developments in somewhat more detail in following chapters; at this point it is merely important to note that with reference not only to matters affecting school district organization but also to almost all other educational administrative concerns, the State Agency is playing an increasingly key policy and regulatory role.

In deciding these kinds of issues, it is usually the enlightened self-interest of student personnel that makes the case; at least, it is such interests as interpreted by whomever has the power to decide. As suggested, that power is increasingly concentrated in the State Education Agency.

Accessibility to Education

As the case is in school district reorganization, involvements with, and about, student personnel are truly the "bottom line" so far as public school administration is concerned. While the whole idea of "students" may seem to be the least of the day-to-day problems that confront the typical school superintendent, the fact is that students are the fundamental issue from which all others derive. Certainly, the "central office" administrator is somewhat removed from the actual technical level of instructional activity in the school and the classroom itself, and, certainly as well, the increasing complexity and bureaucratization of school organization tends to obscure this fundamental concern. Yet the truth is that matters related to the *general delivery of instructional and auxiliary services to students remain the prime basis for all administrative activity*.

The typical school administrator must think not only in terms of what enrollments are like in his or her system, how many students are transported and the costs associated with that, how well this district's students are doing on achievement tests, and so forth, but also in terms of the general dimensions of the "larger" national picture in all these and many other regards. Thoughtful

Table 2-1. Enrollment: Grades 9–12, Public and Nonpublic Schools, and Comparisons with Population Ages 14–17, Selected Years 1890–1976

School Year	Enrollments, Grades 9–12			Population: Ages 14–17	Total Enrolled per 100 Persons, Ages 14–17
	All Schools	Public Schools	Nonpublic Schools		
1890	359,949	202,963	94,931	5,354,653	6.7%
1900	699,403	519,251	110,797	6,152,231	11.4
1910	1,115,398	915,061	117,400	7,220,298	15.4
1920	2,500,176	2,200,389	213,920	7,735,841	32.3
1930	4,804,255	4,399,422	341,158	9,341,221	51.4
1940	7,123,009	6,635,337	487,672	9,720,419	73.3
1950	6,453,009	5,757,810	695,199	8,404,768	76.8
1960	9,599,810	8,531,454	1,068,356	11,154,879	86.1
1970	15,226,000	13,886,000	1,340,000	16,279,000	93.5
1976	15,823,000	14,388,000	1,435,000	16,896,000	93.6

Adapted from U.S. Department of Education, National Center for Education Statistics, *The Digest* (Washington, D.C.: GPO, 1976).

recognition of these more general patterns provides the balanced frame of reference necessary to move toward the policy determinations that prove best for any particular system.

Increasingly, the "general" picture is more difficult to rationalize, not because good data are not available but because increasingly sophisticated computerized retrieval technologies tend to provide too much! How does one decide what is required? Our view is that the more generalized portrayals are the best. For example, examine Table 2-1, a historical picture of enrollment data. Considering the general accessibility to secondary education, it is interesting to note that in just about the space of one lifetime, of those young persons aged 14 to 17 (and for whom secondary education is principally targeted), the proportions exercising that accessibility rose from only about 7 percent in 1890 to more than 93 percent by 1976, a testimony to humankind's efforts to provide any type of mass institutionalized education to the young.

Nonetheless, the idea of accessibility to a basic qualitative education remains yet unfilled in the largest measure and remains, in our view, an undertaking that should involve all professional school administrators. That dream has come much farther in the United States in 1980 than in any other country in the known world, and the fundamental *idea* of accessibility—though perhaps not yet too clearly and fully perceived in its ultimate value for some—remains the most fundamental purpose toward realization of the final achievement of the free, public, mass educational experiment.

How close are we? Not close enough to be sure. Although almost all the eligible youth are "in" schools, too many, in some categories, are not, or they become disenchanted and leave. Consider two examples of school-aged populations that remain underrepresented with reference to accessibility—the handicapped and the minorities.

The Handicapped. Among the "handicapped," data remain questionable. For one thing, it has only been since about 1970 that intensive and sophisticated analyses of the general scope of these types of persons have been pursued actively. Yet not nearly enough "handicapped" persons have reasonable access to public education. In examining Table 2-2, note the relatively consistent *proportions* of the handicapped population *in school* as proportions of the total school enrollment—between just under 6 percent to just over 7 percent. Yet the proportions of handicapped persons *known to us presently* in each of the age groups delineated is disproportionately greater when the aggregate from those aged 5 to 25 is considered. So what? Well, there are always two immediate "articulation" problems that must be put aside when dealing with the handicapped; the first of these is age. Age does not always mean very much when dealing with certain types of handicaps. One cannot presume that a 12-year-old retarded child can be dealt with in the same fashion as a 12-year-old normal

Table 2-2. Estimated Handicapped Population Ages 5 to 25 Years, by Age Group, Enrollment Status, and Specific Handicap, 1976

Item	Total, 5–25 Years	5–13 Years	14–17 Years	18–25 Years
Total population	80,091,000	32,701,000	16,745,000	30,645,000
Total population enrolled in school	58,244,000	31,215,000	15,917,000	11,112,000
Handicapped population	5,409,000	2,007,000	1,224,000	2,117,000
Handicapped as % of total population	6.8%	6.1%	7.3%	7.1%
Handicapped population enrolled in school	3,712,000	1,954,000	1,127,000	631,000
As % of total enrollment	6.4%	6.3%	7.1%	5.7%
Specific handicap				
Retarded	423,000	143,000	97,000	183,000
Hard of hearing	310,000	177,000	65,000	68,000
Speech impaired	292,000	188,000	43,000	61,000
Sight impaired	281,000	137,000	55,000	90,000
Emotionally disturbed	208,000	88,000	45,000	75,000
Crippled	436,000	135,000	120,000	181,000
Heart trouble	246,000	101,000	70,000	75,000
Respiratory disorder	759,000	381,000	199,000	179,000
Other handicaps	3,074,000	914,000	662,000	1,497,000

Adapted from Jeffrey W. Williams, *Students and Schools,* Table 1.6 (Washington, D.C.: National Center for Education Statistics, 1979), p. 18.

child or even, in many circumstances, a 12-year-old physically handicapped child. A second issue has to do with the extent of additional "services" required to deal with almost any manifestation of handicapped persons.

All these and still other considerations notwithstanding, however, passage of P.L. 94-142, "The Education of All the Handicapped," now places both resources and responsibilities on public schools to provide the quality of education necessary so that "accessibility" continues to be expanded as an idea and a reality.

The Poor and the Minorities. A continuing source of frustration that confronts most school administrators relates to attempts to provide equal educational opportunity to impoverished and minority children. Too frequently, of course, these terms typically apply to the same child, for the likelihood is that, if a child is black or Chicano, that child is also poor.

Minority Education and Integration. There are two sets of rather impressive data regarding the "minority" educational issues that must interest the prospective and practicing school administrator. Both really concern, again, the notion of "accessibility," but they have differing patterns. First, there is the simple, general pattern of whether, and to what extent, schools are or are not racially balanced. Based on data depicted in Figure 2-2, integration is progressing in the southern and border states, but racial isolation has increased in the Northeast and integration has made only marginal progress in the West. Some would argue that the proportion of minority students is far less in the western than in the southern and border states, especially of blacks, but under normal circumstances, this would suggest that minority integration ought thereby to be easier and less costly. But any such arguments, either way, tend to oversimplify the issues; moreover, regional data such as that depicted in Figure 2-2 always obscure what may or may not be happening not only in a particular state but especially in particular school districts as well.

Still, depiction of the general situation is useful and does clearly reflect the fact that racial integration in public schools is being accomplished better in the southern and border states than elsewhere and that racial isolation (i.e., where 90 to 100 percent of enrollments are minorities) is greatest in the Midwest and has tended to increase (over the four years from 1970 to 1974) in the Northeast.

Related to Poverty. As indicated, poverty and minority groups seem too frequently in our otherwise affluent society to go hand in hand. To some extent, this relationship is demonstrated in Figure 2-3. It will be noted that the predominantly southern region of the nation continues to have the largest average number of children from impoverished families. While the national poverty rate has remained relatively unchanged—at least during the first half of the decade of the 1970s—other data disclose that poverty has declined appreciably in the South and that at least two southern states—Oklahoma and Virginia—have enjoyed

Figure 2-2. Distribution, Black Students in Public Elementary and Secondary Schools by Geographic Region[a]

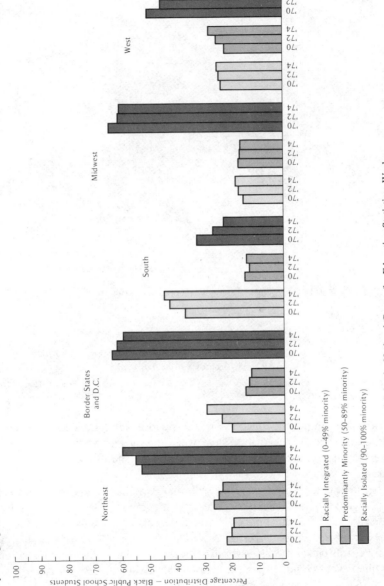

[a]Source: J. W. Williams, *Students and Schools*, National Center for Education Statistics, Washington, D.C.: U.S. Department of Health, Education, and Welfare. 1979, p. 15.

Figure 2-3. School-Aged Children (Ages 5 to 17) in Families Below the Poverty Level, 1975

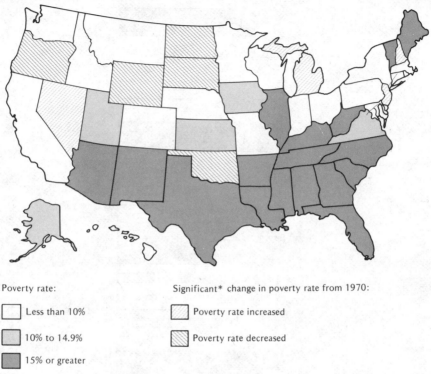

Poverty rate:

☐ Less than 10%

▨ 10% to 14.9%

▨ 15% or greater

Significant* change in poverty rate from 1970:

▨ Poverty rate increased

▨ Poverty rate decreased

*Statistically significant at the 0.05 level.

From Jeffrey W. Williams, *Schools and Students* (Washington, D.C.: National Center for Education Statistics, 1979), p. 13.

statistically significant reductions in the poverty rate. In Michigan and New Hampshire, on the other hand, there were significant increases, and these are somewhat representative of the upper midwestern and the northeastern states as well.

The point is that, in those states with relatively high proportions of minority population, poverty is more prevalent, which compounds already difficult issues related to the adequate financing of public school systems and the levels of achievement that characterize minority children. Even a superficial analysis of Figure 2-4 discloses the disparity in achievement among all school-aged groups of whites, blacks, and Hispanics. In not a single subject area, for any age group, did blacks and Hispanics perform up to the national mean on achievement tests in the five areas recorded. And as the age increased, these young people tended to fall even farther behind. These findings suggest significant challenges to both management and leadership activities of school administrators.

Figure 2-4. Achievement in Subject Areas by Age and Racial/Ethnic Group, 1971–72 through 1974–75

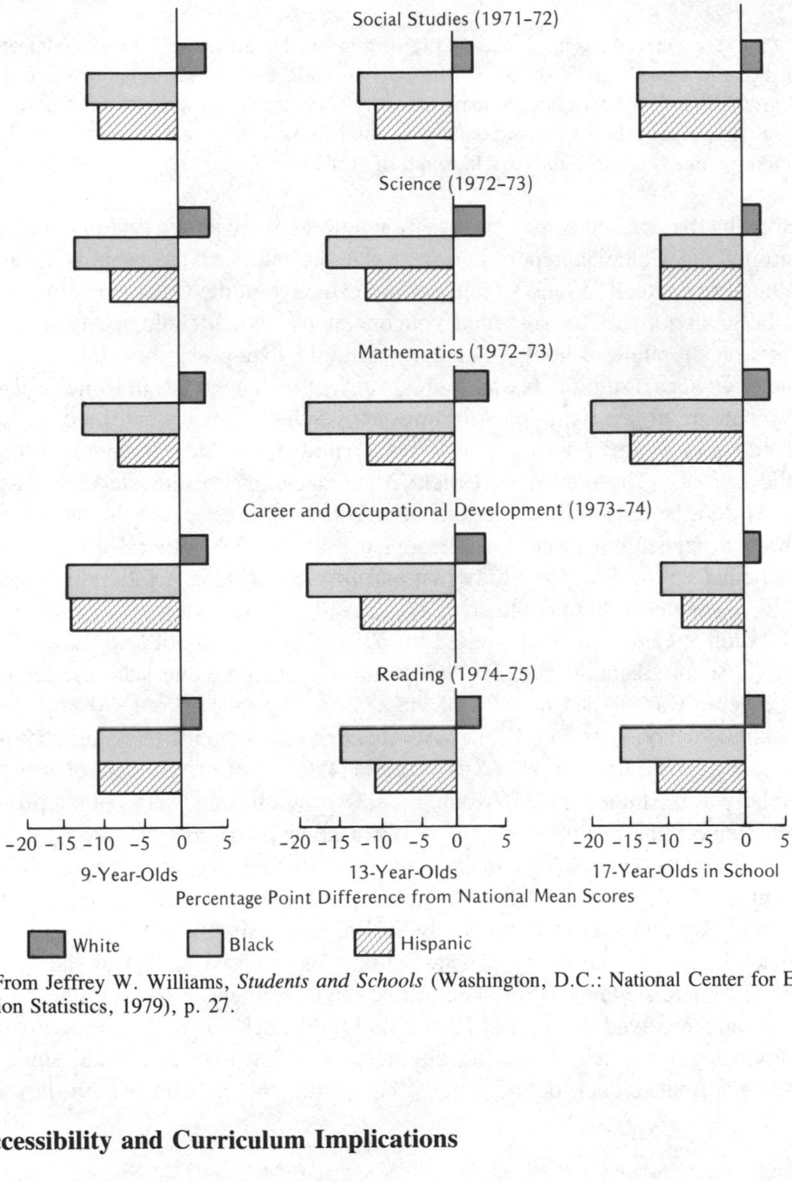

Social Studies (1971–72)

Science (1972–73)

Mathematics (1972–73)

Career and Occupational Development (1973–74)

Reading (1974–75)

-20 -15 -10 -5 0 5   -20 -15 -10 -5 0 5   -20 -15 -10 -5 0 5
9-Year-Olds   13-Year-Olds   17-Year-Olds in School
                 Percentage Point Difference from National Mean Scores

■ White   □ Black   ▨ Hispanic

From Jeffrey W. Williams, *Students and Schools* (Washington, D.C.: National Center for Education Statistics, 1979), p. 27.

Accessibility and Curriculum Implications

The disparity in achievement between minority children and others is further complicated by the increasingly apparent recognition that in some curricular areas, *all* school-aged persons are doing more poorly, and by the findings of the most recent Coleman report that private schools seem to be doing a significantly better overall job in the education of youth than are public schools.[29] Yet according to one critic, the most recent report is cause for some celebration, since it establishes clearly that schools have a positive effect.

For 15 years, since the appearance of the original Coleman report in 1966, educators have been reminded repeatedly that 'schools don't make a difference' and that family background heavily determines educational achievement. The new Coleman report dramatically reverses this pessimistic conclusion and finds instead that schools *do* make a difference, regardless of family background of students.[30]

But what has caused some consternation among many public school personnel regarding the Coleman report is a fear that because private schools (mostly Parochial ones) tend to look so much more effective in the Coleman study there will be great support for so-called voucher plans, which could see further deterioration of public schools. There is certainly that possibility. The various voucher devices or tuition–tax measures—any of which would, in some fashion, allow parents to send children to almost any schools they please and pay for that education with a voucher or a tax write-off—would effectively cripple public schools. The data from Coleman seem clearly to indicate that private schools do a better job in education; however, to a large extent this is because of both a curriculum issue and an advising attitude. In other words, it was documented in the Coleman study that enrollments in science and math courses are much greater in the private schools. Consider these patterns, as pointed out by Ravitch:[31] Geometry was studied by 53% of public school seniors, 84% of Catholic school seniors, and 77% of seniors in other private schools; second-year algebra was studied by 42% of the seniors in public school, 70% of those in Catholic schools, and 66% of those other private schools; trigonometry was studied by 22% public, 44% Catholic, and 42% other private school seniors; chemistry was studied by 37% public, 53% Catholic, and 51% other private school seniors, and so on down the list of academic subjects that are generally regarded as "solids." The same pattern held (though the percentages varied) for physics, calculus, and other subjects. A quite important corollary to these data was also pointed out in the study: There was a significantly different kind of disciplinary climate in the private schools as opposed to that in the public schools. Where students were asked to rate the effectiveness of discipline, Catholic schools received the highest ratings and public schools received the lowest.

Obviously, there are mitigating circumstances that help to explain some of these performance data; public schools have little choice about whom they en-

---

[29]James S. Coleman *et al. Public and Private Schools* (Washington, D.C.: National Center for Education Statistics, Department of Education, 1981), 233 pp.

[30]Diane Ravitch, "The Meaning of the New Coleman Report," *Phi Delta Kappan*, Vol. 62, no. 10 (June 1981), p. 718.

[31]Ibid., p. 720.

roll, and there are unquestionably circumstances in which youngsters who have been something of a problem to the private schools have been denied admission or continuation in such schools and public schools have had to accept them. Moreover, public schools have had to deal with many youngsters who simply cannot meet the standards of "keeping up" in other scholastic environments, and public schools have had as students the least well prepared of minority and other impoverished children, who, although the school may indeed be making a difference for them as the Coleman report concludes, are still poor in comparison with students in private and parochial schools. The fact remains, however, that the curriculum in the public schools is much more elective, with fewer required units than in the private sector, and required course work is less demanding.

TEACHING PERSONNEL

Between 1976 and 1977, the total number of full- and part-time classroom teachers declined slightly (see Table 2-3).

While nonpublic school classroom teachers, in the aggregate, increased during this one-year period only by about 2000 teachers nationally, the overall pattern seems to begin to reflect the trend toward declining enrollments. The number of *public* school classroom teachers was up in 1976 from 2,155,448 in 1973–74; thus, clearly 1976 was a watershed year. The overall general pattern of public school educational personnel in 1973–74 is provided in Table 2-4.

By early 1981 it began to be accepted that there would be teacher shortages again in certain areas—principally in mathematics and the sciences. Although these shortages could become severe by 1982, they are not due to enrollment increases but rather to the economics of teaching. A person with an appropriate math background can earn at least twice as much in careers outside teaching, which is also true of those with science backgrounds.

Table 2-3. Full- and Part-Time Classroom Teachers, Fall 1976–1977

	Public	Nonpublic	Total
Fall 1976	2,193,000	247,000	2,440,000
Fall 1977	2,178,000	249,000	2,427,000

From National Center for Education Statistics, *Statistics of Public Elementary and Secondary Schools, Fall 1977* (Washington, D.C.: NCES, 1978), p. 3.

Table 2-4. Categories of Total Educational
Personnel in Public Schools,
1973–74 (FTE)

Personnel Category	Total Full-Time Equivalents
Total, all instructional staff	2,425,445
Principals/asst. principals	100,455
Consultants/supervisors	37,738
Classroom teachers	2,155,448
Librarians	44,242
Guidance/counseling personnel	55,743
Psychological personnel	9,326
Other supervisory and instructional personnel	22,493

From National Center for Education Statistics, *Statistics of State School Systems, 1973–74* (Washington, D.C.: NCES, 1977), p. 4.

SUMMARY

The most encouraging conclusion to be drawn from these personnel data, and from the other matters raised, for the school administrator is that, after almost forty years of suffering through a "growth industry," we are now approaching a more propitious "economy of scale." The teacher-pupil ratio is becoming more manageable and the FTE (full-time-equivalent) relationship between special instructional services personnel (supervisors, consultants, librarians, etc.) looks favorable for an improved trend for instructional support services as well.

Unquestionably, the costs related to delivery of better instruction continue to increase. And profound jurisdictional, attitudinal, political, and assessment issues continue to influence school managers who must effect more efficiencies and know-how in the system. At the same time, and this cannot be overemphasized, school administrators must do so with full cognition that they remain at the service of the most humane and genuinely sensitive of all modern institutions. Nonetheless, it is within this sometimes perplexing environment of competing values, issues, and dilemmas that the contemporary school administrator finds his greatest satisfactions.

In subsequent chapters, we will provide information on the significant parameters that confront both the management and leadership phases of the school administrator's role.

EXERCISES

1. You have just been appointed to a superintendency in a district with three high schools. Enrollments in all three are declining; each was designed for between 1200 and 1500 students in the upper three grades. Current enrollments are 1160, 930, and 740, respectively. There has been much controversy about the expense of maintaining three such schools, but sentiment is high about eliminating any of them. What alternatives should be considered and what kind of information are you going to need to make a solid recommendation?

2. As principal of a middle school, you have been approached by a group of local citizens with three fundamental evangelistic ministers as spokespersons urging you to introduce moral and spiritual values into your curriculum with "scriptures" as the basis. While you are aware of the legal questions, what are they specifically and how can you handle the request so as not to have it grow out of proportion? What historical data are useful to you?

3. You are the assistant superintendent for instruction and have just examined achievement test data for ten elementary schools; in two, with about 30 percent and 16 percent minority children, respectively, the scores are disproportionately low. This information is also known to a minority female board member, and she has asked you what you intend to do about it. How are you going to respond?

4. As the new superintendent in a community school district with 6500 students K–12, you have been asked to address a dinner meeting of civic leaders on the general topic of your "educational point of view." You will have about thirty-five minutes; outline the speech.

5. Among five school principals under your supervision as a director of curriculum and secondary education there is one who is very conservative in her educational attitudes; she does not follow the curriculum courses of study too closely, preferring instead to emphasize an elitist and heavily academic program at the expense of general and career education programs that the district strongly supports. She has a strong following among parents whose children are not doing well. She also does not enjoy strong cooperative relationships with other principals and tends to "put them down." There is, however, support from most teachers in her school, but the situation is heading for serious community debate. What are you going to do? What do you need to know?

SUGGESTED REFERENCES

Blumberg, Arthur, and William Greenfield. *The Effective Principal: Perspectives on School Leadership*. Boston: Allyn and Bacon, Inc., 1980. See especially the case chapters, Chapters 4–11.

Daignon, Arthur, and Richard A. Dempsey. *School: Pass at Your Own Risk*. Englewood Cliffs, N.J.: Prentice-Hall, Inc., 1974.

Gordon, Margaret S. *Youth Education and Unemployment Problems*. Berkeley, Calif.: Carnegie Council on Policy Studies in Higher Education, 1979. With a chapter by Martin Trow.

Monahan, W. G. *Theoretical Dimensions of Educational Administration*. New York: Macmillan Publishing Co., 1975. See especially Chapters 3 and 10.

Ross, Patricia. *Trouble in School*. New York: Avon Books, 1979.

Spring, Joel. *The Sorting Machine*. New York: David McKay Co., Inc., 1976.

Van Til, William (ed.). *Curriculum: Quest for Relevance*. Boston: Houghton Mifflin Co., 1971.

Chapter 3

Aspects of the Structure and Function of Contemporary Schools' Administration

INTRODUCTION

This chapter is designed to clarify the contemporary operational definition of the role of the local school district administrator, including not only the chief executive officer—the superintendent of schools—but also the chief unit administrators, school principals, and the total professional support staff typically required to achieve an effective organizational team. Our emphasis will be on the "central office" executive personnel. We will also touch on some general theoretical and practical concerns for the effectiveness of the division of labor that is, in our view, essential to effective management within school district patterns. As is typical with this text, we will express our notions of the "general" and leave it to the student and the professor to draw the more specific and applicable implications.

A GENERAL PATTERN

The definitions of the duties of public school officers and teachers are included in the "school laws" of the various states. Although these vary according to state, their general flavor is similar. Almost all of these statutory provisions hold that the "superintendent shall act as the chief executive officer of the board and execute . . . all of its educational policies."

Any generalized, statutory definitions only peripherally imply the organizational components of the roles and statuses that characterize the administration and technical levels of activity for schools. Definitions of these roles are further specified in documents, policies, and "academic program" statements related to certification and licensure (for example, in such documents as "State Standards for the Preparation of Educational Personnel").

In a number of states, these "standards" are drafted in the form of "competency" statements, and, in pursuing a program of studies aimed at eligibility for a superintendent's credential, a college or university is authorized to recommend such a person for certification after its "program" has been evaluated rigorously and "approved" by the state department of education. All related educational roles are also subject to still further—usually complementary—definition through a similar national evaluation by the National Council for the Accreditation of Teacher Education (NCATE). National accreditation is *voluntary*, but accreditation is important if an institution of higher education wants to maintain a regional or national reputation in professional education.

The point is, however, that whereas legal language remains appropriately broad, "professional" influence is explicit and functional. But, despite the disagreement that exists within the education professions regarding process and pattern, there is wide acceptance of the ultimate condition and each professional group jealously guards its own right to be involved in the drafting of standards and their revision and the activities associated with implementing them.

These various "standards" generally provide an operational definition of the areas of competence that the school administrator must possess and range from ability to define goals that result in adequate instructional programs, communication skills, personnel recruitment and assignment, fiscal management, human relations skills, evaluation procedures, understanding of school law, and facilities construction and maintenance.[1]

STRUCTURE AND FUNCTION

All definitions of administrator or teacher roles, regardless of source or circumstance, can only specify what is consensually regarded as minimal, and all posit the "qualifications" that must be met upon entry to the professions. No such standards or consensually recognized definitions can consider the real be-

[1]The state of West Virginia, for example, approves academic programs for the superintendency certificate based on thirty-five different "competencies" that require from thirty to forty-five semester hours of work beyond the bachelor's degree. *Standards for the Approval of Teacher Education Programs; Supplement: Educational Personnel* (Charleston, W. Va.: State Department of Education, 1976), pp. 76–77.

haviors that are actualized in the process of performing the role. Certainly, evaluation techniques are frequently reflective of ongoing performance; but in large measure the superintendent must delegate the oversight and supervision of the major tasks to a responsible staff and, in turn, be ultimately accountable for that staff's efforts.

Consequently, one of the most important management decisions that the school administrator makes concerns the structure and functions of the executive staff, and this always relates with some varying degrees to the size and scope of the system.

THE ORGANIZATION OF SCHOOL SYSTEMS

All school systems, regardless of size, must meet the same fundamental purposes, and all school systems must confront the same generalized internal and external exigencies. Increasing size and scope of activity merely complicate the management of these imperatives and necessitate additional labor for monitoring what classical management theorists refer to as "span of control." In a very small school system, say, one with 200 pupils in grades K–6 (an "elementary" district), all the executive functions may be managed by a single superintendent and a competent school secretary. At the other extreme, a school system such as in Los Angeles (which transports more pupils than there are residents in the entire state of Iowa) employs many hundreds of professionals within the executive function. Such large systems have found it effective to decentralize administrative activity by compartmentalizing the district into "areas" and by placing an area superintendent in charge of each area. These persons, in turn, constitute the primary figures in an executive cabinet or some similarly labeled major policy determination body.

The great majority of American school systems are between these extremes, with a "central office" bureaucracy that varies in scope, again according to size. Among school systems in cities of over 100,000 population, school superintendents have their own national organization and meet together periodically during the year to share ideas and intelligence. Most such systems—and for that matter, all systems with at least as many as 10,000 or more pupils in average daily attendance—have a fairly generalized central "structure." The *table of organization* of such systems will look something like that shown in Figure 3-1.

There are always some variations, of course. In school systems toward the small end of the 10,000 student or more range, there will likely be only one or perhaps two assistant superintendents, and generally these will be responsible for instruction and curriculum and administration and finance, respectively.

Figure 3-1. Typical Central Office Pattern

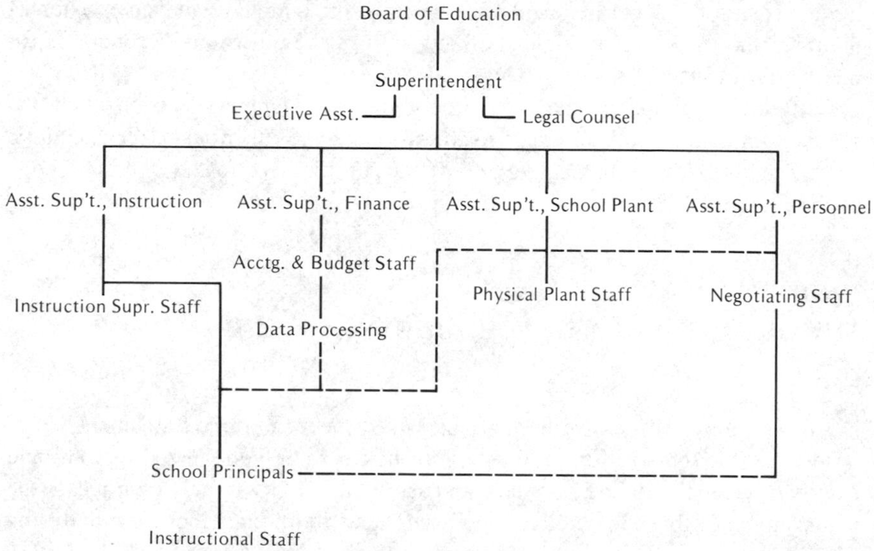

Board of Education

Superintendent

Executive Asst.

Legal Counsel

Asst. Sup't., Instruction   Asst. Sup't., Finance   Asst. Sup't., School Plant   Asst. Sup't., Personnel

Acctg. & Budget Staff

Physical Plant Staff   Negotiating Staff

Instruction Supr. Staff

Data Processing

School Principals

Instructional Staff

Somewhat larger systems—say, 25,000 pupils—may also utilize only two high-level assistant or associate superintendents and then, in turn, utilize the title of "director" for other major functions reporting through these executives. Still other arrangements involve one associate superintendent "for operations" and may utilize a variety of other titles for key personnel within the structure.

The point is that, while there is no one clearly superior pattern of structural hierarchy, there is a generalized similarity, and this is true because there is always the need for determining some appropriate division of labor that does two fundamental things well: first, that the major functions of the school system are carried out responsibly and within a manageable and articulated scope of work and, second, that the distinctions between authority ("line") and consultation ("staff") are explicated clearly and are workable.

Line and Staff

To help clarify the distinctions between the concepts of "functional responsibility/scope of work" and "authority/consultation," we will outline the principles of line and staff.[2]

---

[2]It would be helpful to this discussion to review the section "Ideal Types of Bureaucracy in School Administration" in Chapter 7; W. Lane, R. Corwin, and W. G. Monahan, *Foundations of Educational Administration: A Behavioral Analysis* (New York: Macmillan, 1967), pp. 189–201.

Whereas the general idea of "line and staff" is associated with the traditional literature of organizational bureaucracy, the concept owes its genesis to the military and somewhat less to the Roman Catholic church, which applied these operational principles to a nonmilitary institution. This should emphasize the notion that certain conceptualizations—whatever they might be labeled—are established by virtue of natural utility for the more effective pursuit of purposes of complex organizations, regardless of other considerations. That seems to be the case with "line and staff." In any event, the idea holds simply that, with any system of roles and regardless of size or function, two functions occur: One is action, the other is advice. But as organizations grow in size and complexity, individual contributions must be ordered in some rational fashion if whatever is aimed at does in fact happen. In early military systems, which, after all, were the only major manifestations of relatively massive organizational phenomena, it became apparent that actual battle could not be carried out effectively without organization of both the "support" structures necessary to that as well as some reasonable dependence upon informed advice to commanders about everything from intelligence about enemy strength to logistical help with the massive movement of men, animals, food, and cannon and to assistance with distributing the "fruits" of victory (if there were any). The "staff" operation thus probably owes its generally informal function to the very earliest efforts of *any* kinds of human enterprises of reasonably massive scale.

Clearly the military and the church were, throughout the first dozen or so centuries A.D., authoritarian institutions that perceived human beings merely as the means to some predetermined end and encompassed a "doctrine of command, control, direction, and communication through prescribed channels [and] philosophically derived [when] absolutism prevailed";[3] still, even though the legacy of the "line-and-staff" concept persists "in the terminology of management far beyond its usefulness . . .,"[4] it remains a still rational and fundamental notion of organizational division of labor.

When the factory system came into existence and the Industrial Revolution began in earnest, the only persons around who had experience with large numbers of men were those with military backgrounds. As a consequence, strict adherence to the military model of line and staff became a commonly accepted and useful principle in the early development of industrial management. Unquestionably, certain aspects of strict adherence to such a principle resulted in some forms of oppression of those who worked in the mills and factories, for the military model of efficiency required unquestioned obedience to command and employed the status differentiations that are characteristic of hierarchical organizations. The "line" people were definable in a clearly descending order of importance and authority, from owners to foremen; staff people were increasingly recognized as important not so much in terms of the exercise of command

---

[3]Lane, Corwin, and Monahan, op. cit., p. 6.
[4]Loc. cit., p. 6.

authority as in terms of the exercise of technical expertise, as, for example, with marketing, accounting, and engineering.

Beginning around the turn of the twentieth century, the more oppressive aspects of "line and staff" and the classic "bureaucracy" legacy found some intellectual support through a movement that has come to be known generally as "scientific management."

This movement had particular appeal in an increasingly industrialized America, and almost no aspect of American life was not touched by this prevailing mentality. (Even the care and feeding of infants was presumed to be governed by such principles: One fed the infant according to principles of time and sequence, whether the child was or was not hungry or thirsty. Of course, most infants thrived on that principle: Lying helpless, they exercised their instincts and responded accordingly.)

But by 1930, these "push-pull, click-click" notions of human existence were superseded by theories developed at the Harvard Business School, based on experimental work conducted by Elton Mayo and his associates at the Hawthorne plant of the Western Electric Company in Chicago, Illinois. The Hawthorne studies were designed to measure "worker fatigue," and Mayo's findings led to the conclusion that the social aspects of the work group were far more important than anyone had previously considered. In addition, the Mayo studies ushered in a rather new attitude toward management, namely, the "human relations" movement.

Human Relations and School Administration

It must be remembered that, even in 1930 or 1935, school administration was still an emerging profession. The Mayo work was being reported in the few professional journals of the time and through some books and monographs, and some of his findings were, by the mid-1930s, being incorporated in the general educational literature developed by William H. Kilpatrick, George Counts, and John Dewey. As a consequence, the "human relations" movement was incorporated in an emerging philosophical attitude toward school administration that seems best characterized by the idea of "democratic school administration."

Curiously, no one ever really defined "democratic school administration" beyond encouraging the school administrator to behave "nicely," and this left academic mentors in something of a quandary. Most of those who "trained" school administrators liked the flavor of this new ideology, but they were unable to provide any principles of administration based on it. Somehow, the older notions of "line and staff" persisted, if only as a reasonable pattern of organizational response. Thus by the end of World War II, the view that *some* utility of line and staff made sense *if* moderated by a genuineness of human sensitivity seemed to constitute a reasonable epistemological compromise as well as to serve as a fuzzy basis for administrative principle.

The truth, of course, now is that the contemporary administrator must know much about the *generalized* patterns of line and staff to ensure, as best he or she can, finding competent persons who can perform the technical duties required with genuine sensitivity and commitment to the more noble idea of valued personhood.

This being the case, however, the contemporary school executive regardless of level of operation must also know much about the importance of the organizational structure as it complements the effective pursuit of organizational purpose. It is in this regard that contemporary clarification of the older notion of "line and staff" is, in our view, quite important. Whether organizationally exact or not, the school principal is a "line" officer and, as such, must know that he or she reports through another equally well-established "line" in the central structure—that role may be installed in the superintendency itself or in a designated deputy; but the general pattern of "action" as opposed to "advice" is always reasonably clear if not explicitly defined.

Accordingly, a pattern of responsible and accountable "line" relationships vis-à-vis the executive functions in a school system is, in our view, imperative. One cannot function with effectiveness otherwise. Thus, within the general table of organization, administrators can monitor the management of a variety of behaviors that characterizes the contemporary complex school system. Even if some "part" of the system tends to function with a level of autonomy (e.g., a funding agency or a politically influential individual), the organizational pattern will provide the executive with a useful tool for corrective action.

The generalized table of functions is a much more useful tool in administrative management than is generally recognized. For this reason, we should give such schema much more careful attention.

The Ideal and the Real

It is important to recognize that an organization chart tends to portray someone's notion of what the *ideal* structure is for that particular system. But, quite obviously, an organization chart almost always discloses things as they ought to be, not things as they *really* are. It has frequently been found that analysis of the way the organization actually functions when compared with the "blueprint" pinpoints trouble spots and reveals sources of difficulty.

In one upper midwestern school district, the organizational chart for the system was instrumental in demonstrating to the board of education and its executive staff that the *informal* organization had become more active in the ongoing business of the school system than the so-called *formal* organization as described in the official "chart." Figure 3-2 depicts this system as it was presumed; Figure

3-3 provides a more accurate description of the reality. The inconsistencies illuminated were the following:[5]

1. The chart clearly shows teachers are responsible to principals. Yet, according to the chart, the superintendent is responsible for supervision of teachers. . . . The teacher is automatically caught between the principal and the superintendent.
2. The teachers are further caught between the principals and the assistant superintendent (in charge of elementary education). . . .
3. According to the chart there are several division heads who are directly responsible to the superintendent [such as] physical education and athletics . . . even though athletics is primarily a function of secondary schools.

Other inconsistencies became apparent when comparing the "ideal" and "real" patterns; whereas the assistant superintendent for elementary education had authority for such special curricular areas as music, art, curriculum supervision, and special education, there was no apparently similar concern for such areas in the secondary programs in the central office structure. Also, the business management function was designated as an assistant superintendency, yet this role was depicted as reporting directly to the board of education, and the same was true, in reality, for those "areas" of concern for which the board of education has established standing committees.

Following its study, the consultants recommended a more reasonable organization chart (see Figure 3-4).

An Example of the Utility of Theory

The preceding situation exemplifies the concept that "theory is a practical tool," and although the general theoretical aspects of school administration are not a major concern in this book (and are better treated elsewhere[6]), it is helpful in the case of this discussion to point out how theory is both applicable and explanatory.

The Anthropology of School Systems. School systems are designed to support that larger cultural institution to which we felicitously refer as Education. In all cultures, primitive or complex, education is, in one or a variety of ways, promoted by a "culture" simply because some established mechanisms or activities must be designed to inculcate the young so that the group, or tribe, or state is sustained. In primitive cultures, this inculcation is simplistic and diffused, and institutionalization of specialization for educational purposes is un-

---

[5]Ibid., pp. 192 and 194.
[6]See, for example, W. G. Monahan, *Theoretical Dimensions of Educational Administration* (New York: Macmillan, 1975), esp. pp. 301–305.

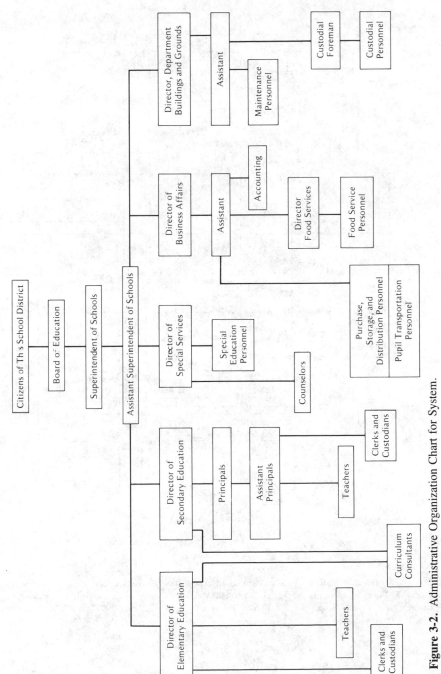

Figure 3-2. Administrative Organization Chart for System.
From W. Lane, R. Corwin, and W. G. Monahan, *Foundations of Educational Administration: A Behavioral Analysis* (New York: Macmillan, 1967), p. 196. Used with permission.

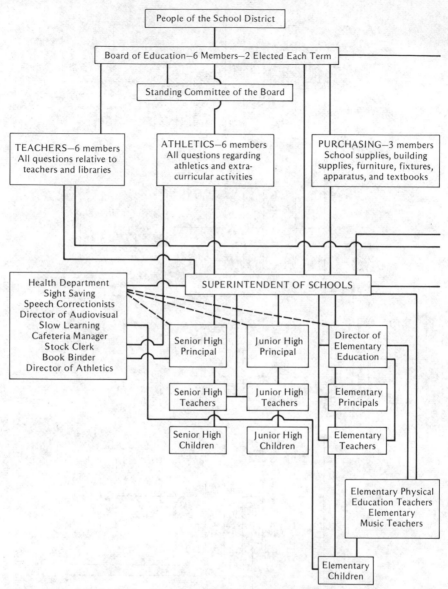

Figure 3-3. Administrative Organization as Interpreted in Actual Practice.
From W. Lane, R. Corwin, and W. G. Monahan, *Foundations of Educational Administration: A Behavioral Analysis* (New York: Macmillan, 1967), pp. 194–195. Used with permission.

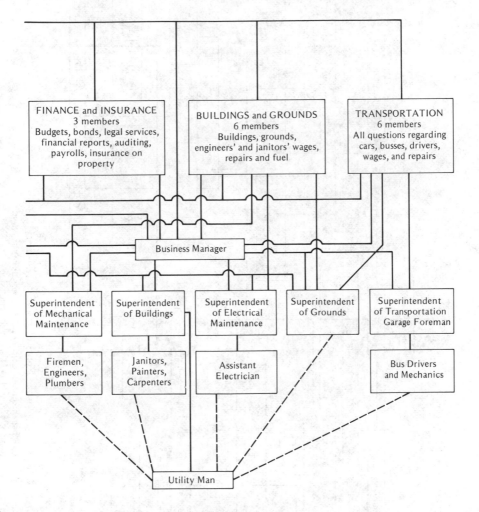

necessary; in complex, industrialized nations, on the other hand, institutionalization requires the elaborate mechanisms of specialization that we have come to know as the "educational establishment." Regardless of political style or pattern of governance, an identifiable and systematic "establishment" can be characterized.

There exist certain generalizable principles and concepts that have application to the institutionalization process no matter what the frame of reference—primitive or complex—or the essential ingredients that together constitute the values of that group, tribe, or industrialized nation. Now this "level of abstraction"

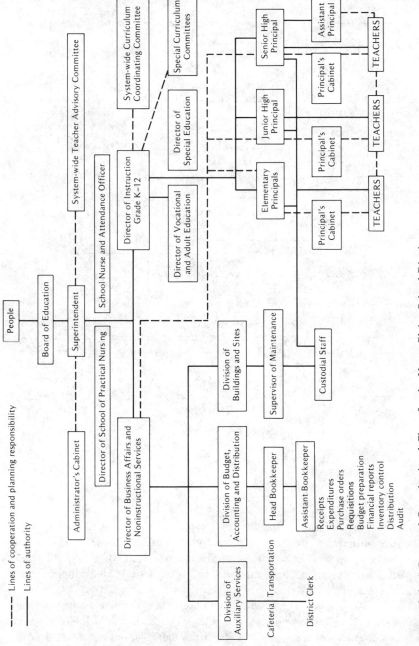

- - - - - Lines of cooperation and planning responsibility
———— Lines of authority

Figure 3-4. A Proposed Organizational Chart for the Upper Plains School District.
From W. Lane, R. Corwin, and W. G. Monahan, *Foundations of Educational Administration: A Behavioral Analysis* (New York: Macmillan, 1967), p. 199. Used with permission.

Figure 3-5. The Malinowski Model of Institutional Structure and Function.

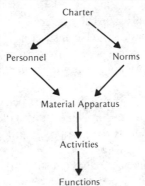

is one of the characteristics of many theoretical conceptualizations because theoretical utility is judged by the extent to which a scheme is applicable to the "smallest" as well as the "largest" *piece* of that institutionalization; accordingly, such generalized conceptualizations—if they can be invented—employ the abstract to help explain the concrete.

One schema that meets these conditions—an "institutionalization model"—was conceived by the late anthropologist Bronislaw Malinowski.[7] We present that model (see Figure 3-5) and explain its applicability to the "organizational chart" discussed previously.

Explaining the Model

The key to understanding this diagram concerns the relationship between what we might like to have happen—the "ideal"—and what in fact actually does occur—the "real." This becomes clear when the particular elements of the scheme and the relationships among them are explained.

The "charter" of any organization or systematized social configuration specifies the system of values for the pursuit of which the entity was initiated. It is something like a constitution, although obviously certain aspects of a charter may or may not be formalized. In other words, the extent to which an organization is progressively institutionalized, or some legal definition of its legitimacy is clearly established, may have a bearing on the necessity for stating its purposes in writing.

The charter defines what *ought* to be accomplished, and what ought to be

---

[7] This discussion is drawn from Bronislaw Malinowski, *A Scientific Theory of Culture and Other Essays* (Chapel Hill: University of North Carolina Press, 1944), esp. pp. 83 ff.

accomplished obviously relates to some identifiable group of people, the personnel. In addition, this system of values must be defined or structured operationally in some fashion so that the prescriptions for pursuing these values are known to the personnel. This is usually determined in formal organizations by policies, regulations, and rules. In the institutional sense and for less formal social arrangements, the determination is by normative standards that are internalized by the personnel. Again, these norms or rules specify *ideal* behaviors or activities.

In any type of organized activity, there must be some manner of interaction with the environment; there must be some apparatus for carrying out the rules in pursuit of the charter's ideals. Even a bridge group must have playing cards and scoring pads and a surface for play.

The final two components of the diagram shift from what *ought* to be to what *is*. Just as the norms are designed to specify the particular behaviors that are appropriate and desirable, the activities are manifestations of reality. These represent what the personnel *actually* do. Finally, the functions or outcomes represent the real or actual results.

The functions are the *real* and demonstrative manifestations of the charter, and the activities are the *real* and demonstrative manifestations of the rules. The charter specifies *what* ought to happen, and the rules specify rather precisely *how* it ought to happen; the activities, on the other hand, represent the way we actually go about the *doing* of "it," and the functions constitute the reality of the results.

Let us review this interesting model in terms of some simple "if-then" statements.

1. If the activities deviate too far from the rules, then either the rules must be modified or the activities must be "brought into line."
2. If the functions, or outcomes, deviate too far from the system of values specified or otherwise internalized by virtue of the charter then the functions must be either sanctioned, whereby the charter must be modified, or restrained or otherwise inhibited, so that the integrity of the charter is reasonably sustained.

What are the generalized consequences of these hypotheses? Malinowski has shown us how change takes place over time. Moreover, he has provided us with a definition of organizational equilibrium. It remains for research to provide us with definitive data for predicting whether the charter will be revised or whether the outcomes will be sanctioned; all the same, a theoretical pattern is outlined. If some set of activities deviates so much from the rules that a state of disequilibrium exists, then obviously adjustments must be made. Either the rules must be modified to accommodate the contemporary activities or the contemporary activities must be made to conform with the rules. The same is obviously true of the functions—either the manifest functions, if they are clearly too deviant from the charter, must be brought back into conformity with the charter or the charter must be revised to accommodate the deviance in outcomes. In effect, there is a compromise between these two extremes. Change occurs consequently more by evolutionary modification than by clear-cut revolutionary destruction, but even the latter is accounted for. Revolutionary behaviors may indeed occur, but significant disruptions are the exception rather than the rule. Because the overriding objective of organizations is survival, anything that threatens that survival will be as risky to the rebel as it is to the ritualist.

Applicability to "Upper Plains"

Whether or not the consultants who worked with the "Upper Plains" school system were familiar with Malinowski's notions about the "ideal" and the "real," they behaved intelligently according to that model. The structure that was presented to that district's board of education (Figure 3-4) was for all practical purposes a manifestation of the theoretical pattern of the Malinowski model. In other words, these outside "experts" saw the imbalances between "charter and norms" and the "activities" and "functions" and suggested a pattern to bring these dimensions into equilibrium.

Any active school superintendent can take a few minutes to make a similar analysis of the "blueprint" of his or her school system and determine the inconsistencies that emerge over time as a consequence of the strains that evolve between conformity or nonconformity to the "charter" and "rules." It is a useful activity and, in almost *every* case, will uncover areas needing adjustments in the structure, not only in terms of the depiction of pattern but also in the redefinition of duties, responsibilities, and the "flow" of authority. Depiction is useful, and it is unquestionably essential, but the definition of the role system itself is much more so. The rather simplistic applications of "theory" that we have set forth are vital to the insightful preparation of school, or other institutional, administrators.

THE BOARD OF EDUCATION

The general authority and functions of local boards of education are well established in the school "codes" of the various states, as are those of the state board. The language is usually general, specifying the number of members, methods of election of local boards (or, in rare cases, appointment), eligibility, terms of office, organization procedures, and meeting issues.

The conditions differ somewhat from state to state, but in the main the "general authority" of school district boards of education is similar and the legal language typically specifies the control and management of all schools and school activities, school closings and consolidations, and authority to require that records be kept, including the receipts and disbursements of funds, to provide for transportation, to provide for insurance at public expense, to employ personnel and legal counsel, and, of course, "to sue and be sued."

Twenty or more years ago, state codes regarding the duties, responsibilities, and authority of local boards of education would have required no more than two or three pages in the published "school laws," but because of the social turbulence that has affected schools in recent years, today's codes can have as many as fifty different "sections" and more than fifty pages of text.

The Nature of School Boards

In almost all cases, members of district boards of education in the United States are elected by nonpartisan popular vote from the district at large. Some school board members are still elected from elector districts or wards, but these cases are rare. In some districts—typically very large urban or metropolitan school systems—members of boards are still appointed, usually by the mayor or city council but always subject to quite intensive advice and consideration for a careful "mix" of ethnicity, sex, and other related factors. (The Pittsburgh, Pennsylvania, system changed from appointed to elected school boards in 1977.)

School board members usually number five or seven, although quite small school districts may have as few as three and a few large systems may have as many as seventeen.

A "composite" of a typical board in larger school systems is the following:[8]

1. Representative of the entire district
2. A seven-member board
3. Elected
4. Members serving four-year staggered terms
5. Male dominated
6. Meeting twice a month
7. Operating with standing committees
8. Operating without salary compensation to members
9. Served by a superintendent designated as secretary of the board
10. Selecting replacements by board vote to fill the position vacated until the next election.

If anything is changing in this picture it is the fact that the extent of male domination on boards of education is considerably diminished. As of 1978, the

[8]S. J. Knezevich, *Administration of Public Education,* 3rd ed. (New York: Harper & Row, 1975), p. 332.

number of females serving on boards was estimated at about 35 percent, up from 15 percent in 1965.

The number of school board members has declined in appropriate ratio to the reduction in the number of school districts, but while some districts are in process of being reorganized, it is common for all those board members who served the separate systems to act as a board of the whole for the proposed reorganized district. While this is a temporary governance pattern, it is not uncommon for a board to be composed of twenty or more. (In one Pennsylvania system undergoing unification some years back, a prospective teacher was interviewed by fifty board members!)

Terms of Office. The term of office is usually from three to five years, with four years being the norm. In almost all cases board members may succeed themselves and most do. While data on the extent of those serving more than one term or on the average length of total service are not reliable, it is typical that more than one term is served. However, the turbulence that characterizes today's school environment has resulted in shorter overall service and increasing defeats of incumbent board members.

Functions of School Boards

As with the general pattern of all fiduciary boards, school boards are primarily policy-making bodies. As such, a board must act *as* a body (i.e., no single board member has any authority to act for the board as a whole, and actions must be taken in official sessions where a quorum is established). This precludes a board from engaging in information-sharing sessions or from conferring with school officials and school patrons as individuals—on the contrary, responsible board members typically seek such information in recognition of their role as a policy (rather than as an administrative) body.

Policy Clarification Issues

Although the generally accepted notion of "separation of powers" acknowledged in the literature in educational administration that holds that the board *makes* policy and the school administrator *implements* it is more ideal than real, this notion of functions, roughly analogous to legislative and executive roles is a useful basis for a discussion of functions.

If school codes could simplify the distinctions of organizational roles so easily, not only the courts but every other vested interest would intrude in the affairs of schools to such an extent that chaos would prevail. Yet, like all such fundamental and well-indoctrinated normative "principles," the policy-making, policy-implementing myth is useful.

It is well established by practice that perhaps the single most important decision of any board of education relates to its choice of a superintendent. At the same time, the *idea* of "policy making" derives from the more fundamental understanding that the complexity of school systems today prevents boards of education from doing little else but devoting attention to goals and purposes and considering the best and most effective ways in which the school system can pursue those purposes. Quite obviously, that includes some derivative and related functions:

1. To keep constituents informed through a willingness to appear and speak out at public meetings, on "talk shows," and with media and to engage in this *responsibly*.
2. To know and understand as well as possible both local and educational issues as well as state and national concerns.
3. To always be cognizant that one represents *all* the people of a district but owes fundamental responsibility to children and youth.
4. To be informed and aware that the board bears major responsibility for all those activities associated with obtaining adequate financial support for schools.
5. To strive for policies that encourage the recruitment and retention of excellent staff.
6. To require the availability of accurate and meaningful data and information necessary to informed fiduciary action.
7. To consider the need for safe and effective facilities.
8. To know what various rules and regulations require of officials in oversight roles.
9. To have clear and rational understanding of roles vis-à-vis school administrators and other school personnel and to learn to argue in safety and disagree in comfort.
10. To participate actively in, and take seriously, the common wisdom accessible from state, regional, and national associations of school board members.

These guidelines are rather general, but in the week-to-week processes in which school board members are involved, they provide, we think, helpful dimensions of performance as a basis for the actual behaviors and deliberations in which school board members engage.

For that reason, the policy-making function of boards should not be too easily dismissed as merely a pro-forma event. On the contrary, an important study conducted in the late 1950s remains seminal in characterizing the policy-making process.[9]

[9]Lavern L. Cunningham, "A Community Develops Educational Policy: A Case Study," unpublished doctoral dissertation. Eugene, Ore.: School of Education, University of Oregon, 1958.

The study identified five phases through which a board progresses as it moves toward the development of a policy: (1) initiation, (2) definition, (3) deliberation, (4) enactment, and (5) consequences. While the extent to which any of these stages occupies more or less of any board's time will vary depending on the issue and the advice of administrators, the process itself is generalizable and stable.

Although many people stand for election to boards of education for the proverbial purpose of "throwing the rascals out" or for personal vendettas, these cases are almost always exaggerated by their visibility. The truth seems more on the side of reasonably responsible citizens who, for whatever reason, want to help to make a positive difference in the more effective education of children and youth.

Certainly the role of a school board member is, in the aggregate, a relatively selfless community commitment. Almost none are compensated and the time that must be dedicated may be many hours each month. Still, *most* new board members learn rather soon that "things" are not so easy as they had presumed and, given tolerant and subtle orientation by more experienced board members, go on to become responsible and effective without sacrificing ideology and point of view.

The Working Relationship

There is no better-established working relationship in American institutional structure than that between school boards and school administrators. While it is normally presumed to be a sensitive relationship, it works best when the professional—the superintendent—maintains his or her professional demeanor and exercises his or her training. After all, it is the board itself that is ultimately responsible to the electorate.

SUMMARY

Concepts such as "line and staff," "division of labor," and "scope of work" as well as those related to "tables of organization" may indeed be far more overemphasized in administrative "trivia" than they deserve, but the fact remains that the administrator performs a function that characteristically places him or her in a direct chain of authority and accountability. Thus to have clear and consensual understanding of the dimensions and boundaries of all of those roles that together reflect both the limits and opportunities for effectiveness really constitutes the fundamental bases for delegation of authority and the effective control of power in school organizations.

Administrators must take those notions seriously; consequently, they give serious attention to what their meanings really are.

In addition, within the formal "table of organization," the administrator must effectively internalize the meaning of his or her relationship to the board of education for, as we have pointed out, this body is the principal link with the ideology that American education is the product and the possession of the people.

EXERCISES

1. As the superintendent-elect of a 4000-pupil district, your "staff" consists of one administrative assistant and two secretary-clerks. In conversation with the board it has been indicated that you can have additional staff—how many people and what kind are you going to request?

2. Recognizing that the general organizational structure of a medium-sized district (10,000 students) is no longer appropriate, you have appointed a committee of teachers, administrators, and student leaders to study the organizational structure and suggest a different pattern. You have provided them with all kinds of information and have met with them several times but not always; they have convened with reasonable regularity for a full half-year and have provided you with a report that makes recommendations that you are convinced are *not* sound. What are you going to do about it?

3. A local newspaper reporter who has always supported you as the superintendent calls you during a fairly routine school board election campaign to ask you "off the record" whom you are supporting. What is your response? Is this something that deserves a systemwide administrative policy bulletin? If so, what should such a policy statement comprise?

4. Two new members of the board of education have spoken with several custodians in the school system and have agreed to a flex-time policy for the custodians on behalf of the board. What is wrong with this and, as superintendent, how do you propose to handle it?

5. As a new superintendent and with a board composed of two hold-over members and three new ones, you are asked to share with the board your views regarding the use of outside consultants; recognizing that there has been some criticism of the previous administration and board in this regard, what *should* the posture of an organization be with reference to consultation, and what are you going to say in this instance?

SUGGESTED REFERENCES

American Association of School Administrators. *Administrative & Supervisory Evaluation*. Arlington, Va.: The Association, 1977. Executive Handbook series; see especially Chapter 1.

American Association of School Administrators. *Roles and Relationships: School Boards and Superintendents*. Arlington, Va.: The Association, 1980.

Knezevich, S. J. *Administration of Public Education*, Third Edition. New York: Harper & Row, 1975.

Lane, W. R., R. G. Corwin, and W. G. Monahan. *Foundations of Educational Administration: A Behavioral Analysis*. New York: Macmillan Publishing Co., 1967.

Rudy, Willis. *Schools in an Age of Mass Culture*. Englewood Cliffs, N.J.: Prentice-Hall, Inc., 1965.

Chapter 4

Education and the Judiciary

THE ROLE OF THE COURTS IN EDUCATION

The extent to which education and schools have become involved in litigation has increased dramatically over the past fifteen or twenty years. The field of "school law," while not foreign to the curriculum for preparing educational leaders, has nevertheless assumed new importance, so much so that the contemporary academic program frequently includes special courses devoted to the role of the courts, to liability issues affecting educational personnel and due process issues, and to collective bargaining. While the last is not a matter of "school law" per se, the fact that so many problems require litigation or demand legal proceedings causes us to tend to think of money matters and "welfare" issues related to contractual negotiation as part of this growing context of education and law.

In the late 1950s, Dr. Robert Hamilton, then dean of the College of Law at the University of Wyoming, addressed a convocation of Kentucky school superintendents and heralded the need for such leaders to give more careful attention to matters of the liability of public school officers and teachers, opening with the observation that "I am always pleased at such sessions as this to see that so many school superintendents are still out of jail!" We were then at the threshold of an era marked, as much as by any other set of developments, by the intrusion of the courts and the proliferation of legal issues in the management of educational enterprises to an extent unforeseen even by Dean Hamilton.

Despite the expansion of school-related litigation, the courts seem reluctant to become involved centrally in educational issues that have traditionally been the proper concern of political and sociological mechanisms. Some years ago, in 1967, U.S. Court of Appeals Judge J. Skelly Wright, in the case of *Hobson v. Hansen,* concluded his opinion with the following "Parting Word":[1]

It is regrettable, of course, that in deciding this case this court must act in an area so alien to its expertise. It would be far better indeed for these great social and political problems to be resolved in the political arena by other branches of government. But these are social and political problems which seem at times to defy such resolution. In such situations, under our system, the judiciary must bear a hand and accept its responsibility to assist in the solution where constitutional rights hang in the balance.

This statement might be seen as a declaration of a new reality because it was an incisive description of things that were already well underway in education.

One cannot discuss the recent role of the courts in education without discussing its evolution, of which there seems to be five stages:[2]

1. *The stage of judicial laissez-faire.* From 1789 to about 1850 the federal and state courts ignored education. Federal courts viewed education as a state and local matter, and state courts were rarely called upon to intervene in a school matter.
2. *The stage of state control of education.* During the period 1850 to about 1950, state courts asserted that education was exclusively a state and local matter. Few cases affecting education were presented to the Supreme Court of the United States, and consequently a body of case law developed at the state level which permitted, if not actually sanctioned, educational policies and practices that failed to meet federal constitutional standards and requirements. More serious than the absence of any firm doctrinal support for this theory of state action are its potentialities for the future. Its failing was a principle of decision in the realm of Fourteenth Amendment concerns.
3. *The reformation stage.* Beginning about 1950 (and continuing until today), the federal courts, the Supreme Court in particular, recognized that educational policies and practices as they had developed under state laws and state court decisions were not in conformity with federal constitutional requirements. This is the period of federal court infusion of constitutional "rights" into existing educational structures.
4. *The state of "education under supervision of the courts."* Concurrent with the "reformation stage," there has been a discernible tendency of the courts, federal and state, to expand the scope of their powers over the schools (e.g., intervention in matters affecting the administration, organization, and pro-

[1] J. C. Hogan, *The Schools, the Courts, and the Public Interest* (Boston: D. C. Heath, 1974), p. 5.
[2] Ibid., p. 6.

grams of the schools; retaining jurisdiction over cases until their mandates, orders, and decrees have been carried into effect). It is therefore clear that a new judicial function is taking place.

5. *The stage of "strict construction."* Beginning March 21, 1973, there has been a further development that will affect the role of federal courts in education: the landmark decision in the school finance case, *San Antonio Independent School District* v. *Rodriguez,* wherein the Supreme Court of the United States declared: "Education is not among the rights afforded explicit protection under our Federal Constitution. Nor do we find any basis for saying it is implicitly so protected." (Piele, 1973, p. 211) This "strict construction" posture of the Nixon Court is bound to affect the trend of federal court decisions concerned with the organization, administration, and programs of the public schools which has so clearly marked the period from about 1950.

According to one study, approximately 40,000 court cases affecting the organization, administration, and programs of the schools were decided between 1789 and 1971. This includes decisions reported by state courts, federal courts, and the Supreme Court of the United States. The total number of federal court cases affecting education has increased in every period since 1897, with sharp increases for the periods beginning in 1956 and in 1967. On the other hand, the total number of state court decisions affecting education, while still substantial, has decreased since 1956.[3]

What may be called the "classical view" of the role of the courts in education endured until about 1950; for that period of over one hundred years, education was viewed as a state and local matter—but not exclusively and entirely free from federal involvement. The argument was sometimes put in this form: the states control public education because the Constitution of the United States does not mention education as a function delegated to the federal government. Under the Tenth Amendment, those "powers not delegated to the United States by the Constitution, nor prohibited by it to the states, are reserved to the states respectively, or to the people."[4]

Court interpretations of this language were consistent: Education was a state function and the power over the public schools was vested exclusively in the state. While the "classical view" held that the state controlled public education, it also recognized that the general government was empowered to tax and spend money for educational purposes. This federal power was implied from the broad language of the "general welfare" clause of the Constitution: "The Congress shall have Power to lay and Collect Taxes, Duties, Imposts, and Excises, to pay

---

[3]P. K. Piele, *The Yearbook of School Law* (Topeka, Kan.: National Organization on Legal Problems of Education, 1975), p. 259.

[4]J. Ferguson, *Elements of American Government* (New York: McGraw-Hill, 1968), p. 104.

the Debts and provide the common Defense and general Welfare of the United States'' (Article 1, Section 8). This was interpreted by the courts to mean that Congress was not limited in the expenditure of money to direct or express grants of legislative powers found elsewhere in the Constitution. Hence, Congress might tax and spend money in aid of public education for the "general welfare" of the people. However, state control of public education and the power of the general government to spend money for educational purposes, as noted, were to be exercised subject to constitutional requirements and limitations. Thus, state or federal actions affecting education, in theory at least, must be consistent with the general provisions of the Constitution.

Unique to the "classical" period was the *laissez-faire* attitude of the courts toward the schools, epitomized by the phrase "leaving education to the educators." It was this disinterested, hands-off attitude that resulted in the development of a body of state case law that permitted state and local educational policies and practices that failed to meet minimum constitutional requirements under the First and Fourteenth Amendments and that first attracted federal court attention to the schools.

One need only compare the extent of court involvement in education in, say, the 1940s with court involvement in the schools as it existed in 1973 to appreciate the significant change that has occurred. The roots of this new judicial function can be traced to about 1950, when erosion of the "classical view" of education as a state and local function exclusively began in earnest and when the federal courts (the Supreme Court of the United States, in particular) recognized that certain policies and procedures of the public schools failed to meet constitutional requirements of the First and Fourteenth Amendments.

The two main ways for obtaining federal court jurisdiction in cases affecting education are by questioning the validity of a state or federal statute under the U.S. Constitution or by alleging that some constitutionally protected right, privilege, or immunity of the individual has been violated. Otherwise, any case will normally be confined in the state courts.[5]

MORE RECENT DEVELOPMENTS

The main thrust of educational jurisprudence since about 1950 has been concerned with enforcing the constitutional "right of the individual" to receive education on equal terms regardless of race and national origin and, more recently, sex or handicap. There is also a corresponding constitutional duty im-

[5]Eugene Jones et al., *Practicing Texas Politics,* Fourth Edition (Boston: Houghton Mifflin, 1980), p. 53.

posed on the states to afford each of the citizens "equal protection of the laws."
Until 1938, the courts said that this duty was satisfied if the state provided
"equal" public schools, even though they might be "separate." The *Plessy* v.
Ferguson case (1896), upon which the "separate but equal" doctrine had rested,
was expressly overruled on May 17, 1954, when, in a landmark decision in
Brown v. *Board of Education,* the Supreme Court held that racially segregated
public schools were inherently unequal and a denial of equal protection of the
laws. In a historic opinion, Chief Justice Earl Warren asked a deceptively innocent question: "Does segregation of children in public schools, solely on the
basis of race, even though the facilities may be equal, deprive the children of
the minority group of equal education opportunities?" His brief answer: "We
believe that it does."[6] Federal and state courts have construed this as a clear
constitutional command to eliminate state-imposed segregation from public
schools.[7]

Other provisions of the Constitution regarding the rights of individuals were
subsequently made applicable to the states through the Fourteenth Amendment.
Thus, a broad new area was opened up for federal court regulation, and it
explicitly included education through the medium of student and teacher rights
and other school activities that might be in violation of any of the first ten
constitutional amendments.

Yet, because of the *laissez-faire* attitude that the courts had traditionally held
toward education and the schools, federal court activity in this "new" area was
only nominal until about 1950. Since then, a new judicial function has emerged
that involves increasing supervision of the schools by the courts to assure that
constitutional "minima" required by the First and the Fourteenth Amendments
are met.

It is becoming increasingly clear therefore that the modern trend in decisional
law is toward "education under supervision of the courts." A new judicial
function is, in essence, an activation of an old judicial principle—that of protecting the individual's rights as they relate to the Bill of Rights.

The Supreme Court of the United States since about 1950 and until 1973 has
adopted an "activist posture" toward education by accepting and deciding cases
that have had significant impact on the schools, and it is logical to conclude
from the great stress placed on education in the first *Brown* decision, and in
subsequent cases, that this has not been merely an *a posteriori* interpretation of
constitutional law but, rather, reflects a changing conception the Supreme Court
itself has of its role in educational matters and other socially related policy
matters where jurisdictional values can be brought to bear.

[6]P. K. Piele, op. cit., p. 108.
[7]T. R. Brown, *Government in Our Republic* (New York: Macmillan, 1968), p. 314.

COURTS AS EDUCATIONAL POLICYMAKERS

When this tendency of the court to involve itself in educational matters first became visible, some justices warned about the possible problems of the Supreme Court's becoming a "super school board" supervising all the schools and school districts in the country. Thus, as long ago as 1948, Supreme Court Justice Jackson referred to the zeal shown by the court for its own ideas of public school instruction and the danger of becoming such a super board:[8]

To lay down a sweeping constitutional doctrine as demanded by complainant and apparently approved by the Court, applicable alike to all school boards of the nation . . . is to decree a uniform, rigid and, if we are consistent, an unchanging standard for countless school boards representing and serving highly localized groups which not only differ from each other but which themselves from time to time change attitudes. It seems to me that to do so is to allow zeal for our own ideas of what is good in public instruction to induce us to accept the role of a super board of education for every school district in the nation.

And Justice Harland in 1899 had observed that education in the public schools[9]

is a matter belonging to the respective states, and any interference on the part of Federal authority with the management of such schools cannot be justified except in the case of a clear and unmistakable disregard of rights secured by the supreme law of the land.

Other members of the Supreme Court, however, at other times have obviously felt otherwise, as the trend in decisions until 1973 clearly shows.

The apparent willingness of certain individuals and groups to accept greater involvement of the courts in the educational process is evident; perhaps it is because of the growing financial and other crises in public education, and there is certainly more general agreement that major reform is needed in the way schools are operated. Yet both teachers and administrators sometimes express feelings of powerlessness as individuals to do very much about this turn of events, even unable to provide sound educational consultation to court decisions affecting the schools. They have, in general, accepted the new role of the courts in education albeit with much complaint; but many educators and the public at large have welcomed it in such areas as desegregation and with reference to the whole broad area of "due process."

[8]Hogan, op. cit., p.12.
[9]Ibid., p. 12.

THE CAPITULATION TO ADJUDICATION

Local school boards, many of which in the 1950s vigorously resisted the implementation of court orders (e.g., desegregation), by the mid-1960s were moving toward compliance with the letter, if not always the spirit, of the court decisions. The year 1966 represented a major turning point in southern school district compliance with court orders. It showed a willingness of school boards, even if under compulsion, to accept the new role of the courts in education.[10] And since that time the courts have required many school districts to provide explicit plans for effecting equal educational opportunity and, frequently, finding such plans inadequate, have taken it upon themselves to provide such plans—almost all requiring massive "busing" operations. Many school districts have appealed these directives and have resisted for a variety of reasons, not without logic and reasonable cause in some cases. But, in the main, the patterns established by the courts have been sustained.

The changing role of the federal courts in education, particularly in the southern states, is illustrated by a few examples:

1. A federal court ordered the appointment of a black assistant principal at a Louisiana high school where the student body was two thirds white, and the order was upheld on appeal. (*Smith* v. *St. Tammany Parish School Board*)
2. A federal court ruled that a state in integrating its school systems should make provisions for a plan governing the assignment and dismissal of teachers and said that such a plan should establish objective, nondiscriminatory standards and procedures for evaluating teachers; the plan should contain definitions and instructions for the application of standards to be given teachers and should set forth methods by which teaching is to be evaluated. (*Moore* v. *Board of Education of Chidester School District*)
3. There are numerous examples of federal courts' ordering student and faculty assignments, such assignments to be made according to a plan that complies with the principles of Supreme Court decisions. (*U.S.* v. *Perry County Board of Education*)
4. There are federal court decisions that restrict the transfer of students and hold that, where there is a scarcity of space in the schools being desegregated, majority to minority transfers have priority over other transfers. (*Northcross* v. *Board of Education of Memphis City Schools*)

---

[10]Ibid., p. 11.

5. Federal courts have ordered that formerly segregated school districts must operate as "unitary systems" for several years before students may be assigned within the system on the basis of achievement test scores. (*Lemon* v. *Bossier Parish School Board*)

As these illustrations show, there is already a considerable body of federal law affecting the organization, administration, and programs of the public schools. While directed primarily at southern schools in earlier years, more recent decisions have been concerned with the larger northeastern and midwestern cities that have operated de facto segregated schools for many years. Recent evidence clearly indicates that integration has proceeded more uniformly in the south than in any other section of the country.

THE SCOPE OF JUDICIARY IMPACT

Roughly 6,000 to 8,000 judges in the United States are assigned to federal and state courts that have jurisdiction over cases involving the schools and education. Certainly not all these judges have participated in decisions involving schools. In fact, some experts suggest that a very small minority of the judiciary and an even smaller minority of the total lawyers in the country are making the decisions that call for sweeping changes in the operation of the public schools. This view maintains that their power stems, in great part, from earlier (post-1950) decisions of the Supreme Court of the United States that supported and sanctioned and, in some instances, required explicit policy determination activity.

In support of this notion, some of the basic changes that have taken place in judicial thinking about the role of the courts in education are persuasive:[11]

the power of courts to reopen schools closed to avoid segregation—

the power of courts to require levying of taxes for support of schools—

the power of courts to assign teachers and students to specific schools to achieve racial balance—

the power of courts to require special programs for the underprivileged—

the power of courts to enforce student and teacher rights of freedom of expression.

[11]Piele, op. cit., p. 84.

COURTS AS EDUCATIONAL GUARDIANS—THE OTHER VIEW

Despite the obvious recognition that courts are now and have been in recent years involved much more intimately in educational policy matters than ever before, the presumption that the judiciary is, for all intents and purposes, administering the schools and determining educational policy is perhaps an overstatement of its role.

According to a 1978 article on desegregation, the high court seems to be developing a more conservative posture in its policy determination patterns. The author demonstrates that, although the Warren court was remarkably consistent and all but one of the thirteen decisions of the Warren court involving desegregation issues was unanimous, in the Burger court, of eleven decisions in this area, only six have been unanimous.[12]

Again, although this analysis concerned only desegregation, the speculation that courts—at least the Supreme Court—may be withdrawing from a central, activist role in educational decision making is implied; Hudgins states[13]

As a group, the justices have been unwilling to put their full force behind a total desegregation effort. They apparently recognize that there may be other instruments that are as effective—or more so—in establishing a unitary school system.

It looks as if the Court will continue to rule on a decision-at-a-time basis with little predictability. This in itself is a major departure from the style of the Warren Court.

This modest retreat from a posture of activism in educational policy determination may not be due so much to the different make-up of the Supreme Court under Burger as to the changes that together have defined American civilization as we enter the last two decades of this century. As with most such explanations, the truth lies more likely within a combination of things. Among these, schools have come upon hard times just owing to those changes in demography that we discussed in earlier chapters; and this creates other kinds of logistical problems that both have impact on, and are complicated by, any requirements to move pupils about. At the same time, the costs of education and any proposals for changing it are the same victims of skyrocketing inflation as are all other goods and services. Also, courts have learned much about many areas of constitutionality and of individual rights, and with all expanded knowledge comes a greater tendency toward more thoughtful reflection. Finally, the enormously expanded regulatory apparatus that is the product of legislative and congressional attempts to adjust law and government action (sometimes directly responsive to court

---

[12]H. C. Hudgins, Jr., "The Many Voices of the Burger Court and School Desegregation," *Phi Delta Kappan*, Vol. 60, no. 3 (November 1978), p. 167.
[13]Ibid., p. 168.

decisions, sometimes in anticipation of it, and mostly just as the natural consequence of a confusing but expanding bureaucratic socialism) also helps to
explain a growing reluctance of the judiciary to continue to exercise visible and
influential leadership in policy manipulation.

Not only at the federal level but also at the level of state and district courts,
the judiciary seems now more willing to take a somewhat conservative attitude
toward the relationship of schools to individual rights.

An example of these variable points was a case involving a Mississippi teacher
who had been a vocal "thorn" in the district's and school's tender administrative
flesh and on the basis of a principal's recommendation was consequently terminated. She sued the school system in the U.S. district courts, alleging that
the dismissal was illegal because it was a result of her exercise of free speech.
Based on the earlier important case of *Pickering* v. *Board of Education* (391
U.S. 563, 88 S.Ct. 1731), in which a teacher who had written a critical letter
to a local newspaper was fired, sued, and was sustained by the Supreme Court
on the basis of his exercise of the constitutional right of free speech, the district
court ruled on behalf of the Mississippi teacher and the case was appealed. The
U.S. Court of Appeals, Fifth Circuit, reversed the district court ruling, however,
on the grounds that this particular teacher had not—as Pickering had done—
made "public" comment about the things that had disturbed her nor had she
done other than to complain to her superiors (she had written no pamphlets, had
participated in no radio talk shows, had written to no newspapers, or had made
no remarks at public meetings). In essence, said the court, an employee's privately voiced opinions and unhappinesses are not covered or protected under the
First Amendment.

Also interesting with regard to the importance of regulatory apparatus is the
fact that today this teacher would be protected under the provisions of Title VII
of the Civil Rights Act (1964), which was made applicable to schools in 1972.
Thus, courts are not as likely to engage in direct jurisdiction of many issues in
the future when increasingly much is covered under regulations.

As a final comment to support the "retreatist" view of the courts, a case
adjudicated recently involved two students in the Chicago schools who were
suspended for about a month (one for smoking marijuana and the other for
wearing an earring). Because they were suspended without a due process hearing, a suit was brought against school personnel, not against the school district.
The suit went through the district court, to the Court of Appeals, and to the
Supreme Court. The unanimous ruling was that under Section 1983 of the Civil
Rights Act of 1971, the intent was "to provide compensation for individuals
who had suffered constitutional deprivation but not designed to provide purely
punitive relief."[14]

---

[14]T. J. Flygare, "Schools and the Law (the Free Speech Rights of Teachers . . .)," *Phi Delta Kappan*, Vol. 60, no. 3 (November 1978), 242.

REGARDING THE ISSUES OF SCHOOL FINANCE

An important and vital field in which the courts have become very much involved with the administration and policy dimensions of public education concerns equitable funding of programs. In this area, again, the Supreme Court has, as of this writing, adopted a "hands-off" policy if only on the basis of what may be referred to as "technicalities." Yet this is a looming issue and, unquestionably, litigation is far from done.

With reference to the financing of education, two landmark cases engendered a great deal of attention in educational circles between 1971 and 1973. One, decided in 1971 in the California supreme court, was *Serrano* v. *Priest*. The court held that the previous method of financing public schools, namely, taxing real property within the school district, was unconstitutional. The objection was that tax money for schools coming from the real property tax varied radically from district to district, thereby causing an inequity and that it "invidiously discriminates against the poor because it makes equality of a child's education a function of the wealth of his parents and neighbors." After *Serrano*, a number of federal and state courts considered the same problem and, in general, reached the same conclusion until the U.S. Supreme Court, on March 21, 1973, in *San Antonio Independent School District* v. *Rodriguez,* decided this issue otherwise.

The *Rodriguez* case dealt with Demetrio P. Rodriguez, the son of a poor family in the Edgewood school district in San Antonio, Texas, and the court held in the opposite view from *Serrano* v. *Priest,* namely, that education, like voting, was a specially protected right. In *Rodriguez,* the U.S. Supreme Court (by a 5–4 vote) emphasized the absence of any reference to education in the federal constitution. The California constitution, by contrast, as do many state constitutions, includes specific references to the importance of education to both individuals and society; indeed, it gives education first call on state revenue. Such provisions, common in state constitutions, appear to provide precisely the sources of fundamental right so obviously absent at the federal level. Henceforth, challenges to school financing systems can be expected to be brought on state constitutional grounds only.

While the U.S. Supreme Court was able to get "off the hook," obviously states cannot. Partly owing to *Serrano* in California and *Rodriguez* in Texas (and other cases) but as well to a consensus among acknowledged scholars in the field of school finance, there has been a strong school finance reform movement building in the last ten years. We will discuss some related dimensions of this reform movement and the quite explicit conditions that help to motivate it in Chapter 9. At this point, however, and before leaving the relation of the judiciary to school financing problems, one final case and some other comments may be useful. We refer to the New Jersey court action known as *Robinson* v. *Cahill,* for it has resulted not only in a massive attempt at financial reform but, in the process, has illuminated some of the monstrous obstacles toward realizing that.

In brief, like *Serrano* and *Rodriguez*, the *Robinson* v. *Cahill* case highlighted the inadequacies of programs for schools' support based on property taxation. The principal argument in all these cases holds, quite simply, that the property tax pattern discriminates against the poor and those who live almost anywhere other than in suburbs or relatively small, self-contained cities.

The New Jersey situation is still a special case, however. When the decision was rendered that the state's schools were not "thorough and efficient," state funds provided only about 17 percent of the almost $1.5 billion of public educational expenditures. The rest was provided from local property taxation. In New Jersey, the courts had set a deadline for the refinement of the public school financial procedure—that was in 1972. An act was finally passed by the New Jersey legislature in 1975 but without a funding formula. The law was acknowledged as constitutional, and the New Jersey supreme court established a new deadline of July 1, 1976. But the legislature could not agree on a taxing plan and the deadline passed. Consequently, the supreme court ordered schools closed until a funding pattern was passed. The schools were closed for a week (only about 60,000 summer school students were affected), and the legislature did indeed come up with a plan. Yet in seven years since the original decision in *Robinson* was rendered, the quality of urban education is acknowledged as being "essentially unchanged."[15]

In all the cases cited, despite the absence of dramatic changes, the fact remains that these court decisions have indeed generated some reforms and certainly significant interest and concern. There is little question as well that still more activity will occur that will owe its origin to the recognition by the judiciary that no other branch of government can more effectively motivate action or shape *needed* policy than can the court.

In a particularly incisive treatment of the role of courts' intervention in school finance reform, Walter Hack has observed that[16]

Judicial intervention has tended to increase in tempo as cases have been recognized as having merit. Once heard, most cases have been decided in favor of the plaintiff and have been appealed with many eventually being heard by state supreme courts. Courts show some tendency to monitor the remedy specified and thus become involved in more than only deciding a narrowly defined issue.

---

[15]See, for example, David E. Weischadle, "Thorough and Efficient Education: School Finance Reform in New Jersey," *Phi Delta Kappan,* Vol. 60, no. 2 (October 1978), 121–123.

[16]Walter G. Hack, "Intervention of the Courts in School Finance," *Theory Into Practice,* Vol. 17, no. 4 (October 1978), 336.

Certainly this observation was precisely the case in New Jersey and, this "monitoring of remedy" has been well established by courts in desegregation issues.

With reference to school finance reform, which some advocates thought early on was an all but dead issue as a consequence of the *Rodriguez* decision, Hack has another instructive observation:[17]

The intervention of the courts . . . suggests the possibility that a revolution in school finance is indeed occurring. It is, however, a revolution characterized by [a front] extending through all the fifty states, by a set of carefully tested and precisely defined questions and issues, by use of strategies which have become integrated with judicial principles, and roles which have broadened the purview of the courts and which now involve legislative and executive bodies in the final resolution of the school finance issues. It has, in many ways, become a popular revolution rather than a judicial assault.

THE ISSUE OF DUE PROCESS

No commentary on the role of the courts in education matters would be complete without mention of certain other developments in the area of student and teacher rights under the First and Fourteenth Amendments. These developments have involved attempted regulation by school authorities of personal "liberties" of students and teachers. For example, the courts have been asked to review the constitutionality of school rules and practices pertaining to "freedom of expression" (pure speech and symbolic expression), hair styles and grooming, behavior and campus discipline, pregnancy, corporal punishment, admission and graduation requirements, and suspension and expulsion. Also, school district use of test scores for pupil placement and teacher employment and promotion procedures and other long-standing educational practices have been challenged successfully in the courts. Because of the long period of *laissez-faire* and the apparent lack of interest of state and federal judges in school matters, there developed a body of decisional law at the state level that has permitted school authorities to make rules and regulations governing student and teacher conduct but that failed, in many instances, to meet minimum constitutional requirements.[18] Much of the recent federal court activity in this area, therefore, has been to correct this situation.

The "analytical tools" used by the courts to make this correction involve the standard of review and question of who endures the burden of proof. Whereas formerly, the party attacking the statute, educational practice, or school rule

---

[17]Ibid., p. 340.
[18]Hogan, op. cit., p. 79.

carried the burden, now, where a First Amendment or a Fourteenth Amendment right is alleged to have been infringed, school authorities must carry the burden of proving that the "intrusion by the state is in furtherance of a legitimate state interest." Thus a different level of scrutiny, which affords special protection to First Amendment rights, has evolved from the earlier view of the "preferred position" of such rights. Some courts have characterized a student's hair style as a "personal liberty," and the burden is on the school authorities to justify regulation of that liberty. In the pregnancy cases involving students, education itself is characterized as a "basic personal liberty or right" and school authorities must bear the burden of justifying any rule or regulation limiting or terminating that right. School rules that restrict student "freedom of expression," symbolic or otherwise, must likewise meet a stricter test, namely, that they are necessary to prevent conduct that would materially and substantially interfere with the orderly operation of the school, and the burden of justifying such rules is placed on the school authorities. The leading Supreme Court case that has reflected a changing attitude of courts toward cases involving student and teacher "freedom of expression" is *Tinker* v. *Des Moines Independent Community School District,* decided in 1969, in which some public school pupils in Iowa were suspended for wearing black armbands to protest the government's policy on Vietnam. Said the court (Justice Fortas speaking), "their conduct was within the protection of the free speech clause of the First Amendment and the due process clause of the Fourteenth."[19] It was reaffirmed that students in school as well as out are "persons" under our Constitution. They are possessed of fundamental rights that the state must respect, just as they themselves must respect their obligations to the state. Justice Black dissented, however, declaring that the *Tinker* decision marks the beginning of "an entirely new era in which the power to control pupils by the elected 'officials of state supported public schools . . .' in the United States is in ultimate effect transferred to the Supreme Court." And he added that, if pupils in our schools can "defy and flout orders of school officials," it is the beginning of a "new revolutionary era of permissiveness in this country fostered by the judiciary."

Although Justice Black was consistently concerned about the court's intervention in policy, the rest of the court was also careful in the handling of various student-related issues to emphasize that student rights are tied intimately to their responsibilities as well. James Shaver has observed that[20]

In the *Tinker* case, for example, the Justices were mindful of "the need for affirming the comprehensive authority of the states and school officials, consistent with fundamental safeguards, to prescribe and control conduct in the schools," to insure "appropriate

---

[19]Ibid., p. 84.
[20]J. P. Shaver, "Democracy, Courts, and the Schools," *Theory Into Practice,* Vol. 17, no. 4 (October 1978), 287.

discipline" in order to avoid disruptions that "would substantially interfere with the work of the schools or impinge on the rights of other students."

One immediate consequence of the *Tinker* decision was the ruling in September 1970, by a three-judge federal panel, that provisions of the California Education Code restricting student expression on school campuses were unconstitutional. Following this determination, the California legislature in 1971 added new sections to its education code dealing with the right of students to exercise free expression on school campuses. The *Tinker* decision has had far-reaching effect, not only for students but also for teachers, and has been the basis for decisions in several subsequent cases.

Yet again, in dealing with the rights of teachers, the court has emphasized the important distinctions between the adjudication of disputes and the policy-making authority of fiduciary boards. In a case involving a school board's termination of teachers who were striking in violation of the law, the Supreme Court upheld the board even though the striking teachers contended that they were denied trial type safeguards. The court said:[21]

Policy making is a process of prudential judgment and we are not prepared to say that a judge can generally make a better policy judgment, or in this case, as good a judgment as the School Board, which is intimately familiar with all the needs of the school district, or that a school board must, at the risk of suspending school operations, wend its way through judicial processes not mandated by the legislature. More important, no matter what arguments the Board may make to the *de novo* trial judge, as we noted earlier, it will be the School Board that will have to cope with the consequences of the decision and be responsible to the electorate for it.

EDUCATIONAL QUALITY AND THE LAW

Beginning in the early 1970s, a new type of litigation began to emerge that raised the unique question concerning the relationship of quality of education and the legal liability of school districts and schoolteachers for failing to instill in their students certain basic skills. One case in California involved a lawsuit brought by the mother of a boy who, having graduated with a B-minus average and receiving a high school diploma, was not competent to read at the fifth-grade level. When his mother discovered his plight, despite assurances by school authorities that her son was attaining the proper reading level, she decided to sue the San Francisco Unified School District. The suit contended that the young

[21]Cited in J. Elson, "Pedagogical Incompetence and the Courts," *Theory Into Practice*, Vol. 17, no. 4 (October 1978), 308. Reference is to *Hortonville Jr. College Dist. No. 1 v. Hortonville Educ. Assn.*, 426 U.S. 482, 497 n. 5 (1976).

man graduated "unqualified for employment other than the most demeaning, unskilled, low-paid manual labor" and that under California law the school district was required to ensure that he met certain minimum requirements prior to being awarded a high school diploma.

In essence, this case illustrates that syndrome of criticisms and issues that have together come to be described by the term "accountability," and, explicitly, since the primary legal basis upon which such cases as this one are pursued has to do with assertions of negligence on the part of school officials, accountability is interpreted in terms of *malpractice*.

In this particular case (*Doe* v. *San Francisco Unified School District*), the plaintiff, Peter W. Doe, wanted to prove negligence under tort law, which required demonstration that (1) a legal duty existed on the part of the district and that duty was breached, (2) the plaintiff suffered *injury in fact*, and (3) the breach of duty by the defendant district was the cause of the injury. The court held that there was no workable standard in this situation whereby the conduct of the defendant district (or its officials) could be measured, nor was their any reasonable certainty of injury; equally important, the court was not satisfied that any causal connection was established between the alleged injuries and the conduct of the schools. What is difficult to decide in a case such as this concerns whether a school's "failure" to teach primarily affects a student's ability to read and write adequately. There are many other potentially "primary" and substantial factors involved such as home environment, cultural disadvantages, and psychological phenomena. Quite obviously, there were many other students who did acquire the skills at issue.

In still another malpractice case (*Donohue* v. *Copiague Union Free School District*), the New York court raised several interesting policy implications of such cases were they to be decided for plaintiffs. If a school district were found to be liable for malpractice, the litigation that would ensue would be significantly expanded; there would be the inevitable feigned injuries; there would be enormous economic considerations concerning how much in damages a school district can afford to pay; and perhaps more important, there would be problems associated with the *foreseeability* of teachers and other school officials of harm to any potential plaintiff. Clearly, as this New York court indicates, malpractice with reference to the explicit responsibility of schools for inculcating scholastic competence in pupils is an extremely complex matter—almost impossible to prove.

But having noted that, it should also be emphasized that courts have a notorious record for seemingly writing decisions at the bottom of the page and building logic down to them. Consequently, *if* a court decides to hold a school system legally accountable for malpractice, it can probably find a legal basis for doing so. That is one reason why the judiciary system has incorporated the elaborate appeals system; on the other hand, one is also well advised to be forewarned and take action accordingly.

The Doctrine of Immunity.   In these various issues, however (and dozens of others), even though courts have upheld schools, they have fairly well established the precedent that the older *laissez-faire* attitude toward immunity from tort liability is no longer much of a basis for protection of public agencies and officials. This doctrine derives from English common law and, in effect, holds that "the king can do no wrong." In American common law, the *doctrine of immunity* was merely extended to governmental systems and holds that, in the performance of official duties, public administrators and officials need to enjoy a kind of blanket protection (under the Eleventh Amendment, which holds that a state cannot be sued without its permission) for their acts and decisions to pursue their official purposes. While this doctrine has been helpful, the doctrine has also been a shield against litigation for all kinds of bizarre behaviors and has provided protection for all manner of irresponsible acts. In many such instances, suits were not brought simply because the immunity doctrine precluded their likely consideration.

This is another example, we think, of a traditional principle that, according to the courts, has apparently outlived its usefulness and in which courts have thereby set about to find "legal pegs" upon which to "hang" that conclusion. Or, as we have said, write the decision first, then build the logic down to it.

In a number of situations, courts have accomplished this by examining the "proprietary" aspect of governmental agencies and officials. With reference to schools, for example, a school system may lease its facilities for use by external groups—say, its football stadium for an exhibition by teams that are unrelated to the school district itself; if some personal injury results to a spectator, the courts will likely waive the "immunity" protection (and have done so) because the school district is engaging in "proprietary" activity (i.e., activity for which compensation is paid).

When the immunity doctrine became increasingly set aside by courts for almost any trivial reason because it was becoming viewed as contrary to other more substantive contemporary logic, school districts quickly discovered the value of thoughtful new policy development and developed a renewed interest in insurance coverage.

Liability of Teachers and Other School Officials.   Not only was the doctrine of immunity a comfortable legal protection for school personnel twenty or thirty years ago, but when damages might easily have been pursued under tort law, another realistic condition prevailed—teachers and school officials, in large measure, were not paid well and were counted in that enormous group of Americans who were considered "judgment proof." In other words, you cannot get blood out of a turnip. Recognizing that, many potential lawsuits were never brought. But that is no longer the case, and liability insurance for malpractice is increasingly as important to educational officials as for other professions. More important, a better understanding of the law as it affects schools is essential.

Some Further Implications of Malpractice

As has been pointed out, the notion of malpractice derives from the larger frame of reference of accountability. Roueche has observed that accountability implies a responsibility on the part of schools to provide equity of potential for all of education's clientele, including "those who come to school well prepared to share its benefits, and those who have nothing in their backgrounds that would equip them for a successful learning experience."[22]

In a real sense, these rather new viewpoints increasingly cast the student—at whatever level—in the mold of a "consumer." Students have begun to ask the courts to determine whether schools and colleges are delivering the education that seems to have been promised. There is thus rather deep concern, especially among college students, as to whether "consumer rights" are being protected properly and appropriately. It is a small step from college-related concerns to those of the more massive elementary and secondary levels. Since the fundamental bases upon which consumer-oriented litigation is advanced concern negligence, breach of contract, and fraud, schools and colleges must give much more detailed attention to their catalogues and curricula statements; Sheldon E. Steinback, staff council of the American Council on Education, has warned, "If you say this course is going to do something and it doesn't, you've got a problem on your hands."[23]

Thus, while the growing edge of the consumer movement has been aimed primarily, in education, at colleges and universities, the implications of the accountability syndrome have had perhaps greatest impact on legislative interest in public elementary and secondary education and specifically in terms of minimum levels of competency and ways for ensuring it.

The Competence Movement

Interestingly, the "competency movement" is seen by some educators as an invitation to more malpractice litigation, while to others the legislation of such standards may prevent such litigation. This issue, however, which we discussed in Chapter 1, reflects the current interest in the effectiveness of basic skills education, and those who see the installation of minimum competency standards for high school graduation as a hedge against malpractice may be terribly naïve. Those, on the other hand, who see such legislative mandates as merely providing still further complications with the work and purposes of schools are typically

[22]J. E. Roueche, G. A. Baker III, and R. L. Brownell, "The Concept of Accountability," *Accountability and the Community College: Directions for the 70's* (Washington, D.C.: American Association of Junior Colleges, 1972), pp. 3–8.

[23]Cited in P. Semas, "Students Filing 'Consumer' Suits," *The Chronicle of Higher Education*, Vol. 11, no. 11 (November 24, 1975), pp. 1, 10.

more concerned about methodology, implementation difficulties, and educational philosophy than of the questionable relation between such standards and legal guarantees of scholastic success.

Yet, as of this writing, seventeen states have adopted minimal competency graduation standards, and in some of these, litigation has already occurred.[24] In Florida, one student had passed through twelve years of school but had failed that state's "literacy test" and did not receive a diploma. In early summer 1979, the Florida federal district court ruled that he and some almost 3,500 other black and 1,342 white students be awarded their diplomas. The judge in this case pointed out that the test had been initiated too recently for students to be cognizant of it, to be in any way prepared for it, and even though the court did not throw out the tests outright, it did mandate that their implementation would be delayed until the 1982–83 academic year so that general familiarity with the intent and function of such tests was ample.[25]

It is already apparent that the intent of those legislatures that have mandated some kinds of competency requirements in the form of tests or similar assessments is extremely complicated to carry out. Almost all who have done so are wrestling with a variety of unforsen problems, not the least of which concerns the old vexing question, What education is of the most worth?

To some extent, the competency versus graduation movement asks that question in the reverse: What education is of the *least* worth? This seems so because the attempt has been almost universally aimed at some workable definition of "minimally acceptable" performance. Trying to develop a test that will provide that is enormously difficult, for who is wise enough to know?

Not Like G.E.D. Testing

Some have used the well-known G.E.D. (general educational development) program as a defense for advocating graduation competency standards. After all, say these proponents, almost a half-million Americans without high school diplomas take the G.E.D. tests each year and 280,000 of them pass it.

But there are some important considerations that this comparison ignores; the average age of the G.E.D. recipient is 30, and the process is voluntary—no one *has* to take the tests and even though many special programs have been established for helping persons to prepare for the tests, there is *no* attendance requirement in any state; moreover, these are not easy tests—the high school

[24]When state board of education action in this area is added to that of legislation, thirty-six states have joined this dubious bandwagon.

[25]Reviewed in S. J. Mercer, "Malpractice and School Effectiveness," unpublished term report, School Law Seminar, College of Human Resources and Education, West Virginia University, 1979, pp. 2–3.

equivalency tests consist of a five-instrument battery and require a total of ten hours.[26]

Test taking is a pervasive American pastime, yet tests, of whatever persuasion, are not always the best or only solution to assessments of performance and skill—sometimes they are the worst; but requiring a "test" seems often to be the simplest avenue for attacking a problem. At least, such devices provide useful information, but to determine one's future or one's adequacy on the basis of tests is hazardous.

SUMMARY

The role of law and courts in the history of American education has expanded dramatically during the past two decades. To large extent this has reflected a more activist and socially conscious judiciary and one that has been far more willing to exercise intrusion into the affairs and policy determination authority of school systems than in the first two and a half centuries of U.S. history. While the activist approach of the courts has abated somewhat in very recent years, the courts will continue to be an important factor in schools functions and activities.

To some extent, an observation by the late Justice Hugo Black, who was a consistently reluctant voice in all issues coming before the U.S. Supreme Court where decisions tended to intrude on local authority, has not impeded the intrusion of the judiciary in the development of educational policy. In 1968, Justice Black warned:[27]

However wise this court may be or may become hereafter, it is doubtful that, sitting in Washington, it can successfully supervise and censor the curriculum in every public school in every hamlet and city in the United States. I doubt that our wisdom is so nearly infallible.

One could apply Black's caution with equal concern to state legislatures, for these bodies, too, have become much more prescriptive and jurisdictional in the statutory treatment of education.

All these developments have reduced much of the autonomy of local boards of education and the administrators who serve as their executives. But while there are always reasons to be concerned about the reduction and subsequent

[26]See Evelyn Witter, "G.E.D. Teachers Are a New Breed," *Phi Delta Kappan*, Vol. 60, no. 2 (October 1978), 110–111.
[27]Hogan, op. cit., p. 2.

rearrangements of that authority, there is also little doubt that the accomplishments of the courts have been on behalf of the rights and responsibilities of citizens. Whether the same is true of legislatures remains doubtful, even though yet to be seen with much clarity. It has always been something of a comfort to know that courts adjudicate on the basis of law and constitutional provision as best they can interpret dispassionately. Legislatures, on the other hand, *fashion* the law from all manner of vested interest and popular pressures. It is for this reason that school administrators and school boards acting through their professional associations must always exercise informed vigilance within the legislative process, for prevention of a bad statute is always preferable to rescinding it.

Yet it needs be said as well that, even with the impressive expansion of school-related litigation and the enormous proliferation of rules by regulatory agencies, the opportunities for effective educational management and administrative leadership are still great, and the potential for affecting the well-being of youth is still most impressive. The work of the administrator is probably not more difficult than in other times—only considerably different; thus training and preparation call for different content and different skills. Certainly included in both is this matter of public education and the law.

Certainly, as well, the trends and concerns of the courts must reflect the concerns and perceived injustices of the people, for it is with people that the great majority of rules really begins. By the same token, changes in pattern of legal interest will continue to occur; even as this book is going to press, there is already reason to predict that, with the coming of the Reagan administration, there will be a softening of the liberal flavor of the courts. Evidence of this is the recent initiative in California that disclosed massive negative attitudes toward forced busing and its subsequent support by the California supreme court; the ink was hardly dry on that decision before the Los Angeles school board voted (with only one dissenting member) to eliminate forced busing. Similarly, there is a more obscure case that may have significant long-range implications for a ''hands-off'' attitude at least from the federal sector. Dean Gordon Gee of the College of Law at West Virginia University in a recent speech before a statewide Phi Delta Kappa group pointed to this situation as follows:[28]

There is an interesting case which was brought by the National League of Cities, I believe it is called . . . and in that case, Justice Rendquist dug up the Tenth Amendment and in a real sense gave that obscure amendment a ''born-again'' quality for in essence, his opinion states that those things not expressly referred to in the Constitution and therefore left to the states, which is what the Tenth Amendment is all about, you know . . ., well, his conclusion is that if it is left to the states, the Federal government has nothing to do with it *at all*.

[28]Gordon, Gee. ''Education and the Law,'' unpublished address at Phi Delta Kappa Symposium on the Law and Education, Morgantown, West Virginia, March 13, 1981.

We believe that we are now likely to see a withdrawal of interest and concern by the appellate courts in favor of a return to a kind of judicial *laissez-faire*. Not anything so remote as that characterized earlier in this chapter but certainly similar as the present mood of the country seems to want the federal establishment and the federal role reduced significantly.

Even though that is rather clearly the mood of both the country and the general ideology being promulgated by the Reagan people, it is somewhat dulled by the announcement by President Ronald Reagan of his appointment of Ms. Sandra O'Connor to the United States Supreme Court; at least, there have been some notable "conservatives" who tended to conclude that Ms. O'Connor's previous position of nonopposition to abortion could be interpreted to mean that the highest court itself was not going to take a sudden sharp turn to the right. Whether there will in fact be something of a lessening of the scope of litigation and regulatory activity that has been characteristic of all levels of education during the past twenty or so years obviously remains to be seen. There is, quite clearly, a manifestly established intent on the part of those at the topmost levels of government to see that the extent to which schools and other educational agencies are subject to a variety of rules and regulations of federal regulatory and enforcement agencies is reduced. The price of that also seems quite clear: significant reductions as well in federal financial support in almost all areas and almost outright elimination of the familiar categorical grants in aid. Even for schools it begins to look as though there is no such thing as a free lunch.

SUGGESTED REFERENCES

Bybee, Roger, and Gordon Gee. *Violence, Values and Justice in American Education*. Boston: Allyn and Bacon, 1981.

Corns, Alexander, and Walter McCann. *Public School Law*. Minneapolis, Minnesota: West Publishing Co., 1979.

Valenti, William D. *Law in the Schools*. Columbus, Ohio: Charles E. Merrill, 1980.

EXERCISES

1. Your school system is centrally located in the state and you have an excellent football stadium. You have been approached by two parochial schools to allow them the use of the facilities for a state championship football game. What are the legal implications?

2. As the assistant superintendent for instruction, it has been brought to your attention that a teacher in one of the middle schools is accused, by parents, of administering corporal punishment to a 12-year-old girl by paddling her bare-handed on her buttocks. The principal's investigation discloses a flat denial by the teacher, and he is convinced the teacher is telling the truth. Yet there are unmistakable signs of the "punishment" and the child so accuses said teacher. There were no witnesses, but two other children corroborate the fact that the teacher openly threatened to spank the child. There is an allowable corporal punishment policy in the system. What are you going to do? What will your own investigation seek? You have a meeting day after tomorrow with the parents and their attorney—how should you prepare for that?

3. A child who was walking home from school apparently broke the windows in a parked automobile. Because the child lives only nine tenths of a mile from the school, he is ineligible for transportation by board policy; the parents hold that, since the child is technically still a "pupil" on the way to and from school, the school is liable for the damage. Is there any basis for this contention? What is your response to be, and how will you arrive at it?

4. In the midst of considerable student reaction over the transfer of a popular athletic coach to another school in your system, students have walked out of classes in protest. The principal, convinced that the transferred teacher's wife (a school employee) was involved in instigating the strike—and with reasonable evidence, dismissed her on the spot and is appealing to you as superintendent for support. Was he within his rights? What are you going to do now that it is obvious that the teacher is going to "fight" it?

5. A school bus in your district was involved in a serious accident that resulted in bodily injury to five children. It is now established that the vehicle had eighteen safety violations and should not have been put in service since two of these had to do with faulty brakes and steering. In your state there is the doctrine of immunity whereby the state cannot be sued. But you are being sued as the superintendent among others, and you were totally unaware that this vehicle was returned to service. What is your status in the matter and what are you going to do about the situation otherwise?

Chapter 5

The State Education Agency

INTRODUCTION

It is generally acknowledged that a signal strength of America's unique system of mass education is that it is regarded as a function of the states rather than of the federal government. This pattern has been expanded and sustained by a persistent attitude of democratic "local control," and thus even the role of the states has traditionally been subordinate to local district interests.

Let us look at scholarly observations about the role of the states with reference to the control of education. In the early 1960s, for example, one reputable text on educational administration had this to say:[1]

> there are divergent views on how [states] should carry out their responsibilities. These views range from that of the extreme "centralist," who advocates strong state administration with little or no responsibility shared by school districts, to that of the extreme "localist" or "decentralist" who would endow the districts with great freedom and wide powers while limiting the state education agency to record-keeping and advising.

These authors did, however, note "a general trend toward centralization of control [by] the states." That was in 1961. During the twenty years since then, that "general trend" has become fairly well established. Today, the authority and functions of the state departments of education (SEAs) are almost universally

[1]C. Grieder, T. M. Pierce, and W. E. Rosenstengel, *Public School Administration*, 2nd ed. (New York: Ronald Press, 1961), p. 31.

more dominant than ever before, and, in collaboration rather directly with the federal apparatus, the locus of educational policy formulation has shifted away from the "local" school system in significant ways.

Discussing this turn of events, two writers recently had this to say:[2]

Because local school boards are prominent in most communities, and because the issues that come before local boards sometimes receive extensive publicity, it is easy to over-estimate the extent to which schools in this country are controlled at the local level. But in reality, much of the time and energy of local boards is dedicated to implementing, or reacting to, decisions made elsewhere—the local, state and federal legislative bodies and agencies, the courts, and a wide array of non-governmental (or quasi-governmental) organizations and groups.

These writers also view the shifts away from the much more autonomous local control and toward state-federal and other organizational interests as a kind of "confederation" phenomenon and thus see "these interorganizational patterns [as] an alternative to traditional public bureaucracy."[3] While we would agree that a variety of groups, interests, and organizations are involved in the governance of schools (professional and bureaucratic as well as informal), we would also argue that professional groups and other nonbureaucratic interests exercise a disproportionate amount of time and energy in reacting to or implementing (or trying to resist) decisions, rules, and prescriptions "made elsewhere." And increasingly "elsewhere" means the state education agency and the federal government. We will give consideration to the impact of the federal government in Chapter 6; now we want to examine the nature and functions of the state department and its relationship to school system management.

EVALUATION OF THE STATE EDUCATION AGENCY

As we have suggested, it has only been in the past fifteen years or so that state departments of education have assumed status in the general operation of schools. Yet it was due to the very early efforts of a handful of energetic and committed state school chiefs that the great system of mass common schools came into existence in the first place. It is also remarkable that because of these early efforts local control was able to assume the burden of continuous devel-

---

[2]R. G. Corwin and R. A. Edelfelt, *Perspectives on Organizations: Schools in the Larger Social Environment* (Washington, D.C.: American Association of Colleges for Teacher Education and Association of Teacher Educators, 1978), p. 25.

[3]Ibid., p. 25.

opment with state departments in a much less visible status throughout our nation's history from about 1870 to 1955.

Certainly when examining the accomplishments of such giants in education as Horace Mann (in Massachusetts), Henry Bernard (in Connecticut and Rhode Island), Gidion Hawley (in New York), and Calvin H. Wiley (in North Carolina), one has to be impressed with the statesmanship of these early educators.[4]

Perhaps it is sufficient to note that while the education movement started in local communities and in sections of the state and by groups interested in culture or the common man or the worker, it was not until the state took action by making provision for a state school officer that the forces of and for education were consolidated into a movement that did not stop until free common school education became a reality.

The Thurston–Roe book remains the single most comprehensive treatment of state-level schools administration (and the only one to our knowledge other than Elwood Cubberly's 1927 work on this subject), and although now more than twenty years have passed since its publication, it provides an excellent frame of reference for understanding the underlying conditions whereby state education agencies have come so strongly and centrally into the mainstream of educational policy determination in the last dozen years.

Between 1900 and 1950, state departments of education were, with few exceptions, concerned primarily with "inspectional and regulatory" functions[5] and were relegated to relatively insignificant-seeming roles in the affairs of public education. While this assessment is widely accepted, it is typically exaggerated, for although it is true that these departments in many—perhaps most—states endured a long period of low visibility, they were nevertheless providing important leadership and advice in many areas—in school finance and budgetary procedures; school transportation; school plant planning; schools consolidation and attendance-area reorganization; accreditation and/or program approvals; teacher and other education personnel licensure and certification; textbook adoption regulations; research and data collection; library acquisitions; legislative guardianship and the promotion of effective legislation; teacher preparation; school lunch and food concerns; rehabilitation concerns; vocational education; and curricular interests.

All these matters quite naturally proceeded with "fits and starts" from one state to another. Some state departments were simply more active than others, and this itself was somewhat a function of factors unique to the states themselves.

[4]L. Thurston and W. H. Roe, *State School Administration* (New York: Harper and Row, 1957), p. 49.
[5]John Guy Fawlkes, "Editor's Introduction," in ibid., p. vii.

THE INTRUSION OF "POLITICS" AND STABLE LEADERSHIP

As with any other state-level agency, SEAs have, until recently, confronted the usual problems and prospects of state political machinery, the darker dimensions of "patronage," and other consequences of basic party politics. In fact, for some years, SEAs endured a reputation of marginal competence as a consequence of the blatant intrusion of "politics" into their affairs.

To a large extent, much of the political meddling was owing to the fact that the chief state school officer (CSSO) was an elected official and the position required no professional qualifications except that one be a native of the state and of a certain age and stood innocent of capital crimes. Moreover, the pressures on SEAs during those years prior to the 1950s were no less from state politicians than were those on other state agencies, and the reciprocities of favors and debts were prolific. Accordingly, SEAs had some difficulty maintaining a core of professional staff, especially at the level of bureaus or directorships, so that relatively long-term plans could be initiated, much less carried out.

As recently as 1955, twenty-six chiefs were elected by the people, four were appointed by the governor, and eighteen were appointed by the state board. Of course, appointment by the board was preferable, for even though only about half of those served a definite term, all were subject to reappointment. It was exceedingly rare that a gubernatorial appointment lasted through a change in executives, and not all those who succeeded to the office by popular vote could serve more than one term.

Kentucky, for example, still allows only one four-year term, and although some of its chiefs have been elected subsequently and have served more than once, state constitutional processes do not allow successions. This means that continuity of leadership is impossible at the level of the chief. In other states—Michigan, for example—the term of office was for only two years but with right of succession.

It has been recognized for many years that appointment of the CSSO is preferable and that has been the trend since 1960. Typically, the appointment is made by the state board of education, which itself may either be appointed or elected, but there is at least an opportunity for continuity of leadership. In West Virginia, the members of the board are appointed by the governor with staggered terms (so that, in theory, no *one* governor can appoint a majority) and they, in turn, appoint the state superintendent.

The greater stability of the professional staff secured through more precise civil service statutes and increasing regulatory provisions based on affirmative action and civil rights regulations has further helped to establish SEAs as professional and leadership-oriented bureaucracies. In addition, the emergence of the National Chief State School Officers Association has provided a powerful force at the federal level for increasing both the influence and the authority of SEAs in the definition of educational practice.

Thus, by 1975, the CSSOs and the SEAs they head had come just about full circle; from their early role in the determination of educational policy, through a long period of ineffectiveness, to a present visibility and status that can impact many local and related educational interests.

THE GROWTH OF STATE EDUCATION AGENCIES

From 1890 until 1920, the total "staff" of SEAs in the nation increased from a total of 129 to 836; by 1955, the total staff had increased to 15,375.[6]

As SEAs have grown in size, they have also grown in influence and prestige. Traditionally, the development of these state agencies has been seen as having passed through three stages: a statistical, or record-keeping, stage in the beginning and until about 1900; an inspecting stage from about 1900 to about 1930; and a leadership stage since 1930.[7] Roe points out that the inspecting function of state departments was so routine and predictable that it was easy to estimate the total staff required. However, given that importance rests on the amount of funding allocated by the legislature,[8] the "leadership" stage has required a gradual redefinition of the functions both of the agency and its personnel. In the case of personnel, emphasis was on professionally prepared persons with much more extensive preentry training and greater identification with outside reference groups.

As we now look back on the development of SEAs, the three stages identified by Beach and Gibbs seem too imprecise. Certainly there is no argument with the first two, but the leadership stage is far more subject to debate. While there may have been a few state departments of education that were exercising leadership prior to 1930 and a few others fairly soon thereafter, in the main, this function did not emerge until well after World War II—in about 1950. We think it is accurate to add a fourth stage after inspection and before leadership; this stage we would characterize as *supervisory*.

[6]F. F. Beach and A. H. Gibbs, cited in Thurston and Roe, op. cit., p. 117.
[7]Ibid., 75 ff.
[8]Thurston and Roe, op. cit., pp. 116–117.

SUPERVISION AND LEADERSHIP

"Supervision" is an honorable term in American education that is frequently used to conceptualize those aspects of administration that deal with instruction as separate from, say, business management. In this context, Eye and Netzer define supervision as "that phase of school administration that deals primarily with the achievement of the appropriate selected instructional expectations of educational practice."[9]

If, in this definition, the reference to instruction is omitted, it describes our view of the supervisory stage in the development of SEAs, which we place in the period from about 1935 to 1950.

The reasoning is fairly clear. During this period, legislatures began to expand their mandates in the education of children and youth and required the state department to provide supervision over them. In the early part of this functional period, state department staffs exercised these supervisory chores with some tentativeness, yet the intent of the legislatures was aimed clearly at failures of local schools to provide effectively for certain educational concerns. Thus a central agency close to legislative supervision was required both to see that mandates were carried out and to provide help to the districts in doing so. What we have called the "supervisory" stage in the development of SEAs stemmed from the distrust by legally legitimate state interests of local discretion.

The late Paul Mort provided incisive analysis of this situation:[10]

Often the reason for failure of local discretion to give satisfactory results may be found in the conflict of personal interests and public interests of the citizens. This is doubtless what has accounted for the removal of discretion from the hands of local communities. . . . Experience showed that local school districts could not exercise discretion wisely.

Mort pointed out that, even though only a few districts may not have responsibly exercised discretion, an optimist-pessimist condition operates in such situations and cautioned against this tendency toward centralized authority: "In extending such regulation there is always the danger that the communities capable of exercising discretion will be unduly hampered by the precedential requirements that were really established from [those shown] incapable of using freedom wisely."[11]

[9]G. G. Eye and L. A. Netzer, *School Administrators and Instruction* (Boston: Allyn & Bacon, 1969), p. 9.
[10]Paul Mort, *Principles of School Administration* (New York: McGraw-Hill, 1946), p. 172.
[11]Ibid., p. 172.

This notion of what most scholars now acknowledge as the first real attempt to establish a theoretical basis and theoretical treatment of educational administration was later formulated more precisely by Alvin Gouldner as the application of "general and impersonal rules."[12]

But Mort also calls attention to the fundamental basis for the emergence of SEAs as significant forces in educational affairs and, in doing so, spells out the basis for the transition from the supervisory stage to what Beach and Gibbs have characterized as "leadership."[13]

Today it is impossible to operate adequate schools locally without some degree of support collected by and distributed from a central agency. This follows from the fact that there are vast differences in the ability of school districts to support their schools. Requiring the communities themselves to support the schools results in inequities and in some cases actually denies adequate educational opportunities because of a lack of economic resources.

It was, then, the emergence of the state as a major partner in the financing of schools that really gave principal impetus to the concomitant emergence of the SEAs as a dominant force in educational administration. As Louis Brownlaw observed more than forty years ago, "It is fundamentally true that the essential control of the administrative process is in the hands of him who holds the purse strings."[14]

At just about the "supervisory" stage in the development of state departments of education, the field of instructional supervision itself was entering a new era. Writing in the 1948 yearbook of the Department of Elementary School Principals, then affiliated with the National Education Association, Henry J. Otto, a renowned authority at the University of Texas, said: "Supervision is no longer direction and inspection. Supervision has become leadership."[15]

POWER FOLLOWS MONEY

It is, as Brownlaw asserted, true in capitalistic societies that power follows money. On the other hand, if the idea of free public education can have any

[12]See, for example, Alvin Gouldner, *Patterns of Industrial Bureaucracy* (New York: Free Press, 1954), pp. 172 ff.

[13]Mort, op. cit., p. 313.

[14]Louis Brownlaw, "City Halls to Capitols," *State Government*, Vol. 7, no. 2 (February 1935), 28.

[15]"The Elementary School Principalship—Today and Tomorrow," Twenty-seventh Yearbook, *The National Elementary Principal* (Washington, D.C.: Department of Elementary School Principals, NEA, 1948), p. 271.

real meaning and if this is presumed to be a state responsibility, then some acceptable "standard" of education ought to be presumed. This principle was articulated in a study authorized in New York State in the 1920s. Strayer and Haig who authored that significant investigation said it this way: "States should set up a minimum program below which no locality shall be allowed to go."[16]

To our knowledge, this was the first published expression of what have become well established in the literature of school finance as "foundation programs." The idea, quite simply, was that a minimum foundation of educational adequacy would be defined and the state would guarantee some level of funding to provide it. The patterns that actually developed from this basic notion were almost as varied as the states themselves; yet this fundamental principle has endured. Moreover, the time required to move in that direction equaled a generation. Many states merely provided "flat grants" by totaling the number of children by a school census or some similar procedure, dividing the revenue available by this total number, then allocating to the district that amount multiplied by a district's school population.

During the 1930s, guidelines for school finance were emerging, which expanded the role of the state department of education. Because the implementation of new and relatively complex formulas for state aid required the amendment of state constitutions, the activity associated with these various efforts clearly established the SEAs and, specifically, the CSSOs in leadership positions.

The implications in the disbursement of substantial sums of money for expanding the authority of the SEA are obvious. It was through this expanded function that SEAs emerged as increasingly powerful and influential organizations:[17]

State departments of education distributed approximately $2,923,000,000 to local school districts during the school year 1953–54.

It must be regarded as axiomatic that . . . annual distribution of three billion dollars . . . is most influential upon the quality, character, and availability of public education throughout the state.

These developments, as we have indicated, were uneven over time. The southern states were leaders in the movement toward more systematic state support for schools mainly because, historically, these states had not instituted the practice of local taxation for school support. Consequently, most of the southern states had been providing most of the money for schools for many years. And, unlike states in the North and Midwest, where local tax levies for schools provided the bulk of funding, schools in the South were acknowledged

---

[16]George Strayer and R. M. Haig, *The Financing of Education in the State of New York* (New York: Macmillan, 1924), p. 173.

[17]Thurston and Roe, op. cit., p. 158.

to be of poor quality—facilities were inadequate, teacher salaries were lower than in any other region, and overall achievement of pupils was comparatively lower. Accordingly, these states' central agencies—state departments—grew to positions of authority and power earlier than in other general regions.

PRESENT STATUS

Beginning in the 1960s, the more active fiscal and regulatory role of the federal government in education created new postures and new demands for professional staff in SEAs, thus extending their authority and bureaucracy. In 1979, with a relatively well-established pattern of federal-state collaboration through the state departments, CSSOs have emerged as almost the most powerful group of educators in America. Moreover, as more states move away from the pattern of popular election to the appointment of these officials, the continuity of leadership deemed essential to stable and long-range effectiveness is more assured.

Personnel in the various bureaus of SEAs are extremely well prepared, many holding doctorates; they are well compensated and are active in state, regional, and national professional organizations.

The danger in this emergence of SEAs as the dominant educational organization has to do with what Paul Mort characterized many years ago as the "principle of prudence." Mort cautioned that with greater influence and power comes the likelihood of greater regulation: "When requirements become so detailed that their purpose is lost sight of, such regulations actually hamper the schools in meeting demands."[18]

SUMMARY

State education agencies have grown both in scope and influence in recent years from their beginnings as primarily record-keeping and inspecting bodies. With greater supervision and more legislatively authorized regulatory power, and with greater control over the definition and allocation of state funds, SEAs are a dominant force in American public education and, in the administration of it.

[18]Mort, op. cit., p. 173.

EXERCISES

1. In your state there is a proposal to change from an elected to an appointed state school chief. You are currently the elected president of your state's association of school administrators and have been asked to serve on a panel at an upcoming state convention of another powerful education-related group on the pros and cons of this issue. Your own association is divided on it. What is your position and how did you arrive at it?

2. Through strong efforts by your state's SEA, there is a proposal to require a competency examination of all high school seniors. While the proposal has enjoyed wide deliberative participation by citizens and teachers, few school superintendents have been consulted, since it is well known that, as a group, superintendents oppose it. You are personally close to the state school chief, and you have been generally supportive of his efforts; you are also in the midst of delicate negotiations with state department personnel to secure an important Title III grant. Your associate superintendent was interviewed by the state's leading newspaper and it came off as an explosive *blast* at the proposal, more emotional than authoritative. When you return from lunch, there is a "While You Were Out" note indicating that you are to call the state superintendent. What are you going to say?

3. You have been a reasonably successful superintendent in three different school systems for fourteen years total and have just earned your doctorate from the university. You were asked if you would be interested in joining the state department of education as an assistant state superintendent responsible for a piece of its large financial and administrative division. The salary is better than you are getting now. What factors and issues, apart from personal ones, enter into your decision?

4. As a superintendent of schools, you are completely dissatisfied with your state's present system of allocating funds. A legislative study has been mandated, and while its recommendations do not completely satisfy you, you are convinced that it is better than what exists. Your state department is vociferously opposed to the study recommendations, but it has no plans to suggest its own legislation. It is also clear that several powerful members of the legislative finance committee are "after" high officials in the SEA. You have been invited to testify before the next finance committee hearing as one of some influence among the state's school administrators. Would you accept the invitation? If so, what will your strategy be? If not, what should you say when you decline?

5. You have been asked to assume the chair of a major task force on "The articulation of relationships between the state department of education and

the local school district." The purpose is to explore ways in which the SEA and the LEA can collaborate and cooperate to improve educational services. You have relatively unlimited initial freedom to organize and design the efforts of the task force. How will you proceed? Who will you ask to serve? What kind of a "product" will you aim at achieving? What important dimensions of "articulation" will you try to emphasize?

SUGGESTED REFERENCES

Corwin, R. G., and R. A. Edelfelt. *Perspectives on Organizations: Schools in the Larger Social Environment.* Washington, D.C.: American Association of Colleges for Teacher Education, 1978.

Johns, R. L., and E. L. Morphet. *Financing the Public Schools.* Englewood Cliffs, N.J.: Prentice-Hall, Inc., 1960. See especially Chapters 1, 7, 9, and 11.

Miller, Van, George R. Madden, and James B. Kincheloe. *The Public Administration of American School Systems.* New York: Macmillan Publishing Co., 1972. Chapter 1.

Smith, Richard N. *Development of the Iowa Department of Public Instruction.* Des Moines, Iowa: Department of Public Instruction, 1969.

Thurston, Lee M., and William H. Roe. *State School Administration.* New York: Harper & Row, 1957.

PART II

The Management Context in Administration

Chapter 6 ――――――――――――――――――――

Management Concerns
and Management Issues

INTRODUCTION

The broad management concerns that confront the educational administrator are, generally, little different from those affecting any enterprise. These concerns include production, communication, training, personnel relations, resources acquisition and allocation (and planning and budgeting), distribution problems, time management, capital improvements, maintenance and operation, and public relations—to mention just some of the more obvious ones.

Missing from the general list are merchandising and sales, even though it could be argued that the manager of any educational operation also deals with some "market" issues. The tendency to equate public kinds of administration with corporate management in the private sector probably breaks down more fundamentally on this point than any other, however. And, as has been pointed out elsewhere, one of the characteristic differences between "administration" and "management" as fields of study and perhaps even as disciplines is that management "is primarily oriented to the use of capital to accumulate capital whereas administration is . . . the use of capital to meet socially mandated needs."[1]

Accordingly, marketing activities are of little concern to the educational administrator. But that the role requires selling talent is unarguable. By the same token, analogies to "product" and "production" are far less appropriate to the language of the school administrator, and the tendency to compare the processes

――――――――――――――――――――

[1]W. G. Monahan, *Theoretical Dimensions of Educational Administration*, New York: Macmillan and Co., 1975, p. 1.

113

of educational management with the traditional "factory model" is a tempting oversimplification that understandably upsets the reasonably sophisticated educational theorist. Children are not inanimate objects and school programs are not assembly lines. Yet schools and school systems do engage in *producing*. Thus certain aspects of production management consume heavy proportions of school managers' time and certain "marketing" techniques are incorporated in the schools that are managed.

ADMINISTRATION QUA ADMINISTRATION

In other areas of management, problems are differentiated only by the contexts in which they occur, and even though techniques must be adapted to the context (whether in a school or a hospital or an engineering firm), the issues and problems can be treated within the same principles. It is this point of view that led to the attitude several decades ago that the principles of administration were pervasive and general, that is, a "good" hospital administrator employs the same principles as a "good" school administrator, as does a "good" business administrator, and so forth.

Unfortunately, this argument is only half true, and the part of it that is true tends to obscure the part of it that is not. Consequently, educational management, given its abstract ingredients, must be pursued in terms of its unique characteristics in the climate within which it functions. Let us briefly discuss the unique flavor of some of these abstractions and then, in more detail, deal with what we consider to be the larger dimensions of specific concerns in succeeding chapters.

PRODUCTION IN EDUCATIONAL ADMINISTRATION

Someone once observed, "There has been an alarming increase in the things I know nothing about." That view reflects the feelings of the contemporary educational administrator. Unquestionably, the division of labor and specialization in education today demands that management personnel know more and more about less and less. To an extent, this trend toward specialized expertise is a function of the management of production that stems from the proliferation of mandated tasks and processes imposed by the orderly pursuit of program purposes.

If, for example, we characterize production as the more familiar tasks associated with instruction (and the delivery of it), it is easier to see how division of labor becomes an important management issue. First, there is the current heavy emphasis on specified target populations such as the handicapped, the vocational and career oriented, and the college bound and human service oriented. Then there are the programs for adult education, paraprofessionals, and a variety of other activities ranging from peer-tutors to right-to-read enthusiasts. All these interests—and ones as yet unanticipated—have a heavy involvement in the production activities of schools. Some of these activities are well established and bring resources into the school settings to assist in the implementation of objectives; others are faddish and emotional and fade into oblivion.

Typically, the division of labor for production resides first with the teaching staff and school principals and then with the central office support personnel and management hierarchies. Whether the division of labor is centralized or decentralized, the other concerns of management intrude: namely, communication, public relations, personnel relations, budgeting, and so forth. None of these other concerns exists separately from the programs, initiatives, and responses related to production factors. In the context of school operations, production concerns the entire process of providing appropriate instruction (and the evaluation thereof) to all clientele served by the system.

Given this rather generalized description of production as a managerial concern in educational organizations, the term itself is not very appropriate to the activities of scholastic management. We prefer to translate that idea into the more familiar concept of "instruction" and will use that term in subsequent discussion. By the same token, we distinguish that broader function from "training," as training—as a managerial concern—refers, we believe, to internal management and the problems generated therein. Examples include establishing and adhering to certain accounting patterns and procedures, utility of data processing memoranda, communication and correspondence styles, leave and vacation policies, security procedures, hierarchial relationships and courtesies, and unique role expectations that, regardless of vocational training, sometimes require extensive orientation training to adapt to the idiosyncrasies of particular organizations. All these conditions (and many more that we could not possibly know) require some ongoing attention to "training" that distinguish them from the larger instructional purposes of school systems that characterize them as *special* indoctrinational organizations.

DISTINCTIONS AMONG ORGANIZATIONS

With reference to such generalized concepts as production, communication, training, marketing, transportation, and so forth, it is useful, in our view, to remind the reader that a little theoretical analysis of organizational differentiation is sometimes helpful in the difficult transition from the abstract to the specific.

In the case of management issues in school systems, we believe that the tendency is too great to presume that the *likenesses* across all types of organizations obscure the unique management problems they generate when, in fact, it is the particularities of organizations that characterize their management effectiveness.

For example, we can talk about the *generalized* value of worker motivation as a vital factor in any organization's efficiency and effectiveness; we can feel quite comfortable with research data supporting the relationship between motivation and effect and thereby adopt conclusions (too) simplistically posited on the basis of theoretically abstract postulates about Theory X and Theory Y organizations.[2]

On the other hand, when confronted with a particular crisis in, say, personnel management at some particular moment in time and in some particular organization and for whatever reason, theoretical conceptualizations provide little basis for the immediate decision that must be made. By the same token, the proverbial "intervening variables" of organizational idiosyncrasy frequently render the larger theoretical postures irrelevant to the situation confronted.

For these reasons, it will be useful to provide some distinctions among different kinds of organizations so that we may discuss the management issues unique to schools.

Clearly any organization confronts the functions of all other; thus, if the major function is indeed the replication of standard products, that organization also needs to give attention to creating new ideas and changing habits and the distribution of services. The purpose of this example is to demonstrate the major significant categories of organizational purpose and the acknowledged criteria of effectiveness by which such systems are assessed. Accordingly, it was immediately acknowledged that schools, as indoctrinational organizations, should not be judged solely on the basis of the number of clients leaving, for surely many clients leave prior to the presumed fulfillment of that organization's purposes (i.e., those who graduate). Yet "dropouts" figure always into efficiency ratios of schools and the "holding power" of schools is a vital statistic in anyone's efficiency analysis of such organizations.[3]

That schools are indoctrinational systems with the major function of changing behavior may not seem to agree with what many school personnel define as

[2]See, for example, Douglas McGregor, *The Human Side of Enterprise* (New York: McGraw-Hill, 1960).

[3]It has been pointed out that the "number-of-clients-leaving" criterion can be too easily a direct function not of the desired changes in behavior postulated and verified as in, say, the case of a mental institution but, rather, of the pressure of others to get in! Consequently, if there is a fixed capacity, those who are dismissed may depend on those waiting to be admitted, and when that pressure is acute, decisions made regarding clients leaving may be (and frequently are) based on judgments about who is the more deserving. For schools there is a well-established pattern of movement "through" the organization for any client (from kindergarten through twelfth grade), but the variable pressures of demand and supply can still have unanticipated consequences. Anxiety about "dropouts" is not as likely to be manifested when there is a long line of folks waiting to fill the vacancies.

their conception of schools' functions and purposes, yet the pattern as presented is rational. Schools *are* viewed as behavior-altering organizations, and they *are* judged frequently by aspects of their leaving clients, surely not only by quantity but also by how many go on to college (with scholarships) or into the armed services, or into the world of work, and so on. The number of "clients" leaving is thus a reasonable general criterion of effectiveness. Indoctrination is, on the other hand, a defensible function because almost from the beginning one of the overriding aims of American education has been to prepare young persons for adult roles in the society. At the same time, both within generalized educational goals and the abstractions of the typology in Table 6-1, the *idea* of indoctrination is posited as value free; that is, indoctrination is seen as a process rather than as some subtle, or subversive, pattern of shaping behavioral thought along some ignoble dimension. Consequently, it is better conceived as a behavior-modifying system aimed at controlled growth.

OTHER SPECIFIC MANAGEMENT CONCERNS

Just as there is some generalized measure of productivity that characterizes the effectiveness of any formal organization or the larger institution it serves,

Table 6-1. Typology of Organization

Type of Organization	Major Function	Examples	Effectiveness Criterion*
Habit	Replicating standard and uniform products	Highly mechanized factories, etc.	Number of products
Problem solving	Creating new ideas	Research organizations, design and engineering divisions, consulting organizations, etc.	Number of ideas
Indoctrination	Changing peoples' habits, attitudes, intellect, behavior (physical and mental)	Universities, prisons, hospitals, etc.	Number of "clients" leaving
Service	Distributing services either directly to consumer or to above types	Military, government, advertising, taxi companies, etc.	Extent of services performed

*These effectiveness criteria are oversimplified. Obviously, organizations set up multiple criteria and have to coordinate them. The criteria specified here were selected for their accessibility to quantitative terms and their formal significance.

*From W. G. Bennis, K. D. Benne, and Robert Chin, *The Planning of Change* (New York: Holt, Rinehart and Winston, 1961), p. 442. Used with permission.

there are fundamental managerial subcomponents of functioning that such organizations must maintain to remain vital. Certainly, the "type" of organization has much to do with determining the specifics of management; for example, the administration of personnel relations varies dramatically between "professional" and "nonprofessional" organizations.

In dealing with highly professionalized systems, it is well established that there are greater commitments by incumbents to outside reference groups, more advanced pre-entry training, and greater individual control over work. Therefore, the extent to which the organization itself can dictate conformity to procedures and conditions governing "work" is much less than is that in so-called nonprofessional systems. By the same token, the reciprocity of greater responsibility by the individual professional somewhat offsets the need for closer and more conforming supervision. Nevertheless, professional organizations are far less tolerant of bureaucratized rules and routinized role expectations. This is also the case even when the "professional" organization may be only a subcomponent of a larger system as, for example, the research and development division of a traditional company.

The researchers in such units who usually hold doctorate degrees and utilize sophisticated equipment and facilities are not treated the same as other personnel. Typically they are not confined to the same rules regarding the time of work, nor are they limited by access to facilities, nor are they expected to conform to norms of dress and habit. They are typically evaluated differently and are not judged by any familiar formula for productivity—one idea that turns out to be marketable may easily justify an entire career for a single researcher.

Consequently, while *some* personnel procedures must be abided, the nature of these obviously varies in terms of the functions performed and the purposes pursued.

Personnel Relations: The General Context

In the case of school systems, and to some extent depending on size and type, personnel relations have seen impressive formalization over the past twenty years. While it is not easy to document the precise causes of these changes, as an area requiring some unique management training for educational administrators, courses in "personnel" in traditional graduate curricula appeared well before 1950. Yet it has been since then that the management of personnel considerations have become a major component of all schools' management.

In the preface to one of the better recognized texts dealing with the "personnel function" in school systems, William Castetter emphasizes a significant dimension of this set of administrative concerns:[4]

---

[4]William B. Castetter, *The Personnel Function in Educational Administration,* 2nd ed. (New York: Macmillan, 1976), p. vii.

[The] general restlessness among organization personnel about the relationship between the governors and the governed is gaining momentum in the public sector. Teacher organizations are demanding, and in many instances gaining, the right to share in the development of policies and in the shaping of practices governing the conditions under which they work.

Castetter also observes that "there is increasing concern . . . about how to remake organizations and to modify existing administrative practices so that they will contribute better to the welfare of both the individual and the system."[5]

Interestingly, these two statements seem to us to characterize the essence of the contemporary sources of fundamental anxiety not only in the management of school personnel relations but in general, although we have presented them somewhat in reverse order. Unquestionably there has been a strong thrust for a greater "voice" in the control over work and an urge toward a more coherent balance between organizational and individual satisfactions. This has been true in all kinds of organizations.

In the second of these considerations—the balance between organizational and individual need satisfactions—there is reflected a scholarly interest in organizational behavior that both transcends particular organizations and particular times. The interest in both theoretical and empirical analysis of the relationships between individuals and organizations traces its genesis at least to the late 1920s in the work of Elton Mayo and his associates in the Harvard School of Business who pursued studies on worker effort and motivation.[6] Since those landmark studies, other scholars, particularly in the 1950s, theorized and systematically investigated a variety of provisations on the same theme. Much of this work led to particular study in educational administration; in leadership there were studies by Selznick,[7] Stogdill,[8] March and Simon,[9] and Bennis[10] among others. In small-group dynamics, work by Bales,[11] Homans,[12] and Cartwright and Zander;[13] in general theory and middle-range analysis, work by Talcott Parsons,[14]

---

[5]Ibid., p. vii.

[6]See, for example, Elton Mayo. *The Human Problems of an Industrial Civilization* (Boston: Macmillan and Co., 1933). Also, review Chapter 2.

[7]Phillip Selznick. *Leadership in Administration* (Evanston, Ill.: Row, Peterson, 1957).

[8]Ralph M. Stogdill, *Individual Behavior and Group Achievement: A Theory* (New York: Oxford University Press, 1959).

[9]J. G. March and Herbert Simon, *Organizations* (New York: John Wiley, 1958).

[10]W. G. Bennis, "Leadership Theory and Administrative Behavior: The Problem of Authority," *Administrative Science Quarterly*, Vol. 4, no. 3 (December 1959), 239–301.

[11]Robert F. Bales, *Interaction Process Analysis* (Reading, Mass.: Addison-Wesley, 1950).

[12]George Homans, *The Human Group* (New York: Harcourt Brace, 1950).

[13]Dorwin Cartwright and Alvin Zander, eds., *Group Dynamics: Research and Theory* (Evanston, Ill.: Row, Peterson, 1953).

[14]Talcott Parsons, *The Social System* (New York: Free Press, 1949). See also "Toward a General Theory," in R. Merton, L. Broom, and L. S. Cottrell, Jr., eds. *Sociology Today* (New York: Basic Books, 1959).

Robert Merton,[15] Alvin Gouldner,[16] Peter Blau,[17] and Robert Dubin;[18] in studies that either focused directly on educational administration or were the primary heuristic basis for such scholarly inquiry, there was the work of Jacob Getzels and Egon Guba,[19] Andrew Halpin,[20] Richard Carlson,[21] and Daniel Griffiths.[22]

But these various behavioral science scholars are only representative of the immense productivity that characterized the proliferation of interest in "organizational behavior" following World War II. This interest was a consequence of several things, including the work of Mayo that spelled the end of an era that for more than thirty years had given almost rigid reverence to Frederick W. Taylor's principles of "scientific management." During World War II research on leadership saw more urgent and pragmatic application, but the theoretical postulates that guided some of that work were still anchored in the earlier conclusions about the importance of human relationships and the pervasiveness of the phenomenon of "social systems."

Much of the empirical knowledge accumulated between, say, 1939 and 1946 found no widely accessible outlet—some of the work was routinely "classified," and much of it was so specific to the war effort that problem solving was awarded a higher priority than analysis. Yet much analysis did transpire; much "theorizing" did take place.

What did emerge as a consequence of such single-minded activity was an enormous expansion of methodological and instrumentation sophistication. The development of sophistication in research sampling, scaling, statistical analysis and data treatment, interviewing, and large-scale experimentation in a variety of attitudinal and behavioral concerns was enormously advanced during the war. And all of this accumulated expertise after 1946 found its way into the literature of management and administration. Yet the nagging, unresolved issue of the organization versus the individual remained.

Using the newly discovered psychometrics, researchers were able to measure both more precisely and more intricately those aspects of manifest behavior that prior to the war years they merely muddled. With the availability of an emerging computer technology, the opportunity was realized for processing previously

[15]Robert Merton, *Social Theory and Social Structure,* rev. ed. (New York: Free Press, 1957).

[16]Alvin Gouldner, ed., *Studies in Leadership: Leadership and Democratic Action* (New York: Harper and Bros., 1950).

[17]Peter M. Blau, *The Dynamics of Bureaucracy* (Chicago: University of Chicago Press, 1955). See also P. M. Blau and W. R. Scott, *Formal Organizations* (San Francisco: Chandler, 1962).

[18]Robert Dubin, ed., *Human Relations in Administration* (Englewood Cliffs, N.J.: Prentice-Hall, 1961).

[19]Jacob Getzels and Egon Guba, "Social Behavior and the Administrative Process," *School Review,* Vol. 65, no. 2 (Winter 1957), 423–441.

[20]Andrew Halpin, ed., *Administrative Theory in Education* (New York: Macmillan, 1958).

[21]Richard Carlson, "Barriers to Change in the Public Schools," in R. Carlson et al., eds., *Change Process in the Public Schools* (Eugene, Ore.: Center for the Advanced Study of Educational Administration, 1965).

[22]Daniel Griffiths, *Administrative Theory* (New York: Appleton-Century-Crofts, 1959).

unmanageable scopes of work, and consequently more theoretical models began to emerge. While the *summary conclusions* were not forthcoming, much was learned and much that was previously speculative or assigned to calculable chance was predictable. New techniques helped to delineate the difference between "variables" and "constants," and because the former could be isolated, their impact could be measured and the outcomes predicted.

Moreover, techniques in multivariate analysis improved our predictions. As a consequence, a "science of human behavior" was aborning, and while it may have taken many apparently disparate directions (e.g., Skinnerian operant conditioning versus Rogerian openness), the pattern itself was relatively singular. It accommodated, however roughly, a fundamental paradigm that in its oldest form observed thesis, antithesis, and synthesis and in its newer, hypothesis, postulate, and assessment. The newer form, or point of view, however, demanded some acceptable demonstration of methodological rigor, for from about 1958 to 1968, emphasis at the scholarly level had been given too much to methodological precision at the expense of theoretical and syllogistic discipline. By about 1970, that began to change and more attention has begun to be given to the more expanded potentiality of imagination and concept.

Some Other Factors

Now having taken the reader through this synopsis of a very small piece of the "sociology of knowledge" vis-à-vis the study of organizational behavior, the issue of the contest between the individual's and the organization's needs remains, of course, unresolved. To pursue the question only a bit further, we suggest two additional possibly helpful considerations.

Beginning in earnest in the late 1950s (though probably much earlier than that if we were to take the time to ferret out its development), there was a decided emphasis both academically and culturally on the importance and the sacrosanctness of the "self." As early as 1934, George Mead had pointed out that the individual's "consciousness both of himself and of other individuals is equally important for his own self-development and for the development of the organized society or social group to which he belongs."[23] This brief passage introduces Mead's fundamental notion of "taking the role of the other" and reflects, at least to some extent, the anthropological origins of an emerging "liberal" redefinition of the older Christian ethic that one is, indeed, one's brother's keeper or, if not his keeper, at least his brother's reflection, and vice versa.

The notion of "self" in the sense of personality was well advanced by Sigmund Freud, but it remained for people like Mead to articulate the "self" in a

---

[23]G. H. Mead, *Mind, Self and Society* (Chicago: University of Chicago Press, 1934), p. 253.

well-developed societal and cultural context and thereby to establish the fundamental reciprocity of the idea; that is, whatever the "self" is, it is defined by what others determine that it is for us.

Consequently, interest, study and multidisciplined cultural analysis regarding the "self," the individual, personality, culture, social system, and organization, and the myriad interactions and interpenetrations among all of these phenomena, proliferated through the twenty years from 1934 to 1954. And while it is true as well that much of the theoretical underpinnings for substantial aspects of this new thrust in the analysis of human behavior was laid down in the late nineteenth and early twentieth centuries, the fundamental paradigm that holds human behavior to be best understood in the interactions between man and social systems is of relatively recent origin.

AUTHORITY AND IDEOLOGY: POLITICS AND ECONOMICS

Given the premise that organizations are social systems composed of individuals and that the behavior of organizations, as they pursue legitimate purposes, involves the transactions between the individual and the "system," it is not difficult to recognize transition that came about with reference to the definitions and functions of authority.

It is not our purpose here to trace the intricate patterns of thesis, antithesis, and synthesis among the seminal conceptualizations that together now constitute a "developed version of the relationship between individual and society."[24] Nor do we have the space, need, or capacity to do so. Suffice to say that, as a consequence of that mysterious process whereby thought and analysis somehow find their way into action and caveat (and who can ever know which precedes, which follows?), that by perhaps 1955 or 1960, the definition and the actualization of *authority* had been significantly revised in the direction of egalitarianism. By this we mean only to imply that autocracy, no matter how "benevolent," had begun to yield, measurably, to democracy. Consequently, consensus began to counterbalance unilateral decision making; economic rewards were to be more broadly shared, and the sharing was to be more systematically determined; and participatory policy determination was increasingly to be reversed from up-down to down-up (not because of a great renaissance of benevolence and selflessness on the part of "ownership," although there was

[24]Jesse R. Pitts, "Introduction," in Talcott Parsons et al., *Theories of Society,* Part III. *Personality and the Social System* (New York: Free Press, 1961), p. 685. The student interested in pursuing these explications is urged to read Pitts's literate and lucid account of this "developed version" and how it, more or less, came about. It is at once an excellent review of the relevant thought and, as well, an aid in fathoming the impact of an enormous intellectual movement. It nicely synthesizes enough of what any nonexpert might feel the need to know. We do think, however, that at least this much is needed.

some of that, but because with a shift in the definition and locus of authority there was a concomitant shift in the locus and function of power and force). Finally, we mean to imply that, when authority—and the potential power it generates and legitimizes—is more broadly disbursed and diffused, it renders control and order more fragile. Thus, power thrusts are somewhat more random, and while this state of affairs invites increased bickering, feuding, and struggling for pivotal spheres of diluted influence, there are predictable consequences: change is accelerated and less orderly; leadership is more transient and therefore based more in emotion than reason; bureaucracy intensifies and proliferates because it is seen as normatively essential and fills the vacuum created by political naïveté; regulatory apparatuses are multiplied; and short-range solutions, which appeal to impulse, are almost universally favored over longer-range rationality.

At the same time, such conditions disrupt the economic stability that ultimately characterizes orderly societal growth and subsistence. The immediate consequence is a contribution to run-away inflation in the economic sphere and a reciprocal weakening of the political structure necessary to bring control mechanisms to bear to restabilize some condition of productive and progressive order.

THE RIGHTEOUSNESS OF THE ADMINISTERED

Now it is a fact that ideology is among the most pervasive of human sentiments. In the scenario that we have outlined, ideology is a base phenomenon. Ideology fuels fundamental dissatisfactions with any one form of governance; ideology promotes still another in its place. Yet ideology does not develop incidentally or without substantial evolutionary intensity. It may come about more quickly in contemporary times as seemingly do other emergent moods and, probably, because of the conditions to which we have alluded; still, any ideological system, with all the values, norms, and commitments that are necessary to the development of a custodial point of view about life, politics, power, and personal trust, requires at least a generation to gestate into a "cause." And the ideology of the late twentieth century as it has come to affect the management of schools (and other public activities) seems to hold almost sacred the attitude that the employee employs and the fiduciary function belongs to the fiduciated. In the private corporate sector, this ideology is advanced through the rationale that control over work is, if not synonymous with control over profits, at least a significant voice in the distribution of them. But in the private sector, profit still determines policy.

Among public systems—as in schools, for example—the problem of ideological commitment to this "righteousness of the administered" has generated a paradoxical version of a non-zero-sum game; quite simply, a collectivity of committed subordinates withholds services in favor of demands for expanded welfare benefits (salary, pensions, working conditions, etc.). The services are withheld from a "system" that has no elastic maneuverability for generating any reasonable bases for negotiating these conditions; this is especially true when the primary sources of dissatisfaction involve additional resources. It is a non-zero-sum game simply because the two "opponents" do not have access to the same conditions required to "win" or "lose." Accordingly, the public officials have no solid "currency" with which to negotiate and are immediately caught in that most discomfiting trap of yielding what they neither have nor can guarantee. The ploy is, of course, to bypass these authority-laden "officials" in favor of the sentiments of the public itself, which theoretically ought to result in a public's willingness to assess itself to generate the additional resources required. It works that way only rarely enough to sustain the plausibility of the strategy.

This pattern has at least two or three strategic leverage points. First, it magnifies the power of the disenchanted simply because to demand of someone what is not within that person's power to give is to prolong and enhance the disruption. Second, to "go public" frustrates an inadequate structure and ensures some form of gain, again, simply because the service is societally presumed. After all, says the established mandate, it *must* be done! That is especially the case with teachers and fire-fighting and constabulary forces: It quite simply *must* be done! Third, it recognizes the capability for immobilizing any social structure. A basic raison d'être of governance and therefore of order in all societies is the protection of a people from violence and chaos. Whether governments are effective in terms of much, or little, regulatory order and thus whether "liberal" or "conservative" and regardless of style and fashion is irrelevant; the ultimate faith of the governed has to do with some basic level of confidence that protection against chaotic and random disorder is secure. When that confidence is shattered, new governments are formed. And whether ideological revolution or systematic redefinitions of power and authority are or are not relevant is of little concern to the "multitudes"; they opt in favor of an officialdom that allows the least disruption of their daily lives. In "civilized" countries, these changes typically came about peaceably and routinely, although not without occasional palace revolts. But, on the whole, ideology makes its emergent demands known and rejoices in the changes it effects within the limits of existing roles and systems. Yet its nuances are visible and its purposes are acceded.

By 1965, this ideology, vested in the curious worldwide individualism that transformed, say, China from an almost anarchic to an absolutist socialistic society between 1945–1955 and took on a much more American "proletarian" flavor among youthful intellectuals in our own country in the early 1960s had resulted by 1968, in a new order—the culmination of political and economic consequences of a developing ideology beginning in the 1930s that held that the individual's needs within organizations not only deserved consideration but recognized that productivity was as much—and more—a function of personal motivation, satisfaction, and ideological attitude than of the older and growingly anachronistic notion of patriotism and moral conformity to the idea of an older capitalistic work ethic.

The Protestant ethic, which held that work, thrift, loyalty, and divine providence (and guilt) constituted the basis for effort, was dying. For some its passing was traumatic; for most, it was a welcomed loss. The "new" attitude is more hedonistic—live for *now* for the world is in a hell of a shape! But take full advantage of the rules. In the new ethic the traditional heroism that modern cultures have tended to attach to the underdog has been supplanted by the view that there need not be underdogs.

The development of philosophical ideas, social commentary, political sentiment, technological advances, and economic theory have all and more led the world into "postindustrial" society. In a paper entitled "The Reluctant Death of Sovereignty," Arnold Toynbee helps to explode the myths of tradition as follows:[25]

An individual can defeat the power of a state if he is willing to suffer . . . for the governments of states, being human, are as prone as any other human beings to commit crimes and sins that ought not to be condoned by their subjects. Far from being divine, states are nothing but man-made public utilities. They are as unsuitable as gas-works and water-works for being made into objects of worship and into focuses of emotion.

While Toynbee speaks in the context of the larger national entities, the same sentiment holds for local governance units—the key to his observation is the notion that an individual can *endure* victory. The "suffering" is a necessary ingredient in the pattern, and if it is not real, it needs to be fabricated; after all, one cannot hope to overcome without that necessary recognition.

In the accepted sense, the acknowledgment of the arrival of some form of a postindustrial society is dependent upon "[shifts] in the kinds of work people do, from manufacturing to services (especially human and professional services) and a new centrality of theoretical knowledge in economic innovation and policy."[26] Yet, even for Daniel Bell, this is too simplistic a definition, for it does not do well enough in terms of that "new centrality of theoretical knowledge" except to imply a lot. That is why Bell devoted a book to describing the postindustrial society and followed that with a series of essays that stood in "dialectical relation" to it, called *The Cultural Contradictions of Capitalism,* in which he expands on the conditions, anomalies, and tensions of the postindustrial world by a somewhat different "theory" of modern society than is typical among most social scientists.

Rather than conceiving of society as some kind of composite "system," Bell

[25]Arnold Toynbee, "The Reluctant Death of Sovereignty," in *The Establishment and All That* (Santa Barbara, Calif.: Center for the Study of Democratic Institutions, 1970), p. 73.

[26]Daniel Bell, *The Cultural Contradictions of Capitalism* (New York: Basic Books, 1976), p. 14. See also Daniel Bell, *The Coming of Post-Industrial Society* (New York: Basic Books, 1970).

holds that analytical progress is better pursued by viewing modern society as a most uneasy set of competing and corroborating realms:[27]

> The argument elaborated . . . is that the three realms—the economy, the polity, and the culture—are ruled by contrary axial principles: for the economy, efficiency; for the polity, equality; and for the culture, self-realization (or self-gratification). The resulting disjunctions have framed the tensions and social conflicts of Western society in the past 150 years.

There is some justification for viewing the contemporary teacher as a *pur sang* epitome of the postindustrial person. Caught up in a politics that gives primacy to equality and a culture that legitimizes self-gratification, the contemporary teacher is pivotal in the growing transformation of a labor-intensive to a brain-intensive work environment. And while that can also be said of a great variety of other professional and quasi-professional roles, the teacher/educator is a special case. The teacher is still a purveyor of the culture and is a striking example in the curious redefinition of the reversals of the traditional means-ends values that surround his or her effort. According to Daniel Bell, in commenting about the passing of the old Protestant virtues, "the culture was no longer concerned with how to work and achieve, but with how to spend and enjoy."[28]

SUMMARY

We have not given attention to other important management activities such as transportation, purchasing, physical plant administration, and auxiliary services, for example, because these are primarily technical functions. We have focused, instead, on the conditions that have dramatically changed the social order within which the school must function in contemporary times. We discuss the human aspects of these changes in Chapter 7.

We have tried to provide a general frame of reference within which the educational manager must function; that frame of reference does include some concern for the more common notions of production, marketing, and quality control, but because educational organizations are largely human enterprises whose functions are to change human behavior and whose abstract criterion is the number of (educated) clients that the school system deposits to assume adult roles in the larger society, we have given major attention to the general patterns of relationships affecting the "persons" in such organizations and some brief

---

[27]Daniel Bell, *The Cultural Contradictions of Capitalism,* op. cit., pp. xi-xii.
[28]Ibid., p. 70.

discussion of the cultural factors that together imply a quite different configuration of personnel interests, concerns, and contingencies.

In the following chapters, these concerns will be discussed in a task and functional context.

EXERCISES

1. You have been a new superintendent for only two weeks and in that period you have had only a little time for observing the general routine in the central administrative offices. That includes seven professional staff people and a clerical-secretarial force of twelve persons. You have scheduled a one-hour meeting with the latter to "orient" them to what you expect of them in terms of their organizational behavior. Outline the points you intend to go over (correspondence style, telephone routine, etc.).

2. With a total staff in your central administration operation of twenty-six, you must move to different and still unsatisfactory facilities; of seven of your top executive staff, three must be housed in offices that have no exterior windows, and this has become an issue of status. How can you resolve this problem with the least amount of "territorial" disruption?

3. While several of your secondary school principals are resentful of the "production" analogies that some members of your school board have applied to school functions, you have been supplied hard data by your internal research personnel that discloses a 7 percent increase in the dropout rate at the high school level. What kind of management implications does this have?

4. Your assistant superintendent for buildings and grounds has indicated that the costs of fuel and transportation have necessitated a pooling of B & G workers so that several will be transported simultaneously to some jobs even though, among them, some may not have anything to do at a particular job site. His point is that, while it may look like a few people are standing around doing nothing, it is more cost effective than having the "taxi" return to physical plant headquarters repeatedly to drop off and pick up. He explains that this will apply only to routine maintenance. You know you are going to get calls as soon as people notice two men working and three watching them, but the union is very strict about which workers can do what. What is your reaction? Is there a better way to deal with it?

5. As superintendent in a large suburban school system, you have been presented with a proposal for a flex-time pattern within the central administrative offices: some personnel report for work at 7 A.M. and leave at 3 P.M.; others work from 9–5, 10–6, and 11–7. There are seventy-five classified (nonprofessional) and twenty professional employees at the center. The argument

is that, by avoiding increasingly heavy peak traffic, employees can get to work and residence quicker and work more effectively. What will you look for specifically in any such plan and what questions should you anticipate that your board will ask when it is presented to them?

6. Two days after a long meeting with a principals' council at which a super-intendent diplomatically chastised them for exceeding their equipment budgets, he learns that one of them had processed an order for a limited word-processing "memory" typewriter that further exceeds his budget. The business manager indicates that in his initial inquiry the principal's secretary complained that the computer-generated accounts records disclosing all fund balances were always sixty to ninety days late. The superintendent reprimanded the principal, indicating that regardless of turnaround on records, he should make it his business to know the status of all accounts and that the order was being rescinded. The machine was being installed at the time of the phone call. If you were the principal, what would you say and do? Was the superintendent right? Wrong? Why? What should he have done? What should he do now?

7. A superintendent needs to appoint an assistant superintendent for internal affairs, which includes all nonprofessional personnel matters. Two principals are interested, although the job pays no more than they are earning. Each is qualified and would do well. Assuming that all affirmative action provisions are otherwise satisfied, the superintendent decides to name neither of them on the basis that they are serving the organization better where they are. They both regard the position as a promotion, but the superintendent plans to bring in a person from outside. What do you think of that decision? How would you have handled it?

SUGGESTED REFERENCES

Likert, Rensis. *The Human Organization: Its Management and Value*. New York: McGraw-Hill, Inc., 1967.

McGrath, J. H. *Planning Systems for School Executives*. Scranton, Pa.: Intext Educational Publishers, 1972.

Monahan, William G. *Theoretical Dimensions of Educational Administration*. New York: Macmillan Publishing Co., 1975.

National Society for the Study of Education. *Behavioral Science and Educational Administration*. Daniel Griffiths, Ed. Sixty-third Yearbook. Chicago: University of Chicago Press, 1964.

Price, James L. *Handbook of Organizational Measurement*. Lexington, Mass.: D. C. Heath and Co., 1972.

Chapter 7

Personnel Administration: The General Dimensions

As we have noted, the size of a school organization quite obviously has an effect on the scope and character of the administrative support structure required to achieve the on-going purposes of the system.

Accordingly, while the essential hierarchy of roles remains that of students, teachers, principals, superintendents, and boards, in the last thirty or so years, there has been a remarkable decrease in the total number of school systems and, as a consequence, a concomitant expansion in the number and definition of positions necessary to complement those basic ones. This trend toward consolidation of many smaller school systems into larger ones involves the more effective delivery of required and useful schooling accompanied by a clear recognition that greater functional value is purchased for the dollars expended.

Certainly it may be argued that there is some point at which increasing size and organizational consolidation produces diminishing returns. This is simply due to the fact that schools and school systems unlike corporate entities must still provide established services to a present and definitive clientele in particular numbers and in particular places called classrooms and laboratories. The distribution of these persons—students and teachers and administrators—always constrains the organization by "how many" and under what circumstances "they" can best be accommodated. In the case of schools, the goal is relevant indoctrination. Corporate entities must deliver services or products, but its work force is generally determined by market demands. Schools, on the other hand, while enduring some fluctuation in the pattern of demands for services as enrollments increase or decrease, in large measure have a more stable work force.

THE PERSONNEL MANAGEMENT STRUCTURE

The function of personnel management in school systems is relatively unique, whether there is a specific staff or line role for managing the personnel functions or that responsibility, as in quite small units, is absorbed by principals and/or superintendents as a part of their regular duties.

What are these dimensions? In our view, they include recruitment and selection, induction, appraisal, development (and advancement), compensation, assignment, transfer and termination, and *systematic contractualization*. We emphasize systematic contractualization because that seems to include an entire spectrum of issues and concerns that have become the major focus of attention in public organizations in recent years. Because these factors are of such interest, we will treat them separately in Chapter 8. The other issues we consider now.

The Dimensions of Hypothetical Structure

The frame of reference for the following discussion assumes a school district with at least 10,000 students; it is organized with at least two major senior high schools, four junior high schools (or middle schools) and eleven elementary schools. The system also provides several sites for preschool, early childhood instruction (beginning at age 3 years but with special constraints in the availability of these services). It employs a small central office staff consisting of one major associate superintendent; directors for both secondary and elementary education, respectively; a director of special services (whose activity is increasingly preoccupied with exceptional children, mainstreaming, psychometrics and psychological services) but who is also responsible for continuing education or in-service programs; a director of personnel services; and a business manager. The staff support for these professionals is an appropriate, but typically inadequate, complement of secretarial-clerical persons most of whom are very efficient, plus several technical people such as a data processing coordinator, a buildings and grounds coordinator, and a transportation coordinator.

RECRUITMENT AND SELECTION

The first consideration of the personnel administrator is to be sure that, when school opens in the late summer, enough teachers have been hired to meet the schedule. That concern has taken on a curiously different complexion in the last few years. As recently as 1965 or 1970, the personnel administrator in our hypothetical system would have approached late summer with a high level of anxiety; he or she would probably still have as many as ten teaching positions unfilled—perhaps several elementary people, a K–12 art teacher, a special education teacher for the "educable mentally retarded," a couple of high school math teachers, and maybe a couple of others in fields such as social studies or physical education. At the same time, the system would still need a couple of school principals or assistant principals and maybe some people who could coach basketball or debate, or handle the yearbook, or direct dramatics.

By 1979 or 1980, the personnel administrator's problems were almost reversed. Data indicated that enrollment projections were down, and surprisingly so in some areas. The board of education and the superintendent were seriously looking at closing at least one elementary school and were considering the combining of schools. The personnel director was having to decide who would be transferred or terminated or reassigned. A very few new teachers may still have been needed, but how was the director to deal with the dozens of inquiries and applications coming each week from prospective teachers from all over the state?

Recruitment and selection is just as important in a buyer's as in a seller's market. Certainly in a buyer's market, the recruiter enjoys the luxury of being able to choose among the best of the several applicants for a position. But given such a range from which to choose does not guarantee that the right choices will be made; on the contrary, the competitiveness of the situation may merely ensure that some candidates will be better at the game than others who might make the better employees. Related to that, perhaps we look for the wrong virtues, or perhaps our general systems of appraisal are bad (or perhaps we are measuring the wrong things). Or perhaps the overall general quality of all available applicants is not good enough. Maybe even a combination of all these. And certainly the increased regulatory requirements under "affirmative action" and civil rights legislation require far greater justification activity than ever before, sometimes creating a compliance mentality that may elevate equity to a higher priority than competence.

In truth, the general quality of applicants for available jobs in teaching does seem good; moreover, personnel directors report that they are getting better people—people not only well prepared but more conscientious, more eager to do a good job, and so forth. As one personnel director has reported, "these people are more polite, better dressed, more business-like in their approach to the interview, more willing to do more than is normally asked of them, and certainly more articulate."[1] But there is another "truth" as well. Apparently,

[1]Keith Esch and W. G. Monahan, "An Analysis of Personnel Directors' Concerns in Medium-Sized School Systems," College of Human Resources and Education Special Papers, Morgantown,

(Footnote cont. on next page)

school systems that have initiated institutionalized recruitment and selection patterns have been reluctant to discard them for at least two reasons: first, even though such systems have reduced the scope of these efforts (i.e., visiting fewer and less distant campuses), they still believe they get better results that way. And, second, too many of the "fugitive" applications they receive are not of any better quality than they ever were—there are just many more of them. One director of personnel in a 26,000-pupil school system put it this way:[2]

I am always impressed by the data about supply-and-demand of highly skilled manpower generally, and from the conversations I have had with people like me in our meetings around the country and with what the news media have to say about our overproduction of teachers—I knew from all this about all that and as I say, am convinced that we ought to be confronting a big glut of available great people, but it's crazy . . . when push-comes-to-shove, the people we have to choose from—and there are certainly more of them—are just not that good. I think most of them are also included in the files of 90 percent of the school systems in our general (geographic) area but we've discovered that we still do best when we go to the colleges and universities we've always gone to— we don't need as many people as, say, six or eight years ago but we are just not getting any better people without those deliberate, old, recruiting efforts.

These (and other) comments seem to support the view that institutionalized recruitment and selection patterns still have a fairly high payoff for school systems. That being the case, how should school executives direct that process? The following seems a reasonable procedure.

The Importance of Planning and Organization

The first requirement for systematic personnel administration is the development of a reasonable policy relating to both short-span and long-span personnel needs. Short-span planning concerns the requirements for filling immediate vacancies. This is the most critical problem that confronts personnel administra-

---

West Virginia, 1978 (25 pages mimeographed), p. 46. There is general agreement among college and university administrators that the country will face particular teacher shortages again in the early 1980s and somewhat severe ones in some areas by 1985. In a paper prepared for a briefing of Chief State School Officers in the Appalachian region, Dean J. T. Sandefur of Western Kentucky University's College of Education recently pointed out, "data projected by the national Center for Educational Statistics . . . (project) a forthcoming shortage in the late '80s." [J. T. Sandefur, "Labor Force Supply and Demand: Teaching," Regional Services Program, Appalachia Educational Laboratory (Charleston, W. Va.: The Laboratory, 1981), pp. 2–3.] Sandefur attributes the shortage to a reversal in the trend of declining school-aged youngsters and an increase of about 7 million by the year 2000; to the effects of competency testing, which will limit access to teaching by many students; to the reluctance to enter teaching because of better pay for the same skills in other areas and because of discipline problems; to high turnover for a variety of reasons; and to increased job opportunities for women in other fields.
[2] Ibid., p. 48.

tors. Long-span personal services planning is typically more satisfying because it allows a more comfortable and thoughtful analysis of personnel needs over time. It encourages greater consideration of "fit" with other ongoing plans of the organization and promotes more exacting definitions of jobs and role expectations. Yet, in general, it is the short-span issues that not only create the most frustrations but, in a sense, have greater determination on the longer-ranged effectiveness of the organization; thus the short-span problems require the most care and the most skillful policy planning.

We suggest the following "rules" or concerns in short-span planning—we call it "personnel contingencies." Clearly, these notions turn out to be part of the longer-run concerns.

1. Initiate and develop a catalogue of priorities; that is, list the kinds and types of personnel that are currently in highest likely demand (these may be special educators, coaches, science teachers, etc.).
2. Develop a file, in conjunction with school principals, of current and immediately anticipated (next year and the year after that) position requirements; update this file every three months.
3. Hold regular conferences for modification of work force needs (i.e., if a person like X is needed now, what will that role be like next semester or next year—not beyond that). Such conferencing obviously also provides more intelligent thinking about long-span needs as well.
4. Develop a system for dealing with sudden vacancies. It can take a variety of patterns—the important thing is that the executives involved (principals, supervisors, etc.) know and contribute to procedure. The first review always concerns the available pool of professional personnel that can be transferred, or have been furloughed, or have indicated availability and are waiting their turn.
5. Know—at least by March or April—what the established needs will be for the following fall, so that there will be ample time to deal with the contingencies that everyone knows will occur in late July or early August.
6. Meet frequently and try to anticipate the worst!

The six considerations are presented to illustrate the importance of both organization and planning, not just to recruitment and selection but to the entire personnel function. It is apparent that the personnel function is a shared responsibility throughout a school system. The function is usually delegated by the chief school officer to a staff administrator; yet it is the superintendent who must provide the board of education with information, advice, and recommendations regarding personnel and who must justify and defend all these recommendations.

As we have suggested, this responsibility may be carried out by the superintendent in several ways, depending upon the size and complexity of the system. But, as with most such concerns, the responsibility may be shared but cannot be avoided.

Some systematic planning and organizing of the personnel function is thus essential. As a general pattern, *recruitment* processes are centralized; *selection* processes are decentralized. In other words, the central office staff has responsibility for the overall direction and management and coordination of activities, but principals or other site-specific administrators exercise the major decision-making responsibility for selection. Consequently, few aspects of the overall personnel function do not require established and active communication between key people in "central personnel" and those in the schools or auxiliary units—the latter for selection and supervision of service personnel.

In the systematic planning activity, at least three major components need to be included: work force analyses, personnel policies, and performance procedures. Within the context of recruitment and selection, let us examine these components of a plan.

Work Force Analyses. Although the scope and complexity of work force analyses may vary from highly systematic to highly informal, these analyses serve to calculate, with as much accuracy as possible, the probable gross difference between available supply of personnel in all categories and the demand for them. Planning on this level is likely to be of reasonable utility only for about a five-year time span and should be updated annually. The data required for devising such a plan accrue from at least these major sources: (1) The established goals (and plans) of the school system itself. Changes in the objectives of the school as an organization quite directly affect the need for changes in work force projections. For example, if a system decides that it is going to move heavily into an "open space" curriculum, or emphasize instructional teams, or move more heavily into experiential education or work-study programs, or any of a dozen other possible redirections of its overall educational plan, the type of personnel required will be a significant factor in the achievability of such revised goals. Thus, a work force analysis like any other "plan" begins with the articulation of a statement of goals and objectives. (2) A careful analysis of the clientele environment. Again, depending upon the complexity of the system, for a small, stable school system, this may involve little more than a relatively simple linear projection of enrollments, or for very complex systems, it may require sophisticated analyses of in- and out-migration patterns, special service needs such as residence and location of handicapped, internal audit trails on current personnel changes (promotions, transfers, retirements, resignations), and subanalyses of certain sociological and industrial patterns (or anything similar) that might serve to predict and anticipate the gap between supply and demand. (3) Data that describe and define the codification of jobs and roles that together constitute the organization. These data do not need to specify precisely the exact number of positions so much as the general categories of personnel;

in this respect, careful attention needs to be given to auxiliary or service personnel and, again, in terms of the generalized mission of the school system as operationally defined in its statement of goals and objectives.

Personnel Policies. A second major component of systematic planning for the personnel function is the codification of personnel policies. These policies, although emanating from board of education deliberations, are typically more specific at the level of a particular organizational function and thus may be viewed as administrative guidelines for the management of the function. In any case, these include clear definitions of the duties and expectations of recruiters; procedures for handling applications, interviews, appeals, and grievances; conditions governing transfers and early retirements; and role expectations for different categories of employees. Procedures and guidelines must be reviewed regularly, as they have an important bearing on overall work force analysis and planning.

Performance Procedures. While personnel policies and the goals and purposes that guide the day-to-day activities of any school system reflect the importance of reasonable intelligence regarding quality control, the assessment of performance is a more explicit aspect of the personnel function itself. Within this function, there are two equally important considerations: Evaluation of performance and professional development. All school systems have always evaluated the performance of personnel in some fashion. It has only been during the past ten years or so that performance assessment has become increasingly formal. To some extent this is a consequence of recognizing the importance of evaluation; to some extent as well it has become more urgent and compelling because "evaluation" has just become an increasingly expected activity in public organizations.

Regardless of the causes, performance appraisal is an accepted and essential aspect of personnel administration in contemporary times. As a result, the procedures that define the way in which performance is appraised together with the instruments and consequences of it must be carefully spelled out in the systematic personnel planning process. Related to performance appraisal if not generated wholly by it as a consequence, there is also growing concern and attention now being given to "professional development." Professional development can certainly imply several things. At one time, it was known merely as in-service education. It now means that and more (for example, continuing education, advanced preparation, staff improvement). In other words, a school system accepts some responsibility to improve the current competence of its professionals. If a school system has the authority to assess the quality of its instructional competence, then it must also give some attention and resources toward assisting any individual professional in the remediation of weaknesses or help in preparing such personnel for new instructional strategies or for different roles in the system if those presently being performed become obsolete or changed. It is really as simple as that.

Implications of Systematic Planning

The implications of systematic personnel planning are obvious: the need for additional or different personnel is identified in part by the definitions of roles specified by work force analysis, by the nature of the purposes to be pursued by the system, and/or by the particular units within it. Good policy guidelines for recruiting and selection give the prospective employee a clearer understanding of the system and what it expects. Finally, assessments of performance indicate how well the system is approaching its goals and ensure the potential employee that some form of ongoing professional growth is sanctioned by the system and encouraged.

INDUCTION OF EMPLOYEES

As with most other organizations, especially the "professional" ones, there are three major categories of personnel: managerial, professional/technical, and service or auxiliary. While "professional" does not necessarily imply that either the managerial or the service categories are not also professionally prepared, it does distinguish the essential functions performed. In school systems, of course, the professional component is largely made up of those who deal directly with instruction—mainly teachers. In many systems, a new category of employees is developing that is referred to as "technical"; these are also prepared professionally to the extent that some specialized pre-entry training is required. Examples of such employees are data processing specialists, graphic arts and media specialists, educational TV personnel, and some highly skilled facilities personnel like engineers, and draftsmen.

Effective utilization of the talents of all new personnel requires rational procedures and thoughtful planning. Too frequently, we presume that orientation in any formal sense merely requires explicit instruction about the job, the salary and fringe benefits and introducing people around. That presumption seems also to hold that the informal organization will take care of those concerns, whatever they are. There is little question that the lack of a well-planned induction procedure is an important reason why so many new employees in school systems—and especially novice teachers—have so much difficulty in the first couple of years and of these, at least partly, why so many fail at it. The same is also true of service personnel. The role expectation in those cases is less diverse, but

whereas many of these personnel also suffer from the lack of effective introduction (the system as well, thereby), the consequences are less visible. Moreover, in the case of service personnel, our ongoing informal organization helps
to induct the employee into the system (e.g., crafts personnel who frequently
work in small groups or are closely identified with small groups: carpenters,
plumbers, electricians, mechanics).

On the contrary, the teacher is relatively invisible. Neither parents nor supervisors "see" what the teacher does day in and day out. And, whereas students
"see" it every day, their perspective is quite different. For example, the concept
of academic freedom encourages teacher autonomy in the classroom. When
parents give over to a teacher the psychosocial care and feeding of their off-
spring, they must be assured that these surrogate mentors are reasonably moral
people. But this activity for some two hundred days every year can lead teachers,
especially first-year teachers, to become very possessive of their classes and use
that dependency as a mechanism to avoid full involvement in other aspects of
the profession. Equally and perhaps more important, this circumstance can also
inhibit a teacher from requesting help when it is needed and can lead to mistaken
or destructive behavior.[3]

The increased practice of team teaching, open-space innovations, and other
collaborative arrangements have reduced the negative aspects of the self-contained classroom. Yet problems of all kinds can be significantly minimized with
a well-planned induction program. And any such program presumes some *a
priori* generalized orientation to the education profession itself

Induction into the Profession

Professional education must be far more than mastery of an area of knowledge
and development of instructional skills. The teacher is obliged, in a democratic
society, to be a constant proponent of individual development within the social
context. Certain practices are implicit within such an obligation. The teacher
today must be a continuing student, a devotee of intellectual activities. (Such
has not always been the case in our society.) The teacher must have a highly
developed empathetic sensitivity if he or she is to communicate effectively with
students. And, finally, a teacher must have a sense of history, an identification
with the continuous development of humankind.

---

[3]See, for example, Jules Henry, "Attitude Organization in Elementary Classrooms," in W. W.
Charters, Jr., and N. L. Gage, eds., *Readings in the Social Psychology of Education* (Boston: Allyn
and Bacon, 1963), pp. 254–263. Henry describes a classroom in which a bizarre process was
initiated under the guise of teaching fourth-grade children to be "better citizens" but which assumed
all the manifestations of the classic witch hunt. It is an excellent analysis of latent intergroup
aggression and the ease with which a teacher can exploit feelings of vulnerability, docility, and fear
of rejection.

Essential Elements of Preparation Programs. A complete professional preparation program designed to accomplish these ends is seldom found. Certain
elements that could contribute to these ends are seen in numerous institutions
throughout the country, but generally they appear most frequently in programs
of advanced graduate study rather than in teacher education programs. Two such
elements appear to be basic and deserve comment.

First, programs for professional preparation should be client centered. That
is, the program through which teachers are prepared for entry into the practice
of education is meaningless unless it is seen in terms of its effect on the student—
the "client." If a program is so designed, it will provide opportunities that
capitalize on the interests, needs, and abilities of the student. In that way, the
program will assist the student in developing an adequate perception of self and
peers, encouraging the examination of his or her own values, needs, attitudes,
and abilities as they relate to the panorama of values and needs indigenous to
a pluralistic society such as ours.

The second basic element necessary to an adequate program of professional
preparation is an implicit expectation of high achievement. It appears to casual
observers that professional education is less than challenging. Often such has
been the case, just as it has been and is with many other professional programs.
Without built-in expectations of full commitment and development, however,
a program falls short of its preparatory function, no matter how well conceived
and designed it might be. To be effective, expectations must be shared by both
the student and the teachers. "Achievement" must be understood and defined
in individual terms. And, once understood, it must be coordinated with achievement as defined by "professional standards." One without the other is meaningless in the context of an individually centered, democratic society. It is for
service in such a community that young persons are being prepared.

The Administrator and Programs of Preparation. How does the administrator encounter preparation programs? How is one to become knowledgeable
enough about them so that one can make a contribution to their development?
The point of contact is frequently only through recruitment and employment
practices of the individual administrator, by visiting campuses and by issuing
de facto evaluations of various programs. But many administrators have found
this experience to be less than complete. Contact with colleges of education can
and should be augmented in many ways, for example, through student teaching
programs.

Hardly a preparatory program today does not include preservice teaching
experience in a regular classroom situation. A few institutions maintain laboratory schools on their campuses to accomplish this end, but most solicit the
assistance of the public schools. Almost without exception, practicing educators
have found these experiences to be challenging and meaningful. Arranging for

and planning with colleges of education to initiate and coordinate such programs provides many opportunities for administrators and teachers to become not only better informed about programs of professional preparation, but also to participate actively in their completion. It seems that such opportunities should be actively sought out.

In addition, professional growth programs should be considered. Although we have referred to this previously, it is appropriate to relate professional growth activities to the total professional preparation spectrum. Inasmuch as continued preparation and study is becoming more and more necessary to the competent discharge of professional responsibilities, the administrator can avail himself or herself of many opportunities to plan with the staff for such activities. In so doing, both the administrator and the staff will become more familiar with activities and programs of colleges of education.

The administrator may also serve on advisory committees. Many departments and colleges of education have one or more regularly functioning advisory committees to assist in program revision and development. Membership is customarily by invitation and includes outstanding practicing educators from the field. The opportunities for becoming informed and for making positive contributions to programs of teacher preparation through this vehicle are clear. They should be accepted eagerly when they are made available.

And finally, through the use of consultants, colleges of education have provided expert assistance to practicing educators in many forms. Special consultative service is frequently available, and in many forms. Institute and faculty meeting speakers, study committee resource people, and specific project assistance are some of the better known activities of consultants. Each of these activities can be expanded to include the whole of the preparatory function simply by utilizing consultants broadly when they are on specific assignments. Such a development will not happen incidentally, however. The interested administrator must find ways and means of capitalizing on such opportunities. And in doing so, discussion related to mutual opportunities for improving professional induction can be fruitful.

Certification. It is assumed that adequate professional preparation leads to legal recognition of the right to practice one's profession. In fact, the nature and scope of preparatory programs are related directly to certification requirements in the several states. Therefore, the interest of the school administrator charged with personnel responsibilities cannot be directed at one without involving the other.

The effect of certification practices on the individual contributes either to the demeaning or the upgrading of the service offered society by the profession. For instance, licensure provisions that focus on the mundane (i.e., state history and other specific course titles) tend to penalize the individual who is capable of a significant professional contribution. Similarly, the proliferation of certification requirements within and among the states tends to freeze professional educators geographically, with the very real possibility of stifling continued personal-professional development. For reasons such as these, the administrator's interest in certification must be broader than solving the specific problems of staffing a given school.

Licensure is not unique to the profession of education. It is a means of protecting society against charlatans and incompetents. It is a proper function of society as a whole conducted through society's duly authorized agents.

Certification involves the codification of the minimum essential requirements for professional competence. It represents the means by which the service rendered by a profession may be continuously enhanced. Furthermore, it defends the duly licensed practitioner from encroachment by and unfair competition from the unprepared individual and the quack. It is, therefore, an area of vital interest to all who teach, not the least of which are those responsible for the administrative affairs of local school systems.

Professional Orientation.   It is increasingly likely that the novice teacher will have participated in several student organizations at the college level that provide much information about the teaching profession. Organizations such as the Student National Education Association (SNEA) and honor societies such as Kappa Delta Pi (KDP) have become very active in recent years. The two organizations cited specifically provide a balance between an activist, welfare-oriented point of view (SNEA) and a broader philosophically, intellectual frame of reference (KDP). Other extracurricular activities are also likely to draw preservice students in terms of particular programs; student organizations in speech pathology/audiology, special education, art, music, physical education, mathematics, and so forth also provide some orientation to professional practice. In these last cases, many teachers continue active membership in their various subject matter organizations after accepting full-time positions.

While much of the professional orientation in extracurricular organizations may be viewed as having too narrow a concern with the "teachers movement" and other vested interests, there is nevertheless greater attention given to many aspects of the professional role of "education" as an establishment.

As every personnel administrator knows, a part of the on-site school system induction will also include activity by the local classroom teacher affiliate of a state's education association or teachers' union as the case may be conducted by the local affiliate's own officers and, theoretically, on its "own time." Yet some coordination of these activities with other aspects of the induction plan can be useful and mutually productive for the individual professional employee and for the school system even though the primary thrust of associational presentations emphasizes the merits of individual membership in the teacher organization.

Figure 7-1. Linkage of Phases, Agents, and Activities of the Individual Induction Sequence. From: William B. Castetter, *The Personnel Function in Educational Administration*, New York: Macmillan Publishing Co., 1981, 3rd edition, p. 202. Used with permission.

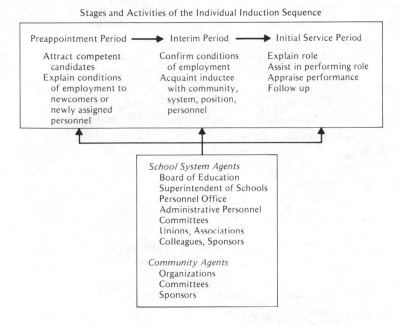

Stages and Activities of the Individual Induction Sequence

Preappointment Period ⟶	Interim Period ⟶	Initial Service Period
Attract competent candidates	Confirm conditions of employment	Explain role
Explain conditions of employment to newcomers or newly assigned personnel	Acquaint inductee with community, system, position, personnel	Assist in performing role Appraise performance Follow up

School System Agents
Board of Education
Superintendent of Schools
Personnel Office
Administrative Personnel
Committees
Unions, Associations
Colleagues, Sponsors

Community Agents
Organizations
Committees
Sponsors

Induction into the System

According to Castetter, induction "may be defined as a systematic organizational effort to minimize problems confronting new personnel so that they can contribute maximally to the work of the school while realizing personal and position satisfaction."[4] That is, the induction process lasts from recruitment through the completion of the probationary period.[5] Thus, the presumption that one is pretty well finished with the bulk of induction concerns prior to the beginning of the first week of school is erroneous. He conceives of the total induction process as given in Figure 7-1.

In essence, the induction process employs information, assistance, and support so that new employees can better adjust to and deal with problems related

[4] William B. Castetter, op. cit., *The Personnel Function in Educational Administration*, 3rd ed. (New York: Macmillan Publishing Co., 1981), p. 189.
[5] Ibid., p. 208.

to the community, the school (and school system), the job, and personal concerns. In few situations will all of these not be interrelated. For example, one needs to know as much as possible about the community, not just to gain a better feeling for the curriculum and teaching expectations but to feel more comfortable about finding a place to live, work, shop, dine, and so forth.

The pattern of organized activities that achieve effective induction varies greatly, depending on the kind of school and community—if metropolitan in nature, one kind of pattern is required; if rural or suburban, another. Some activities are fairly universal; conferences, the assignment of an experienced teacher as a helper or sponsor, brochures and information about the school and community, and orientation toward policies of immediate interest (such as compensation patterns, promotion, insurance, retirement programs, and annual leave provisions), staff development opportunities, probationary periods, and expectations. This kind of information is typically provided both through scheduled early meetings and through individual conferences.

Responsibility of the School and System

While most of our discussion has emphasized the organization's attention and responsibility in the induction process, certainly the individual employee has a responsibility as well, specifically, to seek answers to any questions or express whatever concerns are not otherwise resolved and to assume the responsibility of providing the employing system the most effective effort possible.

At the same time, the school system must recognize that, for any new employee to provide the most effective performance of which they are capable, the school must observe some essential and reasonable guidelines to ensure that the induction process is effective. These guidelines include at least the following:

1. Assignment of initial workload must be done with care. It is too frequently the case that the novice teacher not only is assigned too heavy a workload but also often must endure those extracurricular details that others in the staff with seniority can ignore. The novice should be assigned a slightly less than normal workload and should not be coopted into assuming the ''bad'' details.

This pattern of preferred status is not nearly so mythical as some school administrators like to believe. It happens even in the acknowledged ''better'' schools and leads to some of the militant demands of some teachers' associations for relief, even though some of those who argue most against the pattern also participate in it. A responsible system of probationary monitoring of first-year teachers must reciprocate by recognizing that there is an enormous amount of normal pressure on the beginning teacher.

2. Experienced teachers new to the system also need adjustment. Even though someone may have substantial experience in another school system, that person requires attention too. As a matter of fact, the transferred teacher typically has some unlearning to do and must be guided away from the tendency to refer to

past operating procedures. The conditions and treatment are different from that of beginning professionals, but the need is there.

3. Deliberate attention must be given to careful work relationships. Employees new to any organization are vulnerable to existing norms and relationships about which they are basically ignorant. Consequently, assigning such people to a team or unit where previous personality problems have existed or to intimidating circumstances can be devastating. A staff needs to be reminded repeatedly to be helpful to the newcomer, particularly in the case of support personnel such as media center staff, custodial staff, librarians, counselors, supervisors and consultants, and clerical staff.

4. Social activities and school-sponsored public functions should not be minimized as sources of reinforcement. New employees should be encouraged to participate in official functions, and experienced staff should be reminded to make them feel welcome. Acclamation is facilitated when someone assumes the responsibility for guiding that process—someone who volunteers to accompany the new employee to an athletic contest or encourages their sense of belonging.

5. New employees should be consulted regarding their suggestions for improving the induction process. It is both useful and reinforcing to seek the advice of new employees regarding the strengths and weaknesses of the plan itself. Whereas most appraisals involving new employees are *from* the system and *to* the employee, the system is likely to learn much that is useful *of* the system and *from* the employee.

Service and Technical Employees

It is obvious that the quality of the services necessary to the maintenance of a school system depends primarily on the quality of the personnel most directly involved in the delivery of instruction. Increasingly, however, the need for, cost of acquiring and maintaining, and appropriate use of sophisticated equipment and facilities is a major dimension of a school system's budget. Consequently, careful selection and development of service personnel that can reduce turnover is becoming much more important to school systems each year. Accordingly, the development of an induction plan must give serious attention to this category of personnel and provide for specific activities that complement their roles.

THE APPRAISAL AND DEVELOPMENT OF PERSONNEL

Whether highly centralized or deliberately decentralized, two extremely important dimensions of personnel administration relate to both the appraisal of performance and the continuing development of competency. These concerns are treated together because they are closely related.

The New Emphasis on Appraisal

Until recently, systematic and organized performance assessment was not common among school systems. The current trend relates to the "accountability" movement that emerged in the late 1960s and led to our preoccupation with measuring—or attempting to measure—performance. (You will remember that the accountability movement derived from public distrust, on the one hand, and the growth of cybernetic sophistication that led to the development of entirely new models of rationality, on the other hand.) It is interesting that the demand for proof that public dollars were being spent properly was accompanied by the availability of new techniques capable of satisfying that demand. Only rarely, even today, however, are these techniques a productive basis for measuring performance except in a production-oriented setting. And we doubt if they are accurate predictions of performance of teachers or students.

Another contributor to the emphasis on appraisal is political. With the advent of unionization and the adversarial climate that unionization has encouraged between teachers and fiduciary authority, school administrators have been forced into more formal and more institutionalized processes involving performance appraisal. In that activity, teachers have reciprocally insisted—properly so in our view—on some reasonable participation in the process and the formatting of it. Finally, there is some logical basis for presuming that, theoretically, as organizations grow in size, scope, and complexity, dependence on less formalized and normative mechanisms for assessing all aspects of its functions must give way to more impersonal and formal ones. Funding from external sources, whether state or federal, brought with it specific requirements for both "formative" and "summative" evaluation, and as staffs became more and more familiar with (and less threatened by) such expectations, a sort of subculture of evaluation developed. These various realities have contributed more or less to a "cult of assessment," and administrators have little choice but to accommodate it albeit with increasing complexity and frustration into their systems.

Appraisal Procedures

It is our melancholy conclusion that there is no best or parsimonious way in which to manage a performance appraisal system that is either generally acceptable or that does what it arbitrarily aims to do. There are, however, several underlying assumptions for any such process that seem valid:

1. Appraisal is designed to provide information to the employee so that strengths and weaknesses can be clarified.
2. Appraisal is not designed to be punitive or self-serving.
3. Appraisal involves procedures that bring the appraisee and the appraiser into closer understanding of reasonable expectations.

4. Appraisal is designed to clarify and define reasonable "targets" of achievement.
5. Appraisal is a legitimate and responsible activity, the fundamental consequences of which are to improve the delivery of effective instruction.

No one likes being "rated," especially when it is suspected that the assessment may color more sensitive decisions about merit and pay. Moreover, because of the work teachers do, it is almost impossible to determine with precision what "effectiveness" means. This knotty problem was put into perspective by Fattu:[6]

A difficult problem . . . has been whether to assume that effectiveness is a statement about an attribute of the teacher in a particular teaching situation, or to assume that it is a statement about the results that came out of a teaching situation.

Fattu (and others)[7] point out that most studies of teacher effectiveness seem to presume and seek some properties of the teacher but that there has been little success in this approach simply because testing the fundamental assumption involved would require "a longitudinal study with repeated measurement of the same teacher on the same criteria under a wide range of teaching conditions."[8] To our knowledge, no such study has been conducted.

Probably the most exhaustive study of teacher characteristics was that undertaken by D. G. Ryans,[9] who, with his associates, engaged in at least 100 different studies that involved more than 1,600 schools in 450 different school systems and some 6,000 or more teachers; they manipulated the data in a variety of ways—factored it, correlated it, tested hundreds of hypotheses, and provided a great deal of information about teachers that was useful, interesting, and important as bases for other innumerable studies—but its value with reference to teacher effectiveness (which was not among the various studies' major concerns) is still moot. A not so surprising finding was that, based on a 300-item inventory of a variety of self-reported interests and concerns, teachers who were themselves good students scored higher on most of the scales, as did teachers from larger schools and larger communities (except for those from the extremely

---

[6]N. A. Fattu, "Research on Teacher Evaluation," in J. E. Heald, L. G. Romano, and N. P. Georgiady, (eds.), *Selected Readings on General Supervision* (New York: Macmillan, 1970), p. 281.
[7]See, for example, A. S. Barr and R. E. Jones, "The Measurement and Prediction of Teaching Efficiency," *Review of Educational Research*, Vol. 28 (June 1958), 256–264, and H. H. Remmurs et al., "[Reports] of the Committee on Criteria of Teacher Effectiveness," *Review of Educational Research*, Vols. 22 and 46 (June 1952 and May 1953), respectively. While these reviews were published some years ago, the patterns of methodology and questions raised by them are still being asked today, and despite much greater methodological sophistication and data analytic capacity, the questions remain unanswered or if answered, only tentatively so, for argument abounds.
[8]Fattu, op. cit., p. 281.
[9]D. G. Ryans, *Characteristics of Teachers* (Washington, D.C.: American Council on Education, 1960), 416 pp.

large cities—those of 1 million or more). So what? Well, we have yet to develop a system that does all or many of the things that assessment or appraisal plans aspire to do.

Yet, as we pointed out, the use of formal appraisal procedures is now very much the rule. In a survey conducted by the NEA's Educational Research Service in 1968, only 17 of 235 responding systems enrolling 16,000 or more pupils, at that time, had not established some kind of formal procedures for evaluating teachers and that study classified different procedures into two major categories with six and two variations, respectively. Type A procedures consisted primarily of observation, postobservation conferences, and a unilateral rating by the evaluator-observer against prescribed standards. Type B procedures involved cooperatively established and agreed-upon objectives by evaluator and evaluatee and a rating was subsequently made with reference to those goals.[10]

While some school systems will engage in formal appraisal programs only for probationary teachers, the majority of opinion (and practice) is that it applies to all, and to administrators and central office staff as well.

Roles of Key Staff

Regardless of the details of appraisal, the general function of the various key positions in that process need to be considered and understood.

Superintendent. The superintendent must see that the process is initiated and implemented. This role's key function is to deal with the board of education directly. (This may mean that either the board initiates the interest in systemwide appraisal or the superintendent initiates it with the board.) However it is accomplished, once a decision is made, the superintendent needs to develop a policy statement that authorizes the process and, in turn, begins the implementation of the detailed planning. In these efforts, the personnel administrator has the major coordinating and planning responsibility.

Principals. The administrator involved most centrally in the smooth functioning of the system as well as the manager of the units most affected is the school principal. In large measure, it is at the building level where most of the appraisal activity takes place and where it obviously has the greatest impact. Accordingly, principals must be involved throughout. This is typically managed in two ways. First, there is need for meetings periodically with all principals. And, second, representatives of the principals need to be involved in all major planning sessions. This serves not only for a first-time implementation but—as is more typically the case—for ongoing analysis of the plan, revisions, changes, and monitoring.

---

[10]National Education Association, "Evaluation of Teaching Competence," in Heald et al., op. cit., pp. 292–301.

Teachers. Teachers are the major targets of appraisal systems, and reasonable procedures must be established to ensure their positive participation in the process. No teacher should feel that he or she did not have ample opportunity to understand and contribute to it.

Consultants. In the initiation or implementation of appraisal plans, outside consultation and technical assistance is a wise use of resources. Appraisal plans, even when effective, may require some objective assessment. In major overhauls or revisions, consulting advice is particularly helpful, since these are very time-consuming efforts that can easily monopolize too much staff time.

Throughout any appraisal process, emphasis and attention must remain on its purposes and its value rather than on the process itself. It is all too easy for the system to become an end rather than a means.

The System Philosophy

We have emphasized the importance of articulating the goals and objectives of the formal appraisal process. But it is equally or more important to give attention and discussion to the philosophy from which such objectives emerge. For example, a district may feel that personnel ought to be evaluated on the basis of certain criteria of achievement—that is, that targets are determined concerning some specific levels of improvement in basic skills such as raising reading norms to the level of some familiar criterion like grade level. Although some goals may be forced on a school system by, say, legislation, it is better to approach the appraisal process with a desire for progress toward improvement rather than emphasis on the consequences of such progress. Because this point of view seeks to keep the process dynamic and flexible, we need to consider all real and existing variables that characterize the different levels of attainment in different schools and different sociocultural situations that are automatically built into a set of assumptions (whether articulated or implied). A key statement in one school system's *Handbook for Teacher Evaluation* reflects this attitude as follows:[11]

Personnel evaluation is a cooperative and continuing effort undertaken for the purpose of improving the quality of education. Education is a process with specific goals and as such, evaluation is an integral part of that process. Therefore, in order to provide for the maintenance and orderly growth of . . . schools, performance review and evaluation must be considered an essential part of an employee's contractual obligation. The method of evaluation should provide statements of what is expected . . . and measurements of what is actually achieved. *It should provide direction for . . . performance improvement; stimulate . . . the spirit of cooperation, self-examination, self-confidence, and desire to*

[11]*Handbook for Teacher Evaluation*, rev. ed. (Charleston, W. Va.: Kanawha County Schools, 1979), p. 9. (Emphasis added.)

Table 7-1. Summary of Teacher Evaluation Process*

Steps	Probationary Teachers	Tenured Teachers	Deadline
Step 1—Room Visitation			
Principal visits room to become acquainted with classroom environment, including teaching techniques and organization.	X	O	October End of week 2
Step 2—Preliminary Conference			
Principal and teacher confer to discuss the principal's observations, any concerns the principal may have, and the concerns of the teacher.	X	X	
Teacher and principal together identify areas for improvement for the current year.	X	X	October End of week 2
Step 3—Establishing Objectives			
Teacher establishes specific performance objectives for items chosen as areas for improvement.	X	X	
Teacher then shares these objectives with principal in either oral or written form.	X	X	November End of first 9 weeks
Step 4—Observation and Progress			
Principal visits classroom for purpose of making observations, including three formal 30-minute observations followed by conferences.			
Formal observation and conference no. 1	X	X	November End of first 9 weeks
Formal observation and conference no. 2	X	X	January End of second 9 weeks
Formal observation and conference no. 3	X	X	February End of third 9 weeks
During conferences, observation will be discussed as will progress on performance objectives.	X	X	
Step 5—Final Appraisal			
Teacher and principal each completes evaluation form.	X	X	

Table 7-1. (*Continued*)

Steps	Probationary Teachers	Tenured Teachers	Deadline
Teacher and principal share evaluations and develop consensus.	X	X	
Principal completes final evaluation form during conference and both principal and teacher sign and receive a copy.	X	X	
Form is received by central office.	X	X	March 1
Performance objectives for next year may be identified at this conference.	O	O	

Handbook for Teacher Evaluation, rev. ed. (Charleston, W. Va.: Kanawha County Schools, 1979). Used with permission.
*X indicates a required procedure; O indicates an optional procedure.

grow; and should assure accountability of all personnel. Acceptance of the preceding concepts implies that through evaluation come the establishment, change, and improvement of stated goals and objectives, thus assuring quality education within the system.

All school districts that are involved in formal appraisal planning and implementation utilize manuals for they provide the policy statements, philosophy, goals and objectives, guidelines, design, calendar, forms, and directions for usage of the process. The manual is first and foremost a statement of the point of view and value of the process. Table 7-1 is a summary of the appraisal pattern.

THE ENVIRONMENT OF THE PERSONNEL ADMINISTRATOR

One recent study, which observed the general climate within which school personnel directors function, helped to define, through a series of Q-sort statements, three types of personnel administrators: "processors," "policy brokers," and "linkers."[12] While our main interest in the following section is not so much with these types of personnel administrators as with subsequent information that was elicited from telephone interviews, some brief descriptions may be of interest.

[12]Esch and Monahan, op. cit., pp. 2–4.

Processor types were persons who, either because of role definition by superiors or because of role performance, were greatly involved in the paperwork of personnel functions. This type spent much time on procedures and was much more concerned with the drafting, revision, and management of policies and administrative memoranda than with the design and development of policy (i.e., with *initiating* it). This type spent a much greater proportion of time at the desk and was not nearly so involved with seeing people as were either of the other two types.

Policy brokers were found in larger systems. (*All* of those in this category were from the largest systems—30,000 or more students—although all the subjects in the study from districts of this size category were not in this factor type.) This type was characterized by very high status in the organization, typically at the associate superintendency level; they spent more of their time seeing people—one common response from this type, for example, was "too many appointments." More time was taken up in conferences and meetings, and in all cases, this type spent disproportionately more time with the chief executive. The principal functions of this type of administrator involved bringing various other officials together in initiating policy issues, expediting them for the superintendent, or resolving conflicts over them. It was clear to us that such persons had fairly large staffs directly reporting to them and, among which, there was, presumably, an adequate complement of processor types.

Linkers were similar to policy brokers (as were both in many ways similar to processors), and vice versa. But while policy brokers spent time with internal interactions, linkers spent time with activities and personnel outside the immediate central office environment. The most distinct characteristic of linkers was their intimate involvement in professional negotiations and/or collective bargaining. Moreover, linkers were more to be found in the medium-sized school systems in the study (districts with 15,000–30,000 students). There were incidences of linkers in the smallest category of systems (8,000–15,000), but there were none from the largest category. Medium-sized districts represent the greatest incidence of this type, we believe, because there is less professional staff support and an apparently greater likelihood that the personnel administrator will have more responsibility in all kinds of interrelationships.

Finally, whereas processors were found across all three size categories, our subsequent telephone interviews revealed that among this type in larger school districts, "processing" behaviors were probably somewhat misunderstood. Thus although these items were sorted similarly, apparently that was the case in larger districts because some of these persons perceived that as a function of the office rather than of the person.[13]

In closing, we wish to emphasize that no one should generalize with either much comfort and confidence about these factor types. However, the information

---

[13]It is intriguing to consider characterizing *offices* of the personnel function according to these same categories, but that is another study, and we resisted the urge to pursue the idea.

gleaned from follow-up interviews with some of these subjects proved useful for understanding the nature of the environment in which such administrators function, and in all such cases, it is apparent that this role is a critical one in the ongoing management of school organizations.

Increased Responsibility

In all cases, the chief administrator for the personnel function is very high in the administrative hierarchy, higher apparently than has been the case in the past. This role now has a "line" rather than a "staff" orientation. Among the reasons for this increased responsibility is the proliferation of regulations and due process procedures that must be honored in all formal organizations but especially in those that receive federal funding.

Another set of concerns that has had significant impact on the personnel administrator relates to the elaborate systems of evaluation and performance appraisals discussed earlier in this chapter. Regardless of the size of school districts, the personnel administrator must be involved in these procedures. In larger systems, the office of personnel performs a facilitative function in performance and evaluation activities; in smaller systems, administrators are involved even more directly.

And considering the increasingly sensitive problems of termination and transfer, always with the likelihood of formal appeals and legal redress, personnel administrators must be viewed as full partners in policy development and highest-level discussions within the chief executive's cabinet or team. All the administrators interviewed noted that few aspects of their function require more careful attention than do those related to personnel termination, transfer, and demotion. All persons with professional responsibility within the personnel functions are trained in the management of policies related to these activities, and procedures are continuously reviewed, revised, and assessed. Attorneys are involved in discussions, and court cases or other methods of handling problems are shared with staff to be as certain as possible that "just cause" and "due process" concerns are covered fully.

Negotiations

In all cases, the personnel function has also become the central focus of activity with reference to professional negotiations or collective bargaining.[14]

As one associate superintendent for personnel in a large midwestern school system put it,[15]

---

[14]The distinction between these terms is increasingly less meaningful, and we deal with this important area in some detail in Chapter 8.
[15]Monahan and Eseh, op. cit., p. 28.

In a system such as ours, all personnel administrators are quite involved in the negotiations process either directly or indirectly; in our case there are four such persons, and although it is our pattern *not* to have the chief personnel officer sitting at the negotiating table, we do have our Director of Classified Employees sometimes more directly involved and even occasionally sitting at the negotiating table—that's because he has considerable previous expertise in that aspect of the process and also, the whole pattern with classified personnel is a quite different area.

As the chief personnel officer, I am quite intimately involved in the process but I work quite closely with what we call the "negotiating council." This council meets regularly with the actual negotiations team and, in effect, fashions the "bullets" that the team will "fire." It's a very complicated process and it does take a lot of time.

In smaller school systems, it is not uncommon for the personnel administrator to be involved more directly in bargaining and, in some cases, to perform the role of negotiator. In larger systems, the more general pattern is to have someone on the staff who is designated to perform this function and who carries a title such as "assistant to the superintendent for professional relations." Some districts employ, on retainer, an outside negotiator.

It is the view of these authors that, unless a board of education has little choice, neither the superintendent nor other members of the regular executive staff should act as the board's negotiator and especially not the superintendent himself or herself. Although the superintendent is not a disinterested party, he or she should be in a position to confer with the board and its negotiator(s) to advise, suggest compromises, or otherwise provide a source of temperate reason. If involved too directly and intimately, the superintendent or any other member of the regular executive staff can become too committed to ownership of positions and statements and thus the probability of arriving at "impasse" is greater.

We will discuss other aspects of this important dimension of personnel administration in Chapter 8.

Technical Proficiency

The personnel function is now also marked by the need for a high level of technical competence. Not only must one be well versed in the codes, rules, policies, and guidelines that are both imposed on personnel management from without by state and federal regulatory agencies and from within by policy formulation, but one must have expertise in the areas of evaluation and performance appraisal, retirement and accounting information and fringe-benefit packages, recruiting activities, and the enormously expanded importance of the record-and-file system that is the lifeblood of such a function.

All the personnel administrators we interviewed indicated a lack of adequate computerized systems for information storage and retrieval. In all cases as well, the problems not only were those of hardware but of retaining the skilled work force necessary to the programming and optimal maintenance of the machine systems required. We do not refer to the repair and maintenance of equipment, although that is always a continuing source of some difficulty for any operation; instead, we refer to the maintenance of the system itself, its monitoring, revision, and improvement. These kinds of human and mechanistic resources are very hard to come by in public school organizations, and although quite dramatic innovations have been developed and installed, the need for effective and efficient ongoing data processing systems seems still to be far from what is really available.

It is interesting, however, to note that just as several personnel administrators observed that the exigencies of collective bargaining have created new problems for them, this process has also resulted in improvements in staffing and in systematic procedures. This has also been the case in smaller school systems where central office staff needs previously provoked only a half-hearted response from some boards of education. Speaking to a statewide meeting of school superintendents and state agency executives in West Virginia in 1975, Dr. Elmer Gast, superintendent of the Ardsley, New York, public schools, observed that "You can say what you like about having to deal with the tough-mindedness of unions, but I'll guarantee you that when you do, your boards are going to be far less reluctant to provide some of those staff people you've been asking for."[16]

In general and apparently with little regard for size of district, the personnel function is characterized by increased visibility and responsibility in the hierarchy of executive concerns; by increased tension as a consequence of emerging interest in and critical monitoring of promotion, salary, due process, affirmative action, and collectivization; and by significant expansion in the nature of the technical competence required in such roles.

Termination and Dismissal

A final comment relates to the termination of employees. Although the personnel administrator may be the most directly involved in that painful and always complex process, all administrators must at one time or another confront the anxieties that the termination decision generates—both in themselves and in those who are the subjects of it.

There are a few circumstances in which termination is a consequence of that cliché, it is "beyond our control"; typically that means that funding is no longer available, programs must be canceled, or enrollments are declining to the extent

[16]Elmer Gast, "A New Game with New Rules." Address at School Executive's Round-Up, Morgantown, West Virginia, October 11, 1975.

that layoffs are unavoidable. Yet even in these circumstances, the face-to-face confrontations that simple ethics and humane management require are still disquieting, and much more so when termination is the result of poor performance.

We know of no one who does not face such confrontations with dread—at least any good and effective administrator will. Dismissing some persons undoubtedly strengthens the organization, and some administrators are better at it than others. But even under the most deserving of circumstances, it is unlikely that anyone enjoys it. Whenever possible, this task should be done with the greatest sensitivity and, except in the rarest circumstances, face to face.

SUMMARY

In summarizing this chapter, it is particularly apropos to recall the observations made by William B. Castetter in the preface to the 1981 (third) edition of his excellent book in the area of education personnel; he said:

The decade of the seventies was characterized by changes in the management of educational systems that were more numerous and of more import than in any other decade in recent memory. Dramatic decreases in school enrollments, staff reductions, union-system discord, changes in the mandatory retirement age, personnel stress on security, surging demands for the abolition of tenure, sharp upturn in the cost of human resource time, client insistence upon return on investment, upheaval in human attitudes, new approaches to human resource planning, accelerated personnel expectations, and the flowering of the psychology of human entitlement are recent developments that have generated organization problems and modifications in the way they are resolved.[17]

Such reflects the enormously more complicated nature of the personnel management issues that characterize the contemporary school system. At the same time, the rampant nature of the inflationary cycle on cost-of-living issues has further complicated many aspects of personnel administration in school systems and not the least of these has been the impact on, and of, teacher strikes. Although the inflation rate had dipped below the double-digit level by summer, 1981, it is generally unarguable that salary and economic issues accounted for the major concerns in most of the labor difficulties in schools during most of the 1970s. The situation in 1978–79 was typical; of this, Richard G. Neal observed:

As of mid-October there had been at least 130 strikes by teachers in public school districts in 21 states. . . . The total number of students affected was 1,898,594. . . . There is no

[17]Castetter, op. cit., p. vii.

doubt that inflation is having a devastating impact on teachers. A great many, particularly those who have been on the top of the scale for the past several years and do not earn annual increments for years of service, actually have less purchasing power today than they did five years ago.[18]

The advent of public sector collective bargaining is only about two decades old. The first state to initiate such legislation was Wisconsin in 1959, and it was in 1962 that John F. Kennedy issued Executive Order 10988, which granted federal employees the right to bargain collectively. But in no case has the right to strike ever been a part of the federal employees' privileges, and although more than two thirds of the various states have authorized the right to bargain, few of them have legalized the strike. Yet, in the summer of 1981, government-employed air traffic controllers went on strike at the risk of the loss of their jobs after having rejected a negotiated contract that would have compensated them at three times the salaries of school teachers. It is little wonder that teachers have become sometimes militant in behalf of collective bargaining, and this set of concerns constitutes the major focus in personnel relations in contemporary times. It is for that reason that we treat it separately in the following chapter.

Nevertheless, it now appears that in the 1980s, issues related to both salary and collective bargaining will not so totally preoccupy the education personnel specialist as they have done in the past ten years. On the horizon are the emergingly important issues of continuing education, competency testing, and other aspects of performance assessment.

EXERCISES

1. A formal performance appraisal system has been mandated in the system where a superintendent is in the first year of a three-year contract. An elaborate process of elections was worked out to determine the make-up of a committee of teachers and others to develop the procedures and instruments. The committee has been meeting regularly for almost six months, and nothing much in the way of progress has occurred. The chairperson of the committee advised the superintendent that two females are clearly delaying implementation until several of their colleagues can be tenured; these several teachers are very actively organizing the teaching staff in behalf of a collective bargaining agreement with the board and are generally acknowledged as marginally effective teachers. The superintendent met with these two

[18]Richard G. Neal, "The U.S. Teacher Strike Scene," *Phi Delta Kappan*, Vol. 60, no. 4 (December 1978), p. 327.

persons and urged them to be less recalcitrant. They managed to have this meeting and other aspects of the committee and its task written up in the newspaper with the implication that, if they didn't "go along" with what the superintendent wanted, they would be fired. This was based on a rather loose translation of his observation to them that this committee "was really in the long-range best interests of teachers and if some of the teachers couldn't endure a process in which their own peers had fundamental influence, perhaps they shouldn't remain in the profession." What went wrong? What would you have done in a similar circumstance? How could the issue have been managed differently?

2. Two custodians were fired because they were observed at eleven-thirty, one evening, one sitting at a principal's desk reading his correspondence and the other using the telephone for a personal call. Both appealed on the basis that the one was really not reading anything and whatever was left on a desk could not really be private anyway; the other claimed that the use of the telephone should not be denied. What do you think ought to be the result of the appeal and why?

3. At a meeting of the principals' council, the discussion concerns aspects of a system's induction procedures for new teachers. One elementary principal is arguing against a proposed policy for a lighter load for beginning teachers while a junior high principal is arguing in favor of it. The elementary administration holds that teachers are supposed to be fully prepared to assume a probationary appointment initially and it is costly in dollars and personnel relations to ask other already heavily loaded teachers to "nurse" them along. The second principal argues that it saves money and effectiveness over time to make the first year as painless as possible and the school has an obligation to do so. A third principal suggests that this aspect of induction be left up to each school. Is that acceptable to you? If not, why not?

4. In a school system with 13,000 students, the personnel director advised the superintendent that six clerical personnel could be eliminated and a significantly increased efficiency in personnel records could be achieved by computerizing the system at a total initial cost of $175,000. The annual salary savings would amount to about $60,000 the first year and that, even with the addition of one technical employee during the second year, the salary savings over time would more than offset the technical costs. What kinds of questions must be answered to seriously pursue this idea? What advantages and disadvantages does it imply?

5. As superintendent of a large metropolitan system, you must close twelve schools next year because of declining enrollments and a revised school integration policy. How should you go about planning for the termination of about four hundred teachers and the transfer of another three hundred? What considerations must be included in such a plan?

SUGGESTED REFERENCES

American Association of Personnel Administrators. *The Personnel Executive's Job.* Englewood Cliffs, N.J.: Prentice-Hall, Inc., 1977.

Beach, Dale S. *Personnel: The Management of People at Work*, Third Edition. New York: Macmillan Publishing Co., Inc., 1975. See Chapter 4.

Bolton, Dale H. *Evaluating Administrative Personnel in School Systems.* Totowa, N.J.: Teachers College Press, 1980.

Castetter, William B. *The Personnel Function in Educational Administration*, Third Edition. New York: Macmillan Publishing Co., Inc., 1981.

DeSatnick, Robert L. *The Expanding Role of the Human Resources Manager.* New York: American Management Association, 1979.

Fawcett, Claude W. *School Personnel Systems.* Lexington, Mass.: D. C. Heath and Co., 1979.

Merriott, Dave. "A Sociologist Looks at Induction," *Personnel Review*, Vol. 3, no. 1 (Winter 1979), pp. 4–9.

Chapter 8

Collective Bargaining and Affirmative Action

INTRODUCTION

In the practice of educational administration in contemporary times, there are two significant sets of "new" dimensions of reality to which institutional administrators and fiduciary authority must give increasing attention. One is the emergence of organized collectivization of teachers and other school personnel; the second concerns the establishment of a complex regulatory apparatus aimed at monitoring and enjoining activities of all employing organizations with reference to discrimination and equal employment access in areas of race, sex, religion, and national origin.

Although these two sets of emerging personnel issues are not related immediately in any direct fashion, they are at least theoretically of similar origins. Both collectivization and affirmative action are of interest because they have gained prominence of attention in the day-to-day activities of personnel management. But they are of still more interest because they reflect what Daniel Bell has referred to as "norms of self-realization that are now central in the culture."[1] Bell sees this as being in conflict with the norms that are required in the economic "realm" and sees in these conflicts some important tensions. He further states that[2]

one can discern the structural sources of tension in the society: between a social structure (primarily techno-economic) which is bureaucratic and hierarchical, and a polity which

---

[1]Daniel Bell, *The Cultural Contradictions of Capitalism* (New York: Basic Books, 1976), p. 15.
[2]Ibid., p. 14.

believes, finally, in equality and participation; between a social structure that is organized
. . . in terms of roles and specialization, and a culture which is concerned with the
enhancement and fulfillment of the "whole" person.

It is in this same context of conflict that we confront similar issues in the
management of schools—between what the system must do and what the individual worker wants (between the welfare of the system and the welfare of the
worker). In that way these two phenomena are related. Yet collectivization and
affirmative action represent different levels of response to the emerging conflicts
between the individual and the system. They have therefore taken different
avenues of development and require different patterns of response with reference
to administrative concerns. For those reasons, we treat them somewhat separately in the following discussions and return to their relationship in the "Summary."

THE COLLECTIVIZATION OF EDUCATIONAL PERSONNEL

On a very pleasant day in May 1970, the majority of classroom teachers in
the Keokuk, Iowa, community school district went on strike. Although by 1970,
public school teachers' strikes were certainly not unique, this particular one was;
it was the first public school teachers' strike in the history of the state of Iowa,
and at that time, strikes by public employees were explicitly prohibited by law;
moreover, the prolonged "discussions" leading up to the strike "were on an
extra-legal basis [since] Iowa at that time had neither a legal basis for salary
negotiations with public employees, nor did the state have legislative guidelines
providing for settlement of irresolvable issues in the event of" any possible
formal disagreements.[3]

It could be surmised that this otherwise obscure event heralded the arrival of
the collectivization movement in American public education. Although teachers'
unions were well established long before 1970 and there had been many strikes
(some sanctioned, some not) during the 1960s, the Keokuk strike was significant
in many ways. First, it occurred in a district that had a tradition of "confer and
consent" between the local teachers' unit and school administrators and in which
the general treatment of teachers' concerns for salary and working conditions
had been better than the average for the state. Second, Keokuk, Iowa is, and
was then, not the kind of community that one would expect to be the locus of
such a dramatic controversy. Keokuk is a decidedly rural community with some
industrialization located on the Mississippi River in the southeast corner of the

---

[3]Morris Wilson, "The Keokuk Teachers Strike: A Case History," unpublished doctoral dissertation. Iowa City, Ia. University of Iowa, July 1972, p. 1.

state. In 1970, the district enrolled just under 4,000 students and had always enjoyed excellent support from the citizenry. The first public school in Iowa was established just nine miles from Keokuk, and over the years, the town had enjoyed distinguished programs and leadership. The Keokuk Education Association, not unlike other local teachers' organizations across the country, was until about 1965, something of a "company union." Membership in it was strongly encouraged by the system's administrators, and it enjoyed esteem both by the board of education and the parent state education association. In 1966, under the leadership of a fairly activist president, the association presented the first formal proposal to the board for a salary package. In 1968, "procedural agreements" were consummated primarily due to an enlightened superintendent of schools. This pattern worked reasonably well until the difficulties that resulted in the 1970 strike arose.

It is important to recognize that sentiment against collectivization of teachers was growing during the 1960s, and even in those places in which little formalization of relationships had been worked out, particularly in small and/or conservative communities, an activistic, welfare-oriented perspective was building among teachers and their leadership. Just as predictably, an opposing set of values was evolving with fiduciary authority. Without much significance otherwise, the quite unlikely occurrence of a real honest-to-God teachers' strike in Keokuk, Iowa, on May 6, 1970, reflected the full maturity of that adversarial relationship. Since that time, the presumption of some level and intensity of "professional negotiations" or "collective bargaining" as the case may be is standard. This is particularly underscored by the simple fact that in 1978 the Iowa legislature enacted a public employee bargaining act with the provision of formal arbitration of disputes, explicit negotiation procedures, a nonstrike clause, and "impasse" definitions. What began with some notable intrastate attention albeit illegally in Keokuk in 1970 had resulted in legislative jurisdiction and legitimization only a few years later.

The Issue

It is naïve for any prospective school administrator in contemporary times to believe that, because teachers are professionals with humanistic sensitivities to the moral growth of young minds and bodies, they ought not engage in labor union activities. It is even more naïve to enter administrative roles with notions of "breaking up" the solidarity of teachers' commitments to those behaviors and tactics; on the contrary, that point of view is downright hazardous. The enlightened view is to learn how to deal with that circumstance to gain the most for the continued benefit of children and youth.

There is really nothing either immoral or subversive about collectivization. It is as American as apple pie; it is as worldly as vegetable stew. Collectivization varies not so much in terms of the vegetables in the stew as by the quantity and quality of the meat that might be added. Thus, in some nations, collectivization is totalitarian and rigidly controlled; in others, it is a function of democratic politics; and in still others, it is the only available mechanism for revolutionary change.

In all cases, collectivization is based on the simple principle that there is strength in (organized) numbers. If any category of persons feels the need for redress from arbitrary and immoral treatment, or even for entitlements, collective action is frequently seen as the clearest path toward acquiring some share of the power necessary to have concerns heard and resolved. The key idea in effective collectivization of course is "organization." If collective interests are organized with care and if there is sufficient *commitment* to the purposes and tactics established, collective collaboration has been demonstrated to be effective and successful. It is because collective action is legitimized within the American sociopolitical ideology and it does work well in a pluralistic society that its utility and function in the American labor movement has been relatively formalized and civilized.

Collective Bargaining—The Concept

In the American labor movement, the single most significant manifestation of the effective functioning of organized collectivization is characterized by the concept of *collective bargaining*.

The history of the development and sanctioned recognition of collective bargaining as we know it today is intermeshed with that of the organized labor movement itself. And while it is not appropriate here to trace the events and difficulties in the stream of labor history, suffice it to remind the reader that it is a history of incredible difficulty with many heroes and not a few martyrs.

In his authoritative text dealing with collective bargaining, Harold W. Davey defines it as follows:[4]

In simple terms, collective bargaining concerns two basic subject-matter categories: (1) *The price of labor*, broadly defined to include not only wages as such but any other working conditions or term of employment involving direct monetary outlays, such as pensions, group life insurance plans, paid vacations, and so forth; (2) *a system of industrial jurisprudence*, that is, policies and procedures governing on the job relationships that apply to all workers covered by the contract in like fashion in like circumstances.

More explicit legal specifications of collective bargaining are contained in Sections 9(a) and 8(d) of the National Labor Relations Act. Section 9(a) employs

[4]Harold W. Davey, *Contemporary Collective Bargaining*, 3rd ed. (Englewood Cliffs, N.J.: Prentice-Hall, 1972), pp. 6–7.

the phrase, "rate of pay, wages, hours of employment, or other conditions of employment"; Section 8(d) deals with the bargaining *process* and emphasizes the *duty* to bargain in good faith.

Collective Bargaining in Education

Just as there are value-laden insights and biases of one or another persuasion with reference to organized labor generally, there are also value-laden attitudes toward all categories of workers and regardless of their identification with or relation to some particular union. Whether some category as, for example, "professionals" should "unionize" and thereby bargain with employers collectively can engender strong public opposition merely because that style does not strike many other people as seemly. In circumstances involving police and firefighters, for example, even stronger attitudes prevail.

Certainly, issues of what is in the public good can and frequently do become substantive bases for quite explicit constraints on collectivization and on formal bargaining. But even in cases where the public good is not really threatened (perhaps only inconvenienced), such attitudes still carry the strength of intimidation and disapproval. This is still uniquely the case with public school teachers and employees.

In all such cases, the threat of the strike or the withholding of services is the ultimate weapon and hangs always heavily over the bargaining process. Workers argue that, without the right to strike, the entire bargaining process loses its raison d'être—its integrity, if you will. Although this rationale is too simplistic and experience has demonstrated that good-faith bargaining can be effective even when the right to strike is enjoined by law, the fact remains that the strike is so much a component of the collectivization syndrome that it is not infrequently invoked even in defiance of law. When this occurs, the perpetrators are generally quite comfortable with the calculated risks and assume them by knowing full well that they may be able to parlay the heroic ingredients in that risk for more rapid and more satisfactory resolution of an impasse. The point to be made is that the right to strike is statutorily forbidden to certain categories of workers not only (or even very rationally) because the enterprise cannot meet its public and critical obligations otherwise, but because as well there is a need to sustain the ideology that holds that a "public office is a public trust."

The Constraints of Ideology

Regardless of the fact that public opinion disapproves an organized labor style of behavior by certain public and/or professional employees, the increased incidence of organized efforts by employees to gain various employment advan-

tages has necessitated the initiation of procedures—both legal and procedural—
that are aimed at orderly pursuit of negotiations.

Negotiations versus Bargaining. It is interesting to note that the term
"professional negotiations" is a rhetorical gesture in behalf of public attitudes.
Even teachers who approve of vigorous and militant advocacy of their benefits
find the idea of unionization and collective bargaining distasteful because they
would rather proclaim their status as professionals than do otherwise. The term
therefore has more polite appeal and does tend to follow somewhat less well-
defined and less formal patterns. However, in the larger sense, there is no longer
much real difference between negotiations and bargaining, and the rules and
procedures involved are quite similar.

Among the general constraints and guidelines that have been instituted for
bargaining procedures are these: exclusivity of representation, fact-finding, mediation, arbitration (binding and nonbinding), impasse (and impasse procedures),
and amnesty. Such terms are familiar in the general literature of the organized
labor movement, but only since about 1965 or so have they become a part of
the language in educational administration.

These various terms merely reflect pieces of the development of reasonably
orderly procedures in the formalization of educational relationships between so-
called management and so-called workers—so called because the older models
in collective bargaining in the corporate sector still do not quite fit the public
sector. Who really is management? Who are workers? The categories are imprecise. Yet a pattern has emerged that requires the imposition of generally
accepted rules and norms that had to be adapted from the experience and history
of adjudication and resolution that has "worked" elsewhere.

Harold Davey has noted some of the (then) new problem areas in collective
bargaining that were not "even on the horizon in 1951 or in 1959."[5] Among
these new problems are the following:

Collective bargaining by nurses and public school teachers.
Coalition or multiunion bargaining with conglomerate employers.
Bargaining in the public sector at federal, state, and municipal levels.
Collective bargaining as a vehicle for raising farm prices.
Use of collective bargaining as an instrument for improving the economic status of the
"working poor."
Alternatives to the use of economic force for resolution of disputes over future contract
terms, particularly in the public sector where the public interest (has made) the strike
and the lockout anachronistic.
Impact of Title VII of the Civil Rights Act of 1964 on collective bargaining dealing
with so-called male and female jobs and related matters.

Davey lists fifteen new problem areas that were not factors before 1970, and
we recommend study of his work by any educational administrator who is likely

[5]Ibid., p. 23.

to be involved in highly organized employer-employee relationships whether or not there is unionization of teachers and/or other public school personnel categories.

Because bargaining patterns seem increasingly prevalent regardless of the specificity of a "bargaining agent," let us now discuss the terms that we have suggested as important and move from that to a discussion of the management implications and postures that we think are useful in that context.

Exclusivity. Increasingly, there is competition with reference to the right of representation. In other words, certain competing vested interests have become so potentially disruptive of ongoing work that resort to plebiscites for legitimizing a "bargaining agent" have become relatively common. In such circumstances, teachers have the choice of voting as to whether, say, the NEA or the AFT shall have exclusive representation in bargaining or negotiations. More typically, this has become a matter of contention at the community college or collegiate level wherein the American Association of University Professors (AAUP) has been a factor. In the public elementary and secondary sector, the issue of exclusivity has more typically followed the pattern of majority membership (i.e., where NEA or AFT have, respectively, dominated membership, the one or the other thereby is likely to gain exclusive bargaining rights). Obviously the importance of dealing with only one "bargainer" is essential to management, and the trend in thinking currently is careless—it does not matter all that much so long as one knows that multiorganizational representation is not a factor. Most school systems will generally admit that the differences are miniscule and that dealing with NEA is not much different than dealing with AFT.[6]

When there are competing or even overlapping memberships in organizations representing the "enlightened self-enhancement of teachers," a board of education has the right to expect that it will only enter into negotiation with one or another of them—not all.

Fact-finding. Fact-finding, another familiar phrase in the negotiations process, generally defines some reasonable boundaries within which information, research, comparative analysis, and appropriate information are brought to bear on the good-faith pursuit of resolution. It may or may not relate to wages

---

[6]We use the designation AFT (American Federation of Teachers) only as a convenience; this does not mean to suggest the AFT is the only teachers' union. In New York City, for example, the designation is the UFT (United Federation); we are only implying that one union is pretty much like another and that AFT, at last count, is the more universal. Most school administrators would further assert that NEA behaves so much like a union that it, too, is relatively indistinguishable in attitude and behavior from any otherwise explicitly designated labor union. That is not necessarily the view of the authors—only a statement of general opinion.

or other compensatory issues. Typically, fact-finding is not invoked until some status of impasse has been reached.

Impasse and Impasse Procedures. In most cases, impasse is operationally defined within some agreed-upon provisions. But substantially it simply means that some point is reached in the discussions, negotiations, or bargaining at which the parties cannot possibly agree; no further purpose can be served by continuing the negotiations, and the parties agree that the impasse has occurred. In most formal, procedural agreements governing the negotiations process, impasse is operationally defined in some such fashion as we have characterized it.

Mediation. When impasse is declared, some form of mediation is the next logical step. Mediation differs from arbitration in several ways. First, mediation is just that—acting as a go-between and seeking for relatively neutral assessment of bases for arranging a settlement; the ground rules for mediation always involve an objective third party (one who presumably understands the institution and the issues but who has no demonstrable vested interest in anything other than a reasonable, fair, and honorable settlement). Also, typically, the choice of a potential mediator is also spelled out in the agreements governing the negotiations process. Usually, this means that each party presents the names of acceptable persons, and the lists are matched when one or more names become common. Also, terms of compensation for mediation are addressed—each party pays half, and so forth. If the first agreed-upon mediator cannot and will not act, the next is contacted and so forth until one is appointed.

Arbitration. Mediation differs markedly from arbitration in that the mediator cajoles and negotiates between contending parties without recourse to anything other than some possibility of agreement between parties. Arbitration, on the other hand, is defined more institutionally and carries more neutral sanctions. Whereas an arbitrator may not, under statute, require parties to agree (except under provisions of "binding arbitration"), he or she has much more influence on forced settlement than does a mediator. Those who submit their disputes to arbitration commit themselves to a much more severe test of reconciliation than with mediation. Typically as well, except where statutory provisions apply, arbitration is invoked with explicit presumption of an imposed settlement proposal. Thus, the arbitrator takes into consideration the "distance" between the parties and recommends a neutral settlement—the parties may accept or reject it except in those rare circumstances when such person's recommendations are statutorily binding. The mediator, on the other hand, has little basis for imposing a compromise and must go back and forth with offer and counteroffer.

Amnesty. Although amnesty is *never* an explicit provision of the process, it almost always becomes a negotiable issue, after the proverbial smoke has cleared. Largely this concerns the likelihood of retaliation, and in cases where clearly illegal acts have occurred, amnesty becomes paramount. In mature circumstances, that is, where districts have engaged in formal bargaining for several years, the ground rules are well understood and generally closely followed, so it is rare that resort to illegal acts is either useful or likely.

The Costs of Collectivization

Calculating the costs of the collectivization movement among education personnel is difficult. Yet the question of costs frequently arises and just as frequently is answered in terms of whichever set of biases prevail. Those who find the collectivization movement improper or who advocate injunctive regulation to restrain it are likely to cite statistical data running on into the millions of dollars. Those who defend it or advocate statutory legitimization argue with equal vigor that it produces impressive gains in competence and more successful work performance.

We know of no purposeful and objective study that has attempted to deal with the costs of collective bargaining among teachers, nor can we agree on what a rational set of research hypotheses would postulate in such a study. Certainly there have been interesting analyses made of the costs to teachers themselves of prolonged strikes, but these are rather easy computations to make and are of passing interest only. Beyond such interests, the costs are much more typically cast in the context of "social" costs.

Social Costs. The concept of social costs is a much easier argument to invoke and, regardless of the pattern it might take, is also a much easier argument to support. In both cases that is because it is difficult to disprove. Thus while the "purer" cost-effectiveness argument requires at least passably plausible hard data and is thus difficult to mount initially in any persuasive fashion, it is thereby very easy to discredit. The social cost argument, on the other hand, is easy to mount and difficult to discredit because it begins with a point of view and takes advantage of retroactive interpretations to support that point of view.

Explanations in hindsight are seductive devices for public consumption simply because such explanations are always plausible. Thus, for example, if a prolonged teachers' strike occurs in School District X, it will ultimately begin to have some kind of impact on the circumstances of high school seniors who may plan to enter college in the following year. By the same token, there will be first graders who will not be ready for second grade, ninth graders who will not be ready for senior high school, and so forth. And, of course, there are the social cost arguments about children's observing "illegal" adult behavior.

It is also fairly well established that the longer the strike, the more public sentiment tends to turn against the strikers, no matter how defensible the griev-

ances of employees may be. Even so that is the best and most effective weapon available to justifiably aggrieved employees in the strike; the fact that disruption of the public's interest is too painfully endured makes it also a dangerous alternative.

The Scar Tissue Issues. We use the phrase "scar tissue issues" when we refer to the residue of bitterness and recrimination that seems almost inevitably to follow a strike. Even when there is an accepted history of contract bargaining as, for instance, in the case of the United Mine Workers, the residue of employer-employee bitterness makes anticipation of each new three-year contract negotiation most anxious.

The constitutions of teachers and other education personnel are more delicate by comparison. And those of us who have come more lately into the bargaining encounter have learned much from those who pioneered in establishing the rules. Yet it is a great mistake to assume that the process is not wounding. It is for that reason above all others that administrators and teachers alike must see each other as reasonable adversaries. The coolest heads should prevail, and all should beware of the individual whose enthusiasm for the contest obscures judgment. Although the attitude is very difficult to cultivate, anyone associated with the bargaining encounter might be well advised to remember the words of the sixth-century philosopher Lao Tzu: "He who knows others is wise; he who knows himself is enlightened."

The Contemporary Environment

At least thirty-five states now have laws requiring school boards to bargain or at least to confer in good faith with teachers' organizations. It is more than probable that any student reading this text who aspires to be a school administrator—whether in public or private schools—will confront some established pattern of such negotiations. It is indeed a fact of current professional life.

According to *Business Week* there was an anticipation of the NEA that there would be slightly more teachers' strikes in the beginning of the 1978 school year than the 152 strikes in 1977.[7] As it turned out, there were 164 strikes in 1978 and most were not of long duration. Interestingly, those states that do not outlaw the strike (e.g., Pennsylvania with 38) tended to lead in the number, but there were states in which strikes occurred and which had explicit statutory prohibitions. In 1981, there were only 37 strikes but there were more layoffs—44,000 nationally.

According to the National School Labor Relations Service (NSLRS), a joint program of the National School Boards Association and the American Association of School Administrators, the 1979 school term began with strikes in 18

[7]"Why Teachers Aren't in Turmoil," *Business Week*, September 18, 1978, pp. 24–25.

states involving more than 45,000 teachers and affecting more than 1 million students. The hardest hit, according to the NSLRS, was Michigan, with 25 strikes of about 20,000 teachers that affected 375,000 students. Other strikes occurred in Alabama, Alaska, California, Connecticut, Illinois, Indiana, Louisiana, Missouri, New Jersey, New York, Ohio, Oklahoma, Oregon, Pennsylvania, Rhode Island, Vermont, and Washington. As pointed out in the *NSLRS Newsletter,* only Alaska, Pennsylvania, Oregon, and Vermont of those states in which strikes occurred have statutes wherein such strikes are legal and even those states' laws are qualified. According to the NEA, there were 134 teachers' strikes in 1979.[8] It is our optimistic view that succeeding years will continue to see the decline of the strike, as both sides are beginning to learn that it is a resort to be avoided. (In 1981, only six states reported strikes.)

Few people probably realize or remember that the first significant collective bargaining contract covering school teachers was effected in the New York City schools only as recently as 1962. In 1979—only in a period of seventeen years— more than 60 percent of all teachers worked on the basis of collectively bargained contracts.[9] As Mike Lieberman points out, "providing public employees collective bargaining rights similar to those provided private sector employees is undesirable public policy."[10]

Almost prophetically, Lieberman mentions as one of the bases for his rather startling conclusion that public employee bargaining is "undesirable public policy" the fact that "teachers often play an important role in determining who is management."[11] The explanation is that teachers are increasingly active in school board elections (and even in statewide or state assembly elections) and that such "power" is typically neither legal nor practical for private sector employees and quite obviously no longer would any prospective school superintendent be either screened or employed unless "teacher organization" representatives are either members of "search" committees or otherwise consulted and/or involved formally in some aspect of the selection process. In a growing majority of districts this typically means that the candidate is scheduled to meet formally with either a sample of the teaching cadre or with its duly delegated representatives.

We characterize Professor Lieberman's observation as "prophetic" because, in early 1980, a decision rendered in the *Yeshiva University* case held that the faculty at Yeshiva was *not* entitled to any legal redress of its several complaints against the administration of that institution because the faculty itself was so intimately involved in participatory governance that in a real sense, the faculty

---

[8]*National School Labor Relations Service Newsletter,* Vol. 1, no. 2 (October 1979) (a joint publication of the National School Boards Association and the American Association of School Administrators, 1620 I St., Washington, D.C.).

[9]See, for example, Michael Lieberman, "Eggs That I Have Laid: Teacher Bargaining Reconsidered," *Phi Delta Kappan,* Vol. 61, no. 6 (February 1979), 415.

[10]Ibid., p. 415.

[11]Ibid., p. 415.

is the administration.[12] The case, which is becoming something of a *cause célèbre* in higher education circles, has not yet evoked very much comment in the literature of public elementary and secondary administration, though it will certainly have, in our view, rather substantial impact.

The implications of the *Yeshiva* case are both provocative and administratively delicious. In terms of the curious process through which professional- or technical-level employees have increasingly demanded (and been granted) a greater share in the internal governance of institutional policy and, as well, a significant and often explicit role in the development of that policy itself, it is apparently now open to question as to who is, in reality, the "management." In this case the court merely said, in effect, "How can you possibly say the institution is so badly at fault when you are so much in evidence yourselves *as* the institution?"

Perhaps the lesson to be learned immediately from this decision is that, if grass-roots parliamentarianism shall abide, then a new issue for bargaining is exactly to what extent shall policy development and policy management be distributed among "employees" and "employers"—and, more to the point, how shall it be defined operationally as to *which* is exactly *which*?

Bargaining in General

In the *American School Board Journal*, hardly an issue does not either include a major article on public school bargaining or some substantial information sharing about it.[13] Some aspects of bargaining also garnered space in *Education Digest, Today's Education, Phi Delta Kappan, The NASSP Bulletin,* and *The Christian Century* as well as in the excellent weekly *Education USA* and in the American Association of School Administrators' monthly, *The School Administrator*.[14]

[12]N.L.R.B. vs. Yeshiva University. 100 S.Ct. 856, U.S. Supreme Court, 1980. Also see, for example, S. G. Kramer and M. L. Goldstein, "Faculty Employment Status at Private Colleges and Universities After NLRB v. Yeshiva University," *Business Officer*, Vol. 20, no. 5 (May 1980).

[13]For example, from a major article by Lieberman in October 1977 ("How to Bargain Effectively"), and including another by Lieberman in February 1978, there were major pieces in the *American School Board Journal* in March, and two each in the April, July, and August issues in 1978 alone.

[14]See, for example, B. S. Cooper, "Collective Bargaining Comes to School Middle Management," *Education Digest*, Vol. 41, no. 4 (December 1976), 16–19; Terry Herndon, "Collective Bargaining," *Today's Education*, Vol. 65, no. 6 (November–December 1976), 46–49; NEA Governmental Relations, *Why Teachers Need a Federal Collective Bargaining Law* (Washington, D.C.: National Education Association, 1976). And, Tom James, "The States Struggle to Define Scope of Teacher Bargaining," *Phi Delta Kappan*, Vol. 57, no. 2 (October 1975), 94–97; Kenneth Ostrander, "Collective Bargaining Laws in Education," *NASSP Bulletin*, Vol. 59, no. 392 (September 1975), 16–21; and "New Role for Supporters of Catholic Schools," *Christian Century* (March 1978). See also various issues of *Education USA* in 1976–1979, and *The School Administrator* for the same period. As we have suggested, the literature in the area is prolific; the reader should pursue many other avenues of comment.

Small Schools and Large. It is our view that the chaos that has typified bargaining in the past is being replaced by articulation and that the patterns of behavior today include at least the following:

1. Bargaining (and/or negotiation) is better constrained by rules of procedure (e.g., "what" is negotiable is far less subject to nonprevious agreement).
2. Bargaining (and/or negotiation) is defined more clearly at the outset in terms of established issues and agenda (that is, the process itself is now more orderly).
3. The status of middle-management personnel is increasingly established (e.g., principals are either part of management or part of the teachers' system and in most cases these issues are typically established). The situation with regard to principals seems to vary widely—some have chosen to bargain "with" teachers and some "with" management. According to Bruce Cooper, the American Federation of School Administrators (AFSA) represented, at that time, almost 10,000 principals, assistants, and supervisors and that there were an additional 1,224 school districts with some type of middle-management "unions" not officially affiliated with the AFSA.[15] Apparently, and this seems to be of some importance, school principals and unit administrative staffs are unique in that the Taft–Hartley law forbids "industrial supervisors" from bargaining (federal supervisors are forbidden by executive orders); yet school supervisors and unit administrators (i.e., principals) are apparently recognized as "collective bargaining" agents. Thus the issue of whether principals and staff can bargain outside management definitions remains questionable. Our only substantive observation is simply that those who have chosen to do so have apparently been recognized as being legitimate by the school boards that have in fact "bargained" with them. Whether principals are, or are not, management seems only to make as much difference as some boards of education have decided unilaterally to make it; that is, whether the boards bargain or whether they do not. But the fact remains that principals and their staffs (especially if the staff is a large unit, say, more than 1,000 students in ADA) are terribly vulnerable in a highly "bargained" environment. Too frequently, they are left with almost no power in influencing their own compensation; if they attempt to "organize" they are possibly seen as "scabs" and if they do not, they are ignored for their substantial contributions as "company men." Principals are thus "damned if they do and damned if they don't."[16]

[15]Cooper, op. cit.

[16]Mildred Bentsen, "The Principalship: Death by Ambiguity," *The Hoosier Schoolmaster* (Fall 1977), pp. 4–6, cited in: W. H. Roe and T. L. Drake, *The Principalship*, (New York: Macmillan, 1980), p. 320.

Summarizing of Collectivization

Students of education administration must recognize that collectivization is a movement and a trend. Although it is important to determine the status and policy pattern within any board of education's attitudes toward collectivization, it is more important to know that such urges within any staff are both real and reasonably organized.

There is compelling logic in the recognition that well-organized and responsible employee leadership within the professional component as well as within the "classification" categories will relieve the executive administrator of many personnel problems. To a larger extent than both boards of education and school superintendents realize, a relatively precise meeting of the minds in the broad range of employer-employee relationships will significantly remove a lot of paperwork from the superintendent's desk and off the board's agenda. Boards must entrust their executives to exercise authority in negotiating many of these issues through delegation to the contract; when that is not the case, superintendents and boards must determine *a priori* which kinds of issues can be determined and adjudicated by agreement and thus rid the board of having to deal with everyday concerns. The effective executive (regardless of system size) simply says to the board, "under the authority you have vested in me, I've worked these things out and here is what I've committed us to." It is really as simple as that.

At the same time, as superintendent or as chairman of the board, you do not negotiate directly; let others do that even if your system is so small that you must pay someone to negotiate. Only in very rare circumstances, large or small, should the board or its superintendent exercise authority directly to negotiate, since the risks of loss are great.

Collectivization is unquestionably a condition that confronts all of us and at all levels and in all fields in the public sector. How we deal with it depends probably as much on what we are like as personalities as on what we think we know as professionals.

AFFIRMATIVE ACTION AND
EQUAL EMPLOYMENT OPPORTUNITY

Beginning in earnest in the early 1960s, scholastic institutions came under increasing pressures to assist more directly in social reform. Since then, the operational definitions of methods by which social reform has involved all types of educational institutions has continued to expand, and now, not only educational institutions but all public and private corporate entities are required to observe regulated behaviors in many such areas on pain of stringent penalties.

These pressures for an active participation in social reform have many historic precedents for educational institutions. In the public elementary and secondary schools, one precedent is the legal mandate of compulsory education itself. In the area of higher education, the establishment of the land grant universities is clear evidence of a national commitment to broaden the range of opportunities for more of the nation's citizens. In the field of secondary schools, the famous *Kalamazoo* decision is also to be counted among such precedents. Certainly among the most significant of such invocations was the *Brown* v. *Topeka* case, which outlawed separate but equal schools for blacks and which will probably remain as *the* landmark court decision whereby schools were brought centrally into social policy-making postures.

In the 1960s and 1970s, through revisions in existing laws and new ones, and through a highly developed regulatory apparatus to administer and monitor compliance, social reform developments have proliferated (see Chapter 4). *In almost no case that we can think of have the courts required public and private corporate entities to do anything that they should not otherwise have been doing anyway.* Because institutions—schools, businesses, industrial firms, and even governmental agencies themselves—are only communities of persons, however, both persons and organizations are easily guilty of discriminatory practices (frequently nonintentionally but sometimes deliberately). It has become a widely held view that eliminating explicit statutory or traditional barriers to equal access for individual and even corporate rights is not in itself enough to ensure fair and equitable treatment of persons; there must also be established systems and procedures for encouraging affirmative effort on the part of all employers and an appellate structure that provides for (1) adjudication of legitimate issues, (2) redress, if justified, and (3) a system of surveillance or oversight for ongoing compliance.

The Law and the Regulations

To understand the oversights and interests requires some familiarity with the laws and regulations themselves. This is an essential step in dealing with the assumption that citizens deserve protection and that the bulk of such pronouncements is merely an interpretive extension of the Bill of Rights itself.

The following are summaries of major laws, regulations, and executive orders that constitute the basis upon which compliance is ultimately defined.[17]

---

[17]The authors acknowledge permission to excerpt and paraphrase the following nine selected examples of applicable provisions of law and/or regulatory acts from *Affirmative Action Plan*, 3rd ed. (Morgantown: West Virginia University, June 1974), pp. 2–5.

I. *Title VI of the Civil Rights Act, 1964.*

This section prohibits discrimination on grounds of race, color, or national origin by educational programs which receive any federal funds. This legislation includes students, and employment policies and practices are *not* covered explicitly under it.[18]

II. *Title VII, Civil Rights Act of 1964.*

As amended by the Equal Employment Opportunity Act of 1972, prohibits discrimination in employment and includes such areas as hiring, upgrading, salary and fringe benefits, training and other employment considerations, with reference to race, color, religion, national origin, or sex. Whereas, Title VI above is administered by the *Office of Civil Rights,* Title VII is administered by the *Equal Employment Opportunity Commission.*

III. *Executive Order 11246 (Amended by 11375).*

A) Prohibits discrimination in employment as specified above in Title VII, Civil Rights Act, 1964, but explicitly states that such is applicable to any institution with a federal contract exceeding $10,000. It is this Order which embodies two concepts: nondiscrimination as well as *affirmative action.* "Non-discrimination" requires the elimination of all existing discriminatory conditions whether deliberate or inadvertent and a contractor (school or university) must carefully and systematically examine and reassess all of its employment policies and practices to be sure that they do not function to the detriment of any persons on grounds of race, color, religion, sex, or national origin. There must also be assurance that those responsible in matters of employment including all supervisory personnel, are non-discriminatory. "Affirmative Action" requires that said contractor do more than insure employment neutrality but, as that phrase suggests, additional efforts must be made to recruit, employ and promote qualified members of groups formerly excluded and even if that exclusion cannot be traced to particular discriminatory actions otherwise.

The premise of the affirmative action concept as embodied in these Executive Orders is that a benign neutrality in employment practices will tend to perpetuate the "status quo ante" indefinitely unless positive action is systematically initiated to overcome the effects of institutionalized forms of exclusion and discrimination. This order is also administered by the *Office for Civil Rights* in the Department of Health and Welfare.

B) *Guidelines on Discrimination Because of National Origin*—implementation of requirements of Executive Order 11246 and effective February 20, 1973, requires further that *positive* action be taken to insure equal employment opportunities for members of various religious and ethnic groups, "primarily but not exclusively, of Eastern, Middle, and Southern European ancestry such as Italians, Greeks, and Slavs, Jews and Catholics." The guidelines are administered by the *Director, Office of Federal Contract Compliance for Equal Employment Opportunity, U.S. Department of Labor.*

IV. *Equal Pay Act of 1963.*

As amended by the Education Amendments of 1972 in the Higher Education Act, this legislation prohibits discrimination in salaries and including fringe-benefits on the basis of sex. It is administered by the *Wage and Hour Division, Employment Standards Administration in the U.S. Department of Labor.* (It is important to point out that while primarily directed toward post-secondary institutions, the provisions of the Act are applicable to other institutions as well—applicability in all such of these enactments is less a matter

[18]Authors' italics.

of the particular level of educational concern as of the particular nature of violation or complaint based on it.)

V. *Title IX of the Education Amendments of 1972.*

Among the more recent sources of publicized controversy and frustration for all kinds of scholastic organizations, this "title" prohibits sex discrimination against students or others in education programs *and activities.* Patterned closely on Title VI of the Civil Rights Act, "IX" states, "No person . . . shall, on the basis of sex, be excluded from participation in, be denied benefits of, or be subjected to discrimination under any educational program or activity receiving federal financial assistance." Unlike Title VI of the Civil Rights Act however, Title IX also covers the employment practices of educational institutions. It is administered by the *Office for Civil Rights.*

VI. *Title VII (Section 799A) and Title VIII (Section 845) of the Public Health Act.*

—as amended by the *Comprehensive Health Manpower Training Act* and the *Nurse Training Amendments Act, 1971,* prohibits explicitly: a) sexually discriminatory admission of students to federally assisted health personnel training programs; and, b) sexually discriminatory practices affecting employees who work directly with applicants to or students in such programs. It, too, is administered by the *Office of Civil Rights.* (This title is applicable to any public school system which engages in vocational education programs.)

VII. *Rehabilitation Act of 1973, Sections 503, 504.*

—as amended, established the right of disabled persons to challenge employers as regards health care, employment, education, and access. Widely acknowledged as the *first* civil rights act protecting rights of handicapped persons. (Section 504 is primarily known as the "barriers-removal" provision.)

VIII. *Public Law 94-142—Education of all the Handicapped Children Act, 1975.*

This sweeping piece of legislation finally became fully effective on October 1, 1977 and requires provision of services to children with all manner of disabilities in "the least restrictive environment"—in other words, that all handicapped children shall be provided full educational opportunities.

Distinctions of Application

Although the legislation cited does not begin to represent the acts, laws, titles, sections, and so forth that have proliferated over the past couple of decades in our pursuit of the protection and advocacy of a whole variety of civil rights, these are the major ones; and procedural compliance as well as sources of redress are almost universally traceable to one or another of them. By the same token, while some of these various provisions may be targeted more familiarly toward one or another category of roles such as employees as in the case, for example, of Titles VI and VII of the Civil Rights Act and the Equal Pay Act, or primarily toward students as, for example, in the case of the titles cited in the Public Health Act, the Nurse Training Act, Title IX, and P.L. 94-142, such distinctions are not necessarily exclusive. Yet our principal concern here is with reference to personnel relations.

The Concern for Employment Practices

These various provisions of law and regulation—for boards of education and educational administrators alike (and at all levels of the educational enterprise)—constitute a thoughtful, rigorous, and carefully orchestrated plan for the management of school systems. Such sets of policies should undergo a formal review process at least annually and must involve the system's legal advisors, director(s) of personnel, executive liaison (superintendent or assigned deputy), and preferably officially recognized representatives of the instructional staff. It is essential as well that the fiduciary authority be represented (i.e., the chairman of the board of education or, if a large system, the chairman of the board's personnel committee. If the board does not have such a subcommittee, it should consider establishing one).

The "plan" should include at the least: (1) an affirmative action document, (2) an affirmative action officer, (3) a staff advisory committee, (4) a procedurally and regularly scheduled information-sharing meeting at least annually of all "line" supervisors, (5) an appeals and grievance mechanism, and (6) an institutional research or data retrieval system oriented specifically to the issues of concern. Let us turn to a brief discussion of these components and end with some advice on how to deal with the problems that arise despite careful planning.

The Affirmative Action Statement

"Affirmative action" as both a concept and an operational policy is quite clearly specified in Executive Order 11246. But that must be translated into a compact statement that must be filed with appropriate state and federal agencies. In essence, the affirmative action statement is "a plan," and it should include the following:[19]

A) *A clear statement* of the system's Equal Employment Opportunity Policy. Such a statement must unequivocally commit the system to the pursuit of affirmative action to recruit and employ the best qualified personnel and to ensure as well that all present personnel receive education, training, compensation, promotion, tenure, transfer, and other benefits of employment without regard to race, age, religion, sex, or national origin, except where sex (may be demonstrated as) . . . a bona fide occupational qualification.

B) *Personnel recruitment* and selection procedures; this must insure that publicized vacancies are processed but as well that minorities and women (or men, depending on the sexual style) are encouraged.[20]

[19]*Affirmative Action Plan,* op. cit.
[20]In some organizations, nursing, for example, the affirmative action plan tends to emphasize the recruitment of males or may do so.

C) *Documentation* to the effect that all personnel actions reflect defensible judgments of comparable qualifications and, in some cases, if certain characteristic persons—i.e., race, sex, etc.—are not selected, that written explanations be required.

D) *Promotion criteria* are clearly explicated and circulated and appeals of such decisions defined as to basis and procedure. (If "procedures" are neither established nor known, to make them so.)

E) *Compensation* procedures are known and established without recourse to race, sex, religion, etc., and that these procedures are carefully monitored to insure non-discriminatory equity provisions.

F) *Interviewing procedures* now must follow established rules.

G) *Reference evaluation* is proper and the statement of that propriety needs merely to be stated in the plan. *But,* clearly, it must also be stated in the plan that selection and placement decisions are based solely on an individual's qualifications for a position.

H) *Documentation* of all personnel actions must become a part of the file. The visibility and accessibility of the "file" are covered by still other provisions of laws of disclosure and procedural due process; yet, because files have become so sensitive in personnel relations, the need to clearly spell out procedures for documentation is imperative. At the same time, it is reasonable to include a time span within which such documentation is kept—as a rule, a minimum of two years is acceptable.

I) *Employee rating programs* or any other established performance appraisal procedures should be noted in the plan and not in any detail—merely that such procedures are extant and are utilized in the system of advancements and transfers.

J) *A statement rejecting* prejudicial presumptions is also useful in the affirmative action document; for example, a statement of explicit repudiation of comparative employment characteristics such as "women have higher turnover rates," or "women do better in clerical work," or "women have higher absentee rates," or "blacks around here are less reliable," and so forth.

K) *A final summative statement* expressing the general attitude of the system should be included and also should spell out the penalties for anyone found to be deliberately or even inadvertently in violation of the provisions of the plan and a clear explanation of appropriate *complaint* procedures in that event.

Such an affirmative action policy describes the system's attitudes and policies about this serious business of equal employment opportunity and puts the system quite clearly on the line as to its responsibilities and obligations with reference to its genuine commitments to that ideology. It requires any system to work harder; yet it does not ask any good school system to do other than define its procedural commitments. Those that do it poorly will just have much more to do later on and at the risk of loss of substantial federal support. Those that do it well must merely orchestrate the tunes they are already playing.

Equal Employment Opportunity Commission Complaints

Given the most precise and thoughtful consideration for doing what almost anyone with reason might accept as right, the ax still may fall and a system may still encounter an E.E.O.C. complaint. What is that like? Under what circumstances is it likely to occur? And what should be done about it?

The Affirmative Action Officer. In addition to an officially adopted affirmative action plan and a periodic review of that document and of the compliance of supervisory personnel with it, clear and explicit procedures also must be established and understood with reference to the identity and functions of the affirmative action officer and policies that explicitly define due process procedures with reference to termination of personnel.

The affirmative action plan is essentially a statement of *intent* and therefore describes the importance of, and procedures for carrying out, recruitment and placement concerns; the affirmative action officer is a full-time employee whose responsibilities cover not only the monitoring and administration of the plan but also helping the organization to meet its responsibilities in pursuing the integrity of all such efforts. Consequently, this officer has a fairly clear, albeit difficult, role; while an employee of the organization and certainly something of an advocate for it, he or she is also an advocate for "rightness." It is his or her responsibility to identify those aspects of the organization's activities that make it vulnerable and to recommend corrective action; at the same time, this officer (or the person designated to perform this function) should be involved in the development or revision of policies and procedures that spell out grievance adjudication. In most cases, this affirmative action officer will soon learn that the telephone is going to bring all manner of questions and not a few charges against this or that supervisor. Questions most typically will concern recruitment—advertising and notification, for example, in cases where one may want to eliminate a position or add one on some temporary basis and so forth; questions will also arise regarding who shall have access to personnel files and under what circumstances; what needs to be done when a candidate is not selected; what kind of records need to be kept; and whether "search committees" are required for this or that position. It will probably require a good six months for such a person to just "cycle through" the telephone inquiries; by the end of that time, the telephone will probably bring few new surprises.

Other complaints reflect the routine interpersonal tensions that arise in almost any organization. Often, informed intelligence resolves the issue at the outset, and "ventilation" of the problem may be sufficient. In any case, however, a procedure must be available to provide consideration, and in those few where the possibility of a real violation seems evident, the complaint must be followed up. Depending on the complexity of the organization, roles other than the affirmative action officer may also be involved. For example, many large public organizations, especially colleges and universities, frequently have ombudsmen, student-attorney offices, and associational welfare committees, any of which might be involved in some complainant procedure at one time or another. All these persons or committees need to know about each other and their various interrelationships—and it is not always easy or even necessary for all such components to have these interrelationships defined systematically. Sometimes, one must simply depend on common sense.

The Least-Level Resolution Principle. Because almost all formal complaints that are brought against organizations by such external agencies as the E.E.O.C. include a record of past difficulties, problems that seem to include a degree of harassment or discrimination should be dealt with as quickly as possible.

If a problem has gone beyond the stage of discussion between supervisors and employees, the principle of "least-level resolution" is the first logical response. By this we mean simply that any dispute that may require formal resolution should be directed toward that resolution at the level or unit of the organization that is the locus of the dispute. Typically, because this principle strives for unceremonious satisfaction, it reflects common sense by allowing and encouraging the unit's managers to control the environment of the dispute. As an example of this principle, suppose that a teacher voices a complaint about the behavior of a department chairperson or team leader; whether the complaint is voiced to the principal or to an affirmative action officer, it is the principal who represents the least-level concern in this example. If voiced to the principal directly, he or she deals with it directly; if referred by the affirmative action officer (the complainant may not know about least-level resolution), the principal is still the "level" at which immediate resolution is sought. While this procedure presumes informal discussion and probably clarification of rules and policies involved, it is nevertheless essential that the conclusions reached be written up and copies provided to all concerned.

The Fear of Retaliation. It must be communicated that, whatever procedures are established for dealing with disputes, grievances, or complaints, there should be no fear of retaliation, even though this fear is almost always present and is often justified. Moreover, this fear causes some complaints to go outside the organization, which can compound the problem.

There is no simple formula for eradicating the fear of retaliation, and even among the most comfortable and secure personnel, it can become a factor if a particularly disagreeable situation arises. Of course, the best assurance against retaliation is an open and professional style by supervisors and a long enough time in office for that style to have proved a record of fairness and integrity.

Of the many positive and socially redeeming aspects of this emerging process of civil rights in employment relations, one of the most healthy is the tendency among employees to perceive that injustices will be considered and redressed and that anxieties related to retaliation are no longer realistic. To the extent that organizations are humane, professional productivity tends to increase.

The Formal Complaint. Having pointed out these things, we return to our previous question—What if the ax still falls?

Figure 8-1 is a facsimile of an E.E.O.C. "Notice of Charge of Discrimination with Copy of Charge." This is Form 131-A of the Equal Employment Opportunity Commission and the "charge" that is usually attached to it is typically

Figure 8-1. Notice of Charge of Discrimination with Copy of Charge.

	EQUAL EMPLOYMENT OPPORTUNITY COMMISSION

<table>
<tr><td rowspan="2">TO:</td><td>EEOC CHARGE NUMBER</td></tr>
<tr><td></td></tr>
</table>

NOTICE OF CHARGE OF DISCRIMINATION WITH COPY OF CHARGE

(See Section 1601.15, Investigation of a Charge; Section 1602.14, EEOC Rules and Regulations, and Section 704(a), Notice of Non-Retaliation on the reverse of this form.)

You are hereby notified that the attached charge of employment discrimination under Title VII of the Civil Rights Act of 1964, as amended, 42 U.S.C. Section 2000e et. seq., has been filed against you.

No action is required on your part at this time. However, your attention is directed to:

(1) Section 1601.15 of the Commission's Procedural Regulations which provides that persons charged with employment discrimination, such as yourself, may submit a statement of position or evidence with respect to the allegations contained in this charge. If you wish to submit such information in writing it will be made a part of the file and will be considered at the time we investigate this charge. Telephone communication cannot be made a part of the record.

(2) Section 1602.14 of the Commission's Regulations which requires the preservation of all personnel records relevant to this charge until a final disposition of this charge is made; and

(3) Section 704(a) of the Civil Rights Act which prohibits retaliation.

For future correspondence on this matter, please use the charge number shown above.

Enclosure: Copy of charge

CERTIFICATION. I hereby certify that I mailed the original of this notice to the addressee herein and attached a copy of the charge referenced herein.

DATE	EEOC EMPLOYEE *(Signature)*

EEOC FORM SEP 77 131-A   FILE COPY a copy of the letter or statement provided to the regional office of E.E.O.C. to which the complaint was directed.

When one receives such a notice, the first action that must be taken is advising the organization's attorneys, for at this point, a legal matter has developed. As soon as possible, meetings must be held with attorneys and their advice must be abided. It is beyond imagination that an organization would attempt to pursue such matters without advice of legal counsel.

The following actions and activities and/or other considerations are advised then in the case of receipt of such a formal notice of charge.

Review of Prior Events. A formal notice of charge is never a complete surprise to the organization. In any case, the charge(s) are first reviewed, a statement of explanation is rendered, and tentative defense is begun. Attorneys are briefed and they will know precisely what kind of questions to pose in that review.

The Response. Although the second paragraph of the formal notice states specifically that, "No action is required on your part at this time," it is advisable for the notice to be acknowledged. Such a letter should state only that the organization or the person named acknowledges receipt of the notice and pledges full and complete cooperation in pursuing satisfactory resolution.

The Role of Counsel. Legal counsel should handle the entire matter calling upon the organization's officers and administrators as it sees fit—we advise that attorneys should draft or approve the initial response and all subsequent correspondence. It is equally important that attorneys have previous experience with such matters and, if not, recommend a firm or others who have.

Accessibility to Information. Although pledging full cooperation, attorneys should advise, or be present, when any investigators arrive, and the ground rules should be spelled out and understood. The content of the files and their accessibility are complex in matters of law. It is only good sense to have competent legal advice.

The Circumstances of Formal Charges. As we have indicated, it is difficult to predict the circumstances wherein a formal E.E.O.C. charge will be brought, or for that matter a charge under any of the other regulations applicable.

Experience suggests, however, that whenever an organization must phase out portions of its ongoing activities as with the closing of schools (because of budget cuts or declining clientele services, or changes in organizational purpose), proposed reductions in the work force may be accompanied by individual or "class action" complaints of discrimination. (A "class action" complaint is one filed by several aggrieved employees.)

In the process of phasing out personnel, any organization always tries to transfer some of its work force to other units. But when all personnel cannot be utilized, procedures effected for transfer should be thoughtful. Intraorganizational advertisements of the jobs must be distributed or otherwise posted publicly and announced, and whatever policies are operable should be reviewed at the outset to determine that they conform to the affirmative action plan. The affirmative action officer needs to be involved in all such decisions. Often, the system will want to save the "top" people in the phased out program, and these people may well be white males. Management decisions should not reflect fear of an E.E.O.C. suit, but organizations that receive considerable federal support must recognize that they are targets for action. In retaining or terminating personnel, be sure that the qualifications for existing positions are well stated and that the opportunity for consideration (application) is widely known.

Time and Cost. Charges brought on the basis of discrimination, no matter how seemingly groundless, can be expensive to defend and can drag on for months. Where the organization can demonstrate that it followed the rules, charges are likely to be expedited rapidly and dismissed, particularly when the substance of the charge seems to indicate favoritism. Favoritism is not illegal, and when it can be demonstrated that others of the class have advanced, been hired, and otherwise provided equal access and treatment, favoritism can be defended.

It is also not unlikely that somewhere in that process some pressure will be brought to agree to some financial settlement. Corporations have been known to make financial settlements even when they were convinced they did nothing wrong or illegal but wanted to avoid any further publicity. Scholastic institutions or other nonprofit organizations may also be approached for some financial settlement, but an appealing "cash" settlement depends on the ability of the organization to pay. If the decision goes against the organization, back pay and/or restoration of status may be required, and that is always likely to be even more costly.

Clearly, then, consideration of workable policies carefully followed is the best defense against the damaging circumstances of formalized charges.

SUMMARY

We began this chapter by suggesting that, while collective action and affirmative action are not directly related in the concerns of institutional administration (except that these phenomena are a large part of the fabric of personnel management), these emerging sets of activities reflect the tensions that are building between the norms that govern the bureaucratic-economic "system," on the one hand, and the norms of individual self-actualization, on the other.

In the framework of school systems, for example, the role of technology, the changing culture, and the conflicts of individual freedom and equality must be reconciled. It is useful for the institutional administrator to study the conservative theoretical expositions of, for example, Robert Nisbet,[21] as well as those that are analytically challenging, as with Daniel Bell,[22] and those that are philosophically optimistic, as with Lionel Trilling,[23] and those that treat the attitudes and values of working people themselves, as with Studs Terkel.[24] There are many others of course, but it is always useful for us to try to see much more than what is immediately around us.

EXERCISES

1. You, as superintendent, have an appointment at 10 A.M. tomorrow morning to meet with officials from the Federal Amalgamation of Education Employees, a national union, to discuss procedures for organizing (or trying to) a union local in your system. How do you prepare for it?

2. You are on your way to the seventh consecutive board of education meeting in four days. There is no agreement on a teachers' contract because they are demanding an 18 percent salary increase (which is down from an original demand for 25 percent) and have indicated that it is their final offer. The district does not have 18 percent available, and the only way it could be provided is through a 10-mill tax-level increase. Under law in your state, the board has the authority to levy up to that level without a ballot, but if it does, it will have no other opportunities for revenue, and the general revenue from real property is declining.

3. In a relatively small school system, you have been asked to allow a "check off" on the salary for the payment of education association dues; there is no problem with doing so within the capacity of your accounting system. Two arguments prevail on you by your staff. (1) Do it: It will demonstrate good faith and will cost you nothing and will give you an advantage in, if nothing else, goodwill. (2) Don't do it: Save it as a concession in the next bargaining session. You will have to make a recommendation to the board—which way will you go?

[21]Robert Nisbet, *The Twilight of Authority* (New York: Oxford University Press, 1975).
[22]Bell, op. cit.
[23]Lionel Trilling, *Beyond Culture* (New York: Viking Press, 1965).
[24]Studs Terkel, *Working* (New York: Pantheon Books, 1972).

4. In a "professional" negotiation session, teachers have demanded that their organization be consulted and have "significant influence" on the selection of a new assistant superintendent. Does the recent *Yeshiva* decision have any bearing on this matter?

5. As a principal of a large high school, you are invited to make a presentation to the principals' council in a neighboring large suburban school system regarding the issue of whether principals should have their salaries attached as an "index" to the teachers' salary thus enabling them to hitch-hike on teachers' bargaining efforts. You want to present both sides. What advantages and disadvantages will you list in your notes?

6. As part of phasing out an instructional unit due to declining need and resources, you, as assistant superintendent for instruction, have had to terminate two of the five professionals employed; you were able to retain three by transferring them to other positions, but the two persons terminated are females and they have filed a class action Equal Employment Opportunity Commission complaint against you for discrimination. The three persons retained in the system are males. What do you need to be prepared to do about this?

7. In a search committee you have appointed, you happen to overhear one of the members say to another at a coffee break in a small lounge (and in the presence of others who could also easily hear) that they know who they had already decided to recommend so why go "through the motions." What is your reaction?

8. You are the female administrative assistant to an "old-line" traditional superintendent noted for running a "tight ship." He never tires of waxing eloquently about the intrusion of senseless federal regulations and, on several occasions has "needled" you about your having joined "the boys' team." Now he has asked you to assume the additional function of affirmative action officer, but you are not convinced that he takes that assignment seriously. He obviously does respect your competence and he is an able administrator. What should you do about it?

9. A female physical education teacher who also serves as girls' track coach in the high school where you are the assistant principal angrily informs you that she has been advised that her team cannot attend a particular scheduled meet. She has learned that the main reason is that the boys' team has a chance to attend a regional (previously unscheduled) meet and there are not enough resources to allow both. As assistant principal, you have some responsibility for physical education, dramatics, and student publications—it is through this relationship that you are contacted. In the back of your mind, some notions about Title IX are provoked, but you have real authority in the athletic program. What would be appropriate ways of dealing with this matter?

SUGGESTED REFERENCES

American Association of School Administrators. *The School Administrator and Negoti-ation*. Washington, D.C.: The Association, 1968.

American Association of School Administrators. *Critical Incidents in Negotiation*. Washington, D.C.: The Association, 1971.

Castetter, W. B. *The Personnel Function in Educational Administration,* Third Edition. New York: Macmillan Publishing Co., Inc., 1981. Chapter 15.

Davey, Harold W. *Contemporary Collective Bargaining,* Third Edition. Englewood Cliffs, N.J.: Prentice-Hall, Inc., 1972.

Doherty, Robert E., Editor. *Public Access: Citizens and Collective Bargaining in the Public Schools*. Ithaca, N.Y.: New York State School of Industrial and Labor Relations, 1879.

Garber, Lee O., and Newton Edwards. *The Law Governing School Board Members and School Board Meetings*. Danville, Ill.: Interstate Printers and Publishers, 1963.

Lieberman, Myron. *Bargaining*. Chicago: Teach 'Em, Inc., 1979.

Perry, Charles R., and Wesley Wildman. *The Impact of Negotiations in Public Education: The Evidence from the Schools*. Worthington, Ohio: Charles A. Jones Publishing Co., 1970.

Chapter 9

The Fiscal Aspects
of Educational Management

INTRODUCTION

How much is education worth? Such a question always has two possible meanings: What is education "worth" as a financial value (as in "How much is Mr. So-and-so worth?") and what is education worth intrinsically? Either way, the question is unanswerable. One only knows that education is most certainly worthy and that it is a terribly costly enterprise.

In 1980, even with a strong commitment for a balanced federal budget, President Carter's recommended fiscal 1981 education budget alone came to $15.5 billion. So what education "costs" is almost as impossible to understand as what-education-is-worth is impossible to explain. Yet, when considering expenditures for education in *all* spheres—public, private, preschool through graduate and professional schools, "training" in the industrial and corporate sector, and continuing education for adults in nontraditional patterns—the total represents a sizable hunk of America's total gross national product. Various estimates range from 9 to 12 percent.

And yet again, there is good basis upon which to argue that not enough support is provided and unquestionably that, even with what funds are provided, dramatic inequities prevail. Moreover, it is clear that under the Reagan administration, the federal contribution to education will be quite a bit less than at any time since 1950. The proposed cuts came in two phases; in February of 1980 it was announced that there would be a 20% cut in 1982 fiscal year dollars, and in March, the president announced a 25% cut that was to take effect in

September of 1981. Needless to say, since these were general reductions, some schools were hit much harder.[1]

THE ECONOMICS OF EDUCATION

The economics of education is almost as mysterious as the economics of the country; no institutionalized aspect of American society is more pervasive than our system of schools and colleges. Few lives are untouched by some form of schooling. Even for those thousands of Americans who must, by job and service, spend time outside the United States, "schooling" is still an important aspect of their lives. Through the elaborated "dependent schools" systems in the departments of Defense and State, as well as proprietary "American schools" supported by private interests, educational access and process remains a major consideration even among expatriated citizens.

The overall economic commitment to education and at all levels in *only* the public sector has been no better exemplified over the past twenty years than by the fact that the proportion of our gross national product (GNP) dedicated to public education alone has increased from about 4 percent in 1960 to almost 6 percent in 1980. Even allowing for an accelerating rate of inflation over the later years of that twenty-year span, the fact remains that education, as a funded endeavor, and at all levels of government, has significantly increased as a fiscal reflection of national commitment.

Education and the Economy in a General Perspective

Even given an enormously increased proportion of public resources allocated to education at all levels and recognizing that there are defensible arguments for still more resources for education, the general status of the overall economy needs to be considered as an important context within which any discussion of the fiscal dimensions of education must proceed.

Inflation and Energy

The key concepts confronting the American economy in the late 1970s and, surely, into the decade of the 1980s are the related ones of energy and inflation: Almost all aspects of costs increased, including those for food, health services,

[1]D. G. Savage, "Washington Report," *Phi Delta Kappan,* Vol. 62, no. 9 (May 1981), p. 621.

and other aspects of consumership, yet the big sources of accelerating inflation were attributable to energy (oil) and construction.

By spring 1980, the cost of gasoline had reached $1.35 per gallon and the interest rates on housing finances had risen to about 15 percent. The hopes of many middle-income Americans for homes of their own were increasingly shattered; moreover, school districts, with heavy dependence on local real property tax revenues, were also facing difficult times. By the same token, the dramatic increases in fuel costs both for regular heating and for cooling as well as for transportation eroded public school budgets even further.

In an inflationary economy, prices and wages tend to escalate much faster than fundamental wealth justifies. One very important factor in this process is the concept of "growth," which has always been presumed to catch up with and check inflation. When a rate of growth is no longer being maintained, inflation tends to accelerate.

Economic theorists now are questioning not whether growth is or is not likely in a particular sector of the economy but whether growth is, in fact, even a reasonable assumption on which to base economic theory.

To understand these currently vexing economic realities, particularly as they relate to such public enterprises as schools, we should examine the enormous changes that have occurred over the past half-century in the interventions of government in the economy.

The Public Household

Of the three major systems in economic functions, two are classic: the "domestic household" and the "market structure." In relatively recent times, a third and increasingly more important one has emerged that is variously known as the "public sector" or the "public household."[2]

Bell defines "the public household" as follows:[3]

as expressed in the government budget [it] is the management of state revenues and expenditures. More broadly, it is the agency for the satisfaction of public needs and public wants, as against private wants. It is the arena for the register of political forces in the society.

The public household is a mixture of the two older traditions; that is, whereas the domestic household was oriented primarily to *needs* and the market economy

---

[2]See, for example, Daniel Bell, *Cultural Contradictions of Capitalism* (New York: Basic Books, Inc., 1976), pp. 220–282; Richard Musgrove, *The Theory of Public Finance* (New York: McGraw-Hill, 1959); and William Niskanen, *Bureaucracy and Representative Government* (Chicago: Aldine, 1971).

[3]Bell, op. cit., p. 221.

oriented to *wants,* the public household has tended, in public fashion, to cater to both. In an economy oriented primarily toward providing only needed services, whether of farmers or gatherers or even artisans who produced only enough to supply their needs either directly (by consuming all of what they produce) or indirectly by trading or selling, but in which case, the purpose was self-sufficiency, that reflects the classical concept of the domestic household.[4]

On the other hand, the emergence of the *market economy* is primarily an invention of the Industrial Revolution, and even though it is frequently perceived as a mechanism of Western free enterprise, it is, as a mechanism, also prevalent in totalitarian systems because the "market" concept is founded in the satisfaction of wants rather than of needs. Since wants are infinite, the economic principles of the market economy phenomenon are continued production and efficiency of costs so that ever greater expanding wants can be satisfied and invented.

The ideology that has grown up with the development of the "market economy" into the twentieth century quite naturally has placed major emphasis on individualism and thus on limited government. "That government is best which governs least" means, in the market context, that the private sector dominates and that taxation or government interventions discourage individual initiative and interfere with "natural" supply and demand wants. For at least 200 years, another ideology—principally an ethical one (the Protestant ethic)—had provided a form of restraint on the hedonism that market economics promotes. Again, Bell states[5]

In bourgeois society, psychology replaced biology as the basis of "need" satisfaction. It is no accident, so to speak, that the philosophy of bourgeois society was utilitarianism, a hedonistic calculation of pleasure and pain. . . . In Aristotle's terms, *wants* replaced *needs*—and wants are unlimited and insatiable. When the Protestant ethic, which had served to limit sumptuary (though not capital) accumulation, was sundered from modern bourgeois society, only the hedonism remained. [Thus]—the engine which began to drive the socio-economic system (in its Soviet Communist as well as its Western bourgeois form) has been the prodigal idea of private wants and unlimited ends.

The New Tasks of the Public Household. The functions of government with reference to providing for the "general welfare" have a long history (in the United States, the adoption of Henry Clay's "American system" with its emphasis on internal improvements such as roads and canals, in the early nineteenth century is an example). And insofar as governments procured those "needs" that persons could not, the last fifty years have seen the full development of the

---

[4]The current emphasis on "appropriate technology" is, in a sense, a return to much of what is embodied in domestic household as an economic concept. See, for example, Paul DeVore, *Technology: An Introduction* (Worcester, Mass.: Davis Publications, Inc., 1980), pp. 369–375.

[5]Bell, op. cit., p. 224.

public household concept in a much more profound fashion, in large part as a result of economic measures undertaken during the great Depression of the 1930s.

In the post–World War II years, another major thrust involved government more intimately in the support and subsidization of science and technology. It was with this additional intervention that schools and education became a federal concern in a direct and dramatic fashion. Prior to the enactment of the old National Defense Education Act, the fears of federal control so justifiably held by the private economic sector had precluded anything more than quite indirect federal support of education. But when the "national defense" is at issue, how does one argue?

Then, the great social reform movements of the 1960s—from civil rights and environmental activities to health, education, welfare, agriculture, and housing—launched the central government into economic ventures with explicit social policy implications. According to Daniel Bell,[6]

today the public household is more than a third sector; increasingly in the modern polity it absorbs the other two. And the major aspect of the public household is the centrality of the budget, the level of government revenues and expenditures for reallocation and redress. How much the government shall spend, and for whom, obviously is the major political question of the next decade.

Technology and the Limits of Growth

Among academic economists, there is an increasing number who talk about steady-state conditions and who call themselves "bioeconomists." These scholars emphasize the importance of recognizing the fallacies in presumptions of infinite growth. They are principally concerned with renewable resources and hold that growth must be rethought in terms of intra- and infrasystem changes. These scholars also emphasize the necessities for change in human behavior and conceptualization about the exhaustibility of resources rather than their inexhaustibility. A key concept in this contemporary thought is that of a managed and controlled technology. The alternative, otherwise, is clear and frightening: if present trends of increased production, and consumption, increasing population worldwide, concomitant environmental carelessness, and the remarkable, almost exponential, consumption of nonrenewable resources are not changed, we face certain disaster. Hysterical overstatement? Probably not.

The United States alone consumes more energy than does any other country in the world. As Barry Commoner has pointed out,

[6]Ibid., pp. 226–227.
[7]Barry Commoner, "The Energy Crisis—All of a Piece," *The Center Magazine*, Vol. 8, no. 2 (March–April 1975), 27.

The projected production of total United States energy is expected to rise from about 57,000 trillion Btu in 1971 to about 92,000 trillion Btu in 1985 (an increase of about sixty percent) and requiring that annual expenditures for energy rise from about $26.5 billion to $158 billion over that period—an increase of about 390 percent. This trend coupled with the growing inefficiency in the use of energy, means that, if we follow the present course, energy production will consume an increasing fraction of the total capital available for investment in new enterprises including factories, homes, schools, and hospitals.

Another way of putting this matter is to recognize that, based on energy demands in 1979 (and calculating these demands in the exponential pattern that historical linearity empirically predicts), by 1985 energy production (and consumption) alone will devour as much as 80 percent of all available capital.

This is not an overstatement. Consider the following explanation:[8]

To illustrate the impact of exponential growth on non-renewable resources . . . If the amount of energy consumed increases at a rate of 5% per year, then in 14 years the amount of energy used per year will have doubled. This is known as the doubling time. In 23 years the amount of energy consumed per year will quadruple; in three doubling periods the increase will be eightfold. The folly of promoting high growth rates in a finite environment is evident. Yet, most citizens, businessmen, and industrialists are proponents of a 5% to 6% growth rate per year, believing this is the only way to assure a viable society. Consider, however, what happens to population growth in a finite environment and whether we may have reached the point of no return.

Professor DeVore has cited physicist Albert Bartlett's illustration of exponentiality to support his cogent arguments for the necessity of reshaping consumptive behavior (and to support the need for a bioeconomics theory of a reordered economy, and a different conceptualization of modern technology):[9]

Bacteria grow by division so that one bacterium become 2, 2 become 4 and 4 become 8, etc. If we place one bacterium that has a doubling time of 1 minute in a bottle at 11:00 A.M. and observe that the bottle is full at 12:00 noon, when was the bottle half full? More importantly, if you were living in a finite environment and the coal, oil, land, air quality and water were being used up or despoiled at the same exponential rate when would you first realize there was a problem? Would it be five minutes before all resources and space were occupied, 11:55 A.M., when only ¹⁄₃₂ of the resources and space had been used? Or would it be at 2 minutes before noon when only ¼ of the resources and space had been used? What time is it as far as our own global society is concerned? Doubling

---

[8]Paul DeVore, "Appropriate Technology and Education," address at the American Association of Colleges for Teacher Education, Dallas, Texas, February 27, 1980. Used with permission. Also see, DeVore, *Technology: An Introduction* (Worcester, Mass.: Davis Publishing Co., 1980). op. cit., p. 369.

[9]For this illustration, DeVore draws on Albert Bartlett, "Forgotten Fundamentals of the Energy Crisis," *American Journal of Physics*, Vol. 49, no. 9 (September 1978). See DeVore, op. cit. (DeVore's paper is available through the ERIC Clearinghouse on Higher Education.)

time for the bottle, a finite environment like the spaceship earth, illustrates the significance of the problem of growth rates and limited environment and resources. We would probably not even be aware of the problem at 11:59, one minute before noon, because the space occupied by our population would only be occupying one half of the total. Yet, in one doubling time, (one minute) all space would be filled! There would be no more.

The Hazards of "Spin-offs"

Quite clearly, these trends that only a half-century ago were eulogized in a romantic literature of "progress" in private industrialization and were trends both urged and advocated as the fundamental source of America's (and of Western man's) greatness have become questionable. There was even a sort of patriotism attached to rampant growth and resource exploitation whereby the Western world but particularly America, through the benefactions of private enterprise, generated an enormously expanding and attractive level of living and, with it, opportunities for jobs and security, free public education, systematic protection of individual freedom, and accessibility to the "good life" for almost anyone who could internalize the values and ethics of individual initiative and discipline.

It was understandable because it did, in fact, "work." It worked, however, like a telephone works or a carburetor or a computerized linear program works. What is now becoming painfully obvious is that it "worked" at a cost that has "come home to roost." We have fully enjoyed the fruits of that ideology; now the test of our fiber as a people may rest on the extent to which we are capable of a discipline that promotes our capacity to survive its new implications.

The Challenge to Schools

Quite apart from the administrative and fiscally oriented conditions that these rather recent realities require of this nation's educational custodians, it is vital that we emphasize a significant policy prescription at this point in this discussion: for instructional leadership—in curriculum reform and in all those aspects of the frequently unsaid but nevertheless quite authoritative power of the schools to "indoctrinate" and shape behavior—school administrators at all levels of the enterprise must advocate and otherwise bring influence to bear on re-educating the youth of America toward a realization that there are limitations in what we can exploit, that there is need for our consumptive and acquisitive behavior to change. Such a "policy" is best founded in a longer view of civilization's survival. The "general welfare" clause in the U.S. Constitution does more than merely advocate the protection of rights of the living at some moment in time; it also now means that we must give more serious thought to future generations and certainly, while we have always made some sanctimonious noises about that on ceremonial occasions, the bourgeois attitudes that have presumed that all wants are capable of fulfillment must now give way to a more disciplined pattern of survival.

This is probably the most critical measure of long-term effective educational leadership, and although we will discuss it in a different fashion in Part III of this text, without exaggeration, the ability to fashion a different and realistic notion of what shall make this great nation survive probably rests more on the leadership of its schools than on any other single cultural invention. It is a terribly responsible leadership role; the evidence is accruing that the implications of assuming that leadership require a long and responsible view.

It is no exaggeration as well to assert that the long-term future of our survival as a viable social-democratic system rests not all that much on presidents or Congresses or governors or fiduciary policymakers, but on the nature of our enlightened indoctrination of the young. School administrators *must think about that;* they must not get too caught up in the day-to-day "administrivia" not to think beyond the "now" and this year. Leadership must be exerted in behalf of the long view. It is among the most difficult of postures to assume and among the easiest to prescribe. To some extent, it is a matter of managing time; to another, of managing attitude; to still a greater extent, perhaps, of the quality and nature of preparation. In any case, however, the importance of only thinking about these seemingly large matters and talking about them, and provoking others to think and talk about them, is an aspect of leadership that is too easily dismissed in the pressures of the daily working lives of institutional managers.

Accordingly, leadership requires thoughtful consideration of its impact on the total enterprise; leaders who do not consider any of the "eternal verities" have little, or even negative, impact on prolongation of ethical choices. And after all, it is ethical choice that characterizes the validity of effective leadership. We will return to the resources issue again—and still again.

THE PATTERN OF FISCAL STRUCTURE

As was pointed out in early chapters, public school systems are quasi-corporations; they derive their financial support from local, state, and federal jurisdictions.

Certainly the importance of understanding as much as possible about the general economy is useful to any prospective or practicing administrator, and here (and in Part III) we provide some useful perspectives on that. Still, we also recognize that the need for more explicit comment about unique fiscal matters is paramount. Even though any introductory text can only touch upon these aspects of concern, we turn now to a discussion of the parameters of fiscal concern that are of particular interest to such professions. In doing so, we emphasize the presumption that more technical and operational aspects of concepts of school finance and budgeting will be discussed in courses dedicated to those competencies in advanced curricula of educational administration.

Funding Patterns

The earliest pattern of funding for schools was based on relatively crude censuses of eligible persons; in other words, if the law specified persons eligible for education as those between the ages of 6 and 18, each school district conducted a "census" and submitted that data to the state. The state authorities, in turn, calculated the total numbers, divided that figure by its "school fund," and then allocated that many dollars per capita to its various districts according to the numbers of pupils. This system has become known in parlance as "flat grants."

During the late nineteenth and early twentieth centuries, this pattern prevailed. It enjoyed certain advantages, and it encouraged certain abuses. It was relatively easy to "count" persons who might not be qualified, and geography and demography gradually made such simplistic systems unmanageable.

The next major innovation was some form of pro-rated system that adjusted flat grants according both to some local area's ability to pay and/or effort to support (based on local initiative of taxation and real property assessments); thus, the grand concept of "equalization" was introduced. Equalization is still a major component of some state-aid formulas. The fundamental premise of equalization is a mechanistic adjustment of various school district's ability versus effort compared with a "foundation" of acceptable minimum quality.

As a consequence of these manipulations, various programmatic formulas were developed particularly in the 1950s based on the notion that there should be some designated "foundation" of educational support available to all youth regardless of local circumstances as a state responsibility and, beyond that any "local" district could go higher given its commitment and resources.

Although such "foundation finance programs" were typically associated with a particular geographic region, and were given little attention in those states in which the majority of financial support for schools came from local revenue usually as a tax on property, during the 1950s, the general emphasis in school finance was directed toward developing these complicated formulas. The bottom line in all such considerations had to do with how much of what was needed would or could be provided by the state (for schools are constitutionally assigned as a state responsibility) and how much should be provided by a local school district's constituency.

From this activity at least two patterns emerged: one based on the presumption that the bulk of support would come from the state and the other based on the presumption that the bulk of support would come from local taxation. For a variety of reasons—historical, political, economic, and cultural—the pattern of state support predominated in the southern states (which included the border states of Kentucky, Missouri, West Virginia, and Oklahoma), whereas local support characterized the "upper midwestern" states. Western states (California, Oregon, Colorado, Washington, and Arizona) were mixed in their funding formulas.

In the southern states, however, generalizations are more defensible as some variation of the foundation programs prevailed. In a particularly important book published in 1960 (at the edge of the period we have characterized as active), an evaluation of the foundation program concept appears as follows:[10]

> In practical terms, the foundation program concept implies and involves a plan for financing schools that requires equity for taxpayers as well as equity and adequacy of opportunity for students. It means that the resources of each state—and, by implication, of the nation—must be used to provide the financial support required to meet basic educational needs. Thus, the most wealthy citizens and the people in the most wealthy communities should be expected to make as much financial effort to support the foundation program . . . as the least wealthy.

The concept itself, according to Johns and Morphet, goes back to a 1923 study in New York State conducted by George Strayer and Robert Haig of Teachers College, Columbia University:[11]

> To carry into effect the principle of "equalization of educational opportunity" and "equalization of school support," as commonly understood, it would be necessary (1) to establish schools or make other arrangements sufficient to furnish the children in every locality within the state with equal educational opportunities up to some prescribed minimum; (2) to raise the funds necessary for this purpose by local or state taxation adjusted in such manner as to bear upon the people in all localities at the same rate in relation to their taxpaying ability; and (3) to provide adequately either for the supervision and control of all the schools, or for their direct administration, by a state department of education.

What happened, of course, is that the *idea* of foundation programs was adapted to the particular concerns of states quite different from New York. Of course, it is no accident that, among the educational leadership in many states, the idea of some rational combination of state and local support was becoming increasingly evident as a necessity, since both compulsory education and high

[10]R. L. Johns and Edgar Morphet, *Financing the Public Schools* (Englewood Cliffs, N.J.: Prentice-Hall, 1960), p. 263.
[11]George Strayer and R. M. Haig, *The Financing of Education in the State of New York* (New York: Macmillan, 1923), p. 173, cited in Johns and Morphet, op. cit., p. 265.

school graduation were becoming increasingly common. After 1930, if this many persons were going to be literally taken out of the mainstream of noninstitutional life until they were about 17 or 18 years of age, some improved pattern of "subsidy" had to be invented. It should be remembered that up until about World War I a "common" school education of about eight years was the almost universal pattern and that was more especially true in the South; thus persons who achieved that level of education were, until the mid-1920s, universally presumed to be "ready" for the world of work. Because post–World War I years were economically chaotic, many young men and women began to attend public high schools because, first, there was little else available for them to do, and, second, almost as a self-fulfilling prophecy, those who did so enjoyed an enormous advantage in occupational placement.

By the time the Strayer–Haig study was conducted, the numbers of youngsters attending secondary schools, plus the requirements for more adequately accommodating them, created significant need to re-examine ways for funding programs.

The Impact of the Depression of the 1930s

Not too long after the attainment of a "high school education" became something of a norm, the United States entered its worse economic depression. "Education," as both an idea and a sort of public utility, became suddenly prized. This period from about 1930–1939 demonstrated that education (as defined then in terms of a high school diploma) became a prerequisite for upward social mobility, and its fundamental economic as well as ideological value increased enormously. It was, interestingly, the great American Depression that gave to education a quality of universal value that it still retains to this day. And it was as a consequence of this perceived importance that school districts were able to persuade constituents to tax themselves more strenuously to support it.

In the "newer" portions of this country—in the great cities and in the Midwest—that support came more from local initiative than from the state itself. In the South, where a tradition of more centralized state jurisdictions in most matters of social service had developed, there was a tendency for dependence on state control and state administration in schools; thus, in those states, there was an earlier recognition of centralized state responsibility for the fiscal support of schools. This was, to some extent, complemented by the fact that property rights were held with a somewhat different attitude, on the one hand, and the growth of cities was not so much characterized by significant proportions of southern European immigration, on the other. In other words, there was not nearly so much of "new Americanization" in the South. Some basis for this centralized view also is at least somewhat attributable to an older quasi-aristocratic tradition in the Deep South whereby the general attitude toward blacks as well as a still strong (even in 1930) agrarian-elite value system dominated, and these conditions and attitudes probably had some apparent influence on preconceived attitudes of incoming immigrants from Europe between 1870 and 1920. Many preferred the more northern states.

The influx of immigrants beginning in the late nineteenth century and continuing well into the twentieth was characterized by a southern European flavor; many of these were Roman Catholic, working-class people with great motivation to improve the opportunities for their children. As a consequence, the idea of making significant effort on behalf of the support of public schools was both meaningful to and accepted by them. Public school programs responded to their needs and prospered in those regions where they settled; and, as we have mentioned, they tended to settle in the industrialized parts of the United States where more varied work was available.

In the Deep South and in most of the border states, education was still much flavored by an elitist view and the system of "common schools" was slower in developing.

At the turn of the century, in 1903, the condition of public education in the South was characterized by John Carlisle Kilgo, then president of Trinity College (which later became Duke University), as follows:[12]

> There are two prominent difficulties that obstruct the growth of education in the South. The first is the lack of an educational conscience; and the second is the lack of sound educational doctrines and correct educational ideals. . . . The material provisions made for education show that it is not regarded as serious work.

Economic difficulties (hard times were once called "panics" and later referred to as "depressions" and now still more refined as "recessions") did not seem to have a dramatic effect on public education in the South until the 1930s simply because "education" as a public venture was pretty badly depressed regardless of the cycle of good and bad times.

There were, of course, school funds that had built up, but the political culture was such that almost any kind of public fund was fair game for abuse and irresponsible management. In Kentucky, for example, one governor "borrowed" the school fund for other purposes and then, faced with the need to restore it, literally burned the paper notes of that debt on the capitol steps with the explanation that a state cannot owe itself money! In the period from the end of the war between the states to the 1920s, it was common for the leadership at the state level—the state departments of education superintendents—to be ill prepared for the function, to be little more than "clerks" with almost no staff

---

[12]John Carlisle Kilgo, "Some Phases of Southern Education," in William Baskerville Hamilton, *Fifty Years of the South Atlantic Quarterly* (Durham, N.C.: Duke University Press, 1952), pp. 39 and 40.

other than a secretary, and who were frequently politically deserving Protestant ministers who carried out their duties as only part-time administrators. While some among these were extraordinary men who accomplished much in the face of overwhelming odds, most were not very effective.

The Flat Grant Pattern. Thus until well into the twentieth century, the school fund was distributed according to the flat grant pattern. Quite obviously, this procedure was ripe for potential abuse. Frequently, school-aged youngsters "counted" in one county's allocations actually lived close enough to the "line" that they attended a different county's schools. Moreover, since the data were based on census, actual attendance was obscured, and many districts were paid to keep youngsters out of school! If the census provided funds based on 1,000 children but only 500 actually attended schools, this meant that there was twice as much money to spend on those 500 who attended. Thus, if a district could encourage children to attend schools in a neighboring district while it received the flat grant based on their "census," it had more dollars per pupil to provide.

The "Formula" Movement in School Finance. To recapitulate, then, as the demand for schooling increased, with more stringent laws coming into existence to protect children from labor abuse and to mandate compulsory school attendance, it became equally clear that not only in the South but throughout the nation, reforms in methods of financing public education had to be effected.

In all such reforms even into contemporary times, some types of "formulas" had to be invented that took into consideration the following significant concepts:

1. *Equalization.* Obviously some areas had more basic wealth than did others, yet all children were entitled to schooling. How, then, could support be equitably shared?
2. *Effort and ability.* Variables in the process of attempting to develop reasonable patterns of financing schools had to consider both the *ability* of some parts of a state to "pay taxes" as compared with other areas' commitment to support schools in terms of *effort;* thus, if a particular district had a relatively low per-capita tax base but taxed itself accordingly quite heavily, that was greater effort. The issues of ability to pay, and effort exerted, were important variables in any formulas.
3. *Foundation and partnership.* No better terminology seems available to us to present the idea that the financial support for schools had to be based on some reasonable definition of a "pooling" of both state and local resources. Thus, if the local community wanted to provide some "quality" of education beyond that which was otherwise defined as basic or "minimal," it could do so by taxing itself above the required amount accordingly. It was in virtue of this notion that many such foundation plans became known as "minimum foundations." In any case, this idea was forwarded in a variety of ways so

that a formula provided for opportunities to go beyond what was defined statutorily as fundamentally adequate and for which a school district had to pay a greater portion.

Participatory Patterns. Although almost all patterns of combined support between local district and state funding showed serious discrepancies, some effective resolutions were worked out. Some states (Michigan, for example) developed what was generally known as "participatory millage"; this meant, in effect, that, if any school district expected to "participate" in state aid, it had to levy a prescribed millage ratio. If such a district levied, say 10 mills on local property for schools, it was eligible to receive all of its authorized state aid; but if it levied only 9 mills, it was eligible to receive only 90 percent, or if 8 mills, only 80 percent, and so forth. However, if any district levied less than, say, 7 mills, it was eligible to receive no state aid. In a few situations some districts did not really need to levy more than 3 or 4 mills locally to generate enough funds to support local schools regardless of any state contributions, simply because within their district's boundaries were major industrial establishments or major public utilities that provided the lion's share of their district's tax support. Sometimes, however, the less prosperous neighboring school districts were in trouble because most of those who worked in the industrial establishments did not live in those districts but in the school districts that bordered them. These and other problems finally resulted in changing the plan.

This is one example of the important dimensions of the "equalization" issue. Geography, demography, and sociological factors all contribute to the complexities that school finance formulators confront now and have confronted in the recent past, as they wrestle with the dual problems of ensuring some acknowledged level of quality education for all children and yet[13]

provide funds for schools in such a way that those districts least able to finance a program of essential educational opportunities . . . with local funds receive proportionately more money from state resources than the more able districts.

Geographical circumstance is the easiest factor to understand in this dilemma; some parts of states have few landed resources; such areas may have marginal agricultural productivity and little industrialization and, thus, little wealth regardless of whatever measures might be utilized to assess that wealth. On the other hand, many children may go to their schools. At the same time, some school districts may enjoy a disproportionate number of people who send their children to private or parochial schools and, again (because *all* residents pay taxes), more funds are available per capita to children attending public schools.

[13]Johns and Morphet, op. cit., p. 271.

These kinds of difficulties have become exacerbated in recent years by sociological phenomena that have resulted in curious special problems for urban and metropolitan school districts—specifically with reference to "white flight" but going beyond that trend. For whatever reasons, the urban areas that, until about 1965 or so, enjoyed relatively wealthy revenue bases for school funding have come upon hard times due to residential movement out of districts and losses of commercial tax revenues by similar relocations of corporate and industrial businesses. Consequently, whereas twenty years ago, the great urban centers were expected to provide substantial subsidies for "equalization," these districts now require subsidies themselves. Schools in New York City and Cleveland, Ohio are in severe financial crisis. Most very large cities have serious problems in providing government services.

CURRENT STATUS IN SCHOOL FINANCE

The contemporary pattern for financing public schools is now more centralized because the role of the states and the federal establishment have tended to predominate directly, through formulated patterns of subsidy, or indirectly, through interventions by government regulation and/or court determinations.

The Federal Contribution

Beginning in the late 1950s and continuing through the 1960s, federal contributions to the direct support of local school programs have increasingly become part and parcel of local school districts' budgeting procedures. With that, of course, has come significantly increased monitoring of categories of expenditures and increased "auditing" of such funds. At the same time, since state agencies have been allowed more discretion in the applications for, and allocations of, federal dollars, local districts have become more dependent on inadequate local tax-initiated resources and on state and federal dollars as well. As a result, school systems have less autonomy in the allocation of all funds. A consequence of these redistribution patterns is that local school districts have little choice but to lobby more aggressively on behalf of state and federal funding just as they have done previously (and still must do) on behalf of local support.

Aside from the philosophical issues of possible threat to "localized" initiatives, there is the frustrating likelihood that, without continued substantial state and federal support, many large local school districts will have to dramatically curtail programs.

The Passing of the "Local" Public School

We may take some satisfaction in this maturing toward a kind of "national-ization" of the idea of public education, but by the same token, this evolution of nationalization surely characterizes if not the passing, at least some significant dilution of what has seemed among the last truly fundamental opportunities for the "common man" to have direct influence on the nature of his destiny. At present, we must conclude that free and local public schools are no longer quite so "local" or quite so "free" as they were in the past.

Free and Local: Implications of a National Program

As we have pointed out, there is a conviction that holds—and is empirically supported—that "whoever pays will inevitably control." Louis Brownlee pro-posed this principle well over forty years ago, characterizing his conclusions as the "simple truth of history":[14]

It is fundamentally true that the essential control of the administrative process is in the hands of him who holds the purse-strings, and the incessitudes of public finance . . . have completely altered the relationships of local, state, and federal governments with regard to poor relief.

This "simple truth of history" has been challenged persuasively, not so much in terms of its *general* effect but in terms of the "rightness" and productiveness of that effect. In other words, this argument holds that control is essential and moral. It was early pronounced by Mabel Newcomer:[15]

If state revenues are to be returned to the local districts it is desirable that some control should be exercised. For if these funds are not apportioned according to local need there is very real danger that some municipalities, especially those whose local revenues are adequate, will spend their state funds carelessly since these are revenues for which the local officials are not accountable to the local taxpayer.

These comments are more than fifty years old, and no one could have foreseen at that time the extent to which state and federal governments would have intruded into local matters or the extent to which an "accountability" syndrome of auditing activities would have grown up with those centralized funding pat-terns.

[14]Louis Brownlaw, "City Halls to Capitols," *State Government,* Vol. 8 (February 1935), cited in Paul Mort, *Principles of School Administration* (New York: McGraw-Hill, 1946), p. 314.

[15]Mabel Newcomer, "Tendencies in State and Local Finance and Their Relation to State and Local Function," *Political Science Quarterly,* Vol. 43, no. 3 (March 1928), 1–31, cited in Mort, op. cit., p. 315.

What has evolved over those years, and especially since very substantial federal and state support has become the pattern since the late 1950s, is a "terrible dependence" by local school districts on such external funding. Accordingly, no matter how sophisticated certain partnership formulas are, the contribution of federal dollars to local school district budgets have gradually increased to the point that such dollars now reflect about 10 percent of all local school districts' funding. And it is no longer possible for local school districts to function without that additional funding.

Proposition 13 Attitudes

Nothing illustrates this trend better than what we characterize as the Proposition 13 mentality, a term we derive from the State of California's "Proposition 13," which was a drastic popular mandate for local property tax relief. Proposition 13 carried overwhelmingly and resulted in dramatic reductions in tax-supported human services including those for public education. In 1979, a kind of Proposition 13 mentality swept the nation, rejecting school construction bond issues that curtailed operating levies as well as capital outlays.[16]

To some extent as a consequence of these local constraints, efforts to secure still more funding from state and, especially, federal sources increased, and though not without some success, these efforts forced school districts into a still more constrained relationship with the enormous federal establishment.

An important recent study by the Southern Growth Policies Board (SGPB) disclosed that, although the South receives more federal education funds than does the rest of the country, that region spends from all sources quite a bit less per pupil. Recognizing that this general geographic region has more poverty, it nevertheless pays out much less to its needy. Such data are not, in retrospect, particularly surprising, but in terms of schools' funding, some findings are revealing:[17]

In 1976, 38 of 100 southern students dropped out of school, compared to 25 from other regions. Their parents have less education: 42% do not have a high school diploma, compared to 34% overall. Standardized test scores are up especially in reading, but still below national averages. The South leads in the number of children not promoted—over 42% of students are below the appropriate grade for their age.

These facts show up in spite of large federal and state contributions to education budgets. The South receives 13% of its revenues from the U.S. Government. The rest of the country gets 7.4%. Southern schools get another 51% from the state, compared to 41% elsewhere. However, the South spends an average of only $1,468 per pupil, $542 less than the non-Southern states.

[16] In 1970 alone, more than 60 percent of all such referenda were rejected; in 1965, more than 60 percent of all referenda had passed. In 1980, when there were many less referenda as a consequence of generally declining enrollments, still 65 percent of all referenda failed.

[17] See *Education USA*, Vol. 22, no. 25 (February 18, 1980), 188.

In the South, as compared with the non-South, the sources of revenue per pupil are revealing. In the South, state and federal sources contribute 50.8 percent and 13.2 percent, respectively, or a total for decidedly local sources of only 35.9 percent, whereas in the non-South, the decidedly "local" contribution is 51.6 percent and, depending on state and area, that local contribution varies from a bit less than 50 percent to as much as 80 percent.[18]

Relationship of Expenditures to Education Quality

That there is a relationship between the quality of educational programs and their costs is undeniable. However, determining these relationships is difficult to accomplish as measurement of educational quality involves many variables and interactions among them and controlling the variables is almost impossible.

Yet numerous attempts to make such measurements have sometimes been productive. The most tempting criterion for assessing quality is the use of standardized test scores—achievement data. But any attempt to relate test performance to other school variables in a causal fashion has obvious hazards and one open to challenge on the grounds of home and family environment, neighborhood factors, previous student experiences, mobility into and out of schools and neighborhoods, effects of television, and other individual demographic data just to mention some of the more familiar contributing factors.

Regardless of the complexities of such analyses, Johns and Morphet suggest that some generalizations are justified, "on the basis of numerous studies,"[19] among them (1) that today's educational quality is superior to that of the previous generation; (2) that public school quality is at least as good, in general, as that of private and parochial schools; (3) that quality is better where expenditures are higher; and (4) that, even in "higher" spending schools, there "seems to be a strong relationship between expenditures and quality of education."[20]

Again, it is reasonably well established that levels of expenditures correlate consistently with educational quality even though in many cases those factors may be extrapolated into such things as "teacher experience" or "class size" or "school facilities." These types of factors nevertheless reflect costs.

In a more recent analysis of major studies of teacher quality and class size, for example, Bargen and Walberg synthesized twenty-three studies from 1956 through 1972 and concluded that "Nearly all the studies show that per-student expenditures for teachers and teacher-experience or education are significantly associated with student achievement."[21]

It will be noted from the table we have reproduced from the Bargen–Walberg

---

[18]Ibid., p. 188.

[19]Johns and Morphet, op. cit., p. 11.

[20]Ibid., p. 15.

[21]M. Bargen and H. J. Walberg, "School Performance," in H. J. Walberg, ed., *Evaluating Educational Performance* (Berkeley, Calif.: McCutchan, 1974), p. 243.

study (Table 9-1) that teacher salaries and expenditures per pupil were explicitly cited in most of these studies and factors cited in others reflect cost data in one way or another.

The Impact of Inflation

Despite the established long-term conclusion that by whatever criteria utilized expenditures per pupil are the best measure of good school programs and despite, as well, the generalization that today's youngster seems to be better educated than his or her parents were, the contemporary view seems to hold that schooling costs too much vis-à-vis its record of "goodness."

To some extent, the progressively growing rate of inflation now clouds the older stability of correlations between expenditures and quality, on the one hand, and continues to generate both patron discontent and frustration with schools (and other public services), on the other. It was always easy to expect that educational costs would increase as enrollments also increased; yet in the past several years, enrollments in public elementary and secondary schools have been declining while costs have continued to increase and overall quality is more suspect.

Of course, the major villain today is inflation, and the major source of this inflation—the increasing cost of "energy"—impacts schools very directly and heavily. Patrons of schools and taxpayers in general have begun to express their frustrations by literally revolting against "all" government services at the ballot box.

On the heels of the passage of Proposition 13 in California, another initiative was proposed in California—Proposition 9—which, if passed, would have cut that state's income tax in half. As a source of revenue, the California income tax accounts for 25 percent of the total, and cutting that by half would have had enormous implications for the California schools, since about 44 percent of California's state government revenues are utilized for education aid and as much as 80 percent of school district funding comes from state sources.[22]

Lieberman argues for a much more sophisticated "cost-benefit" procedure for education if the trend of citizen rejection of escalating education taxes is going to be reversed. He points out that, in purchasing consumer goods, the individual purchaser can usually discern the relative differences between high and low price immediately. Thus if one buys an expensive luxury automobile as opposed to a "compact," the differences are easily comparable (even though both may be overpriced). However, as a taxpayer, this is seldom the case:[23]

---

[22]See, for example, Myron Lieberman, "Against the Grain," *Phi Delta Kappan* (May 1980), 635–637. Subsequent to this writing, Proposition 9 was defeated in California by a substantial majority.

[23]Ibid., p. 636.

Table 9-1. Major Studies of Teacher Quality and Class Size

Investigator	Grades	Sample	Control Variables	Significant Correlates with Student Achievement
Armor (1972)	6	U.S. schools	SES, background	Teacher salary, verbal ability
Averch and Kiesling (1970)	9	U.S. schools and individuals	SES	Teacher salary, class size
Benson (1965)	5	California schools	SES (district)	Teacher salary
Bowles (1969)	12	U.S. blacks	Background	Teacher verbal ability, education; class size
Bowles and Levin (1968)	12	U.S. individuals	Background	Teacher verbal ability, experience
Burkhead, Fox, and Holland (1967)	12	Chicago and Atlanta schools	Median family income (census), lower-grade achievement	Teacher salary, experience; class size nonsignificant
Cohn (1968)	12	Iowa districts	Prior achievement	Teacher salary; class size nonsignificant
Coleman et al. (1966)	3,6,9,12	U.S. individuals	Background	Teacher verbal ability; teacher experience, education, and class size nonsignificant, but these findings are disputed
Goodman (1959)	7,11	New York State individuals	SES	Teacher experience, observer rating of ability to relate subject matter to student ability and interest, instruction expenditures per student
Guthrie, Kleindorfer, Levin, and Stout (1971)	6	Michigan individuals	SES	Teacher experience, attitude toward teaching, school, and other teachers; verbal ability
Hanushek (1970)	3	California individuals	SES, prior achievement	Teacher experience and education nonsignificant
Hanushek (1968)	6	Northern urban individuals	SES, background	Teacher experience, verbal ability

Study	Grade	Population	Control variables	Findings
Katzman (1971)	6	Boston districts	SES (by census tracts)	Teacher experience, education, accreditation; lack of teacher turnover in school; class size
Kiesling (1969)	6	New York State districts	SES, prior achievement	Expenditures per student
Kiesling (1970)	8	New York State districts	SES	Teacher experience, education—mixed; salary—negative; class size—mixed
Levin (1970)	6	Eastern city individuals	SES, student attitudes, grade aspirations, parents' attitudes	Teacher experience, satisfaction, and attendance at university rather than college; teacher verbal ability nonsignificant; only teacher experience significant when all control variables included in model
Michaelson (1970)	6	Eastern city individuals	SES	Teacher experience, tenure, verbal ability, academic rather than education major in college
Mollenkopf and Melville (1956)	9,12	U.S. schools	SES	Teacher experience and education nonsignificant; class size
Plowden (1967) (Central Advisory Council for Education)	Kindergarten, elementary	British individuals	SES, background	Teacher experience, education; observer rating of teacher quality; class size nonsignificant
Raymond (1968)	College freshmen	Virginia districts	SES	High school teacher salary; class size
Ribich (1968)	High school	U.S. individuals	SES	Expenditures per student
Smith (1972)	6,9,12	U.S. northern individuals	SES, background	Teacher experience, attitude, and verbal ability nonsignificant
Thomas (1962)	10,12	U.S. schools	SES characteristics of home and community	Teacher salary; expenditures per student; class size

*SES refers to socioeconomic status measured by parental or average community education and/or income. Background refers to number of books in the home, appliances, and other factors thought to be related to student achievement.

From Mark Bargen and H. J. Walberg, "School Performance," in H. J. Walberg, ed., *Evaluating Educational Performance* (Berkeley, Calif.: McCutchan, 1974), Table 13-1, pp. 240–242. Permission granted by the publisher.

The citizen "buys" a lump of services for his tax dollars. For the most part, he has little or no idea of the costs and benefits. . . . The impact of a public service such as education is distributed among many individuals, over a long period of time and in many different places. [And] personal experiences . . . is hardly sufficient evidence on which to base a valid conclusion on the service as a whole. On the other hand, the evidence not based on personal experience is fragmentary, fortuitous, and oriented to special interests.

What Lieberman is not so subtly pointing out is the fact that there is an understandable tendency for us to "[obscure] the real costs for the simple reason that most people would regard them as excessive."[24]

Thus, much of the "real costs" such as the values of property and capital outlay and equipment are hidden, and if these were made more readily known, many patrons of school systems might be more favorably impressed by the extent of "their" investments in schools.

It is apparent that those of us who manage scholastic enterprises can no longer have it both ways. Either we do a reasonably adequate job with the resources provided or we do not. Some cost-benefit data no matter how crude are certainly called for and would unquestionably be of great value.

The Energy Bind—Once Again

Among all the fiscal issues that currently confront school systems, none is so increasingly pervasive as those associated with accelerating energy costs. These costs are progressively eroding instructional budgets and program-quality considerations, regardless of the type of school district—large or small, urban or rural, east or west.

Transportation

Apart from the inflationary costs associated with normal public utilities (heating and, in many cases, cooling), telephones, water, sewage, fire protection, and so forth), there is the added crunch associated with the double-bind of transportation. First there are the costs of replacing equipment—buses of all manner of size and "options" have increased in cost by as much as 30 percent in five years; yet the courts have just about unanimously decreed that the best solution to desegregation is massive transportation initiatives. Simultaneously other federal mandates, particularly those with reference to handicapped students, have necessitated the purchase of special transportation equipment so that as much as 400 percent increase in overall transportation costs has become

[24]Ibid., p. 636.

common for many school systems in such categories. Unfortunately, subsidies for the increased costs have not been forthcoming to offset these mandated expenditures. As a consequence, many school districts must use too much of their resources to *get* pupils to schools rather than to instruct them once they get there!

Interestingly, the dramatic increases in the costs of fuels associated with the transportation of pupils as well as the associated increases in costs of vehicles, maintenance, and replacement parts have not captured nearly as much attention among school administrator workshops and professional meetings as have concerns for energy management with reference to buildings and other facilities.

In the fall of 1979, an international conference on energy use management devoted two of its special sessions to energy education. In one of those sessions, Dr. Shirley Hansen, an associate director of the American Association of School Administrators (AASA), said that "Efficient use of energy in school facilities must be a top priority in the United States."[25] In similar vein, an impressive study conducted by two professors at Virginia Polytechnic University that surveyed 136 school districts was devoted almost entirely to energy issues related to school facilities.[26] While it is important to note that, based on the Wormer and Pusey survey, fuel costs have increased by 10 to 25 percent per year over the past five years, their data do not include explicit information on transportation costs for a similar period. They did report, however, that the smallest districts in their survey (less than 299 students enrolled) tended to pay higher rates for gasoline, which suggests to us, at least, that some measures of transportation costs were included.

Considering even the most sophisticated applications of computerized linear programming algorithms that could effect significant efficiencies in "load" and "trip" capacities, the crudest estimates of increased costs for *all* types of student transportation, regardless of racial factors, suggests that since 1960 these overall costs to the nation in gross terms have more than quadrupled; for some school districts, these costs have increased by as much as ten times what they were in 1960 and that precludes districts (quite a few) that for one or another reason may have transported no students in 1960 and substantial numbers in 1980. For major metropolitan districts that have come under court order to effect massive desegregation plans based significantly on transportation into and/or out of attendance areas, the costs of transportation additionally and cumulatively have become almost prohibitive.

In the Wormer and Pusey survey, it was disclosed that among the more notable impacts from spiraling transportation fuel costs was maintenance and purchase of materials and supplies. Clearly, to budget appropriately for fuel inflation, other budget categories have had to be pared.

[25]*The School Administrator*, Vol. 36, no. 8 (August 1979), 6.
[26]W. M. Wormer and R. N. Pusey, "Survey of Energy Cost Impact," cited in *The School Administrator*, Vol. 37, no. 4 (April 1980), 5.

Another important dimension of the problem concerns not only general maintenance of the physical plant but extended periods for the depreciation of vehicles. A study for one state that examined the "typical" repair costs of a school bus over a period of seven years and 100,000 miles indicated that the repairs and maintenance costs increased from $148.66 in 1973—after only one year— to $3,160.74 in the seventh year when the 100,000-mile mark was reached. That state's legislature in 1971 had devised a ten-year bus-purchasing formula based on annual mileage of 10,000 average miles and presuming a bus would be replaced at the end of ten years. Obviously that formula is not appropriate for 1980.[27]

CALCULATING COSTS AND THE FUNCTION OF BUDGETS

School administrators who are likely to get caught up in externally imposed policy dilemmas such as court-determined transportation patterns cannot be advised on how best to proceed in terms of the impact on relatively scarce resources. Nonetheless, prerogatives and alternatives directly consequential to the budget and planning process must be determined. We now turn to a discussion of that important set of tasks and concerns.

The Budget and the Budget Process

The most important vehicle available to the school executive for effective management is, of course, the budget process and the budget document.

Too frequently, we tend to dismiss the budget as an accounting tool needed to "balance" the funding of people, functions, and programs. But the budget process is indeed a basic planning mechanism available to the school executive, and we believe that too few administrators recognize its managerial value.

Exactly what is this notion of a "budget"? Everyone has some feeling for the general idea of a budget even though it is an invention of capitalistic language. *Webster's* defines it, simply, as "A financial report containing estimates of income and expenses."[28] As with most definitions, this one is simplistic. Yet by substituting "plan" for "report," the definition strikes true; one calculates what is probably incoming in the way of resources and calculates, as well, what is probably going to be expended and the two sets of "sums" must balance. *Between* them, one determines what shall be bought and sold. It is in this sense

---

[27]"The Story of No. 87," *State Ed.* (West Virginia Department of Education), Vol. 1, no. 1 (May 1980), 11.

[28]*Webster's Third New International Dictionary* (New York: Merriam, 1966), p. 290.

that it has been said that "the school budget is often defined as a school program expressed in fiscal terms."[29]

School systems "sell" the most comprehensive educational program they can given the resources they can anticipate. Yet within that traditional pattern of buying and selling, the various districts and especially the administrators who make the decisions must weigh many options and consider the funding of initiatives within constraints that are fixed. The targets of opportunity that are always presumed to enhance the "product" and its development are determined through a very complex pattern of discussions and decisions.

Many school administrators are uncomfortable with analogies of capitalistic productivity to their own budget management; they are, of course, correct in those defensive commitments—after all, schools are not at all like factories or assembly-line systems. Human beings are not so easily assessed as machine screws. Yet schools are increasingly being required to demonstrate some measures of success and are being forced into interpolating that success in terms of rather hard-and-fast criteria that make all persons who work with human beings uncomfortable.

Standardized test score data, for example, are becoming of greater importance to school districts as a basis for judging effectiveness, and evidence of success in the "basic" skills—reading, writing, and mathematics—seems to dominate. Yet there are still other bases upon which consequential judgments are brought to bear, including numbers of collegiate scholarship winners; numbers of students going on to higher education; awards at academic fairs and festivals in music, art, science, vocational education, and so forth, and publicized activities of some schools and teachers where innovative and unusual activities result in visible positive attention.

Increasingly, then, these kinds of considerations also count for much in discussions and plans that lead toward the finalization of a budget document. But, regardless of good ideas and strong support for particular initiatives, any budget process is a continuum, only a small portion of which is relatively unrestrained.

The Extent of Budget Flexibility

Recognizing a variety of particular patterns, institutional budgeting is generalizable in terms of five major cost categories: (1) *personal services*, which includes all salaries, wages, and fringe benefits; (2) *current operating expenses*, which accounts for costs associated with utilities, fuels, travel, and supplies; (3) *equipment*, which provides for everything from typewriters to overhead projectors; (4) *capital outlay and bonded indebtedness*, which concerns facilities

---

[29]R. F. Campbell, J. E. Corbally, Jr., and J. A. Ramsayer, *Introduction to Educational Administration*, 3rd ed. (Boston: Allyn & Bacon, 1966), p. 124.

construction, school bus purchasing, and other assorted additions and renovations that come outside routine physical plant concerns; and (5) *maintenance, repairs, and alterations,* which has to do with the day-to-day necessities of sustaining buildings and grounds.

As suggested, the precise nature and definition of such budget categories may vary from state to state, yet in general these categories reflect the major components of the budget and the budget process. It is also true that costs associated with the first of our categories—personal services—account for the most substantial portion of any system's expenditures. In determining the level of staffing and the level of compensation, a school district also determines between 80 and 90 percent of its operating budget.[30]

Despite some flexibility in the overall determination of the extent of personal services, budget planners are increasingly confronted with negotiated contracts that can reduce that flexibility significantly. The *level* of staffing simply means that certain alternatives may be considered whereby additions (or deletions) in guidance counselors or in, say, supervisory personnel may be considered and, thus, a school district may enjoy some variation in its overall personnel costs. Compensation, on the other hand, is frequently established by fixed salary schedules and personnel policies over which the administrator has increasingly less control.

Also, some restraints in the budget process are mandated by law and contract that require fixed and predictable costs. These include the retirement of bonds, interest on debt service, insurance premiums, social security payments, and so forth, which further reduces the available dollars for options and program priorities.

The Annual Budget Cycle

In all cases, some type of budget calendar is followed in pursuing the determination and definition of the budget. In some cases, certain aspects and events in the budget process are defined by law or regulation or are a direct function of other events, such as tax collection deadlines, which themselves are defined by law.

Typically, the budget calendar and process begins early in the school term—in September—with the preparation and distribution of forms and procedures and ends in the late spring when the board of education "adopts" the budget. In many cases, the adoption of the budget is immediately preceded by an open public hearing or vote of ratification of the budget.[31]

In recent years, the complexities associated with the development and admin-

[30]Leo M. Casey, *School Business Administration* (New York: Center for Applied Research in Education, 1964), p. 17.
[31]Ibid., pp. 20–21.

istration of the budget and fiscal affairs of school systems have resulted in the emergence of a specialized field of administrative expertise—school business management—and a substantive literature has developed associated with this role. Many states now provide, and some require, special certification or licensure of school business officials, and this role is represented by its own influential national organization, the Association of School Business Officials.

The Support Structure

As a final comment on the importance of the budgetary process, it is useful to remember that, as public organizations, schools like other units of government depend almost totally on public revenue for their existence—at least that is the case for the public schools.

The significant sources of difficulty in this regard do not have to do with the legitimacy of this pattern: clearly a public school is a public function and must be supported by public taxation. The problems occur with reference to the continuing concerns and debates over the determination of a tax structure that is both equitable and beneficial. It has been noted that these are the two fundamental principles in taxation equity and that equity itself is about the only way in which to deal with the almost universal perception that all taxes are necessary evils. Two authors have put the issue in this fashion:[32]

> Citizens exchange purchasing power for government goods and services through the payment of taxes. Under an equitable system, the level of payments is equal to the benefits derived.

Lee and Johnson point out that the achievement of an equitable system as defined is immensely difficult because of such problems of "exclusionary" issues (i.e., some people pay taxes for services they may neither believe they need nor want as with schools for childless citizens or for national defense but in both cases persons who may not be willing to pay for these services are really not excluded from the benefits that result). And also types of taxes complicate the idea of equity; some taxes, such as those on income and wages are "progressive," whereas taxes on sales, for example, are "regressive."[33]

Even though property taxation is not a significant source of revenue in general, it is still a very important source for local school districts, and thus schools are the most immediately accessible targets for public discontent and rejection of taxes. One has little choice about the imposition of a federal income tax but one can have much to do with what schools get in the way of revenue. Since property

---

[32]R. D. Lee, Jr., and R. W. Johnson, *Public Budgetary Systems* (Baltimore, Md.: University Park Press, 1973), p. 42.
[33]Ibid., pp. 42–43.

tax accounts for about 80 percent of most school districts' locally collected revenue, the equity issue of assessment methods becomes quite important. Jones has pointed out that[34]

There are more than sixty million plots of taxable real estate on local tax rolls. To each of these must be attached a value for tax purposes. The starting point is usually the free market value of a piece of property . . . however, tax assessors place a final value on property for tax purposes [the assessed value] at a fraction of true value. . . . Even in those states which presumably require assessment at a 100 per cent level, the assessed values are likely to be below this standard.

Obviously, then, one of the first concerns in the development of a school budget is the determination of the available revenue. In increasing numbers that determination may not reflect the total of what is felicitously referred to as "the bottom line," but it certainly represents most of it.

SUMMARY

This chapter has been designed to provide a perspective on the fiscal dimensions of educational management. In contemporary times, the resources available to educational managers are linked intricately to important aspects of the overall economy of the nation. And unlike in former times, this linkage is exacerbated by the strong emergence of the "public household" as a major factor in the economy that has brought with it a more intense and sometimes more critical surveillance of schools as public enterprises.

Also more important than ever before, schools are caught up in unique energy difficulties that complicate their ability to continue to provide good programs when overall enrollments are declining but inflation-related costs increase dramatically.

All these concerns mean that funding patterns for schools continue to require additional study and that budgetary procedures demand ever more skillful and well-informed administrative judgment. That is particularly the case when one considers the impact of new federal policies related to a variety of educational funding cutbacks beginning in 1981 and targeted for still more significant cuts in 1982. The rationale of the new educational economics, as in fact is the case with most of the federal participation in human services funding, is to consolidate previously established *categorical* grants or programs into *block* grants. Under "block" grants many programs are consolidated and the distribution of funds as well as the rules governing that distribution will be left up to the states.

[34]Howard R. Jones, *Financing Public Elementary and Secondary Education* (New York: Center for Applied Research in Education, 1966), p. 62.

Even though the block grant bill that passed the Congress in the late summer of 1981 was something less than the Reagan administration wanted, it still consolidated 33 smaller programs into one $589 million package that will forward funds to the states in what is referred to as an "80 percent pass-through" to local districts. This means that as much as 80 cents of each of those dollars will find its way—or could—to local school districts. It also means that rules governing the use and distribution of such funds—its own budgeting, if you will—will be determined by the states. Referring to this, Paul Hill of the Rand Corporation pointed out that this will mean a change in all education program rules.[35] He also pointed out that, "Many compliance provisions have been eliminated although the general principals (sic) of supplement-not-supplant, comparability and maintenance-of-effort have been retained. . . . States may create their own guidelines and regulations . . . but in order to deflect criticism they may have to keep existing federal programs."

There is little question then about one certain impact of the shift away from categorical to block funding regardless of whether one favors the notion or not; that has to do with the fact that budgeting at the school district level will surely be different from what it has been in the past twenty or more years that federal programs and funds have been quite explicitly defined not only by area of support but also by a complex set of guidelines, rules, forms, procedures, and reports. Many school people welcome the possibility of relief from a chaotic regulatory apparatus, but they are not yet convinced that the reductions in funds that have been authorized are worth the relaxed rules; on the contrary, there is no reasonable evidence yet that the states will not be equally stultifying in their requirements for the so-called pass-through dollars.

EXERCISES

1. As a result of President Reagan's planned cuts in educational funding, your district anticipates significant cutbacks in school lunch subsidies. As a rather poor district you face painful but necessary alternatives. What are some of them?
2. You have been asked to make a presentation at a local chamber of commerce meeting on the meaning of "block grants" and how these differ from other kinds of grants in aid; you will want to explain flat grants and others. What are the distinctions?
3. There is a question about the use of a petty cash fund to purchase a part for a piece of equipment in the home economics department of a high school from a local merchant; the part costs twenty dollars and a board member has

---

[35]*Education USA*, August 10, 1981, Vol. 23, no. 50, p. 378.

argued that this was a misuse of the fund. What do you think? What criteria do you suggest as appropriate for such funds?

4. With growing inflation and increasing difficulties with cash flow, you as superintendent have become aware that a number of schools are routinely passing on to parents certain "fees" for materials and supplies. What are the arguments for and against this practice? What should your policy be?

5. You have been invited to interview for a position as superintendent of schools in another state about which you know little; the information provided to you states that the district has "$8,800 available per classroom unit, of which 85 percent comes from state sources." What do you think that means? How would you go about finding out how that district fares in comparison with others in that state? Would you presume this state to be participating in a "foundation" school finance program? Why?

6. For a number of reasons, there is growing sentiment in your school system for initiating a year-round school pattern. Arguments being raised in support include the lost utility of empty buildings versus ongoing utility costs and a growing summer school program. How are you going to "cost it out"? What other sources of information will you pursue?

7. One of the most predictable proposals in times of declining resources is that which calls for curtailment of extracurricular activities; in your system, the board wants you to provide the advantages and disadvantages of eliminating all or some of such activities; specifically, they are concerned about athletics, dramatics, student publications, and academic contests (e.g., debate, science and art fairs, and state and regional music competitions). What are the pros and cons?

8. One of your more respected and experienced colleagues has asserted that there is *no* equitable way in which to finance schools so that the burden of cost is equalized. Do you believe that? If so, why? If not, why not?

SUGGESTED REFERENCES

Alioto, Robert F., and J. A. Jungherr, *Operational PPBS for Education: A Practical Approach to Effective Decision Making*. New York: Harper & Row, 1971.

Greenhalgh, John. *Practitioner's Guide to School Business Management*. Boston: Allyn and Bacon, 1978.

Johns, R. L., and E. L. Morphet. *Financing the Public Schools*, Third Edition. Englewood Cliffs, N.J.: Prentice-Hall, Inc., 1975.

Johns, R. L., and Edgar L. Morphet. *Planning School Finance Programs*. Gainesville, Fla.: National Education Finance Project, 1972.

Jordan, Forbis K. *School Business Administration*. New York: The Ronald Press, 1969.

PART III

The Leadership Context

Introduction to Part III: Toward the Concept of Contextualism

It has been our intent to emphasize throughout this text that institutional administrators are always either the victims or the beneficiaries of the times within which they function. Contemporary culture seems to us to cause the administrator to view himself or herself as more of a victim—of all those conditions and events and circumstances that were characterized in the first chapters of this text as relating to the "administrative environment."

When times are perceived as good and economically expansive, public attitudes are reasonably charitable toward schools and their administrative custodians. Administrative leadership is tested in such circumstances mostly in terms of its actions in moments of crisis. Certainly, for any school administrator, even the best of times presents more than a fair share of opportunities to demonstrate crisis-based leadership, for there will always be the inevitable emergencies that demand immediate decisions. Yet a broader perspective suggests to us that in the 1980s and beyond the school administrator may well experience leadership challenges that will override even the anxieties of daily crises.

There is little argument that in these times not only is public education itself in some special difficulty as a public utility but that it may also be in some difficulty as a concept. Thus, there has never been a time when its leadership (and especially from among its professional executives) has been less well respected or more frustrated and therefore in greater need of unification of direction.

The issue, then, in its broadest dimensions, is not only in terms of well-trained and well-prepared management but also in terms of the mettle of its leadership.

LEADERSHIP

Throughout the evolution of educational administration as a modern developing profession, say, since about 1940, periodic attention has been given to leadership and administrative theory. That attention has fluctuated between periods of great excitement about macronistic notions and particularistic ones. The all-inclusive theory held, for example, that administration is a quasi-science and that a "good" administrator in one type of institution could be equally successful in any other. The notion, all glorious, was administration qua administration.

To use a familiar metaphor, this larger view of administrative activity tended to see "forests" rather than "trees." Broad notions always give little attention to the technical details of substance that in many cases provide operational meaning to the whole activity. But breadth and inclusivity of concern alone do not constitute theory; by the same token, a detailed listing of tasks and responsibilities even if hierarchically ordered—for example, a "taxonomy"—does not constitute a theory either. What *theory* really comprises is a set of assumptions from which can be derived another set of empirical laws.[1]

But what exactly does that mean? Among other things, it means that *interpretations,* which only human beings can execute, are made in the form of assumptions about the way things are. These in turn serve to explain certain "regularities" that, in virtue of being predictably the same, are called *laws.* So a theory is a set of assumptions and lawful derivations useful in prediction and explanation. Thus to the previous definition we have added function; that is, not only what a theory *is* but what a theory *does.*

Certainly we have oversimplified in a few sentences what entire books have been written about and do not mean to imply thereby that theory and its understanding are not quite important. We do want to suggest that in the context of theory, leadership is a concept and as such either it may be fitted into theory or a theory devoted almost entirely to such a concept can be pursued. But that would not change the fact that *leadership* is a real and observable phenomenon and can be studied, taught, and practiced apart from theory itself. By the same token, another concept like *power* and which a leader may exert, is a more abstract concept and is less an attribute of a role than it is of the organization itself. Power can also be fitted into a theory or a theory devoted to it may be conceived, and it may also be incorporated in a theory of leadership.

One other dimension of this discussion is useful for us; in attempting to explain and predict (the two major functions of theory), it is also likely that certain other "ways of knowing" may be brought to bear. For example, in

---

[1]Herbert Fiegl, "Principles and Problems of Theory Construction in Psychology," in *Current Trends in Psychological Theory* (Pittsburgh, Pa.: University of Pittsburgh Press, 1951), p. 182.

explaining some aspect of a phenomenon, it may be important to deal with its *quality;* its goodness or badness, or its truth or falseness, or its reality, beauty, and so forth. These "ways-of-knowing" are included in the general realm of philosophy and there is a branch of philosophy that deals with each dichotomy; thus, *ethics* deals with what is right and wrong, *esthetics* with what is beautiful or ugly, *metaphysics* with what is real, *epistemology* with what is known and knowable, *theology* with what is sacred and profane, and *logic* with what is correct (not necessarily what is true). This latter distinction is a very important one in dealing with theory and philosophy, and in any fundamental understanding of what science itself is all about; that is, there are differences between what is right, what is true, and what is correct.[2] We typically think of philosophy as being speculative and of science as being exact.

There are two ways to think about science; we talk about "formal" sciences and "empirical" sciences and what we refer to with these descriptions is the extent to which there is a correspondence with experience. Some sciences are "empirical" because they correspond with experience. Thus chemistry is concerned with the physical properties of real elements and sociology is concerned with the social interactions of people, and these are therefore "natural" sciences. They are "natural" because the phenomena of interest are related to our experiences in the natural scheme of things. Mathematics (and logic), on the other hand, do not care a whit about experience or natural phenomena; the correspondence of the formal scientist's observations with facts is not of central interest to him. He is interested primarily in the *connections* among things; that is, how statements follow one from another. Experience has very little to do with it.

Finally, our discussion needs to include the concept of "axiology." This concept has to do with the study of *value* and *valuing.* Is something good or bad or strong or weak? It is the axiology of phenomena (or, more accurately, our attitudes of value toward them) that has much to do with the nature of our assumptions (in a theoretical sense) as well as our postulates and hypotheses— our "hunches." Put another way, *value* is what we attach to things that we find necessary, satisfying, or both.

The function of theory, then—to explain and/or predict—is of particular value to us. If we can explain leadership in some fashion such that we can improve on its practice or its development, that is obviously of value. To some extent, it is the intrusion of *value* that has led to the development of philosophical systems that have had utilitarian payoffs. Thus certain particular philosophical points of view could and have been described as "theories." For example, pragmatism and instrumentalism have been seen both as philosophical systems

---

[2]A colleague of one of the authors once paid a $6.00 limousine fare with some one dollar bills and quite a handful of change which equalled exactly $6.00; the driver counted it several times and the professor said to him, "It's correct isn't it?" The driver replied with disdain: "It's correct, Mac, but it ain't right!"

and as theories. Such systems of thought have generated particular practices and have thus provided explanations that have been useful.

The Scope of Theorizing. Another helpful distinction to bear in mind is that although both theory and philosophy tend toward abstraction, theoretical devices do not necessarily require that all aspects of phenomena be included for analysis. In other words, it is perfectly acceptable to develop theory concerned only with a subcomponent or a "piece" of some larger "set." Philosophy tends to be less comfortable with this kind of "component" analysis and works better with wholes. Again, it is in terms of the scope or the "inclusiveness" of the phenomena under study or of interest that theories have been characterized as "macronistic" and "micronistic." This really only implies that the former tends to explain by dealing with the largest aspects of phenomena whereas the latter deals with smaller and more manageable pieces.

It is micronistic kinds of theories that Merton has referred to as "Theories of the middle range." Merton's emphasis is on "special theories," wherein the extensiveness of abstraction is more manageable and more productive than with basic or general theories that are sweeping in their applicability.[3]

ADMINISTRATION AS SOCIAL PROCESS

One such theoretical effort whereby administrative behavior was analyzed in terms of the integration of concepts and particularistic concerns has been referred to as a social process theory.[4] In this notable early work, administrative behavior was theorized as being the product of interaction between two parallel sets of needs and properties existing simultaneously within an administrative context or environment. One set of these prescripts consists of properties of or generated by, the organization—for example, the school or school system—and these were labeled "nomothetic"; the other set of prescripts, properties of the incumbent administrator's own personality, was labeled "ideographic." The theory had to do with the generation of hypotheses derived from speculations about the functions and interactions of these two "sets" of need-evoking dimensions. It is immediately obvious that ways of characterizing administrative behavior on the basis of this "model" have to do with the extent that the behavior is more typical of personality needs or of the organization's needs.

In point of fact, the more conclusive evidence in favor of effectiveness of administrators in a number of studies based on this theoretical work, came down on the side of the "transactional" administrator; that is, one who was signifi-

---

[3]Robert Merton, *Social Theory and Social Structure* (New York: The Free Press, 1957), p. 9.
[4]See, for example, Jacob Getzels, "Administration as a Social Process," in Andrew Halpin, ed., *Administrative Theory in Education* (New York' Macmillan, 1956).

cantly motivated neither by enlightened self-interest ("ideosyncratic") nor by responses to the organization's expectations ("nomothetic"), but rather one who functioned with reasonable tolerance *between* these two extremes.

Probably too frequently overlooked in discussions about some of that early theoretical "model" was Professor Getzel's own fundamental observation: "In any case . . . whether the preparation tends toward one end [nomothetic] or the other [ideosyncratic] behavior insofar as it is *social* remains a function of both role *and* personality, although in different degree."[5]

Thus, while in one or another circumstance, one may act in terms of what is in him rather than what is in the organizational situation. There is always a mix of role and personality. One might presume that the context within which both role and personality are embedded is a key factor all too easily ignored or perhaps taken too much for granted.

So what? There is an implicit conclusion from all of the research based in various formulations that the "leader" who tends to "transact" between any postulated extremes generally functions more effectively. That is surely not a startling revelation, but it would be a great error to presume that it means that effective administrators are "middle-of-the-roaders" or are unwilling to take a stand. On the contrary, we see it as recognizing that because administration may be viewed as a social process and is therefore an essential set of functions within some institutional context, it cannot ignore except at peril, the recognition that it serves the larger purpose of educational growth and development. In other words, it does best when it results in the attainment of educational purposes.

Although that may seem almost to be an axiomatic recognition, its value is all too easily lost on theoretical considerations. The conclusion simply implies that in leadership roles, one reasonably and *thoughtfully,* treads a rather tenuous line between what he or she feels, believes, and knows, and what the organization demands. Interestingly, it is when that is indeed *not* the case that administrators as well as the organizations they serve get into difficulty.

Leadership is, we think, always a curious matter of a complex interrelationship between the personality and point of view of incumbents and the organizational configurations in which they find themselves. Added to that—and sometimes also much too easily ignored—is the *context*. This includes the particular history of the system itself, its environment, and certainly as well, some feeling for policy-determination patterns in a larger sense. Most clearly to us, a feeling for the historic development of policy structures ought to be founded in some understanding of the modern polity of bureaucratic systems. Our feeling is that too many of our professionally oriented students have too little previous academic experience with those variables that altogether characterize contemporary rational systems as other than predictable and normal. Thus by policy structures, we refer to all those aspects of bureaucracy that can be viewed as helping to determine purposes.

[5]Ibid., p. 158. (Italics added.)

In the following brief comments, then, we want to suggest some prerequisites to effective leadership behavior; these have to do with some notions about the usefulness of a sense of historic progression, of some philosophic patterns, and finally of some feeling for the conflicting demands of contemporary life that impinge on our institutional culture and exacerbate administrative effort. We choose to call this *administrative contextualism*.

ADMINISTRATIVE CONTEXTUALISM

Frequently, an administrator may come to the role without taking the time to become familiar with the organizational development of the system that he or she inherits. It is not easy to learn what is involved in the process of organizational history. It is thus important that the prospective administrator of an organization develop insight into the general and specific development of the organization he or she joins.

The Idea of Policy

The word "policy" derives from the Greek *polis,* which means "city." It is from this concept as well that our notion of *police* is derived. The early function of police had far less to do with enforcement of law than it did with the administration and regulation of procedure; the relationship between administration and enforcement is a close one. Thus, "policy" has come to refer to the ways not just cities but all governmental subdivisions tend, formally, to manage their affairs. We provide a more detailed discussion of policy issues related to educational administration in Chapter 12 but at this point some theoretical treatment is necessary.

Since "policy" really deals with the *idea* of regulating organizations and constitutes the rather formal patterns that govern the accepted ways by which they pursue their purposes, policy is obviously, as well, a major source of authority and power. In theoretical parlance, it is essential that the prospective school administrator have a comprehensive grasp of the concepts of power and authority as well as a clear understanding of how these concepts relate to both policy formulation and implementation.[6]

---

[6]For a usefully brief discussion of these concepts in a theoretical framework, see W. G. Monahan, *Theoretical Dimensions of Educational Administration* (New York: Macmillan, 1975), Chapters 6 and 7.

The Functions of Policy Administration. It is abundantly clear in the work of acknowledged theorists in organizational sociology that dominance and submission are facts in the existence of social systems, whether differentiated by large or small scope. Within that frame of reference, bureaucracy is a highly rationalistic and operational paradigm for structuring social systems (particularly formal ones such as schools) and must be accommodated by school administrators and boards of education; thus, the increasing centralization of authority at state and national levels can limit the power and authority of local school district officials. Dominance by a centralized bureaucracy can be realized through a variety of regulatory patterns, not the least of which is the control of funds and the superordinateness of policy. Thus submission to "larger" authority by local school districts is almost always a function of a district's dependence on resources that are external to its own jurisdictions and to the policies to which they must conform. This in turn creates tensions within a local school district simply because its authority as a quasi-corporation, "locally" established and legally authorized, nevertheless forces it to accommodate to "policy" stipulations that seem increasingly to be superimposed from the top rather than initiated locally.

Policy Politics. These various contentions both at local and centralized levels may be at least dimly understood in terms of what we call policy politics. By generalized definition, the development, implementation, and assessment of policy initiatives are all shot through with political insinuation. Policy is itself obviously a political concept, and the maneuvering of any policy consideration through the processes of its realization touches all manner of formal and informal political interests. It is with reference to policy politics that administrative leadership is probably the most tested and challenged. In a paper concerned with conceptualizing some of the dynamics of organizational power as such organizations struggle to "gain control of their environments," Kenneth McNeil stated recently that[7]

The major benefit which institutional economists, legal historians, and others might gain [from Max Weber] . . . is a healthy skepticism about the effectiveness of democratic control of economic power through state regulation. . . . The state can easily manipulate organizations in the public interest through . . . regulation [and] planning.

McNeil is pointing out, as have others, that there is a seductive rationale to the idea that, given quite obvious commitment to democratic values, a state bureaucracy can effect regulatory apparatus in behalf of the enlightened self-enhancement of some of its citizens to the effect that it does indeed "easily

[7]Kenneth McNeil, "Understanding Organizational Power: Building on the Weberian Legacy," *Administrative Science Quarterly*, Vol. 23, no. 1 (March 1978), 87.

manipulate'' and, as well, control localized systems, and its regulatory apparatus is thus seen as both beneficial and protective while, in truth, it can be inhibitive and repressive.

Toward Contextualism: The Philosophic Dimension

Just as policy matters are crucial to administrative functioning, and the feeling for a history of the development and evaluation of particular school systems is an important aspect of our "knowing" how better to deal with policy matters, another and still more pervasive element in a predisposition to effective administrative leadership has to do with philosophical considerations.

What any of us believes, and feels, and wants from schools as well as from our associations with them reflects the cycles of our belief systems, not only as persons but also as professional administrators. Whether filtered through our experiences or our attempts to practice pedagogy, we do not arrive at this moment in time and space without some conscious awareness of the patterns of scholasticism and of traditions of thoughts, ideas, and actions that have shaped us.

Some of the Philosophical Antecedents

To illustrate this argument, let us consider four particular American contributions to the assumptions we currently hold: namely, George Santayana, William James, John Dewey, and A. N. Whitehead.

Santayana. George Santayana was born in 1863, twenty-one years after William James and four years after John Dewey. He outlived James by forty years and died in the same year as Dewey, 1952. Yet Santayana's philosophy was not nearly so "American" or as forward looking as that of the others.

A talented writer, Santayana is best known for his doctrines of skepticism. He was born in Spain but came to America as a child of nine and remained in the United States for almost forty years. He taught philosophy at Harvard (1889–1912), but he was never really comfortable with what seemed, despite his having grown up with America, to be the vulgarity in the American ethos. In large measure, George Santayana was a displaced aristocrat. Philosophically, he was a classicist who was more comfortable with early Greek naturalist thinkers but he liked the solidarity and rigor of scientific thinking. He thought of pragmatism only as a methodology but then he rejected most of modern philosophy. He was as skeptical of aristocracy as he was of the tenets of Roman Catholicism, he never really lost his appreciation for the form of both. Santayana certainly valued democracy and believed it a better alternative in the long run to aristocracy, yet there was always that nagging notion that quality education was probably wasted on the masses.

There are many even today who share the feeling that at least some significant piece of schooling should cater to and develop the "better" minds even if at the expense of the less well endowed.

William James. James (1842–1910) and his novelist brother Henry (1843–1916) attended private schools and traveled to France for further study. There they both came under the influence of the growing field of psychology. Henry remained in Europe taking British citizenship ultimately; Will came home to America, taking an M.D. degree at Harvard and subsequently teaching there until his death.

James came naturally to philosophy from psychology and was impatient with the abstractness of the philosophical systems of the then popular European points of view. Whereas those systems were seemingly concerned with the origins and derivations of ideas, James was concerned about their consequences. When he happened upon an essay written by Charles Peirce in *Popular Science Monthly* in 1872 ("How to Make Our Ideas Clear"), he found the basis for the proofs he was seeking. William James thus launched his own versions of metaphysics based on pragmatism; he was concerned with actual events as the meaning of reality, and that meant for him what is truth now, at this moment. He saw truth as no more objective than beauty or the good—as relative to the needs of man. Truth, for James was a process, and he brought philosophy out into the street and the field; it was an active and lively idea. Said Will Durant,[8]

What James meant to do . . . was to dispel the cobwebs that had entangled philosophy; he wished to reiterate in a new and startling way the old English attitude toward theory and ideology. He was but carrying on the work of Bacon in turning the face of philosophy once more towards the inescapable world of things.

The impact of William James on educational thought probably owes more to his psychology than to his philosophy, and yet the two sets of ideas are complementary. His notions of the mind as an organic concept thus capable of being "prompted to useful conduct" suggested to teachers that there is a stream of consciousness in mental states rather than merely something reflecting the external world. James was not particularly taken by notions of some "external world"—for him, there was enough to consider in what Nietzsche called the rough and uneven contours of reality.[9] According to James,[10]

---

[8]Will Durant, *The Story of Philosophy* (New York: Washington Square Press, 1952), p. 519.
[9]Cited in W. Barrett and H. D. Aiken, *Philosophy in the Twentieth Century*, Vol. 1 (New York: Random House, 1962), p. 23.
[10]Ibid., p. 24.

A pragmatist . . . turns away from abstraction and insufficiency, from verbal solutions, from bad *a priori* reasons, from fixed principles, closed systems, and pretended absolutes and origins. He turns toward concreteness and adequacy, toward facts . . . it means the open air and possibilities of nature, as against dogma, artificiality, and the pretense of finality in truth.

As Santayana was particularly skeptical of all those notions of the older idealism with its presupposition that nothing real exists outside the "mind," James recognized that facts and consequences reflect that "reality" with which men must deal and plunged ahead to consider the consequences of historical change. The stage was thus set for still another philosophical player—enter John Dewey.

Dewey. Born in Vermont in 1859, Dewey was educated in the American East but is much identified with that time when the great traditions of the American midwestern universities were emerging. He taught at the universities of Minnesota and Michigan, coming to the University of Chicago in 1894 where he remained for ten years. It was during this time that he gained prominence for his particular brand of pragmatism with its emphasis on experimentalism and education. He returned to the East in 1904 subsequently to become professor and chair of Columbia University's department of philosophy where he remained for the most part until his death in 1952 at the age of ninety-three.

It is said of Dewey that he gave to pragmatism much of the precision that it had not bothered with as Will James expounded it, and for that reason, Dewey even labeled his philosophy Instrumentalism. Dewey was thus also a positivist, and he came by his significant emphasis on experimentation as a natural consequence of his conviction that philosophy should be far less concerned with knowing what the external world is like and much more concerned with learning how to control it and for what purposes. Thus for Dewey, "man *is* the behavior he exhibits for all to see in situations which any informal inquirer can thoroughly comprehend."[11]

Max Lerner, the syndicated columnist, often said of himself that he was neither an optimist nor a pessimist but a "possibilist"—in that regard, he was much like John Dewey. Of him it is also said that he is neither optimist nor pessimist but rather a "meliorist."[12]

In this sense, just that is meant—to be better, to improve, thus not to just be optimistic but to be always getting a bit better on. In both cases, the implication is the same: we must do the very best we can under whatever circumstances we find ourselves to adjust as well as possible to our complex environment and thereby improve the human condition. It is for these reasons that Dewey believed

---

[11]Ibid., p. 79.
[12]Ibid., p. 80.

in the power of democracy; he knew that democracy is cumbersome and therefore less efficient than, say, monarchy or oligarchy but that, if the purpose of political systems is, in fact, individual self-actualization, democracy provides the best avenues for that. Yet, because Dewey placed such great emphasis on experimentation in his extensions of pragmatism, Alfred N. Whitehead felt that Dewey narrowed James's philosophy.

Whitehead. The fourth person to form the backdrop for what we call *contextualism* in administrative leadership is Alfred N. Whitehead. Whitehead was born in England in 1861, two years after Dewey and two years before Santayana. He went up to Cambridge University at the age of 19 already a very good mathematician and at the tender age of 24, in 1885, was made a fellow in Trinity College, Cambridge. It was during this time that events occurred that affected Whitehead's thinking throughout his long life. It was fairly well presumed at that time that the science of physics was the model for philosophy and it was also presumed that the laws of the universe had been quite nicely worked out by Sir Isaac Newton over the previous two centuries. Whitehead commented that, in 1885, it was generally accepted that just about everything of importance had been worked out except for a few obscure spots like anomalies related to radiation that everyone also supposed would be resolved by at least 1900. Well, of course, those obscurities were indeed worked out, but in the process the whole of Newtonian physics, so well-fixed and presumably everlasting, was just about gone.

This collapse of certitude, for Whitehead, impressed upon him the fallacy of dogmatic finality and, conversely, the significant importance of novelty and imagination. Throughout his writings, the importance of novelty is a recurring theme. It is a part of the explanation of his great admiration for William James of whom Whitehead felt that were he, James, not to survive as a philosophic mind, he would as a man of letters because of the richness of his awareness of the wide scope and interrelatedness of all questions. (It should again be remembered that it was said of Will James that he wrote psychology like fiction.)

But Whitehead's preoccupation with novelty, and with his return again and again in his writing to the events at the beginning of the twentieth century in natural science, which saw every aspect of scientific presupposition in the Newtonian scheme of things enthusiastically questioned, are at the heart of his philosophical perspectives. As a mathematician, he was completely convinced that inexactitude is fundamental and that our need to measure phenomena is only further inhibited by the imprecision of our language. Whitehead was immensely respectful of the dynamics of time and space, and he therefore understood better than most that the universe of phenomena is basically unstable. This conceptualization is perhaps best expounded in his *Adventures of Ideas* published in 1933, although it is more centrally the theme of his earlier *Process and Reality* (1929), which he acknowledged himself as his most difficult work.

In *Adventures of Ideas,* there is a key sentence, translated loosely as "The process is itself the actuality."[13] When asked what that meant to him, he said,[14]

It took a long while, centuries in fact, for philosophers to get beyond the idea of static matter. Certain substances, like water or fire, could be seen to be changing rapidly; others, like rock, looked immutable. We know now that a piece of granite is a raging mass of activity, that it is changing at a terrific rate; but until we did know it, a rock seemed to possess little or no life, though it looked immensely permanent. But, since there was obviously quite a little mind about [it] the older philosophers brought it in from the outside. There seemed to be divisions between one part of the universe and another. But in the light of what we now know, there is no dividing line between the infinitely vast and the infinitely small. The element of time affects it too. Our human bodies change from day to day; certain external appearances of them are the same, but change is constant and sometimes visible . . . whether change occurs in a minute or in a billion years, is merely a matter of human measurement; the fact of change is not affected by our using, as human beings, the only standards of measurement we have, which are necessarily affected by the limitations of our own lives. We exist here under certain conditions of space and time within which we have to function, and these conditions, unless watched, colour our judgments.

Thus for Whitehead, the process of change is the reality and that process is outside our own judgments of it.

In his educational philosophy, he makes a repeatedly strong case against "inert" ideas and sees novelty and imagination as the way through time and space that make the most of the human condition—we can do very little about time as a part of the process of actuality, but we can most certainly make the best of it. So, Whitehead, too, is a possibilist, but he stands much more to the side of optimism in that posture as indeed did William James and, so probably, does John Dewey although Whitehead thought him much "narrower."

It was thoroughly consistent with Whitehead's enthusiastic openness toward the different and the novel that, when the invitation came to him to leave England and join the faculty in Harvard University at the age of 63 and his wife asked him what he thought of it, he said he would rather do that than anything in the world. It was at that point of course that he began a new life and, undoubtedly, the most productive aspect of his career.

Implications for Administrative Leadership

This detour through philosophical terrain has bearing on the development of scholarly concern about administration as a fundamental human activity, though

[13]As cited in L. Price, *Dialogues of Alfred North Whitehead* (Boston: Little, Brown, 1954), p. 213.
[14]Price, op. cit., p. 213.

we have tended to behave as if humanistic phenomena can be made scientific. Unfortunately, the social sciences have not elucidated any solid body of "laws" like those of, say, physics and thus there is probably more (uncritical) philosophizing within behavioral sciences than in any other field of study.

There can be no argument that when human behavior is the fundamental focus of study, the variables involved are almost infinite. Accordingly, there is no real possibility of a flash of insight that will lay out some singularly conclusive explanation; there is no $E = mc^2$ or similar kind of universal formulation imminent for the social sciences. This again is reason to give more energy and attention to those intermediate and special concerns that Merton referred to as "middle range."[15] It is in this spirit that particular interest in the study of leadership has been primarily pursued from sociological and psychological frames of reference and by scholars with such varying interests as mass communications, reference group and personality theory, and influence process. In any case, the concept of leadership is a decidedly social notion, for it automatically presumes an interactive condition—that between leader and follower. We will deal with leadership in this special context and in terms primarily of a rational analysis in the following chapter. For the present, however, we think it also useful to talk about the context itself.

In a sense, the leadership context was at least partially described by R. H. Farquhar, who pointed out at the end of the 1960s that educational administration had about arrived at the point where it was ready to deal more maturely with administrative leadership; he was referring to it in terms of the administrator's personhood. Said Farquhar:[16]

Educational administration as an area of scholarly inquiry came of age during the 1960's. As in many growing-up processes, this development included the observation of rituals, the testing of new powers, and the rejection of old shibboleths. . . . First (there was) the discipline-based 'theory for theory's sake' principle (which) began to be rejected in favor of an approach that focused primarily on contemporary problems (e.g., race relations and teacher militancy) and processes (e.g., sophisticated planning and management technologies). And second, the quest for a value-free science of educational administration began to be abandoned in favor of an approach that accepted the essential humanity of the school administrator.

What Farquhar was suggesting is that the proper frame of reference for the study of administrative behavior—of leadership—includes the humanities as much as the social sciences. There is considerable support for that point of view although the intensity of interest such as it was may be said to have peaked

---

[15]Robert Merton, *Social Theory and Social Structure* (New York: The Free Press, 1957), pp. 5 ff.

[16]Robin Farquhar, *The Humanities in Preparing Educational Administrators* (Eugene, Oregon: The ERIC Clearinghouse on Educational Administration, 1970), pp. 1–2.

between 1965–1970.[17] More recent literature in educational administration does not pursue the work of the late 1960's with reference to the humanities, although there are occasional philosophical acknowledgments and there was one lively literary dialogue that, though theoretically premised, was decidedly philosophical in content and flavor.[18]

There remains considerable comment about values and valuing (we might characterize this as the axiology of educational administration), but in general, scholarly interest in philosophical inquiry regarding educational administration is no longer substantial. In those instances where a "philosophy of educational administration" is provided, it is more in the nature of a rather superficial litany of beliefs or tends to be somewhat mystical and cultish.[19]

It is sometimes easy to forget that if we want very much to be "humane" in the process of learning how to be effective administrators and to be "humanistic" in our practice of it, those disciplines that we collectively refer to as the "humanities" have something useful to say to us. We need to remember as well that "methodology" is not alone the property and activity of scientists. Abraham Kaplan has pointed out that when philosophers talk about methodology, it is not distinguishable from epistemology itself and in that sense, the content of methodology refers to the "most basic questions that can be raised concerning the pursuit of truth."[20] What is important for us to recognize in the relationship of philosophy to science is merely that the directions and even the accomplishments of science are influenced by philosophical viewpoints. Again, Kaplan states:[21]

Descartes' metaphysics . . . was important in the history of medicine for it encouraged viewing even the human body as a material thing. The anatomists who came after Descartes had fewer difficulties getting cadavers for dissection . . . and the concepts of physics and chemistry . . . found readier application to human biology.

At least one problem for the development of a science of administration, then (and consequently of useful applications of scholarship to the effective development of leadership as well), is that we may have become quite sophisticated

---

[17]See, e.g., R. E. Ohm and Wm. G. Monahan, *Educational Administration—Philosophy in Action.* Norman, Oklahoma: University of Oklahoma, 1965. Robin Farquhar, "The Humanities and Educational Administration: Rationales and Recommendations," *The Journal of Educational Administration*, 6, 2 October, 1968, pp. 97–115.

[18]See T. B. Greenfield, "Theory about Organization: A New Perspective and Its Implications for Schools," in M. Hughes (ed.), *Administering Education: International Challenge* (London: Athlove Press, University of London, 1975), and "Reflections on Organization Theory and the Truths of Irreconcilable Realities," *Education Administration Quarterly*, Vol. 14, no. 2 (Spring 1970), pp. 1–24.

[19]See, for example, T. J. Sergiovanni and F. D. Carver, *The New School Executive: A Theory of Administration* (New York: Dodd, Mead & Co., 1973), Chapter 2, "Eupsychian Management: Model for Educational Administration," pp. 45–48.

[20]Abraham Kaplan, *The Conduct of Inquiry* (San Francisco: Chandler Publishing Co., 1964), p. 20.

[21]Ibid., p. 21.

in the treatment and analysis of important administrative phenomena but may not have given enough attention to some philosophical principles that may guide our efforts. In other words, in educational administration, ours is an uncritical philosophy. We have not given nearly as much attention to the application of content from the humanities to the teaching and practice of educational administration as we have to content from the behavioral sciences.

Toward a Philosophy of Contextualism

Although we do not pretend to suggest a particular philosophical "system" that might be specifically applicable to educational administration, we do believe that effective administrative leadership must ultimately come to grips with some more systematic analysis of its philosophical foundations.

If one examines the patterns of thought in American philosophy that we have only very briefly mentioned and that have constituted in several fashions the prevailing ideas that have had enormous impact on American educational practice, it seems to us that there are several currents of importance that characterize a stream of philosophy-into-practice. These currents of importance have to do with time, immediate space, and the events therein; of consequences, of experimentation, of the growth of selfhood, reverence for personality (personhood), and the value of pluralistic polity.

For us these thrusts form a logical and real *context*. This context, most fundamentally, refers to the interrelated conditions in which events occur and is thus a useful term for attempting to characterize the connections and coherences that define the ethics, esthetics, and epistemology of administration as a special kind of human activity.

In *contextualism* we see time as relevant primarily in terms of the immediate now, which includes the recent past, the immediate present, and the near future. We see spatial phenomena in terms of the relevant environment. Thus the relevant environment is dynamic and while at its center is *this* place and *this* organization, there are also relevant dimensions of our administrative space that may be remote but at a particular time equally relevant as is *this* place. For example, events in Washington, D.C., or in the next county may have relevance to the impact of spatial considerations. We also see *contextualism* as recognizing those aspects of pragmatism that have to do with what *works*, and with the implications of seeing ourselves with others as beings caught up in what one philosopher has called the cares of time and history.[22]

The question we ask is not what is administrative man nor what is education nor what is truth or beauty or love; instead we ask, "What is the context?"

[22]W. Barrett and H. D. Aiken, *Philosophy in the Twentieth Century*, Vol. 3 (New York: Random House, Inc., 1962), p. 132.

In this book, although we have tried to be reasonably respectful of the utility of what is practical and of the changed environment within which contemporary school administrators must learn and practice, we have also tried to be true to the idea of contextualism. Thus, we have at least tried to provide some perspective of what the context of contemporary educational administration is like.

The Illusionary Revolt Against Rationalism. What that context seems clearly to imply is that educational administration, like other management fields, has been significantly influenced by a rampant rationalism over the past twenty-five years while trying to maintain something of a focus on what Douglas McGregor called "The Human Side of Enterprise."[23] This has sometimes generated conflicts in our belief systems that have been damaging to the definition of purpose as well as to its orderly pursuit. Also, in our view, it has contributed much to the frustrations of managers in all fields and especially to education.

Why? Because with the decline of the kind of rationalism that was characteristic of Frederick W. Taylor's "scientific management" and that was rather soundly repudiated as a consequence of the emergence of the so-called human relations attitudes in the 1930s, educational administrators discovered that the newer point of view was much more compatible with the development of child-centeredness that had begun to flavor pedagogy even earlier. When Elton Mayo and his Harvard associates, through their work at the Hawthorne plant of Western Electric (and using the most careful empirical methods), concluded that productivity of workers is more a matter of social relationships than anything else, it struck school people as meaningful and useful. For quite a number of years thereafter, a variety of "human relations" thrusts dominated the literature of education, and this still forms an important aspect of the context. The maximization of human potential has itself become a special area of interest and includes (owing directly to the Mayo beginnings) such activities as sensitivity training, assertiveness training, temporary-systems management, conflict resolution, and so forth—all emphasizing "people-centeredness" and having a strong affinity to existentialist-flavored foundations. Yet, beginning almost simultaneously with this human relations attitude, there were other events that followed and enormously expanded the scientific rationalist posture; we refer to the information-processing revolution that generated the growth of computer technology and, with it, a new "cult of efficiency"[24] that fostered an immense growth in the study of systems. Fundamentally based in the quantification of

---

[23]Douglas McGregor, "The Human Side of Enterprise," *The Management Review,* 46, 22–28, 1957.

[24]This phrase is used as the theme of one important statement about the impact of the scientific management movement on Education. See, for example, Raymond Callahan, *Education and the Cult of Efficiency* (Chicago: University of Chicago Press, 1962).

programmatic problem solving and systematic controls, this new rationalism aimed at the ideal of complete predictability. By the reduction of phenomena to a binary simplicity and with the power of electronic technology, it was almost entirely data-based and aimed at systematic elimination of unintended consequences. Thus, in a sense, it was founded in that aspect of phenomenology that in its early states is concerned with the particular and the piecemeal as opposed to the grand speculative metaphysics of the older absolute idealism. At the same time, this phenomenological foundation—uncritically unnoticed, and unknown to some of the modern proponents of rational systems theory—also owes some of its genesis to that idea in the philosopher, Edmund Husserl's phenomenology that holds that consciousness is *always* intentional; thus the phenomenologist was concerned with the pure data open to consciousness.

Again, the seeming paradox between a person-centered attitude, on the one hand, and a data-centered one, on the other, must be understood in terms of the contextualism that includes and accounts for both. For one thing, the person-centered attitude was somehow compartmentalized into a growing literature of organizational *behavior*, whereas the data-centered attitude was compartmentalized into a growing literature of organizational *functions*. Repeatedly, then, we reminded ourselves and, perhaps with increasing lack of conviction, that it is man-the-person who controls man-the-machine. That the system generates predictive *order* and the person-as-leader generates *control*. Curiously, as the order-generating factors grow in utility and scope, there are inevitable clashes and conflicts between these domains. It is these recurring clashes between human and machine control that may constitute the single most urgent intellectual and cultural problem of the next fifty years. We have not, we think, come very much to grips with this in any fashion, much less as a contextual dilemma, that is, one in which connectives and coherence should be the central concerns of our scholarship and the focus of our administrative leadership.

In summarizing these comments, *contextualism* is seen as a way of characterizing the circumstances of administrative life. It recognizes that unlike the physical sciences, the human sphere finds limited value in the precision of an exacting methodology and, with John Dewey, holds that we must resort therefore to history as the source of experimental knowledge. Contextualism also recognizes that the challenges to leadership are *always* those within the immediate reality of the moment of deciding and thus that reality is circumscribed only by what is relevant *at that time*. This involves responsible moral deliberations with what is possible, what will "work," and what will happen as a consequence. In summary, *contextualism*, insofar as leadership is concerned, is a matter of coming to know that the *solution is always in or implied by the situation*. If the situation is well studied, the solution can be determined. Contextualism has only to do with the meaning inherent in the circumstances in which human events of interest occur.

NEXT THINGS

In the following pages, we talk a bit about administrative leadership itself—what others have to say about it and what it means and what it can and ought to be. Probably that discussion will be familiar to many of our readers. But within that too, policy issues, the politics of compromise, the consequences of the centralization of authority, and the essentially moral nature of the educational experience are never far away from the surface of the discussion and are always factors in the articulation of context.

As a final comment, what we are advocating is, we believe, much more than mere eclecticism. There is no philosophical point of view that does not build on what preceded it, just as there is no fully developed theory that can claim no heuristic relationships with what went before it. But if we can better understand the context within which we function, we can surely better understand the nature of the problems we confront and begin to fathom reasonable solutions for them.

Accordingly, organizations are indeed man-made realities and they are multidimensional; a school organization has both qualitatively different and quantitatively different dimensions than does a commercial one or a political one or a religious one—its context is defined uniquely and its variables only partly operationally describe its context. And by the same logic education as an institution has a still different dimensional context. As we begin to explore these configurations that seem, on the face of it, no terribly difficult agenda, we can better fathom the connectedness and coherence of its reality and its truth.

EXERCISES

1. For an important position as assistant superintendent for instructional programs, a search committee has recommended to you, as superintendent, two persons. Both have had similar and appropriate experience, but one is acknowledged as a diligent, practical "doer," whereas the other is acknowledged as having a more theoretical orientation. Both are strong people. If all else were equal, which would you choose and why?
2. Examine the system in which you are currently working as an educator, or the most recent one, and see if you can "contextualize" it. That is, describe it in terms of its structure, function, and content including the value system it prefers.
3. Some members of the board of education have expressed strong support for

the policy of not hiring any prospective teacher who does not have at least a B average overall in all college work; as one school principal, you have been asked to react to this proposal. What considerations are worthy of attention? What possible political implications can you discern, if any? Are the premises upon which this notion is based sound? Why or why not?

4. Someone has observed that what has been discussed as "contextualism" is really nothing more than "cultural relativism." What is the latter view, and of what possible value or use to the study of administration is this whole notion of social and philosophical foundations of education?

5. In a provocative argument at a recent school council meeting, one high school principal asserted that he was weary of hearing about organizational behavior. "What the organization does," he said, "after all the people go home is organizational behavior!" Do you agree? If not, what do you think people mean when they talk about organizational behavior? If all the people go home, is there any "organization" left? When we speak of a law firm, does "firm" mean more or less than the people themselves?

SUGGESTED REFERENCES

Barrett, William, and Henry D. Aiken (eds.). *Philosophy in the Twentieth Century*. New York: Random House, 1962.

Bass, Bernard M. *Leadership, Psychology, and Organizational Behavior*. New York: Harper & Row, 1960.

Bennis, Warren, Kenneth Benne, and Robert Chin. *The Planning of Change*. New York: Holt, Rinehart, and Winston, 1961. See especially chapters 8, 9, and 10.

Farquhar, Robin. *The Humanities in Preparing Educational Administrators*. Eugene, Oregon: University of Oregon and ERIC Clearinghouse, 1970.

Feinberg, Walter. *Reason and Rhetoric: The Intellectual Foundations of Twentieth Century Liberal Educational Policy*. New York: Wiley, 1975.

Graff, O. B., C. M. Street, R. B. Kimbrough, and A. R. Dykes. *Philosophic Theory and Practice in Educational Administration*. Belmont, Calif.: Wadsworth Pub. Co., 1966.

Gross, Bertram M. *The Managing of Organizations*. New York: The Free Press, 1964.

Haas, J. Eugene, and Thomas E. Drabek. *Complex Organizations: A Sociological Perspective*. New York: Macmillan Publishing Co., Inc., 1973.

Ilich, Robert (ed.). *Education and the Idea of Mankind*. Chicago: University of Chicago Press, Phoenix Books edition, 1964.

Kaplan, Abraham. *The Conduct of Inquiry*. San Francisco: Chandler Publishing Co., 1964.

Monahan, William G. *Theoretical Dimensions of Educational Administration*. New York: Macmillan Publishing Co., Inc., 1975.

Nisbet, Robert A. *The Twilight of Authority*. New York: Oxford University Press, 1975.

Ohm, Robert E., and William G. Monahan. *Educational Administration—Philosophy in Action*. Norman, Oklahoma: University of Oklahoma, 1965.

Rubenstein, Albert H., and Chadwick J. Haberstroh. *Some Theories of Organization*. Homewood, Ill.: Richard D. Irwin, Inc., and the Dorsey Press, 1966. See especially Section 3, "Leadership and Morale."

Whitehead, A. N. *The Aims of Education*. (Free Press Edition) New York: Macmillan and Co., 1957.

Chapter 11

Administrative Leadership as Interpersonal Behavior

INTRODUCTION

While the newly appointed administrator must become familiar with the idea and practice of leadership, each member of the professional team is obliged to renew continually his or her insights and understandings of this vital concept. Each educator is called upon daily to display "leadership" in a variety of forms. The manner in which that role is carried out is a primary factor in the degree of success that the individual administrator achieves. And it matters little what position in the organizational structure the administrator occupies, the practice of his or her leadership function is essentially an interpersonal activity. The reality of the administrative situation is simply that the individual administrator cannot escape the whole set of responsibilities that the leadership role and the members of the organization thrust upon him or her. Indeed, the expectations of all individuals with whom the administrator has contact by virtue of his or her position provide the frame in which he or she must begin operation and to which each must return for periodic progress checks.

This chapter is designed to launch the discussion of leadership. To that end, it seems appropriate to avoid an academic approach (i.e., a detailed description of the meaning of "leadership" in its historical and scholarly sense coupled with a thoroughgoing review and analysis of the copious research conducted by scholars in the several specialties of management and administration). Such information is readily available in a variety of excellent publications (see the suggested references for this chapter). Rather, this effort is designed to apply pertinent information to contemporary realities so that the new educational administrator might find tools with which to make the administrative life more productive and, consequently, more satisfying and fulfilling.

The first set of information, then, that appears pertinent to this objective is the reality of the context within which leadership is practiced. Much of this reality has been described in preceding chapters. But a survey of issues as they relate to the leadership function helps to focus attention on some specifics of special concern and aids in providing an appropriate background for a subsequent discussion of the nature of leadership. The latter becomes the topic of the second section of this chapter and is examined in terms of the survival and the success of the individual administrator. The final section of this discussion treats the problems involved in the implementation of leadership when viewed as interpersonal behavior. We discuss that problem as a consideration of the tactics of leadership.

If the objective of this chapter is achieved, the newly appointed principal, supervisor, central office staff member, or deputy or assistant superintendent will be encouraged to develop an operational definition of leadership. And, furthermore, that definition will be stated as an hypothesis to be tested in the daily practice of the administrator's leadership behavior.

LEADERSHIP ISSUES: A REALITY DIMENSION

It can be said that no issue that affects the organization escapes the concern of the individual in the leadership position. It is not too much to claim, therefore, that each administrator is obliged to be alert to the nature of the issues that claim his or her attention. Those that have been identified in the preceding pages can be understood on several dimensions. They can be seen in terms of their primary source, for example, as school based or extraschool based. They can be classified in terms of the time dimension, for example, as immediate or long term. Similarly, they can be considered in terms of numerous other continua, but the interpersonal dimension of leadership calls attention to a unique set of "issues" that is pervasive. A discussion of selected issues follows.

The Problem of Authenticity

The central issue confronting each individual who occupies a formal leadership position is simply "believability." The news media in general have documented scores of instances in which officials, those in public life and those operating in the private sector, have violated both formal trusts and informal confidences. Officials guilty of such violations have ranged from village law officers to White House staff members. Indeed, the presidency itself has not been immune from such acts. The consequences of these revelations have produced, at best, general skepticism in the mind of the public and, at worst, an active distrust of all public officials. Citizens simply have lost confidence in the veracity of individuals who discharge official leadership functions. It almost seems that status leaders are no longer to be followed. Rather, they exist as antagonists to be challenged, if not to be denied. And so society struggles in a crisis of leadership.

The educational community reflects a similar set of symptoms. The confidence of faculty, students, and community alike is withheld from formal leadership individuals in major school districts. Evidence can be found in the turnover in senior administrative positions around the country as well as in community actions designed to restrict the resources invested in education. Concurrently, the unionization of teachers and their aggressive pursuit of higher levels of compensation, as well as control over the conditions of their work, represent an adversarial posture vis-à-vis the formal leadership structure of school districts and has both developed from and of necessity promotes alleged inadequacies of that leadership structure. These factors have eroded the position of those in official or status leadership roles. And so the crisis of leadership is clearly a part of the educational scene.

It is too simplistic to speak of causal factors for the social and institutional malaise. In fact, that analysis is not necessary to the purposes of this text. Even so, the issues posed by the condition can be confronted from the "leadership" point of view. Indeed, to do otherwise is to avoid a primary function of leadership. Consequently, the contribution to the illness, if that indeed is an accurate description of the context, both can and must be examined. We suggest that "authenticity" is a tool of great importance to the understanding of the response of a status leader to the understandable and, at times, deserved denial of confidence and trust that he or she experiences in the discharge of everyday responsibilities. Authentic behavior is that behavior that issues from an individual's presentation of himself or herself as he or she in fact is. It is behavior that is real; that does not misrepresent the person but rather faces joys and sorrows, victories and defeats, with equal integrity. The absence of authenticity in the behavior of individuals occupying formal leadership positions is one of the primary causes of the erosion of confidence by the American public, both on the national and on the local level. Perhaps this erosion is among the unintended consequences of the nation's massive advertising exposure, an exposure that encourages distrust of partial or exorbitant claims on the one hand and resistance to "public" announcements on the other. Perhaps it results in large measure from lack of understanding of the function of leadership by those in official positions. And perhaps a collection of complexities nourishes the roots of whatever sets of causal factors diminish the authentic behavior of educational administrators.

But the issue persists, and the problem of authenticity remains of first-order significance for each individual who occupies a leadership role. What can individuals do about the absence of confidence in their work or performance? How does one examine oneself in terms of the integrity question? How does one behave "authentically" in a conflict-ladened confrontation? How does one enhance the development of an organizational climate of integrity, one that encourages authentic behavior on the part of *all* members of the organization? It is expected that in some small measure this volume will aid in beginning a search for answers to these and like questions.

The Politicization of the School

One factor that has contributed to the absence of authentic behavior throughout the educational establishment is the politicization of the school. Although specific actions of specific individuals designed to persuade nonrationally have been part of interpersonal behavior from the beginning of time, the formalization of such actions to influence educational policy reached a new high as a result of the significant developments of the 1960s. The successful emergence of teachers' organizations into forces demanding recognition and attention is, perhaps, the single development of broadest impact on the internal management of schools. Now, at the beginning of the 1980s, it is almost commonplace to find teachers in major school districts delaying the opening of classes in the fall through an action that withholds their services until their concerns are treated. The civil rights and student activism movements that flowered in the 1960s as well as the national tragedy associated with the war in Vietnam also contributed immeasureably to the modification of decision patterns in the schools. Issues that had, by previous custom, not been of open and direct concern to the educational administrator qua educational administrator emerged to confound the discharge of his or her leadership role. The range of reliable authorities, those to whom appeals for guidance could be referred, suddenly was significantly enlarged. It became increasingly necessary to rely on aid from the legal community, from state and national politicians of influence, from leaders of local and state self-interest groups, and frequently from factions within each category. Increasingly, local problems are born as a consequence of issues national in scope being played out on the national scene. They frequently become operationalized in terms of issues associated with collective bargaining, erosion of local control and an increased regulatory apparatus, and a generally increased level of litigation. Indeed, it has been claimed that we have become a litigious society.

At an ever-growing pace, educational administrators face issues in which there is a conscious effort to use the educational structure to promote and achieve social goals not involved directly with or related to the central purpose of the schools when that purpose is understood in terms of the education of the nation's children and youth. This has resulted in the politicization of the school, the division of the institution, broadly conceived, into contesting factions and adversaries. Of course, it must be recognized that the monolithic set of assumptions and traditions describing the central purpose of the schools in America no longer proved serviceable to many segments of American society. As the decade of the 1960s wore on, representatives of such groups quite properly raised serious questions about the nature and function as well as the purpose of the schools. And these questions were quite frequently posed in contentious form, a form that provoked contentious response. The politicization of the schools has continued unabated and now represents the common condition that confronts the leadership group.

It is not the intent of this work to deny or demean this development. It is necessary, however, to suggest that it creates a new set of leadership problems. In fact, it requires a view of the leadership function that is quite different from the traditional or classical view, the view that is commonly held by a majority of our contemporaries. That is, the leader cannot be seen as a figure of assumed superior wisdom and ability whose words can lead organizations out of their unique wildernesses. Unfortunately, not only do citizens and faculty members expect such results from ''strong'' leaders, but newly appointed administrators frequently expect such performances for themselves and promise it to their constituencies. This posture seems to represent the characteristics of a ''true leader'' in the minds of many people in all factions across society. Quite obviously, a politicized school can seldom be led successfully by such an administrator. Frequently, increased factionalism results and a change is demanded in the formal leadership of the institution.

An even more debilitating consequence is associated with uninformed leadership performance in a politicized school. The nature of the adversarial pattern allows the focus of energies to devolve on operational as opposed to productive activities. In fact, the management of conflict through techniques appropriate to an adversary procedure actually promotes the rewarding of those individuals who possess instrumental skills rather than those whose skills are related more directly to the primary goals of the school. That is, a skillful negotiator is paid more than a skillful teacher of reading. And the politicization of the schools has required that a greatly increased administrative cadre be employed, thereby directing the investment of greater portions of resources in programs related to instrumental objectives.

This issue is related directly to the further obfuscation of the means versus ends dilemma. Too frequently means, that is, operational or instrumental objectives, become the ''end'' or the goal of the institution, for it is claimed by some that *no* goal will be achieved if the institution fails to survive. This is not an issue for the formal or status leadership group of the school alone, for another confounding consequence of the politicization of the school is the development of a plural or a multiple leadership structure. No longer does the superintendent or principal have primary responsibility for the formal leadership behavior in the school. The factional leaders must assume some of that responsibility as well. The issue is found in their refusal or inability to do so, very probably for reasons similar to the failure of the administrators also to fulfill leadership functions with vigor. The danger is that an adversarial stand-off may well develop resulting in either a leadership impasse or a problem resolution that satisfies no one and does not enhance the goal achievement potential of the unit.

The consequent operational issues for leadership can be expressed in question form. Several are suggested by the discussion. For example, how does one minimize the adversarial nature of a politicized unit? How does one involve others in a productive leadership mix in a politicized school? What actions can a status leader invoke to maintain a focus on the primary goals and objectives of the unit in a meaningful way? This set of questions represents a rather different emphasis than would a set that focuses attention on winning contests or playing political games. Indeed, the politicization of the school has raised a rather thoroughgoing set of new issues for leadership in the educational establishment.

THE NATURE OF LEADERSHIP: PATTERNS OF SURVIVAL AND SUCCESS

In a contextual treatment, three approaches can be identified as helpful in understanding leadership: the individual approach, the interactional approach, and the situational approach. The first looks to personal characteristics of the one who has demonstrated something called "leadership." The second focuses on the dynamics of the relationships between the leader and the led. The third attempts to find in the mix of individual, group, and situation ways in which to understand both where leadership comes from and something of its nature. Each is sketched in some detail in the paragraphs that follow.

The Individual Approach

Early attempts to understand leadership, both formally and informally, looked to individuals who were acknowledged leaders. Frequently, novice administrators or persons contemplating accepting such responsibilities start from the same position. That is, they look to leaders they have known or know of for information about their own potential to perform as successful leaders. It is not difficult to understand how examinations of individual traits or characteristics appeared to be the most reasonable place to begin. It often seems that, when viewed from a distance, the individual occupying a leadership position in fact possesses some distinctive ability. Indeed, so strong has that assumption been in the history of organized life that it was long thought that leaders were born, not made. As reputable a thinker as Aristotle subscribed to such a notion.[1] And hereditary leadership provided the basic pattern for centuries. Indeed, this criterion was strengthened by claims of divine authority as well, and such claims have not been restricted to any one segment of the human community or to any one period of human history.

It is not, therefore, to be considered strange that researchers initially looked to the psychological traits and personal characteristics of individuals when they wondered about the nature of the leadership phenomenon in educational and other organizations. However, the singular approach proved less than rewarding. That is, when individual traits and characteristics were studied, it was not unusual for different studies to report findings that were contradictory.[2] Certain traits or characteristics that were found to be related significantly to successful leadership performance in one study could not be substantiated in another. An example might deal with physical characteristics such as size or voice.

These apparently contradictory findings led to a general disaffection with the traits versus characteristics approach to explaining the differences that appear to exist between leaders and their followers as far as researchers were concerned. In fact, the compiled research had demonstrated that the search for an understanding of leadership could not be pursued successfully by an isolated consideration of the personality traits of the individual.[3] A review of 124 studies of psychological traits of leaders led Stogdill to conclude that "A person does not become a leader by virtue of some combination of traits."[4] This finding, though not strange in terms of contemporary conventional wisdom, helped to direct interests of students of leadership to a broader field of study. In the minds of some, it served as the end of the search for an understanding of leadership from the traits and/or characteristics point of view.

But this approach has left another legacy to our understanding of leadership. In spite of the rather general and basic turning away from a search for universal leadership traits, the results of research do offer guidance to the person considering a career involving formal leadership responsibilities as well as to individuals charged with selecting a leader. Stogdill reported six meaningful clusters of traits as follows:[5]

1. Capacity (intelligence, alertness, verbal facility, originality, judgment).
2. Achievement (scholarship, knowledge, athletic accomplishments).

---

[1] See *Politics*, Book I, Chapter 5.
[2] R. D. Mann, "A Review of the Relationship Between Personality and Performance," *Psychological Bulletin*, Vol. 56 (1959), 241–270.
[3] W. K. Hoy and C. C. Miskel, *Educational Administration: Theory Research and Practice* (New York: Random House, 1978), p. 177.
[4] R. M. Stogdill, "Personal Factors Associated with Leadership: A Survey of the Literature," *The Journal of Psychology*, Vol. 25 (1948), 35.
[5] Stogdill, op. cit., p. 64.

3. Responsibility (dependability, initiative, persistence, aggressiveness, self-confidence, desire to excel).
4. Participation (activity, sociability, cooperation, adaptability, humor).
5. Status (socioeconomic position, popularity).
6. Situation (mental level, status, skills, needs and interests of followers, objectives to be achieved).

Other sets of individual characteristics are available in the literature, but these serve to remind us of the significant, albeit neither exclusive nor universal, traits that have been associated with effective leadership. Furthermore, they call to our attention that leadership does reside in an individual while, through the last cluster listed by Stogdill (situation), they keep us mindful of the fact that the individual leader functions in and through a group, an organization. Perhaps the best antidote for the excesses associated with the individual approach to leadership, excesses that culminate in "great man theories" or longings for a "man on a white horse" to ride to the rescue of an organization, is found in the "situational" nature of the leadership function. Lipham, writing in 1964, reported that, in the contest between those who supported the traits and characteristics view of leadership and those whose orientation favored the situational nature of leadership, the latter prevailed.[6]

It must be reported, before leaving the "traits" discussion, something of its posture vis-à-vis the interpersonal behavior dimension of leadership. Although, as reported, the literature does not permit the presentation of a unitary set of traits, the "commonsense" or man-in-the-street view quite regularly assumes that a "good" leader will be tough minded, businesslike, skilled in his specialty, and aware of needs of "his people." Clearly, the assumptions suggest the kind of behavior that Barnard associated with "effectiveness" (i.e., the achievement of organizational goals) as contrasted to "efficiency" (i.e., the satisfaction of individual member needs).[7] Such assumptions place the leader in an elite of sorts and, as a consequence, permit the individual to ignore other elements in the leadership environment. Some of those elements are considered in the two sections that follow.

The Interactional Approach

The shortfalls in the work and position of the "traitists" focused attention on the relation between the leader and the followers. Few individuals who have occupied even the most modest of leadership positions have failed to recognize

[6]James Lipham, "Leadership and Administration," in *Behavioral Science and Educational Administration* (Chicago: University of Chicago Press, 1964), p. 130.
[7]C. I. Barnard, *The Functions of the Executive* (Cambridge, Mass.: Harvard University Press, 1938), p. 55.

clearly that their effectiveness is dependent upon the effectiveness of the individuals in the organization. This recognition is often couched in negative terms and is observed when a subordinate fails to discharge his or her responsibilities. Robert K. Merton observed this characteristic in the following language: "leadership does not, indeed cannot, result merely from the individual traits of leaders; it must also involve attributes of the transactions between those who lead and those who follow."[8] The inevitable tension that develops between the leader and the led forces the interested individual into an examination of interactions between them.[9]

The concern with leadership as an interaction between the leader and the led, that is, the group or the organization, evolved from what has been called the human relations point of view in the study of organization. Most authorities credit Mary Parker Follett's work with introducing this set of concerns into the rational consciousness of organizational life.[10] The highly regarded and influential studies conducted by F. J. Roethlisberger and William J. Dickson at the Hawthorne plant of the Western Electric Company provided great impetus to the human relations movement. Although the primary focus of the Hawthorne studies, as they came to be called, was on factors related to improving worker productivity rather than on the interactions between the leadership group and the employee group, the implications of the findings for leadership behavior were clear. Roethlisberger and Dickson reported their central findings in these words:[11]

It became clear to the investigators that the limits of human collaboration are determined far more by the informal than the formal organization of the plant. Collaboration is not wholly a matter of logical organization. It presupposes social codes, conventions, traditions, and routine or customary ways of responding to situations. Without such basic codes or conventions, effective work relations are not possible.

The educational administrator who reviewed these findings with some care could no longer defend a posture that ignored the dynamics at work within the school he or she served. Neither could an assumption of formal obedience by subordinates be defended based simply on occupying a superior position in the

[8]Robert K. Merton, "The Social Nature of Leadership," *American Journal of Nursing,* Vol. 69 (1969), 2615.

[9]It should also be noted that an interaction between two participants can be examined without reference to the context within which the interaction occurs only at great risk of being misled. Such analyses turn the analyst toward the whole milieu. Indeed, the consideration of something called an "interactional approach" can only be helpful if it is clearly understood as being abstracted from its context. In the present discussion, then, the value of this section must be realized only as a prelude to the section that follows, "a situational approach."

[10]See Henry C. Metcalf and L. Urwick, eds., *Dynamics Administration: The Collected Papers of Mary Parker Follett* (New York: Harper & Row, 1940).

[11]F. J. Roethlisberger and William J. Dickson, *Management and the Worker* (Cambridge, Mass.: Harvard University Press, 1939), p. 568.

organizational structure. The nature of the administrator's interpersonal relationships would have to be significantly modified if the General Electric studies were to have meaning.

The range of the possible changes for such an administrator was suggested by another seminal study. Three highly regarded scholars, Kurt Lewin, Ronald Lippitt, and Ralph White, studied the impact of three different leadership patterns on the behavior of 11-year-old children at the Iowa Child Welfare Station, University of Iowa in 1938. The children met in groups of five after school to participate in handicraft activities. The adult leaders of the groups behaved according to one of the three leadership patterns that were being studied. They were the now familiar *autocratic, democratic,* and *laissez-faire* leadership patterns. All other factors were maintained as constants among all groups. Trained observers monitored the behavior of the children.[12] The findings excited the world of education, especially that segment concerned with its administration, for they generally supported the "democratic" leadership pattern, and this fit well into the child-centered and activity notions being advocated by progressive educators. In addition, the negative impacts of the "autocratic" or "authoritarian" pattern supported the general dislike of the fascist dictators then in power in Europe as the Western world moved inexorably toward World War II. These factors, coupled with the human relations movement in management, can account for the success with which the three-phased description of leadership was greeted. "Democratic" leadership became the *good* type, "autocratic" the *bad;* democracy in school administration became a rallying cry and a movement.

The impact of these activities on an understanding of leadership as interpersonal behavior is clear. From the Hawthorne studies, the notion of the administrator as a manager of the work environment found support. The leader's function as a facilitator of worker efficiency (in the Barnard sense) as a first order of concern was clearly supported by these findings. The interpersonal interactions between the leader and the led must be supportive and so understood by the subordinate if the goals of the organization are to be achieved. And the Iowa studies detailed further the nature of leader behavior that could be so viewed by the worker. For some school administrators, these findings matched well their intuitive response to their leadership responsibilities. Others found the ideas suggesting a collegial relationship to be threatening to their understanding of leadership, and questions of authority and democracy in the leader-led, principal-teacher roles continued to be discussed with vigor.

The interactional approach to leadership assumes that the leader is dependent upon the led for cues to his or her behavior. It recognizes that simply holding a formal leadership position is not enough to ensure favorable responses to one's

---

[12]A complete description of the studies can be found in Ralph K. White and Ronald O. Lippitt, *Autocracy and Democracy: An Experimental Inquiry* (New York: Harper & Row, 1960). This review is taken from Jacob W. Getzels, James M. Lipham, and Roald F. Campbell, *Educational Administration as a Social Process* (New York: Harper & Row, 1968), pp. 36–39.

actions. The compliance behavior of the members of the group, then, is enhanced by confidence in the leader, produced in large measure through interpersonal interactions rather than through formal directives and memoranda.

The Situational Approach

The examination of leadership as the relationship between the leader and the led pointed out the situational nature of such interactions. For purposes of our discussion, it is helpful to conceive of the "situational approach" as one that suggests that leadership depends primarily on the members of the organization and the nature of the circumstances within which the leader and the organization are called upon to perform. One position holds that the group is the primary locus of concern and that leadership emerges from the group in response to specific variables at specific times. A more comprehensive view, one that traces its lineage to systems theories, sees leadership as contingent upon several sets of variables.

Emergent Leadership. The first position to be discussed might be called "emergent leadership." It has been especially interesting to students of educational administration as it developed out of the research on small groups and the interest in group dynamics. The professional nature of educational staffs has proved a fertile ground for minimum amounts of internal organization and consequently for procedures that encouraged individual faculty members to exercise their expertise in a leadership role. It has been considered wise to attempt to secure an isomorphism between the informal organization and the modest formal structure in the practice of educational administration. Each of these conditions has provided face validity for the view of leadership as "emergent" from the group within certain situations. It has been considered as a technique well designed to encourage growth among professional members of an educational organization.

Much of the support for "emergent" notions of leadership was found in the work of George Homans.[13] He used the findings of a study of street gangs as one source of data and produced a number of conclusions about leadership that are pertinent to the present discussion. For example, he found that, "the organization of the large formal enterprises, governmental or private, in modern society is modeled on, is a rationalization of, tendencies that exist in all human groups."[14]

Such findings gave strength to those who translated small informal group practices into relatively large, formal organizations. And the result was not

[13]G. C. Homans, *The Human Group* (New York: Harcourt Brace, 1950).
[14]Ibid., pp. 186–187.

always successful. The situation frequently called forth "leadership" behavior that was not consistent with formal goals or policies of the school and resulted in perhaps unnecessary strain in the interpersonal relationships within the unit.

The leader that emerges from small or unstructured groups was described by Homans, and several of his observations about such leaders and the job of such leadership are instructive, as they emphasize the mutual dependence of the leader, the led, and the situation. For example, Homans reports that the social rank of an individual affords him or her certain advantages in the group: "The higher a man's social rank, the larger the number of persons for whom he originates interactions."[15] Also, "The leader is at the center of the web of interaction: much interaction flows toward him and away from him."[16] Furthermore, "The leader is the man who comes closest to realizing the norms the group values highest. The norms may be queer ones, but . . . the leader, in that group, must embody them."[17]

The relationships among these three elements was brought to the attention of many by such findings. The group dynamics movement, although not explicitly fathered by Homans's work, proceeded to operationalize many similar ideas as a parallel development. The vehicle was "sensitivity training" first developed by Leland P. Bradford at Bethel, Maine in 1947. This was the first human relations clinical mechanism and was called the National Training Laboratory. The NTL movement grew in reputation and scope throughout the 1950s. One observer has reported that the "essence of this sensitivity training was to achieve changes in behavior through 'gut level' interactions which led to increased interpersonal awareness."[18] Not a few administrators, in education as well as in business and industry took advantage of the "Bethel" experience. The consequence was a heightened awareness of both the interpersonal and situational variables in the operational patterns of organizations. To that end, the skills of the administrator were sharpened in functional services to the emergent characteristics of leadership as well as its consequent effectiveness.

The Contingency View of Leadership. The situational approach requires that the leader attend to variables other than those that reside in the interpersonal and small-group contexts of the organization. The set of ideas that permit a more inclusive view of leadership, currently the dominant ideas in the study of administration, is called the contingency theory of leadership. The leadership task in this context is to relate specific leader behaviors to effective group performance and satisfaction. To accomplish that task certain variables intervene. Such variables include those that inhere in the *self* of the leader, those

[15]Ibid., p. 182.
[16]Ibid., p. 418.
[17]Ibid., p. 188.
[18]Daniel A. Wren, *The Evaluation of Management Thought* (New York: Ronald Press, 1972), p. 325.

that are aspects of the *position* the leader holds, those that reside in the *members of the group,* those that deal with the *internal environment* of the organization (purposes, policies, procedures, products, etc.), and those that reside within the immediate *external environment* within which the organization exists. The successful matching of leader behavior with group performance and satisfaction is *contingent* on these variables.

The contingency view of leadership is a consequence of the emergence of systems theory and its impact on organizational and administrative theory. Of course, such a development cannot be explained away in one brief sentence, but it is not appropriate to the present discussion to provide a more detailed description of the development. It is sufficient for our purpose at this point to call to the attention of the reader the primary characteristic of a system. In the words of Parsons and Shils,[19]

The most general and fundamental property of a system is the interdependence of parts or variables. Interdependence consists of the existence of determinate relationships among the parts or variables, as contrasted with randomness of variability. In other words, interdependence is *order* in the relationship among the components which enter into a system.

Contingency leadership, then, must be understood in terms of the interdependent interaction of such variables as the five suggested.

Several examples of attempts to develop schemes to treat leadership in this fashion have been published. It is reported that the theory developed by Fred Fiedler has been "The propelling force in [the] transition to contingency theory . . ."[20] Earlier, Tannenbaum and Schmidt developed a position based on a "range of behavior" for the leader that varied from boss- or subordinate-centered leadership needs. Each of these patterns is discussed now.

Fiedler's Contingency Model. The contingency variables identified by Fiedler were leadership style and three leadership situations. The leadership style variable to be utilized was based on the familiar task-people dichotomy. Fiedler developed a semantic differential instrument through which the leader rated the co-worker with whom he or she worked *least* well. Leaders who rated their least preferred co-worker in a relatively positive fashion were identified as "relationship motivated." Those who rated their least preferred co-worker unfavorably were identified as "task motivated." An assumption basic to the Fiedler theory is that a leader's style is a function of his or her personality and, consequently, is relatively consistent from situation to situation. This position requires that the

---

[19]Talcott Parsons and Edward Shils, "Categories of the Orientation and Organization of Action," in T. Parsons and E. Shils, eds., *Toward a General Theory of Action* (New York: Harper & Row, 1962), p. 107.

[20]E. Mark Hanson, *Educational Administration and Organizational Behavior* (Boston: Allyn and Bacon, Inc., 1979), p. 247.

difference between leadership *behavior* and *style* be clarified. Behavior, Fiedler holds, refers to specific actions of leaders, whereas style connotes underlying attitudes and values that serve to motivate the behavior of leaders in various situations.[21] In that sense, style and personality become practically synonymous, and this factor has been cited as one of the shortcomings of the Fiedler conceptualization.[22]

The three situational variables that comprise a facet of the theory and that intervene between the leader's style and effectiveness are leader-member relations, task structure, and power position. Groups can be classified as either favorable or unfavorable on each of these variables. For instance, if the group members like and trust the leader, the leadership setting is favorable with respect to that variable; if the tasks are clear and procedures for accomplishing them are well known, the leadership setting is favorable; and if the leader occupies a position of power in the formal structure of the organization, the situation, again, is favorable. Of course, the opposite conditions create an unfavorable leadership setting.

Fiedler and others have used the contingency model to study the relationship between leadership and group performance across a wide range of groups. The studies determined the style of leadership, categorized the type of situation, and then determined the degree of successful performance evidenced by the group. The data from many studies were compared that demonstrated that "the appropriateness of the leadership style for maximizing group performance is contingent upon the favorableness of the group task situation."[23] That is, the most favorable situation in which the leader will be able to influence the group is one in which he or she is well liked by the group, is directing a well-structured task or assignment, and is in a relatively powerful position. Fiedler also reported that[24]

task-motivated leaders perform generally best in very "favorable" situations, i.e., either under conditions in which their power control and influence are very high (or conversely, where uncertainty is very low) or where the situation is unfavorable, where they have low power, control and influence. Relationship-motivated leaders tend to perform best in situations in which they have moderate power, control and influence.

The contingency model as developed by Fiedler does describe the interdependence of several sets of important variables and permits a description of leadership as being contingent upon those variables. Although the model does not incorporate situational variables external to the group itself, it does focus attention on three meaningful variables in the internal context of the situation.

[21]Fred E. Fiedler, *A Theory of Leadership Effectiveness* (New York: McGraw-Hill, 1967), p. 36.
[22]Hanson, op. cit., p. 253.
[23]Fiedler, op. cit., p. 147.
[24]Fred E. Fiedler, "The Contingency Model—New Directions for Leadership Utilization," *Journal of Contemporary Business* (Autumn 1974), 68.

It should be noted that the leader-member relations variable deals with the set of concerns we have called the "interactional approach," whereas the remaining two variables, task structure and position power, identify variables related to formal organization of the group. The position adopted by Fiedler regarding leadership style seems definitionally quite insightful. In spite of the criticisms leveled at the technique and fact of its measurement, it does place the personal or "self" element in the contingency mix. The self of the leader was only indirectly approached in the traits and/or characteristics era, the emphasis that we have called the "individual approach" to the consideration of leadership. Yet, the pervasive nature of the self-concept held by a leader is such that it might be considered as the pre-imminent contingency in the whole leadership mix. Certainly the nature of the leader-member relations is contingent upon it, as is the structuring of the work tasks for the organization, and several other variables that the Fiedler model omits (e.g., communication patterns, levels of training, cultural diversity, resource availability, levels of stress, and organizational climate, to suggest but a few). But the work of Fiedler brings this variable to the attention of the novice educational administrator and in so doing adds a significant dimension to his or her understanding of the interpersonal nature of leadership.

The Tannenbaum and Schmidt Model. A "contingency model" received widespread favorable response in the late 1950s before the term itself had been coined. It was the "boss-centered-subordinate-centered leadership model" designed by Robert Tannenbaum and Warren Schmidt and published in the *Harvard Business Review* in the spring of 1958. The "contingencies," although not so identified, were the elements in the problems that a leader had to treat, and they were the variables that helped the leader to vary his or her managerial or leadership style. A basic dimension in the "range of behavior" decision the leader was called upon to make was the question of the locus of authority. "Boss-centered leadership" was characterized by holding all of the authority in the hands of the boss. The boss made all decisions and simply announced them to the group. At the other end of the continuum, the "subordinate-centered leadership" end, a large area of freedom of action was reserved or assigned to the members of the work group. The leader allowed subordinates to operate freely within certain prescribed limits. Between these two positions there were five intermediate spots on the continuum using varying distributions of the authority versus freedom dimension.

The authors held that four sets of factors influenced the manager in selecting a leadership style: forces in the self, in the subordinates, in the situation, and in the external environment. This range of variables that behave as contingencies point out that scholars and practitioners alike recognized the complexity of the leadership phenomenon before the development of sophisticated theoretical approaches. It suggests that there must be a continuing interplay between the person on the front line of organizational life and the scholar for both to improve the practice of educational leadership and the output of the scholar's craft. The enthusiasm with which the boss-centered–subordinate-centered model was received, even though its design was not such that it stimulated research, demonstrates the need for cooperative efforts between the field and the office.

A concluding observation concerning contingency theories noted by Hanson is appropriate at this point. "Perhaps one of the most important implications of the contingency theory of leadership is that in a large measure specific conditions within the organization are as responsible for the success or failure of the leader as the leader is himself."[25]

In fact, the value of the contingency theories of leadership lies more in their attention to the total context within which the individual leader strives both for survival and success than in the degree of sophistication evidenced by their design and instrumentation. And this fact is of special note to the novice in educational administration.

LEADERSHIP STYLES: NOTES ON THE TACTICS OF LEADERSHIP

The three approaches to understanding leadership that were discussed each imply a variety of characteristic behaviors that are demonstrated by individual leaders. A set of particular behaviors can be described as a *style* of leadership, and much can be found in the research and general literature dealing with leadership styles. Before discussing several selected examples, a comment about the nature of "style" is in order. Style, as used in the present context refers to a distinct or characteristic mode of behavior. Leadership or administrative style, then, refers to the distinctive behavior exhibited by persons in formal positions of leadership. This is the sense in which style is used in administrative literature. In some discussions, the presumed difference between style and substance becomes a point of real disagreement. It is held that an emphasis by a leader on style can be interpreted as either an avoidance of substantive issues or an ignorance of their existence. Indeed, individual leaders have been known to avoid analyses of and planning for the use of stylistic considerations on these grounds, that is, on the ground that they would be diverting time and resources from "important" matters by so doing. The discussion of leader styles that follows is in no way intended to diminish the importance of substantive matters. It seems self-evident to us that a proper balance between the two cannot be achieved in the absence of style, for a mindless adherence to a pattern of behavior with the

[25]Hanson, op. cit., p. 248.

intention of displaying a specific style is as counterproductive as is its opposite. One other preliminary observation is pertinent. The literature as well as the experience of the authors suggest that few leaders in education give evidence of behavior that can readily be classified in any one of the categories of the styles that are reviewed in the following discussion. The reader will note that leadership styles are frequently described as contrasting pairs that represent a continuum of behavioral possibilities.

Democratic–Laissez-Faire–Autocratic Styles

The most commonly discussed categories of leadership styles are represented by the trilogy developed by the Lewin, Lippitt, and White child welfare studies described earlier. The democratic style was people oriented but structured, the *laissez-faire* style was without structure, and the autocratic style was rigidly structured and task oriented. Much lip service has been accorded the democratic leadership style, but little has been accomplished in moving it from the realm of rhetoric to the operational level. In fact, this has been one of the major problems with this set of style names. Nonetheless, it has proved to remind administrators about the impact of their behavior on the organizations they serve.

Initiation of Structure—Consideration

In the early 1950s Halpin and Winer, using an instrument developed by Hemphill and Coons at The Ohio State University, identified initiation of structure and consideration as two basic dimensions of leadership behavior.[26] The measurement of the behavior of leaders in terms of these two dimensions permits the identification of an individual's style as understood by the members of his or her organization. Halpin defines the dimensions as follows:[27]

Initiating structure refers to the leader's behavior in delineating the relationship between himself and members of the work-group, and in endeavoring to establish well-defined

---

[26]The instrument, the Leader Behavior Description Questionnaire (LBDQ), is a well-known and widely used device to study leadership. The members of the leader's group are requested to respond to a series of short statements, each of which describes a behavior that leaders might exhibit. A form can also be used to secure responses from the leader about his or her behavior. The former is scored to provide insight to his or her behavior on the dimensions. See the following for further information: John K. Hemphill and Alvin E. Coons, *Leader Behavior Description* (Columbus, Ohio: Personnel Research Board, The Ohio State University, 1950), and Andrew W. Halpin, *Theory and Research in Administration* (New York: Macmillan, 1966), pp. 86–127.

[27]Andrew Halpin, *Theory and Research in Administration* (New York: Macmillan, 1966), p. 86. (Emphasis added.)

patterns of organization, channels of communication, and methods of procedure. *Consideration* refers to behavior indicative of friendship, mutual trust, respect, and warmth in the relationship between the leader and members of his staff.

It is clear that the essential difference between the two dimensions is the task-people emphasis. The administrator whose style favored the initiation of structure dimension would be appreciated by his or her group because they would have a clear understanding of their role in the organization, of the performance levels expected of them, and of the rules and regulations that guide the organization's procedures. The administrator whose style favored the consideration dimension would be appreciated by the staff by virtue of the attention he or she pays to individual and personal matters, the equal treatment afforded to the members, the administrator's willingness to listen and to accept new ideas, and the administrator's openness and approachability.

It is clear that the style of a successful educational administrator must include at least some elements of both dimensions. A leader cannot gain the trust of members of his or her organization without being able both to plan and organize and to demonstrate genuine concern for the individual members of the organization. A well-organized principal, for instance, one who is "on top of" everything, still cannot provide the most effective leadership if he or she is not readily available to his or her staff and students. And this is what the rather extensive research using the LBDQ has demonstrated. Halpin reports that "The evidence from these inquiries shows that effective leadership is characterized by high Initiation of Structure and high Consideration."[28] The import of these findings for leadership understood in terms of interpersonal behavior is self-evident. The style must display genuine concern for the people in the organization and adequate mastery of the skills pertinent to the leaders role. In concluding the discussion of the Ohio State group's work, it is necessary to heed a warning issued by Halpin. It is an especially informative corrective for administrators who would be tempted to overemphasize the set of behaviors subsumed under the consideration dimension as utilized in the LBDQ:[29]

It is important to note that this concept of Consideration does not include what can be best described as merely "spray-gun consideration." The latter behavior is typified by the PTA smile, and by the oily affability dispensed by administrators at faculty picnics and office parties. Promiscuous Consideration defeats its purpose by its very promiscuity. Genuine Consideration must be focused upon the individual recipient and must be tuned to his requirements at a particular time and place.

[28]Ibid., p. 126.
[29]Ibid., pp. 86–87.

Theory X and Theory Y

Douglas McGregor, a psychologist who also served as president of Antioch College before he developed the Theory X and Theory Y model, was convinced that assumptions a manager (leader) made about people produced behavior in people that confirmed the assumptions. The leader's assumptions became self-fulfilling prophecies. These assumptions about human nature and human behavior were the primary determinants of the leader's style. McGregor identified two clusters of assumptions and called them Theory X and Theory Y.[30] Theory X assumptions represented the classical view, the view that he believed to be predominant in the contemporary industrial world. Theory Y assumptions represented those on which managers needed to operate if they were to bring about an integration of individual and organizational goals.

Theory X assumptions, three in number, can be summarized briefly. The first dealt with the attitude of people toward work and held that they had an inherent dislike of work, avoiding it when possible. The second, following from the first, held that people must be forced and coerced to work for the achievement of organizational objectives. The third held that people prefer to avoid responsibility, like to be directed, and seek security first.[31] Theory X represented the traditional and customary view of direction and control that guided most managers. It is clear that it parallels a "task" or "effectiveness" or "initiating structure" emphasis. Leadership style energized by Theory X assumptions would be characterized by a "full-speed ahead, damn the torpedoes" set of behaviors.

Theory Y assumptions were designed to bring about a "new" approach to leadership style by "changing assumptions about people in order to see that people could be trusted, that they could exercise self-motivation and control, and that they had the capacity to integrate their own personal goals with those of the formal organization."[32] The assumptions McGregor devised to accomplish this end, that is, to create an organizational environment conducive to the integration of personal and organizational goals, called for a new leadership style. They can be summarized as follows: (1) work is as natural for people as play or rest; (2) people can and will be self-directing if working toward objectives to which they are committed; (3) the most significant rewards that lead to such commitment are those that satisfy self-actualization needs; (4) people can learn to seek and accept responsibility; (5) imagination, ingenuity, and creativity

[30]See Douglas McGregor, *The Human Side of Enterprise* (New York: McGraw-Hill, 1960), for a complete discussion of his work.
[31]Ibid., pp. 33–34.
[32]Daniel A. Wren, *The Evolution of Management Thought* (New York: Ronald Press, 1972), p. 451.

are widely distributed in the population; and (6) the intellectual potential of individuals was being only partially used by modern industrial life.[33] These assumptions, singly and as a group, speak to the *potential* inherent in human beings, potential to be productive, contributive members of a formal work group. Although McGregor recognized that a "perfect" integration of personal and group objectives would never materialize, he expected that operations derived from Theory Y assumptions would contribute to an improved organizational climate in the industrial scene.

Theory Y style is similar to the characteristics of the consideration dimension of the LBDQ. It holds much attraction for many educators. Furthermore, it is instructive to the educational leader who is concerned about the nature of inter-personal behavior within the school. At the same time, Halpin's warning concerning promiscuous consideration is also applicable to Theory Y.

The Managerial Grid

The managerial grid developed by Robert R. Blake and Jane S. Mouton as a management and leadership training device, has two axes: concern for people and concern for production. The former refers to warm interpersonal relations within the organization; the latter denotes concern for the successful accomplishment of organizational tasks. Once again, we see these two basic dimensions of leadership style, people and tasks, conceptualized. The similarity to the consideration and initiating structure dimensions of the Ohio State studies is clear. But the interaction of the two through the grid present a somewhat different set of combinations that are represented by different leadership styles. Theoretically, there could be at least 81 combinations in the 9×9 grid, but Blake and Mouton have conceptualized five for their purposes (see Table 11-1). A brief description of each is pertinent to the present discussion.

The *impoverished* style of leadership is characterized by a low concern for people and for production. Leaders demonstrating this style tend to be self-interested and defensive, seldom "rocking the boat." In fact, they demonstrate a lack of leadership. The *task-oriented* style is characterized by high concern for production and low concern for people. An administrator demonstrating this type of leadership believes that people are instruments for the achievement of the organization's objectives. This style is very much like McGregor's Theory X. Relationship-oriented leadership, on the other hand, is similar in some respects to Theory Y characteristics in that people concerns are high and production concerns are low. Leaders tend to find out how the members of their organization want to operate and then try to make that happen. Conflicts, if they develop, are smoothed over through appeasement procedures. The *country club*

---

[33]McGregor, op. cit., pp. 47–48.

Table 11-1. Leadership Styles in the Blake and Mouton Managerial Grid

Style	Characteristics
Impoverished	The minimum effort exerted to get required work done is barely sufficient to sustain organization membership.
Task	Efficiency in operations results from arranging conditions of work in such a way that human elements interfere to a minimum degree.
Middle of the road or balanced	Adequate organization performance is possible through balancing the necessity to get out work while maintaining morale of people at a satisfactory level.
Country club	Thoughtful attention to needs of people for satisfying relationships leads to a comfortable friendly organization atmosphere and work tempo.
Team approach	Work accomplishment is from committed people; interdependence through a ''common stake'' in organization purpose leads to relationships of trust and respect.

From Robert Blake and Jane Mouton, *The Managerial Grid* (Houston: Gulf Publishing, 1964), p. 10.

style is characterized by the group in which this leadership style predominates. The *teamwork* style is characterized by high concern for both people and production. The leader utilizing this style attempts to develop a situation in which individual goals and organizational goals are integrated. This type of leader sees no intrinsic incompatibility between the two, so work is designed to promote mutual understanding, creativity, and high productivity, which encourage the development of high morale. The *balanced* or middle-of-the-road style is characterized by medium but equal levels of concern for people and production. Blake and Mouton found this style to be the most typical in industrial organizations. This style relies on tradition and rules and regulations; it recognizes a basic inconsistency between people needs and production objectives and strives to strike an acceptable balance between them rather than attempting to integrate them; it also recognizes the leader's responsibility to plan, direct, and control, although he or she usually does so by motivating and communicating rather than by directing.

The contribution the grid makes to an understanding of leadership as interpersonal relations is clear. It focuses on the dichotomy, presumed or real, between the needs of the individual and the needs of the organization. It seems that the lesson to be learned by the school administrator is that a leader must be cognizant of these two dimensions, perhaps a self-evident truth. The grid permits the individual to analyze his or her own leadership style and to initiate a self-development program.

SUMMARY

This chapter has introduced the reader to the concept of leadership. To that end, the setting for a consideration of leadership was suggested in terms of two generic issues, two issues that describe the reality within which an individual exercises leadership, the questions of *authenticity* and *politicization*. The *nature of leadership* was then described as it has been presented in a copious literature. A three-level structure organized this section, the focus being first on the individual approach to understanding leadership, then on the interactional approach, and finally on the situational approach. These are seen as differing patterns for survival and success in leadership positions. The last section of the chapter reports selected *leadership styles* as including suggestions for the tactics of leadership.

Authenticity was described as the central issue with which a leader must deal. It becomes a key to producing the trust and confidence necessary to the exercise of leadership. Its absence is present in most incidents of leadership failure. But it has become a very contemporary issue by virtue of the skepticism of all leadership evidenced by the public, and consequently must be dealt with directly by today's leaders in educational institutions. The politicization of educational institutions has brought upon the formal leadership of schools a new set of problems that, in turn, require a new approach to leadership itself. The multiple leadership produced by the factionalization of the schools is one evidence of this set of problems and responses.

The three approaches to understanding leadership began with the individual and focused the personal traits and characteristics of leaders. Research over many years has demonstrated that no specific set of traits or characteristics could be depended upon as describing all leaders, conventional wisdom to the contrary notwithstanding. This led to the examination of interactions between leaders and the followers for additional cues to the nature of leadership. Discoveries about this interdependence suggested that factors within the situation in which leadership was exercised might well add valuable insights. Consequently, the contingency approach to understanding leadership, based as it is on the variables that intervene in the interactions between the leader and members of the unit, emerges as the most comprehensive to studying leadership. An understanding of contingency models of leadership appears to offer the best hope of both survival and success to the practicing administrator.

The manner in which the administrator in fact operationalizes his or her leadership behavior can be described as his or her "style." The literature available to the interested practitioner includes more information on style than on other elements of the study, although the reports are frequently individual memoirs rather than analyses of leadership style. Four examples of major treatments of leadership, each having well-known and respected descriptions of style, were described briefly, the democratic-autocratic styles, the Ohio State studies, which produced the style categories of initiating structure and consideration, the Theory X and Theory Y pattern developed by McGregor, and the managerial grid from the work of Blake and Mouton. It should be noted in summary that a basic pair of emphases runs through each of the examples, namely, a concern for people and a concern for production. Each of the examples treats the two emphases differently, but the thread runs through them all. It can be safely generalized that these two contending concerns are pervasive in the exercise of leadership. The understanding of the leadership phenomenon has grown from a consideration of them in an "either-or" sense, as in the McGregor construction, to thinking of them as representing points on a continuum, as represented by the grid model of Blake and Mouton. The latter constellation fits more appropriately into the contingency theories that are currently looked to for a more meaningful understanding of potentially useful tactics of leadership.

EXERCISES

1. We have said that the absence of authentic behavior in leaders is an important reason for loss of public confidence. Whether or not you agree, during the next week try to observe leaders in terms of whether and to what extent you can ascertain their "authenticity." It might be revealing.
2. Because of a prolonged controversy and power struggle over salaries between teachers and the board of education in one school system, a strong-minded, respected, but obstinate superintendent was subsequently terminated. The teachers were pleased with the dismissal even though the superintendent had clearly been responsible for better facilities and working conditions, an effective affirmative action policy before that was fashionable, and a general reputation of quality education and solid community support. What does this situation suggest in terms of our discussion of "the politicization of the school" in this chapter?
3. The following observation was made during a break at a seminar on personnel management: "A conservative manager is one who's tough-minded and businesslike and gets the damned job done one way or another. Now a liberal manager, on the other hand, is always worrying about the people and things get off track." In terms of Chester Barnard's notion of effectiveness and efficiency, is this observation accurate? Why? Why not?
4. Two students were engaged in a lively discussion in which one held that an acknowledged leader like so-and-so, who had done a superb job as a uni-

versity president for ten years, would do equally well were he a regimental commander or captain of a ship or a Catholic bishop or corporation president; the point was that a good leader is a good leader, *period!* "No," said the other; "on the contrary, a 'good' ship captain wouldn't last a month as the administrator of a huge hospital because the status system would frustrate him." What is your position and why?

5. Dr. Joe Blow has just been handed his administrator's credential, all framed and gleaming, and is now ready for his first administrative post. He gets pieces of advice from two experts: A says to him, "Be sure you cultivate your subordinates so that they will come to have some affection for you— that is the most favorable leadership setting." B says to him, "Be sure you do not become too familiar with your subordinates—an attitude of aloofness enhances the perception of power and that is the most favorable leadership setting." Are both sets of advice sound? Why? What advice would you give by completing the following sentence: If you want to be an effective leader, then _____.

SUGGESTED REFERENCES

Blake, Robert R., and Jane S. Mouton. *The Managerial Grid*. Houston: Gulf Publishing, 1964.

Halpin, Andrew W. *Theory and Research in Administration*. New York: Macmillan, 1966 (especially Chapters 3, 4, and 6).

Homans, George C. *The Human Group*. New York: Harcourt Brace, 1950 (Chapter 16).

McGregor, Douglas. *The Human Side of Enterprise*. New York: McGraw-Hill, 1960.

Roethlisberger, F. J., and Dickson, William J. *Management and the Worker*. Cambridge, Mass.: Harvard University Press, 1939, 609 pp.

Stogdill, Ralph. *Handbook of Leadership*. New York: Free Press, 1974.

White, Ralph, and Lippitt, Ronald. *Autocracy and Democracy: An Experimental Inquiry*. New York: Harper & Row, 1960.

Wren, Daniel A. *The Evolution of Management Thought*. New York: Ronald Press, 1972 (especially Chapter 20, pp. 438–470).

Chapter 12

Administrative Leadership and Boards of Education

INTRODUCTION

The functions and duties of the local board of education, described in Chapter 3, require a unique set of behaviors on the part of the superintendent of schools. The individual occupying that position traditionally has served as the chief executive officer of the board and, consequently, has been responsible for carrying out the decisions of the board. Historically, the superintendency grew out of a need for assistance by board members who were well occupied in their own business and professional affairs. The early functions were frequently more clerical than managerial. Gradually, local boards of education became less and less concerned with the administrative detail involved in providing educational opportunities for the children and youth of their districts and relied increasingly on the advice and performance of a developing professional cadre of managers.

Numerous factors contributed to this development, not the least of which were the growth in size of school districts and, concurrently, the ever-increasing complexity of the organizational context within which "schooling" was practiced. As the twentieth century progressed, the relationship between the board and the superintendent modified in favor of the superintendent, and, in the 1920s and 1930s, several achieved national stature by virtue of the leadership they provided education. The decades of the 1960s and 1970s, however, have seemed to moderate if not reverse that tendency. School boards have become more responsive to the divisive issues and factions that have emerged as American society has grappled with long-standing grievances of its less fortunate citizens, and the consequence has, in part, included a confounding and a confusing of the role of the superintendent and the relationship between the occupant of that role and the board itself.

It is true that large school districts are becoming nearly unmanageable. Furthermore, the functioning of both the board and the administrative leadership has become an exercise in the political manipulation of the forces and factors at work within the larger society. It becomes the task of the formal leadership of the school district—a function that resides in the board of education as a corporate body and its chief executive officer, the superintendent of schools— to operate in a statesmanlike manner within the highly charged political milieu that characterizes all contemporary public enterprises.

What behaviors characterize political statesmanship in the management of public schools? This and corollary questions give direction to the comments that are included within the present chapter. More specifically, the questions that confront the individual occupying the administrative chair are: How can the superintendent enable the board of education to discharge its proper function? What behaviors should that person exhibit that will provide direction for the board? How can he or she provide proper leadership while remaining an appointee of the board? These questions will be considered first by examining selected issues that speak directly to the relationship between the superintendent and board. Next, specific interactions between the superintendent and board that grow out of such issues will be examined. And, finally, implications of the patterns that emerge from those discussions will be developed in a context of applications to several selected operational concerns.

ISSUES

Events, activities, and concerns that are viewed as "issues" are customarily so classified by virtue of the values, understandings, and previous experience of the individuals doing the viewing. It is quite likely that citizens serving on boards of education would define certain events as issues differently than would their chief executive officer, the superintendent, and the professional staff of the school. A primary and enduring issue, then, for the administrator who would discharge the leadership assignment with some degree of success is to examine and treat the question of differing perceptions of such pervasive concerns as the purposes and goals of the enterprise, the nature and use of authority, and the clarification of board and staff member roles that might well exist in the board-superintendent interactions.

For reasons not even yet clarified through much scholarly research, successful leaders have always been able to manage such potentially disruptive and dysfunctional issues as these with aplomb. Some individuals seem to be blessed with the necessary skills and appear to operate successfully almost intuitively. But most individuals who occupy administrative positions find it both necessary and advisable to seek a more reliable base for their performance. An initial approach to this baseline issue is to seek out the assumptions held by members of the board. These are assumptions that guide their particular views, of the proper nature of school organization. Individuals who are unfamiliar with the nature of educational organizations frequently assume that the industrial model is adequate to the functions of schools. That is, the objectives are clear and precise, the technology needed to achieve the objectives is understood and available, and the several units involved in the process are aware of their responsibilities and these are well coordinated and controlled. This is a production-line model, which appears on the surface to be an efficient organizational pattern. And this view is understandable when it is recognized that most school board members are laypersons with mostly commercial and industrial backgrounds.

But, on the other hand, schools customarily operate with unclear or at least very general goals and objectives about which there is frequently vigorous debate. Furthermore, the technology necessary to the achievement of *any* of the goal and objective patterns is amorphous at best, residing as it does in the system of instruction, of teaching and learning, that is the primary responsibility of the faculty. Little is known with confidence about the nature of the teaching-learning technology that can be generalized across an educational institution. Finally, little or no effective control and/or coordination can be exercised over the primary technology of the school. The sanctity of the classroom has long been demonstrated, and properly so. In sum, the nature of educational organizations is simply *different* from most organizations with which board members are and have been customarily associated. The issue for the superintendent is to enable board members to recognize these essential differences and to act in accordance with a useful understanding.[1]

One way in which the administrator can confront this issue is to introduce the board members to an understanding of the school as a "loosely coupled system."[2] Coupling refers to the nature of the relationships within an organization that link its several parts and processes. The common and generally unexamined assumption is that good organizations are "tightly coupled," as in the description of the naval captain who takes pride in running a "tight ship" (i.e., one

[1]A helpful discussion of these understandings is found in Michael D. Cohen, James G. March, and Johann Olsen, "A Garbage Can Model of Organizational Choice," *Administrative Science Quarterly*, Vol. 17, no. 1 (March 1972), 1–25; and Michael D. Cohen and James G. March, *Leadership and Ambiguity: The American College President* (New York: McGraw-Hill, 1974).

[2]This concept was described initially in terms of educational organizations by Karl E. Weick in "Educational Organizations as Loosely Coupled Systems," *Administrative Science Quarterly*, Vol. 21, no. 2 (June 1976), 1–19. We rely on this source in the present discussion.

in which everyone does a prescribed job properly, the sum of which is an organization that is "shipshape"). Loosely coupled organizations, by contrast, are those that by design provide much room for individual initiative. Indeed, it can be said that the purposes and goals of some organizations require that the control and coordination necessary to an appropriate technology be exercised in large measure by the primary operatives. Some observers hold that the school is such an organization. Teachers, who are the primary operatives, function as highly trained and skilled directors of learning for the primary clients of the organization, the students. The role of such operatives requires an environment within which high orders of initiative and inventiveness can flourish if the school is to serve the societally and historically determined purpose of individual development. That is, if this generally agreed-upon purpose of schools is to be achieved, a loosely coupled system view of their organizational characteristics appears to provide a useful and potentially productive set of guidelines.

Schools that represent loosely coupled organization patterns demonstrate such characteristics as tolerance of a wide range of teaching styles, adaptability to local conditions, resistance to imposed change, and low levels of ability to mount concerted efforts, each contributing to an environment that encourages freedom and experimentation as well as individual responsibility. It would not be surprising to find that an individual who works in a much more controlled and directed environment would view a loosely coupled system as ineffectual. Thus, the role of the superintendent involves enabling the board members, individually and as a corporate body, to behave in ways that enhance a productive loosely coupled environment. It is clear that such an environment requires much more nurturing than does one based on a more traditional view of authority and control. The former must be held together by high levels of mutual confidence whereas the latter are bound by formal controls and sanctions. Leadership, then, involves ensuring that the bases of mutual confidence are established and continually maintained in good repair.

Although the level of confidence appropriate to successful organizational performance cannot be prescribed in general, it can be estimated in specific organizations. Attention must be directed to the consequences of the technology— at the outputs of the school if you will. In other words, if goals and objectives, even though imprecise and tentative, can be examined openly and candidly by members of the school, the chances of their being achieved improve. As a consequence, development of an improved level of mutual confidence, the necessary binding agent in a loosely coupled organization, thereby becomes a real possibility. The same speculation can be made regarding the general policies that guide the operation of the school and the manner in which formal authority is understood and discharged within the school. These are central issues that ought properly to be of concern to the local board of education. They might well be the elements through which the superintendent provides leadership for the board. Each is discussed in the following sections.

The Determination and Clarification of Goals:
A Continuing Primary Issue

Board members frequently assume that the purposes and goals of the school are clear, well understood, and generally agreed upon. At least, this was true in the past even though it is a much less reasonable generalization as the decade of the 1980s begins. Just as frequently, professional educators, including superintendents, have become disaffected with discussions of purposes and goals. Teachers of specific subject matter assume that the objectives of education in large measure revolve around mastering a particular field of knowledge, whereas administrators, although verbalizing general purposes, tend to believe that purposes and goals of education have been achieved if the school runs smoothly. Of course, there is a measure of truth in each position. But the general tendency is either to ignore the purpose-goal question on the one hand or deny the need to consider something that seems to be self-evident, on the other. The tendency in any case suggests a primary cause of the erosion of confidence in a school. Consequently, a first and continuing task of the superintendent in providing leadership for the local school board is to embrace this issue.

The question, then, is how can this issue be raised so as to improve the levels of mutual confidence that exist within the school structure? How can the board keep the problem of goal-objective determination and clarification in a dynamic mode without encouraging the development of a negative attitude toward the process and the concept? The key appears to be found in the maintenance of an informal, open, continuing discussion of goals and purposes in terms of activities that are of real and demonstrable possibility within the constraints of local conditions. Such conversations might well be in the form of traditional program achievement reports by teachers, students, and community representatives presented to the board in regular but informal information sessions that are open, of course, to all interested people. The function of such "conversations" is to demonstrate publicly the nature of the "real" objectives of the school, that is, the programs and activities that are in fact being supported by the resources and energies of the school. The function is not an evaluative one; it is an informational one. The assumption is that such a series of conversations becomes a tool through which the superintendent encourages greater understanding by the board of the actualities of the school, greater openness on the part of the staff and students, and, it is hoped, the development of higher levels of mutual confidence.

There are specific issues, however, concerning the goals and purposes of the schools with which the board ought to feel free and competent to deal. It should be noted that there are certain objectives that have been determined on a state and national level that are beyond the review of the local board. Such objectives as a segregation-free society and equal opportunities in employment serve as examples. Specific items differ from state to state and should be examined with care locally. Nonetheless, the question of the scope of the school's role should be of concern to the board and the faculty. For example, is or should the school be all things to all people? Or does it have a more limited role? Should the school be an agent of social change or a guardian of the traditions of the community? Should the school be a vehicle to enhance the values of one segment of society? These and similar questions are debated without final resolution being achieved. They go beyond the ability of a single local school board to resolve. But their impact is still seen in the policy responses and goal determinations made in the routine operation of a single school. Consequently, the leadership group must be aware of the position it is supporting by virtue of its routine decisions on such far-reaching purpose issues as these. And the local board not only cannot escape dealing with these issues, it has the competence necessary to the task. The superintendent's function is to ensure that the goal-objective questions are kept in focus and that the board's competence is released.

The Conflict Between Policy and Managerial Roles and Functions: A Confounding Issue

The discussion of goal determination and clarification issues certainly implies that there is no clear line that separates policy questions from operational issues. A policy decision for one level in an organization becomes an operational procedure for subordinate levels. And that relationship is then repeated for subsequent subordinate levels. Consequently, a confusion regarding this matter in the board-administrator relationship should not be surprising. Still, it is important to the successful operation of the school that potential conflict points be recognized and that measures be taken to minimize the impact.

A clarification of policy is a first measure that both board members and the superintendent must take. A policy is customarily understood to be a formal statement that describes a settled or definite course of action. It is a general statement that describes an intention to act in a given way when confronted with a particular set of circumstances. Policy statements, then, provide guides for future action, enable an organization to display consistent behavior, and serve as a means to avoid or resolve conflict. Policy statements are generally constructed in terms that are broad enough to cover most of the pertinent issues and specific enough to be useful in particular situations. They are customarily implemented through sets of procedures, rules, or regulations. The most important task of the board of education is the development of sound policies to guide the operation of the school. Theirs is the "policy function" both by tradition and sound practice.

The superintendent's leadership function involves the clarification of the elements of policy development. The implementation of the policy guides is the function delegated by sound boards of education to their professional chief executive officer. In addition to stimulating the development process, the superintendent should be charged with the responsibility of determining the manner in which the policies will be implemented. It is his or her task to advise the board in the policy development activity and then to develop the organization and the procedures required by the policy. Hence, the administrative and managerial functions reside in the staff employed by the board and not in the board itself.

A major aspect of this issue develops when individual board members insist on discharging administrative functions and/or the superintendent attempts to write policy for the school district. The potential for conflict in such situations is clear, and the consequences in eroded confidence in the leadership of the school cannot be avoided. This issue develops most frequently from the unbridled ambition of the individuals involved. When self-serving ambition is coupled with inaccurate information about the function and responsibilities of either role, the conflict potential is realized, and the energies of the organization are misdirected and abused in nonproductive activities.

The policy-managerial tension that frequently develops has been compounded in recent years by the aggressive stance taken by teachers' organizations and unions. Collective bargaining procedures have blurred the already gray boundary between policy and operating regulation by requiring that all formalized relationships between the board (or the district) and the staff be opened to negotiation. Such action has materially complicated the policy development function and, according to some observers, subjected it to the uncertainties of the adversarial processes of negotiations or bargaining. Time alone will make possible an evaluation of the contribution of this confounding of the issue.

The Source and Use of Authority: The Basic Operational Issue

Indigenous to each of the categories of issues described and impinging on the board-administrator relationship is the question of authority. It is clear that the board's authority, resting as it does in statutory provisions, prevails. Furthermore, it is clear that the formal authority residing in the superintendency does so by virtue of the action of the board. It is *delegated authority*.

And Some Comments About Authority

Authority is customarily understood as the quality that secures obedience from a specific group of people. In a sense, it is one form of power.[3] Interestingly and frequently not recognized, authority inheres in an individual and is, in

[3]See, for example, William G. Monahan, *Theoretical Dimensions of Educational Administration* (New York: Macmillan, 1975), pp. 147–162.

effect, *granted* to the individual by those who are subordinates. Power, on the other hand, is based on the control of resources that are desired by another individual. In organizational terms, power resides in the *position* or office whereas authority resides in the *occupant* of the position. While something of an oversimplification, power, then, can also be understood as *formal* or *legal* authority. But, authority, as defined, may also be described as *informal* or *technical*. When an individual accepts employment from a school board, he or she accepts that agency's legal authority over all matters dealing with the operation of the school. When an individual is assigned to a specific position in a specific school, he or she accepts the formal authority of the superordinate but may or may not ascribe to that person a measure of technical authority.

Thus, the nature of the authority that resides in the board can be understood as formal or legal authority. The board as a corporate body does not exercise authority because of the expertise of its members but, rather, by virtue of the formal positions they occupy as an agency. The superintendent, on the other hand, exercises both forms of authority. This role has formal authority delegated to the position occupied, and it is expected that such a person's technical skills will be substantial enough to earn the respect of subordinates. The same applies to every other professional employee of the board. And herein lies the source of the issue: simply put, it is the dual nature of the authority of the superintendent (and other staff) and the singular nature of the authority of the members of the board.

The Authority Dilemma

The issue often produces confusion at best and at times even conflict in the relationship between the superintendent and the board. The most familiar example is frequently manifested in attempts of board members to take action as individuals by intervening in behalf of a constituent or an employee. Such action is bound to fail in the larger sense, for it is beyond the scope of the individual board member's formal authority. Other examples are seen when the superintendent provides advice to the board on matters that are beyond the scope of his or her technical authority, and the advice fails to have the support of the members of the staff who possess the appropriate expertise. It should be noted that these "confusions" create stress not only in the relationships between board and administrator but also in board-community and administrator-faculty relationships. When a member of a school board misleads a representative of the community by undertaking activities that are beyond the scope of that role's policy development prerogatives, the confidence of the community in the school is bound to suffer. A similar erosion of confidence can well be assumed when the action involves the administrator and representatives of the educational establishment. Consequently, it is incumbent on the superintendent to confront the authority issue routinely but directly. Only by developing an understanding of the sources and uses of authority appropriate to each level and each member of the school can the confusion be kept within acceptable and, thereby, nondisruptive bounds.

ADMINISTRATOR-BOARD INTERACTIONS

So we would hold that the superintendent can provide leadership for the board initially by confronting three categories of issues that plague the relationship: the confusion regarding goals and objectives, the conflict between policy and managerial roles, and the identification of the locus of authority.

It is clear that attempts to confront such issues involve the participants in interactions fraught with at least a high potential for discomfort (sometimes, even more, an invitation to seek employment elsewhere!). Obviously, disagreements between the board and the superintendent cannot be avoided. Indeed, the absence of a manageable level of tension suggests that the organization (or some major segments of it) just might be asleep. The problem for all parties is one of recognizing a state of dynamic tension as a normal or even valuable condition.

We emphasize that point. Our own experiences as administrators in the education establishment convince us that the *a priori* recognition and acceptance of dynamic tensions is not only a fact of life in administrative reality but that, without it, the system is robbed of the values that govern good education. Prospective school administrators must learn to both accept and channel that dynamic tension—it is their best hope for effectiveness as opposed to efficiency.[4]

If the issues are to be confronted, the administrator must find operational answers to the following questions: How is agreement on the purposes and goals achieved? How is policy developed in a flexible and continuous manner? and How can the board be organized so that its proper functions can be discharged effectively? Each of these questions is treated now as a central contact point in the interactions between the superintendent and the school board.

Purposes and Policies

The Nature of Purposes and Policies. It is appropriate to discuss the goal-policy questions concurrently, for in the operational context of the schools, statements of purpose and of objectives become "policies" that guide the decisions and, consequently, the actions and behaviors of the personnel of the

---

[4]We urge readers to consider the classic work of Chester Barnard, *The Functions of the Executive* (Cambridge, Mass.: Harvard University Press, 1938), which establishes a useful distinction between efficiency and effectiveness.

school district. As described, a policy is most commonly understood as a statement giving direction to a government, an administration, or an institution. Furthermore, it is customarily defined in terms of goals and objectives. After reviewing several descriptions of the nature and function of policy, Bogue and Saunders conclude that "policy describes the general goals of organizations . . . and provides a guide to decision making for achievement of goals."[5]

One way in which to conceptualize this close relationship or to clarify the technical differences is through the classification schema presented in Figure 12–1. This hierarchy identifies levels of policy according to the scope of their applicability. For example, the most general level applies to the total function of the organization. Policies of this nature are properly statements of the overriding or societal purposes that provide ultimate guidance for the school. An example of this level of policy is the claim that the school shall prepare children and youth for productive citizenship. A central purpose is, thereby, articulated.

General purposes such as this seldom cause disagreements between the board and the superintendent in policy development activities. They simply are so general that they permit great latitude in their interpretation and stimulate little discussion. Additionally, they frequently remain unexamined by virtue of the set of relatively unarticulated cultural agreements that sustain much activity in school organizations. Issues arise more frequently at each of the subsequent levels in the hierarchy. *Goals* are derived from statements of general purpose and are intended to initiate the implementation of those purposes by taking the first step in the process of translating them into action. To continue the example, if it is the purpose of the school system to contribute significantly to the preparation of the children and youth of its district for productive citizenship, the goal policies that describe the meaning of "citizenship" must be verbalized. These goals and the policy statements that give them substance must be restricted to activities that can be accomplished within the authority of a given school system. For example, if "productive citizenship" is uncritically assumed to be possible only for individuals with no mental or physical handicap, however defined (as was the case for decades), then the school needs to provide no special services for the handicapped. Again, if the intended purpose is assumed to require full development of special or unique talents of students, then the school's goal policies must direct the establishment and maintenance of a broad range of talent and skill development programs.

It can be seen from this example that the second level in the hierarchy, the goal-policy level, is pregnant with points of possible friction and disagreement. And most of these disagreements involve the members of the board, both as individuals and as a corporate body. It is proper that the board be involved actively and energetically at this level. Indeed, when the board's policy-making

---

[5]E. G. Bogue and R. L. Saunders, *The Educational Manager: Artist and Practitioner* (Worthington, Ohio: Charles A. Jones, 1976), p. 128.

Figure 12-1. A Policy Classification Schema: The Hierarchy of Purposes, Goals, and Objectives

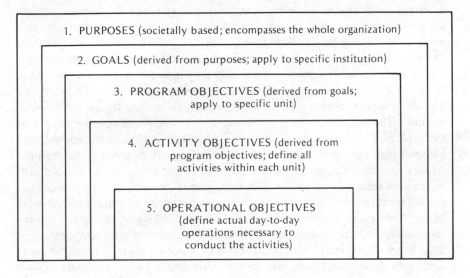

Level 1. General Purposes — are societal in nature and give "purpose" for the existence of all educational organizations.

Level 2. Goals — are institution-specific and define the aspect(s) of the societal purpose that a given institution accepts and/or serves.

Level 3. Program Objectives — are intra-institutional and define the aspects of the institution that each specific subunit assumes or is assigned.

Level 4. Activity Objectives — define the whole range of specific activities required within the subunits by the program objectives.

Level 5. Operational Objectives — are derived from and implement the activity objectives and, consequently, enable the institution to achieve its goals and satisfy its societally defined purpose.

function or role is contrasted to the administrator's executive responsibilities, it is the goal level of policy formulation that is the customary reference. The classification schema demonstrates, however, that no clear-cut differentiation of function between the superintendent and the board can be observed in operation, for the administrative responsibility includes providing leadership for the board in goal-policy matters even when by custom and legal description the board as a corporate body has the formal responsibility. But, working together, with the board's exercising its function both in initiating questions and proposals and in making final decisions while the superintendent provides the necessary information and appropriate analysis of potential consequences, functional goal-policy statements can be developed. When done properly, this is not a casual exercise. Rather, it is one that is both time consuming and tension producing.

The superintendent's primary leadership responsibility in this undertaking is to search for levels of agreement within the board and between the board and himself or herself, agreements that are defensible on both moral and professional grounds. The reference here is not to facile maneuvering or to naïve delight in the absence of disagreement. The appeal is to tough-minded, open confrontation between legitimate differences without resort, overtly or covertly, to personal attacks or petty politicking. Indeed, such forthright engagement of significant differences must rely on an atmosphere of mutual respect, and it is toward the development of such an atmosphere that the superintendent's major efforts must be directed. There is no simple prescription for discharging this leadership responsibility, but the basic tenets of an ethical rationalism provide the structure necessary to a potentially successful endeavor. Such practices as resolving questions with the best available information, willingness to go beyond one's own preferences, respect for the intentions of vigorous opponents, ability to endure ambiguity productively, and the diligent and continuous search for rational solutions represent a portion of such a position.

Levels 3, 4 and 5 in the hierarchy properly belong in the realm of professional decision. That implies a minor role for the board and a major role for the superintendent and the professional staff. Although it is often assumed that the board is not involved in these levels of policy development, it must be noted that it does retain the responsibility of reviewing such actions and evaluating the consequent implementation activities. The actual development of programs and activities is, of course, left to technical staff and is carried out within existing policy. Sometimes the proposal of new programs implies new policy and such policy statements are usually part of the proposal. If, however, the staff or faculty establish a new program such as driver's education or interscholastic swimming, a program that represents a significant departure from existing patterns and, hence, an additional goal-level activity, and does so without the involvement of the board, confusion and probably conflict will result. *The role of the superintendent in all these cases, regardless of the source of the initiative, is to ensure that proper policy determination procedures are followed.* By daily and routine attention to this responsibility, the necessary clarification of roles can be achieved, and unnecessary contention can be reduced to a minimum. In fact, this is the first step in the development of a productive working atmosphere, and it represents a significant accomplishment for the superintendent in the discharge of his or her leadership responsibility.

One more aspect in the management of the purpose-policy interactions between board and superintendent requires comment before proceeding to other matters. That aspect is the idiosyncratic nature of all the actions in the purpose-policy clarification scene. The wise superintendent is the one who is sensitive to the uniqueness of each individual member of the board and the staff and who is not immobilized by that awareness but is able to understand and interpret the sometimes aberrant views that an individual espouses. It is not at all unusual in the life of an organization to find individuals speaking from their highly personalistic and idiosyncratic sets of needs. Similarly, it is not unusual for other members of boards and/or staff to take offense at such positions. And it is this type of interaction that often results in destructive contention within a school system. The awareness and artistry of the superintendent in such cases may enable him or her to mediate the conflict to the benefit of all concerned. That is, the unique view of one member may be turned into an emergent policy-purpose contribution of some significance to the organization if the leadership is able to turn it in a productive direction and to do so within the clearly understood role responsibilities of the participants. But the idiosyncracies of one or a few participants should never be allowed to destroy a productive working environment within the board itself, the staff, or the total school system. To maintain the system in this dynamic tension is a major function, responsibility, and challenge of the leadership of the superintendent. These issues are most frequently engaged at the purpose-policy clarification and development level of operation. It is simply in the nature of policies and purposes to produce such issues for leadership.

The considerations noted help us to understand the nature of policy as demonstrating the following characteristics:

1. A policy is a formal statement rationally determined (i.e., selected from among alternatives in the light of given conditions) describing a course of action intended to guide present and future decisions.
2. A policy in an educational institution is characterized by its dynamics and flexibility, its interpretive ability, and its applicability to ongoing educational programs.
3. An educational policy can be understood as a statement intended to facilitate purpose-goal achievement. As such, it represents the translation of goals and objectives into the operations of an institution.
4. Policies should be understood as servants of the people who comprise the school and not their master.

The Development of Policies and Purposes. It is clear that, while the leadership responsibilities of the superintendent are discharged through each of his or her activities, the development of policies and purposes requires a major portion of his or her energy and attention because of their crucial role in the success of the educational enterprise. We have described purposes and policies as a complex set of direction-giving statements, the development and implementation of which is influenced by a variety of factors. In the words of one student of public policy, "In a pluralistic society, almost any proposal will have advocates and opponents. Out of this conflicting opinion, compromises must be made—and this is public policy."[6] The nature of each local school district reflects the increasingly "pluralistic" nature of American society and the variety of factors that intersect in the policy development activities is consequently limited only by the social complexity of the given district. One can confidently assume that the policy development process must provide for the emergence of rationally defensible compromises, even though the structure of the complexity and of the policy issues appears to be composed of significant nonrational elements and forces. Members of the board of education increasingly represent constituencies either formally or informally. The tendency is that board members become "decision brokers" in all matters of board business, but especially in policy development matters. The superintendent finds that, given such a development, he or she becomes more clearly a compromise producer. To enhance that set of activities, a rational assessment technique must be available, one that provides for as many of the variables and contingencies as possible. Two analysis techniques are described in the paragraphs that follow.

The first technique provides a description of the sequence or flow of activities involved in the process of developing educational policy. Its major elements are presented in Figure 12-2. Thompson suggests that the process of policy formation must first take account of the cultural milieu and its consequent impact on the local situation. These environmental factors are located customarily in forces well beyond the control of the local board. A national political campaign, an economic recession, or an international threat to peace and stability are examples of such factors. The manner in which they influence attitudes and events in a local school district varies from locale to locale, but the fact of the impact is beyond question. An intelligent assessment of their status is an important first step in the policy development sequence of activities. The second step in the flow of activities is a consideration of the background of the local situation itself. Such an analysis calls to the attention of the policymakers local traditions, existing organizations that might be effected by the proposed policy, and those established positions that have been held by local constituencies through legal or quasi-legal agencies. A review of past actions in areas closely related to the proposed development is simplified by the second phase in the development flow. Such information provides an opportunity to avoid stumbling into an unnecessary set of contradictory actions. The third step focuses attention

[6]J. T. Thompson, *Policymaking in American Public Education* (Englewood Cliffs, N.J.: Prentice-Hall, 1976), p. 7.

Figure 12-2. A Policy-Making Sequence in Education

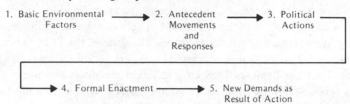

Adapted from J. T. Thompson, *Policymaking in American Public Education* (Englewood Cliffs, N.J.: Prentice-Hall, 1976), p. 16.

on contemporary actions and programs of interested and potentially related agencies. This phase of the sequence represents a "pulse-taking" exercise that assists in developing an accurate estimate of potential responses from key groups in the effected area. Thompson calls it the political action input to the development flow. The actual establishment of the new policy is accomplished in the fourth step in the development sequence. All the previously gathered and analyzed information about the proposed policy is converted at this point, and the policy is formalized. It then becomes one of those formal, direction-giving statements that we identify as purpose-goal-policy elements in the operation of an educational organization. What happens operationally is simply this: the "fit" of the proposal is "tested" first with the overriding cultural values that have been identified as pertinent, then with previous actions taken both by predecessor boards and significant agencies, and finally with the potential impact on contemporary and affected organizations. If it is determined that the fit is acceptable, the issue can be formalized through appropriate action by the board, and policy is born. But the development process does not stop at this point in the Thompson sequence. A fifth step focuses attention on the consequences of the implementation of the newly formulated policy. New situations develop as a result of the new policy, and they represent new and additional needs to be considered, so the policy formation sequence is initiated anew. And ever is it so, for out of identified needs come new purposes, goals, and policies. The fifth step, then, represents the feedback loop in the process.

The second policy development process considers elements similar to those just described, but conceives the process as a continuous and unavoidable cycle. This analysis tool is called the policy development and redefinition cycle (PDRC).[7] A primary characteristic of policies permits the defense of an as-

---

[7]The PDRC has been adapted for the present purposes from H. R. Hengst, "Purposes and Their Determination," *American Journal of Pharmaceutical Education*, Vol. 30, no. 12 (December 1966), 627–637.

sumption that is basic to the PDRC model. Being of a dynamic nature implies that policies are both modifiable and impermanent. The PDRC assumes that a policy is modified by the process of development and application. Simply stated, policies, when examined in the real world of school system operation, are seldom fully implemented or strictly enforced. They serve, it will be remembered, as guidelines for the decision making of teachers, administrators, and board members. They are flexible. They have different meanings and implications at different times according to differing circumstances. If this were not the case, there would be a markedly reduced need for the judicial system in the broader society for that system is devoted in large measure to the adjudication of differing interpretations of policy statements that are called "laws." The point is simply that policies are subject to a variety of forces and factors both in their development and in their application and that these factors help to shape specific policies. The PDRC is intended to take into account this dynamic characteristic of educational policies. To that end, it permits the analysis of both the *de novo* development of a specific policy and the analysis of the life of an existing policy as it functions within the school system. The elements of the four-phase cycle are identified in Figure 12-3.

The first of the four phases is called the *identification phase*. As the name implies, this is the place where officials responsible for the operation of the school system exercise policy development initiatives. To do so requires a particularly alert superintendent and/or board, individuals who do not assume that they are all seeing and all knowing but who have devised personal and organizational techniques for keeping in touch with the ongoing activities of the school system. They are sensitive to the needs of the organization and are routinely ready to receive inquiries and complaints about existing procedures and policies. They screen such information regularly through the existing policies and traditions of the school system so that they might identify with some precision the nature of the condition requiring treatment. When a decision that treatment is needed is reached, the superintendent drafts a recommended policy statement for the consideration of the board.[8] After due consideration, the board instructs the superintendent to initiate the PDRC, and it becomes his or her responsibility to oversee the review of the initial draft as provided for in the second phase.

Phase 2 is called the *potential-testing phase* in the development process. It is intended to provide the information necessary to answer this question: Will the proposed policy work? That is, will it treat the problem it is intended to treat? The draft proposal is then screened through several significant groups and

---

[8]The use of appropriate language is vital to this activity. More is said about it in succeeding paragraphs.

Figure 12-3. Policy Development and Redefinition Cycle

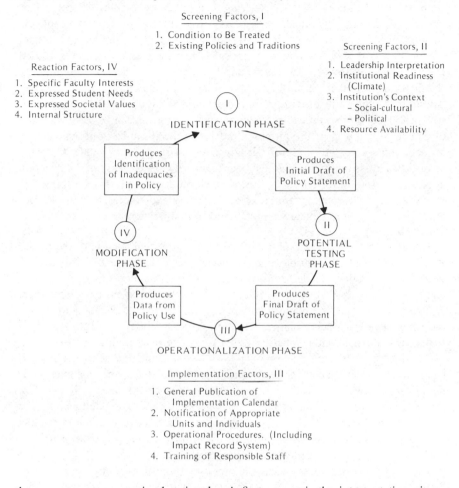

Screening Factors, I

1. Condition to Be Treated
2. Existing Policies and Traditions

Screening Factors, II

1. Leadership Interpretation
2. Institutional Readiness
   (Climate)
3. Institution's Context
   – Social-cultural
   – Political
4. Resource Availability

Reaction Factors, IV

1. Specific Faculty Interests
2. Expressed Student Needs
3. Expressed Societal Values
4. Internal Structure

I

IDENTIFICATION PHASE

Produces
Identification
of Inadequacies
in Policy

Produces
Initial Draft of
Policy Statement

IV

MODIFICATION
PHASE

II

POTENTIAL
TESTING
PHASE

Produces
Data from
Policy Use

Produces
Final Draft of
Policy Statement

III

OPERATIONALIZATION PHASE

Implementation Factors, III

1. General Publication of
   Implementation Calendar
2. Notification of Appropriate
   Units and Individuals
3. Operational Procedures. (Including
   Impact Record System)
4. Training of Responsible Staff

the responses are examined seriously. A first screen is the interpretation given the proposal by the leadership group. How, for example, do the superintendent and his or her agents explain the proposal to those whose reactions are being solicited? Both the substance of the explanation and the attitude conveyed by the leadership have an impact on the understanding and reactions of the response groups, and the superintendent should keep this possibility well in mind. It is also important to be aware of the "climate" of the school system itself. Is, for example, the school ready for the kind of change envisioned by the proposed policy as evidenced by the attitudes the faculty customarily displays toward both the *substance* of the proposal and the *fact* of change? The superintendent is responsible for gauging the institutional climate regularly through both formal and informal measures. Estimates of faculty and student body morale are frequently helpful indices of "climate" and can aid in developing a "sense" of the group's attitude toward the proposal. These informal estimates should be supplemented by discussions with each faculty council or committee and student organization that is affected by the proposal. The same sort of reaction is needed from community groups. The norms and traditions of the school's community should be reviewed in terms of the potential impact of the proposed policy. Additionally, the political realities of the existing situation should be canvassed so an estimate of the political implications of the proposal can be assessed. And of course, the impact of the proposed policy on the resource pool available to the school must be studied closely. It might seem strange to the reader that such a consideration is not included in the board's initial consideration of the question in phase 1 of the cycle. To do so, however, would limit the board's information about resource allocation preferences too severely and, therefore, tend to preclude consideration of development activities that involve reassignment of some already existing resource.

The product of the second phase of the PDRC is a final version of the policy statement itself. The superintendent or his or her agent is responsible for reviewing the reactions of the groups through which the proposal was screened and for incorporating the findings in the final draft as far as possible. That draft is then taken back to the board for its review and action. If it adopts the draft, the superintendent assumes implementation responsibilities. If further study is required, he or she conducts that study by recycling back through phase 2 until a satisfactory draft has been produced. Before leaving the second phase, it should be noted that the scope of the proposed policy determines the extensiveness of the involvement of the potential-testing activities. It seems obvious that a policy development of major proportions requires a more detailed and precise "testing" than one that relates, for example, to a relatively minor personnel procedure. Nevertheless, the function of the second phase, potential testing, is appropriate to all policy development proposals.

The task is now to implement the policy. Too often policy development activities view the formal adoption of the policy statement as the terminal activity in the process. Not so with the PDRC, for it is a basic assumption within this construct that policies live through implementation and die through abandonment to policy manuals. If they live, they change. The first opportunity for such change comes through the development of procedures to operationalize the policy. Hence, the third phase of the PDRC is the *operationalization phase*. It involves all the required start-up activities—the detailing of the operational procedures necessary to the implementation of the policy, the general notification of all people and units touched by the new policy, and any special training needed by the staff members whose responsibilities include operating the policy. One procedure required for the operation of the policy provides for a monitoring activity. The operationalization phase is responsible for observing how the policy "works" as well as seeing that it in fact is operable. The products of the third phase, then, include both a record of the implementation of the policy and a record of its impact on the school itself. This information may be maintained in a formal and detailed manner or in an informal and casual manner. In either case, it provides the data descriptive of the actual application of the policy, information that becomes increasingly meaningful as the redefinition character of the PDRC is approached.

Much of the descriptive information gathered by those who monitor the operation of the policy is produced by the responses of members of the organization. The cycle views these responses as phase 4, the *modification phase,* for the dynamic and changeable nature of educational policy implies that compliance alone is not the proper response of a professional group to an operational policy. Rather, it is properly expected that the users of a policy (or at least those whose behavior is affected by a policy) shall also have a significant evaluative response to that policy. Critical response by a faculty to a policy is acceptable behavior. Procedures to utilize this resource, namely, evaluation through application by the faculty and staff particularly, should properly be invoked by the board and the superintendent to assess the impact of a given policy. The modification phase recognizes the fact that policies seldom see operational "light" in the form that the statement implies. It recognizes that individuals translate policies into their own life spaces differently. They of necessity *modify* the policy as they attempt either to live it out or to ignore it. Faculty members respond to a specific policy in terms of their personal and professional interests, students in terms of their expressed needs, and representatives of community groups in terms of their values. Similarly, the very structure of the school tends to condition some of the responses of members who hold positions of different levels of responsibility and influence. Phase 4 reminds the superintendent and the board, indeed all members of the school system, that operationalization of a policy in a humane organization leads inevitably to modification of that policy. The modification may call for something either modest or severe, a mere clarification of language or major change. Whichever is the case, the product of phase 4 is an identification of the inadequacies of the policy as stated and, by implication, a call for a review of that policy.

And so the cycle is completed. The policy has been designed, screened, put into operation, and its shortfalls identified. It has returned to the first phase, the identification phase. In the case of an existing policy, the case with which we are now dealing, the problem for the administrator is no longer policy development but rather policy redefinition. The board, in its role as the major policy development agency of the school system, must now review the impact of and responses to a specific policy action it initiated at some previous time. In so doing, it examines the problem or condition the policy was designed to treat to see if the need for the policy still exists. If so, it directs the superintendent to embark on the PDRC again, using all the information produced by the modification phase to develop an amended policy statement before proceeding to the second phase. And so the policy itself is kept vital and useful in providing guidance to the school system in its goal and objective achievement activities. If the need that produced the policy in the first place no longer exists, the policy is rescinded and taken from the books. In this way, the operating policies of the school are maintained in a current and viable condition, thereby contributing to the confidence all personnel can place in the management of the local school system.

The process described need not be understood as requiring a vigorously adhered to sequence of activities. It might even be understood as a series of minicycles that loop opportunistically back and forth among the four phases as well as within each of the four. The time involved for the completion of the cycle can also be considered as indeterminate. The operational circumstances within the local district as well as the nature and scope of the proposed policy should guide the "opportunistic" response of the superintendent or the administrator whose responsibilities include managing the policy development system. The cycle may be operated several times before need for major change in a given policy statement is identified.

We have discussed at some length two examples of processes that offer guidance to the superintendent and the board in the development of educational policies. Another significant skill prerequisite to a successful policy development activity is simply the verbalization of policy statements. "Policy" has been defined as a formal statement. To be successful, a formal statement must be characterized by a clarity of expression. It must say what is intended by the board and the superintendent in language that is as unequivocal as possible. The problem becomes the development of clear and meaningful policy statements. Central characteristics of "clear and meaningful" statements are that (1) they are comprised of unambiguous words, that is, words that communicate the object or characteristic or action with little disagreement and (2) they are comprised of words that represent *facts* of the natural or social world rather than referents that have emotionally laden associations.

Several different uses of language can be described to call to the administrator's attention potential problems in the development of clear statements of policy. Frye and Levi identified five different uses of language that we might well be aware of: poetic, expressive, ceremonial, practical, and scientific.[9] When language is used *poetically*, it presents images designed to stimulate contemplation. Also, it is intended to give delight through its sound. When language is used *expressively*, it represents the emotional attitudes and feelings of those who are speaking or writing. When language is used *ceremonially*, it facilitates social intercourse and maintains the feelings of sociability that are the precon-

---

[9]Frye, Albert M. and Albert W. Levi, *Rational Belief* (New York: Harcourt Brace, 1941), pp. 10–20.

dition of human communication. When language is used *practically,* it is intended to arouse emotions and stimulate the activity of those to whom it is addressed. And, finally, when language is used *scientifically,* it is intended to communicate knowledge and information about the natural and social world. The harried administrator and the politically motivated board member (or faculty member or student) might be strongly tempted to express formal policy statements through the "practical" use as defined by Frye and Levi. That is, they might well intend in clear and unequivocal language to stimulate the activity of the members of the school system and community. This is not the function of policy statements, however. It is the scientific use of language, as described, that is appropriate to the expression of formal policies. Administrators should develop the skills necessary to a clear articulation of information about the operation of the school system to those who are involved.

Within the clear and precise structure of policy statements suggested, three other essential characteristics of policy statements should be described briefly. First, the area of activity being treated should be identified. If the policy refers to achievement levels for graduation, for example, the statement should indicate clearly that it relates to academic matters. Second, the conditions under which performance by members of the institution will be assessed as well as the criteria that govern the assessment, the range of acceptable alternatives, and the members (or positions) to whom the policy is addressed should be specified with precision. And, third, the level of generality should also be clear. That is, does the policy apply to the system in general or to some specific aspect of it? The development of policy statements that include these three characteristics (or their equivalents) is a skill that contributes greatly to the level of understanding that exists within a school system. The function of the superintendent in this matter is to ensure that the board has such skilled service available to it, preferably through its chief administrator himself or herself.

The content of educational policies is an important, though too frequently unexamined, aspect of the policy development activities of a local school board. If policies are intended to provide useful guides for action within a school system, it is clear that they must treat all central issues involved in organizing and operating such institutions. Knezevich suggests that a comprehensive set of board policies would include the following:[10]

1. Legal status, functions, organization, and ethical conduct of the board of education.
2. Selection, retention, and duties of the chief executive officer or superintendent of schools.
3. Relations among personnel in the school system.

[10]Stephen J. Knezevich, *Administration of Public Education,* 3rd ed. (New York: Harper & Row, 1975), p. 323.

4. Scope and quality of the instructional program and school services within the system.
5. Function and operation of the school food services.
6. Procedures and other aspects of budgeting, accounting, auditing, and management of school property.
7. Operation of the pupil-transportation system.
8. Selection, retention, and other matters related to the professional personnel.
9. Selection, retention, and other matters related to the non-professional personnel.
10. Identification, admission, promotion, discipline, etc., of pupils.
11. Public relations.

There are other patterns of cataloguing the content of educational policy the relative simplicity of which recommends them. One pattern involves viewing policies in two general categories, those that speak to programmatic aspects of the school's operation and those that encompass the elements that support program efforts. The directness of this two-point pattern is deceptive, for problems develop in defining specific activities as primarily "programmatic" or "support." Still, a successful application of this system maintains the central purpose of the school in clear priority and reminds personnel of that purpose. More customary approaches to the classification problem organize policies according to their content as did Knezevich but use more general categories. For example, the following four categories have been used: (1) personnel administration, (2) school program, (3) business management, and (4) school-community relations. Still another pattern, organized around the relationships of policies to instructional programs, utilizes the following content structure: (1) admissions policies, (2) student charges or fees, (3) faculty and staff qualifications, (4) instructional programs and services, (5) accreditation or recognitions, (6) institutional standards, and (7) business management services. Regardless of the pattern selected by a specific school, the efforts designed to ensure the usefulness of the policy manual will determine in large measure the reception that policies are given by the faculty and staff.

Organizing the Board for Action

The function of the board of education has been described in preceding pages with an emphasis on policy development. Of course, it is more. The board of education is a legal agent of the state with both general and specific duties assigned by statute. Its primary function is the provision of educational opportunities within a local community.[11] As such, each board operates within a set of

[11]The present discussion refers to local operating boards, not to other levels of educational boards that serve supervisory or coordinating functions.

regulations that should be well known to each member. For the local board to discharge its duties successfully, it must operate in a consistent and well-organized manner. That is, the local board must avoid a haphazard schedule of meetings and a casual attention to organizational detail. It must provide opportunities for all controversy to be aired and for all records to be maintained in clear language and in a form that is readily available to the public. Such evidences of orderliness and competence do not occur without conscious and continuing attention to the details of board operational procedures, and boards properly rely on their chief executive officer to provide these services. The superintendent discharges another of his or her leadership responsibilities through assisting the board in its organization and operation. Generally, local boards of education across the country are expected to discharge the following responsibilities:

1. Establish goals and operating policies.
2. Establish the organizational pattern needed to achieve the goals and implement the policies.
3. Appoint the chief executive officer.
4. Provide for the assessment of personnel performance and goal achievement.

Boards must be organized in ways that facilitate the development, conduct, and oversight of activities designed to discharge such responsibilities as these.

State regulations customarily require that the board organize itself at its first meeting each year. A presiding officer, usually called the president, and other officers are elected. It is not unusual for the superintendent to be elected as the board's secretary, even though he or she is not a member of the board and, consequently, has no necessary formal involvement in the work of the board. A regular schedule of meetings is determined, a set of operating procedures (or bylaws) is adopted, and the business of the year is initiated. The role of the superintendent in these matters is key, for that office assumes the implementation detail of the organizational pattern agreed upon by the board.

The Board Meeting. Each administrator and each member of the board must know that the board is a *corporate, deliberative body* that can act *only* as a board. All actions of the board must be taken in formal, regularly scheduled, and public meetings. This condition is an operational imperative. It is violated when an individual board member attempts to commit the board to a specific action or position or when any member of the staff or a citizen appeals to an individual board member to take such an action in any forum other than a regular meeting of the board. The consequences of behavior that denies the corporate nature of the board are serious indeed. Such actions deny the attempt to reach decisions on the basis of the best information available as it relates to the goals and objectives of the school district. Such action substitutes influence and power for the more tedious and time-consuming rational and public approach. It promotes impatience with problem analysis and encourages problem-solving procedures based on political trade-offs. Although apparent gains may be achieved thereby in the short run, the long-run impact on both the work of the board and the well-being of the school district is inevitably negative. Citizens and staff tend to become alienated from the educational activities of the community when their board becomes known for its political dealings. Alienation produces disinterest and disaffection. The consequent erosion of confidence hampers the work of the board by ensuring little more than negative responses by both staff and community. The negative attitudes are seen in the denial of support by the voters of the district and the erosion of morale within the faculty and staff. And, of course, the students are the ultimate victims through a diminished quality of the educational programs.

The regular meetings of the board can become the focal point of a powerful antidote to the development of such disaffection. A second imperative about board operation, one that is reinforced by the power of law in most states, is that all formal actions of the board must be taken in public legally scheduled or called meetings. It is naïve to assume that all aspects of the work of a board can be conducted in a public forum. For example, provision is customarily made to consider personnel matters and matters involved in land acquisition in executive session. The guiding principle is that, when the candid and complete discussion of an issue might do damage to an individual unjustly, the discussion should be conducted in a closed or executive session of the board. Similarly, when the board is considering the expenditure of a large amount of money for the purchase of property, an action that might cause some economic disruption in a local community, that discussion also should be conducted in private. However, even though discussions may be conducted in executive session, any action taken by the board in such matters must be consummated in a public, regularly scheduled or called, meeting. The practice, indeed, the *requirement, that actions be taken in public* provides the board with a significant opportunity to be accountable for the nature of its stewardship. It has the opportunity to explain clearly the rationale supporting each of its decisions and to invite comment prior to taking action. If such a pattern is followed assiduously, a confidence in the integrity (and, it is hoped, also the wisdom) of the board is gradually established and validated continuously. This is the antidote to school and community despair and alienation that the regular meeting of the board both can and ought to make possible.

The meetings of the board should be held in a place that can accommodate observers and representatives of the press. To claim to be holding public meetings without providing adequate space for representatives of the "public" is to make a sham of the whole affair. An agenda for the meeting should be prepared and distributed in advance of the scheduled time to all parties concerned. The agenda should be consistent with a set of operating rules adopted by the board to guide the progress of each meeting. It is deemed desirable to maintain as informal an atmosphere as conditions permit during the meetings, but it is also important that an agreed-upon set of "parliamentary procedures" be used when actions are to be taken. It is customary that a well-planned meeting of the board would follow an order of business that includes the following items:

1. Formal opening of the meeting by the presiding officer at the appointed hour.
2. Roll call of members.
3. Formal noting of the presence of a quorum (the number of board members required by statute or bylaws before business can be conducted).
4. Reading and approval of the minutes of the last meeting.
5. Report of communications received by the board.
6. Receiving of reports from duly recognized delegations to the board.
7. Receiving a report of the superintendent.
8. Clearing of any unfinished business from previous meetings.
9. Introduction of new business.
10. Any additional reports, information, or activity.
11. Adjournment.

The agenda itself might follow this pattern and serve as the order of business for the conduct of the meeting. But its function should go well beyond merely presenting a schedule or sequence of activities, even though such a listing of activities satisfies the commonly understood meaning of the term. The list or schedule should be accompanied by copies of reports, requests, and proposals that would enable the board member to be informed as thoroughly as possible before the meeting. The supplement to the agenda might well be organized according to such categories as reports, old business, new business, action items, study items, and information items.

The success of each meeting should be estimated following each session. The president of the board should be instructed in such matters so that he or she can report regularly to the board and the community on the progress the board is making. Evidence of achievement by the board can be found in the content of each meeting agenda, the response of the board to requests from delegations, the attitude of the members of the board toward the board itself, and the relationships maintained by the board with the faculty and staff.

The Role of the Superintendent. The major interest of the present analysis is the function of the superintendent in the board-superintendent interaction. Several specific responsibilities have been assigned to the superintendency in previous pages and will not be commented on in this section. Rather, attention will be focused on the responsibilities that the superintendent must assume if the formal work of the board achieves success. It is generally agreed that the superintendent as executive officer provides leadership to the board in this aspect of its operation in the following activities:

1. Preparation and distribution of the agenda for each meeting.
2. Supervision of the keeping, filing, and distributing of board minutes.
3. Attendance at all meetings.
4. Provision of advice on matters of policy, regulation, or law.
5. Handling of all official correspondence of the board and district.
6. Preparation of regular and special reports upon the direction of the board.

Other responsibilities, all of which offer the superintendent leadership opportunities, include recommending of faculty and staff for employment, drafting an annual budget and regular financial reports, overseeing policy development activities, supervising the performance of faculty and staff, and the host of details that are involved in each of these activities. The common element in each of these tasks is that they surface formally and are legitimized through the medium of a formal meeting of the board of education. The efficient, prompt, ethical, and humane performance of these staff duties enables the superintendent to make a most significant contribution to the development and maintenance of a productive environment. In fact, it is through such performance that his or her influence can be the enabling factor in the operation of the school system. The superintendent's role is operationalized through the administrative skills its occupant practices and the interpersonal skills that characterize the relationships with board, staff, and community. These skills are especially critical in the productive functioning of the board through its regular schedule of public meetings.

A note should be added concerning the function of the informal relationships that develop within the board also. In most school districts of some size, it is not unusual for members of the board to be elected by different and sometimes contending constituencies. Consequently, board members frequently see each other *only* as occupants of the formal role and fail even to approach developing an understanding of each other as complete, whole human beings. It becomes one of the superintendent's responsibilities to assist, indeed, to lead, the process that enables the board members to move beyond their formal roles and toward becoming a dynamic unit that can address the important educational questions of the day in terms of the specific issues that emerge within their own community. Techniques that contribute to such a development need not be catalogued in these pages because they must rely on specific communities and specific situations to be defined as "appropriate." Certain characteristics seem to be related to potentially successful activities, however. We refer to behaviors that are grounded in personal integrity, professional competence, candor, openness to criticism, respect for differing opinions, and willingness to relate specific actions to general goals and objectives. The occupant of the superintendent's position provides leadership for the board by modeling these characteristics in his or her own behavior regularly and by recognizing and encouraging these characteristics in the behavior of individual board members. The consequences of a successful attempt will be found in a more humane and productive operation of the community's schools. Perhaps even more far-reaching social consequences can be anticipated. We would certainly entertain that hope.

EXERCISES

1. Your board president has been involved in situations in which he has been interpreted as speaking for the entire board when in fact that has not been the case. How do you handle this?
2. Everyone seems to understand the *idea* of the separation of powers whereby boards make policy and administrators implement it, but in one system it is well established that, while administrators recruit, screen, interview, and in general manage all aspects of professional appointments, two of five board members have insisted on the right to interview all applicants. The other three board members are upset, but there is nothing in the policy or procedure that forbids it. In every instance in which these two have voted against an appointment recommendation, the person has been hired by a 3 to 2 vote. Needless to say, even though there is no apparent antagonism toward the superintendent, this situation is becoming intolerable. What would you advise?
3. In a system where you are the superintendent, a board member's nephew's wife has applied for a vacant position in the clerical staff of your office. The board member has called you endorsing her candidacy and the relationship is not covered under any nepotism statutes; moreover, other members of the board apparently have no objections, but you are apprehensive about it because you know that the applicant has a reputation for both gossip and petulance. She is fully qualified. What are you going to do?
4. You need to purchase some materials and a board member who has such materials available through his business volunteers to provide it at cost. Is this a violation of the code that holds that such officials may not engage in commerce with the district?
5. It has come to your attention that one of your high-ranking female central office staff members is having an affair with a married member of the board of education. You have been advised to take the position that what people do with their private lives is their private business so long as it does not

affect work performance. But on two occasions in a single week, the staffer took two hours for lunch and when you mentioned it were told that she was requested to join *a* board member for lunch. So?

6. You want very badly to have two new board members to attend the national meeting of both the AASA and the NSBA, but there is going to be serious criticism from some influential people and the local newspaper regarding the cost. It is important to have these new people exposed to important learning experiences. What is the best way to proceed?

7. As superintendent, you have been particularly troubled by one member of the board who has been consistently critical and sometimes even insulting. This member is running for re-election and you have been urged by influential people in the community to make a public statement that could be interpreted as supporting his opponent. After all you are advised, everyone knows that effective superintendents must be "political." How would you advise the superintendent if you had the chance?

SUGGESTED REFERENCES

L. O. Garber and Newton Edwards. *The Law Governing School Board Members and School Board Meetings.* Danville, Ill.: The Interstate Printers, 1963.

Keith Goldhammer. *The School Board.* New York: The Center for Applied Research in Education, Inc., 1966.

S. J. Knezevich. *Administration of Public Education.* New York: Harper & Row, Publishers, 1969. Chapter 11.

E. L. Morphet, R. L. Johns, and T. L. Reller. *Educational Organization and Administration.* Englewood Cliffs, N.J.: Prentice-Hall, Inc., 1974. See Ch. 11.

Chapter 13 _____

Administrative Leadership at the Building Level: The Principalship

INTRODUCTION

This chapter will focus primarily on the practice of educational administration at the building level. The principal, who is the administrator charged with the formal leadership responsibility at that level, is the concern of this chapter. After describing some critical issues and their consequent problems at the level of the individual school unit, we will sketch the evolution of the principalship, discuss the characteristics of leadership at the front line of educational administration, describe the central function of the principalship as facilitating successful teaching and learning, comment on organizing supporting services in an unobtrusive manner, and examine the question of accountability and evaluation at the building level. As has been the practice in this volume, the chapter will conclude with exercises that provide an opportunity to apply the information.

SOME PRESSING ISSUES AT THE BUILDING LEVEL

Although it is clear that most problems confounding the operation of school buildings are consequences of broader social issues, it is equally clear that they must still be managed by the faculty and staff of each building. They cannot be dismissed simply as manifestations of overriding social problems. Thus their management becomes a central concern of the principal. The issues that plague the building-level administrator are essentially those that derive from contests between and among individuals. They are people-centered issues. The people involved primarily are teachers, students, and parents.

Although many aspects of school life involve the relationships between the principal and teachers, the central figure is the principal. Is the chief function of the principal a managerial one or is it one of instructional leadership?[1] The perspective an individual holds regarding this question demonstrates itself in the innumerable face-to-face interactions between and among the members of the professional staff within the school building. Should the principal attempt to influence the performance of the teachers in the school to the end that instruction might be improved? That is, does the principal adopt the "leadership" position? It is claimed that to do so might cause the principal to trespass on the professional autonomy of the teachers. Such possibilities have increased in the last decade in direct relationship to increasing levels of teacher militancy and the consequent systemwide negotiated contracts that govern many of the relationships among professional staff. On the other hand, should the principal adopt the managerial role and become a superclerk who cares for only the administrative details necessary to keep the school running? In fact, this more nearly characterizes the reported work of principals than does "leadership" activity.[2] The issue is not mitigated by the awareness of its complexity and perversity, however. Confronting it in the guise of "people problems" on a daily basis comprises the major work of the principal. Actually, these represent the most significant and potentially productive set of problems that the principal is privileged to deal with, for they present a person with unlimited opportunities to impact both directly and indirectly on the learning environment enjoyed or suffered by the students.

The central concern for the principal experiencing the problems of which this issue is comprised, then, is his or her own response to them. We fear that too often the principal fails to exercise initiative in such matters and soon finds that circumstances seem overwhelming. A sense of self-direction is lost, and the principal responds as though the "situation" were in control. If this happens, the managerial role soon claims another individual. But this need not happen. Roe and Drake suggest that basic organizational changes be made to provide for a services coordinator who would manage the routine and record-keeping dimensions of the role, thereby freeing the principal for instructional leadership activities.[3] The individual principal, though, can take a significant measure of

---

[1]It is not the purposes of this chapter to review the significant and rather copious published research that deals with the role of the principal. The interested reader is referred to Arthur Blumberg and William Greenfield, *The Effective Principal* (Boston: Allyn & Bacon, 1980), Chapters 2 and 3, and William H. Roe and Thelbert L. Drake, *The Principalship*, 2nd ed. (New York: Macmillan, 1980), Chapter 2, for helpful discussions of this particular issue as well as for reviews of the pertinent research descriptive of the functions and responsibilities of the principalship.

[2]Blumberg and Greenfield, op. cit., p. 36.

[3]Roe and Drake, op. cit., pp. 136–138.

control of his or her activities and need not wait upon major organizational modifications. One scholar suggests that the administrator has two areas of freedom of action of great importance. First, one makes decisions about the commitments one will embrace. Second, one can use unavoidable activities, that is, those that *must* be engaged in, to flatter one's own professional goals and objectives.[4] For the principal, the implication is clear: he or she may decide that the major commitment is to instructional improvement and, consequently, utilize every opportunity to improve skills to that end and utilize *each interaction* with professional colleagues in the light of its contribution to such an objective.

The issues that confront the principal in dealing with students most frequently involve the question of control. In view of the central purposes of organized education in the American tradition, it is unfortunate that controlling the behavior of children and adolescents too frequently dominates the attention of the principal. Contemporary schools tend to grapple with a set of specific behaviors marked as unacceptable. They range from such ever-present problems as tardiness and truancy to more vexing problems associated with alcoholism, drug abuse, and teenage sexuality. These concerns are customarily discussed as "discipline" problems and are regularly marked as among the most serious problems facing schools according to nationwide opinion polls. School vandalism has been discussed previously (see Chapter 1, pages 10–11), and its relationship to the malaise affecting schools is readily observable. So is its relationship to the task of the principal, for, although most acts of vandalism are extensive enough to require the involvement of central office personnel and community agencies, the victimized units are almost invariably school buildings. Not only must the principal be concerned with developing values and attitudes that act as preventives, he or she must also deal with the frequently major disruptions to school routines and educational activities that are the fruit of vandalism. Buildings have been burned, offices and records destroyed, classrooms rendered unusable, transportation systems immobilized, teachers and other officials attacked and brutalized, and students harassed, intimidated, and injured; and, in a majority of such incidents, the perpetrators are themselves members of the student body of the school in which the vandalism took place.

The principal's leadership role requires that he or she treat the issue directly. The novice principal is poorly advised if he or she fails to give the question of "discipline" continuing attention of a very high priority. The nature of the attention and energy so directed varies with the understandings and commitments of the principal.

Certain questions, however, guide the consideration of the control issue: What does "discipline" mean? What are community expectations (and, hence, standards) for student behavior? What are the objectives of the school in relation to student behavior? What "control" techniques are consistent with community

---

[4]Henry Mintzberg, *The Nature of Managerial Work* (New York: Harper & Row, 1973), pp. 50–51.

values, professional knowledge, and the objectives of the school? And, finally, how does a specific principal initiate action in a specific school setting that reduces the need for control actions (or disciplinary action) on his or her part? The question of developing and maintaining an environment that encourages the growth of self-discipline appears to be at the heart of the principal's task as he or she encounters the incidents in which the control issue is manifested.

The third group of people the principal meets regularly are parents. Issues that involve the principal with parents are customarily treated as school-community interactions rather than as principal-parent interactions.[5] That is, general studies of the principalship focus attention on *community* relations rather than on *parent* relations. While it is true that each principal will be involved with individuals from the community who represent a group or an organization, it is also true that most interactions will invariably be between and among individuals. Novice principals and those who are unfamiliar with the community frequently permit ignorance to blind them to the individual concerns that the petitioner presents. In other words, even the representatives of the community who wait upon the principal in the name of a general cause or concern do so to protect or enhance the status of students in the school. And the students of greatest concern are usually the children of the petitioner. All this suggests that the principal's community relations start with parent relations and will achieve success in accordance with the degree of success with which the principal manages those.

Issues involving parents, then, grow out of problems that emerge from the school program itself. At one time, parents seldom raised questions about the instructional program or the instruction itself. But those days have gone with the awakening of social and ethnic consciousness, and parents now quite properly challenge biases within content materials as well as omissions or gaps resulting from unexamined assumptions about social or political policy. So the principal of the 1980s must be ready to deal not only with issues resulting from student behavior and academic performance in contacts with parents, but as well must be ready and willing to encounter issues that seem to challenge concerns that once were the preserve of professional knowledge.

The manner in which principals manage encounters with parents in dealing with this broader range of issues depends in large measure on their interpersonal and administrative skills. It takes a high level of personal and professional confidence to endure with equanimity a withering attack by an enraged parent and still be able to identify and treat the source of the real concern. But to fail to do so causes the loss not only of an opportunity to improve the learning environment for a specific student, it also leads to an erosion of confidence in the principal and the school within the community the school serves. The duality

[5]See, for example, J. G. Cebuka, "Creating a New Era for Schools and Communities," and Rodney J. Reed, "Education and Ethnicity," in Donald A. Erickson and Theodore L. Reller, eds., *The Principal in Metropolitan Schools* (Berkeley, Calif.: McCutchan, 1978), as well as Roe and Drake, op. cit., pp. 33–52.

of potential consequences of parent-principal interactions adds a unique value to them in the opportunities they offer the principal to exercise positive leadership.

Issues, then, that vie for the attention of the principal revolve around the people with whom he or she interacts daily in the regular and routine discharge of responsibilities. They involve facilitating the work of the professional staff, managing the nonroutine behavior of the students, and encouraging the understanding of parents. It should be noted that these "people-centered" issues are found in all school units regardless of size, level, or location. Of course, size, level, and location influence significantly the nature and emphases that are expressed in the form of issues, but teachers, students, and parents still represent the locus of the issues themselves.

CHARACTERISTICS OF THE PRINCIPALSHIP

This discussion of the characteristics of the principalship considers its evolution, its leadership functions, its relation to supporting services, and its relation also to the question of accountability. Throughout the discussion, a primary concern is the behavior and performance of the individual who occupies the principalship.

Evolution of Building-Level Administration

It seems appropriate to recognize briefly that the principalship as we know it today has evolved as the role and function of education in America has expanded. The wise building administrator, indeed, the wise educator, never fails to recognize his or her indebtedness to the contributions of unnamed men and women who have served in earlier times. So it is with the management of organizations in which children and adolescents learn.

The nineteenth century in America saw the birth of the common school and its evolution from a single-room, single-teacher center of rural communities across the land to a graded school with elementary and secondary divisions serving many students in major cities of the nation. By the middle of the nineteenth century, the movement in cities was well underway.[6] The first step came when more than one teacher was involved in a single building. Local school boards or committees of trustees had customarily cared for management details and the necessary supervisory responsibilities, but increases in size required that

---

[6]Blumberg and Greenfield, op. cit., pp. 10–16. The outline presented in this section is based on this source.

they secure assistance. Consequently, one teacher was designated "principal teacher" and was given additional duties, thus relieving the school committee members of certain operational responsibilities. The principal teacher taught a regular assignment, of course, in addition to caring for the maintenance of certain records. It is interesting to note the similarity between this development and the head master system that emerged in England. Both clearly retain identification with the conduct of instructional programs rather than with the management of school units.

Toward the end of the nineteenth century, the building-level administrator became more of a managing director. It will be remembered that the development of high schools was greatly stimulated by the decision in the *Kalamazoo* case (1872). The growth of cities, spurred by industrial developments and increasing numbers of immigrants, provided a fertile ground for an increase in the graded school movement. The need for more direction in specific school units became evident, and the principal teacher became more involved in making operational decisions, exercising control over daily management matters as well as directing the work of teachers. This pattern became the norm by the beginning of the twentieth century in the cities of the land. The adjectival connotation of "principal" was lost by that time.

In the first half of this century two dimensions were added to the role of the principal. No longer was it appropriate to be concerned only with management details and control. Supervision of instruction slowly superseded the controlling of teachers as their programs of professional preparation improved and the democratic values espoused by progressive education gained adherents. Another development born in the child study movement of the last decade of the nineteenth century bore the fruit of the school-community activities. Thus, by the middle of this century, the contemporary view of building-level administration had evolved to include management and supervisory responsibilities and community relations activities.

The Contemporary Position

The present principalship requires the skills of a professional administrator, one whose identity remains with the corp of teachers and represents the first-line administrator in an ever more complex educational system. The problem of identity clouds the question of the role of the contemporary principal with numerous and conflicting alternatives.[7] It is not the purpose here to re-examine that issue. Rather it is our purpose to underscore several "bottom-line" elements of the principalship that have pertinence regardless of the manner in which an

[7]Roe and Drake, op. cit., discuss the question of identity. See especially Chapter 8, "The Principal's Major Task," pp. 131–148, and pp. 388–389. See also Bruce S. Cooper, "The Future of Middle Management in Education," in Donald A. Erickson and Theodore L. Reller, eds., *The Principal in Metropolitan Schools* (Berkeley, Calif.: McCutchan, 1978), pp. 272–279.

individual resolves his or her professional identity problem. These elements are suggested in the propositions that follow and encompass our understanding of the purposes and goals of the contemporary principalship.

1. Inasmuch as the building level is the place at which the primary goals of the school system are achieved, the principal's first responsibility is the provision of instructional leadership.
2. The leadership behavior of the principal is demonstrated through behaviors that facilitate the teaching of teachers and the learning of students.
3. Facilitative leadership is most appropriately expressed in actions that demonstrate deep and abiding respect for individuals.
4. The facilitative principal is one who is skilled in goal identification, objective clarification, and conflict resolution. That person invests time regularly in developing and improving these skills.

The characteristics of the principalship in the coming decades will depend on variables beyond the control of the individuals who occupy the position. Will school systems decentralize and balkanize, reverting to the conditions prevalent at the beginning of the twentieth century? Or will the trend toward larger educational systems with increasingly cumbersome bureaucracies continue unabated? The pattern will probably lie somewhere between these untenable extremes. But the management of the first-line unit, the school, will remain the province of the principal in any eventuality. Certain responsibilities calling on certain skills and values will be required. The remainder of this chapter speaks to those skills and values.

LEADERSHIP AT THE FRONT LINE

Much has been written about educational administration at the theoretical and general levels. And this is as it should be, for the direction the harried practitioner needs comes in large measure from such sources. But the place where all educational philosophizing and theorizing and planning bears fruit is in the school, the front line of the educational enterprise. It is in the classrooms and halls and on the grounds of the school, regardless of its size, location, or sophistication, that opportunities to learn are organized and presented to children and adolescents. And it is to the management of that important unit in the educational enterprise that the principal is called. It is through the exercise of his or her leadership in the individual school unit that the teachers and pupils are able to accomplish the goals that promote individual development.

This form of leadership has been discussed in some detail in other sections of this volume. The key idea in the concept as it is being developed in these pages, however, is *facilitative,* by which we mean the behaviors that consciously enable colleagues who are traditionally described as "subordinates" to perform their assigned tasks. Such leadership is especially appropriate when the work group is comprised of highly trained specialists (professional teachers, for example). Behaviors of the formal or status leader who would demonstrate facilitative leadership evidence a regular commitment to collaborative actions. The facilitative leader invests much time and energy in the identification of potential problems and in designing activities that anticipate and provide options for such eventualities. Further, the facilitative leader is interested in student and faculty development, not control. Priorities would be determined through consensual techniques, not by directive from the principal or pressure from a segment of the school community. Involvement and participation in the major decisions taken in the school unit would be routine as contrasted to fiat. Information would be disseminated informally, regularly, and easily, with memoranda serving to confirm rather than announce important decisions, policies, and procedures. The facilitative leader can tolerate ambiguous situations in the knowledge that openness promotes growth, both for the principal and for the other individuals in the school. The facilitative principal regularly calls to the attention of all members of the school the goals and objectives being sought after, the *ends* of education, while ensuring through his or her behavior that the processes and procedures being utilized—the *means* through which the goals are pursued—are characterized by the highest ethical and moral standards. We see, then, that facilitative leadership is open, collaborative, informal, flexible, people oriented, and goal directed.

The principal does not, of course, practice these grand and glorious behaviors in a vacuum. Large school systems and many of intermediate and smaller sizes describe the responsibilities of the principal in formal "position descriptions."[8] The responsibilities generally include supervising the instructional program and the faculty and students as well as overseeing the system's procedures regarding records, materials and supplies, and the buildings and grounds. A veteran educator told one of the authors as he took a principalship for the first time that his activities revolved around five rather clear-cut areas of responsibility: (1) the instructional program, (2) the needs of the faculty, (3) the growth and development of the students, (4) the daily routines and operational procedures, and (5) the school plant. These five areas of emphasis provide a useful classification scheme for thinking about the functions or responsibilities of the principal.[9]

[8]The reader may wish to review the following for information about job descriptions for principals: National Association of Secondary School Principals, *Job Descriptions for Principals and Assistant Principals* (Reston, Va.: NASSP, 1976).

[9]An example of a similar but more recent conceptualization is found in J. M. Lipham and J. A. Hoeh, Jr., *The Principalship: Foundations and Functions* (New York: Harper & Row, 1974). They identify five major areas of responsibility as (1) instructional programs, (2) staff personnel services, (3) student personnel services, (4) financial physical resources, and (5) school-community relations (p. 203).

The tasks of the principal who would provide facilitative leadership for the school that he or she serves can also be described in this context. This individual would, in the first instance, facilitate instruction. It must be noted that almost every activity carried on in a local school unit has some impact on the instructional program. Consequently, the facilitating of instructional activities involves elements in each of the other areas of responsibility. To facilitate instruction means to make it easier for students and teachers to achieve the objectives of instruction. Faculty and student needs, both in individual and group terms, would then be treated in such a way that their satisfaction would also contribute to the achieving of instructional objectives. Much may be implied from this observation, and the implications are discussed in subsequent pages. The manner in which school routines and operational procedures are managed by a facilitative principal can also be identified. The key descriptor in this instance is "unobtrusive." The facilitative principal would attend to organizing and operating both minimally necessary routines and the appropriate support services (clerical, record-keeping, accounting, maintenance, transportation) in ways that emphasize their instrumental function. The school would not be operated, for example, for the convenience of those whose task it is to maintain the record system nor for the convenience of the principal. A "smooth running" school is one in which the services that support the primary mission—instruction—are notable for their quietness, their unobtrusiveness. Attendance accounting is accomplished with little fanfare; audiovisual equipment is available and operable on demand; teachers and students are invited to use library and laboratory resources; educational specialists (health, reading, counseling) from outside (or inside) the building are involved regularly; custodians keep the facilities clean without intruding on program needs; the transportation system is tailored to the schedule of the school. More examples of unobtrusiveness could be suggested.

To achieve appropriate levels of support service operation requires ingenuity and persistence on the part of the facilitative principal. He or she also attends to the developmental needs of student and staff, needs that treat personal development. The school is a people-oriented organization, and the status leader of that unit must consciously direct his or her own energies and those of the entire school community toward enhancing the total growth of the people involved. Of course, the specific activities designed to promote such development quite naturally fall within the range of the purposes of the school itself. Consequently, this phase of the principal's responsibilities also contributes to the school's goal achievement in a positive way. And, finally, the facilitative principal must find techniques to assess goal and objective achievement, techniques that in and of themselves contribute to the development of the people involved. The key to this set of behaviors appears to be found in the concept "formative evaluation," that is, evaluation of progress toward the achievement of an objective while consciously providing feedback to enable an individual to modify his or her activities. The focus is not on a summative statement—performance is not *good* or *bad;* rather, attention is directed to the tasks remaining to be accomplished not to the individual performer.

Each of the areas of responsibility is described in more detail in the paragraphs that follow.

FACILITATING SUCCESSFUL TEACHING AND LEARNING

We have suggested that the principal who would provide facilitative leadership should involve himself or herself in activities intended to identify, develop, and clarify the goals and objectives that give direction to the work of the school. Additionally, the principal traditionally has been expected to provide supervision of the instructional program. Some observers call such activities instructional leadership rather than supervision.[10] The concern with the supervisory aspects of the role of the principal implies an interest in teaching-learning styles and instructional strategies and a commitment to relate such information to the work of individual teachers. We hold, then, that the facilitative principal is occupied in a major way with these dimensions of his or her responsibility, the clarification of goals and objectives, the clarification of various teaching styles and instructional strategies, and student personnel services.

Goals Clarification

We have frequently indicated that one of the major functions of the administrator is the development and clarification of the goals and objectives that give direction to the school. To fail to do so creates confusion among teachers, students, and parents, confusion that results in lowered levels of effectiveness. The principal's role may well be the critical factor in attempts to avoid such consequences, for he or she is largely responsible for the management of the formal direction-giving activities within the school. Central to that responsibility is ensuring that the staff understands the objectives that energize and give meaning to the school. Unfortunately, it is not unusual to find individuals within the faculty working at cross-purposes. Teachers are prone to assign highest value to their own specialties. Examples of conflicts abound. In elementary schools, schoolwide programs and observances frequently intrude on the time that individual teachers had planned for their lessons or activities. In middle and sec-

---

[10]Roe and Drake, op. cit., pp. 132–133, emphasize the leadership dimension, but we are assuming in this context that all activities of the status leader, the principal, have a leadership component that either enhances or inhibits the work of the faculty and students. Consequently, we may use such terms as supervision and leadership to refer to the same constellation of activities, recognizing full well that in other contexts the more technically precise definition would be desirable.

ondary schools, music, dramatic, and athletic activities frequently compete for the same units of time and often require the time assigned to "regular" classes. Other opportunities for confusion about goals and objectives to be manifested in the daily life of schools exist, but these program-staff examples serve to suggest the scope and the depth of the problem.

The clarification of goals and objectives, then, can claim much of the time and concern of the principal. Goals and objectives are "clarified" when the faculty and staff members who are involved directly in their implementation can translate the elements of the formal statements in which they are expressed into behavioral terms. That is, a teacher understands an objective when he or she can express it in terms that describe the behavior that is required for its achievement. When an individual is able to express an objective in behavioral terms of his or her own construction, and when those terms are in general agreement with the intended interpretation, it can be said that goal-objective clarification has been achieved. It must be noted that failure to pursue the question to the point of actually verbalizing a statement in behavioral terms permits the continuation of reliance on unexamined assumptions. Faculty members frequently find this exercise to be tedious and, in some instances, professionally offensive. The principal's task is to develop an atmosphere within the school that assigns value to the use of time in a planning exercise of this nature. Such an atmosphere would also encourage the regular and frequent exchange of professional opinion in the forming of judgments, thereby raising goal and objective clarification activities to a level of highest significance.

Even though it is not the intention of these comments to analyze the nature or function of goals and objectives, it is necessary to the discussion of "clarification" to address their sources briefly. It can be said without fear of contradiction that educational goals and objectives are derived from the *values* of the society in general, from the profession that provides staff for the schools, from the community that supports the school, and from the individuals who live and work within the school. It is clear to even the casual observer of contemporary America that a variety of often conflicting values finds support within society. And value confusion continues to grow with the increasing diversity and complexity of society. Educational goals and objectives, embedded as they are in broader societal and cultural values, can be expected to reflect some growing levels of confusion. The principal should expect to find differing interpretations of relatively straightforward statements of goals and objectives within the school and its community. Even though the objectives for a specific school may have been developed through participative procedures operated by the superintendent and the local board of education, the principal should expect that the teachers in his or her building will find different implications in them. Indeed, this is not a condition to be decried. Rather, it simply emphasizes the need for clarification activities to take place. Also, it recognizes that the final interpreter of the goals and objectives of the school is quite properly the teacher. The wise principal is the one who not only recognizes this basic operational fact but who also is able to stimulate a continuing professional discussion of the impact of the "teacher as goals source" on the programs of the school.

How might he or she go about discharging this important aspect of the principal's role? Involvement is the key principle—involvement of the teachers on a regular basis in the operation of the school. An environment in which this principle is well established is the first step in a goals and objectives clarification exercise. Such an environment is characterized by mutual respect among the faculty and between the teachers and the principal, a respect that recognizes the professional strengths of each individual and concentrates interactions on those strengths without denying the weaknesses of each member of the group. Of course, the development and maintenance of such a collegial environment is a continuing task (but not one that is onerous!). Consequently, the principal must introduce goals clarification activities into the developmental routines and not wait until conditions are "perfect" within the faculty. Interestingly, this is also the source of greatest satisfaction in the principalship role.

Personal involvement of faculty members, the kind of involvement without which understanding cannot develop, does not relieve the principal of some "structuring" responsibilities. The nature of the involvement of the teachers in the clarification process requires the astute leadership of the principal if it is to succeed. It is the principal who must initiate the activity. Discussions of the meaning and purpose of objectives should have a regular place in the schedule of formal staff planning activities. Similarly, they should be a central feature of the informal interactions between the principal and teachers. Two dimensions of the clarification process are pertinent and should be the responsibility of the principal within that process. The first dimension focuses on the *content* of the goal or objective under discussion. The principal should be the primary source of information about the meanings and intentions of goal and purpose statements. He or she must be able to describe the relationship between relatively specific objectives pertinent to the school unit and systemwide goals. He or she must be able to describe the circumstances and conditions that led to the development of specific goals or objectives and which they were intended to treat. He or she must be able to locate information that aids in the evaluation of goal-objective achievement. The principal cannot delegate the responsibility for providing the content dimension in a goals clarification activity if the faculty is to develop understanding.

The second dimension speaks to the *skills* needed by individuals in the goals clarification exercise. Because this is essentially a problem-solving activity, the skills needed by individuals are those associated with the scientific method, a rational model. They appear in Table 13-1 expressed in goals clarification terms. The skills themselves are typical cognitive skills possessed by all educators in varying degrees. The unique aspect of this proposal is their conscious and intentional application to the clarification of goals and objectives. The realms of application suggested for the set of five skills comprise a sequence of activities that may be called a goals clarification system. The logic of the system implies clearly a sequential relationship.

While the skills of analysis, inference, and evaluation are commonly used in rational models, steps 4 and 5, which involve the explicative and initiative skills, require explanation, as they frequently do not appear in traditional problem-solving sequences. In the present instance, their purpose is to ensure that both the teachers and principal understand the objective under discussion in clearly operational terms. The best test of that level of understanding is the ability to describe the intention of the objective to individuals who either have professional knowledge of it or have a personal stake in it (i.e., colleagues, parents, and students). The final test of understanding is taking action, and the clarification process is not completed until the programs to operationalize the objective have been initiated.

The clarification of goals and objectives should not be understood as a one-time event or activity. Rather, it is properly understood as a significant professional development tool that is continuous. Also, the clarification activity should not be taken as Procrustean. That is, its purpose is not to convince a teacher or faculty that a specific interpretation of an objective represents the *correct* understanding. Quite the contrary. The clarification process is intended to stimulate an examination of the *variety* of approaches that might be taken to achieve a given objective and to encourage that the best professional judgment be utilized in choosing from among acceptable alternatives. To do the former is to demean the intelligence and training of the faculty. To invoke the latter is to recognize the talent that resides in every faculty. The role of the facilitative principal is clear.

Table 13-1.   Goals Clarification Skills

Skill	Application
Analysis	1. Identify major elements in the goal or objective.
Inference	2. Examine alternative implications of goal or objective.
Evaluation	3. a. Compare alternatives with existing practices and situations.
	b. Choose most pertinent alternative.
Explication	4. Explain choice in colleagues, students, and parents.
Initiation	5. Take action in accord with objective as clarified.

The Supervision of Instruction

It has been implied throughout these pages that the development and management of strong instructional programs is the central responsibility of the educational administrator. Indeed, it is more than that; it is his or her calling or vocation. The principal in charge of a school is the educational administrator on the front line, the administrator with the most immediate contact with this central function. This responsibility and these opportunities are described by the idea expressed as the title of this section: The Supervision of Instruction. It is recognized that the term *supervision* frequently connotes such things as directing, controlling, and evaluating the behavior of a group of employees and, further, that the supervisor is accountable for the production of those employees. We find that this use of the term is inappropriate to educational processes and organizations. For example, a group of teachers is unlike a group of employees with a product to produce. Teachers are increasingly a professionally and personally mature group. It has been estimated that the average age of teachers in America will approach 40 years by 1984.[11] Older and more experienced teachers differ markedly from novices in several ways. Research has demonstrated that the former tend to be more professionally committed and involved, more politically active, more insightful concerning the behavior of students, evidence greater wisdom regarding teaching and learning, possess stronger community ties, and provide more stability within the school.[12] The point is clear. As the decade of the 1980s progresses, the principal will be called upon to provide supervision for more mature, experienced, and competent teachers. The quality of that supervision will in large measure determine the degree of success the school is able to achieve.

Another set of factors will make the supervisory tasks of the principal different not only from those that are customary in noneducational organizations but also from those that have been the norm within local schools. Those factors derive essentially from the diminished level of confidence in education demonstrated by the general public and the consequent economic impact. Evidence abounds to support this observation and is amply described elsewhere in this volume. The principal must deal with schools in which teachers carry heavier teaching loads than desirable, have less time to provide individual help to students, and may even be teaching in subject matter fields outside their professional interest or preparation. Additionally, lower levels of support mean that the principal will have fewer resources upon which to call when crisis situations develop, when special program development activities are required by changing socioeconomic circumstances within the community, or when students with special needs enroll in his or her school. In times of economic stress, it can safely be assumed that school districts will provide fewer professional and support staff. The principal and the remaining teachers will be called upon to accomplish as much as they did before with a marked reduction in all resources.

One view of this sort of future was described by two Stanford University

---

[11]B. David Delhanty, "Myths About Older Teachers," *Phi Delta Kappan*, Vol. 59 no. 4 (December 1977), 262.

[12]See Jean Dresden Grambs and Carol Seifeldt, "The Graying of America's Teachers," *Phi Delta Kappan*, Vol. 59, no. 4 (December 1977), 259–261, for references to the research that supports these observations.

researchers who studied the impact of a severe curtailment of funds on a central-city high school and documented a tragic situation.[13] Five major sources of frustration for the teachers who survived dismissal were identified: (1) major increase in the difficulty of the teaching tasks caused by more students in each class and the absence of curriculum resource people from the central office; (2) a concern about being assigned to teach courses for which they did not have competence; (3) being reassigned to a school serving a significantly different community (in the instances of the study, an inner-city school); (4) lack of time to work with students on an individual level; and (5) a fear that there was no way out of the situation, that they were "trapped in a downward spiral," to use the words of the researchers. These are serious problems, problems that over-whelm many individual teachers and principals, not only those in the study school. They suggest the scope of the instructional supervision challenge faced by every principal even though the degree and intensity will obviously differ according to specific school situations. The decade of the 1980s may well be characterized by the set of problems suggested by this case. Duke and Meckel's report concludes with a recommendation that the community be awakened to the consequences of severe cutbacks. They suggest that the only way to correct the problems is to restore adequate resources.

Until "adequate" resources are made available, what does the principal do? How does he or she provide instructional leadership under conditions of depri-vation? What steps can be taken to develop and maintain a system of noncon-trolling supervision of experienced and competent teachers who live with serious levels of frustration and discouragement daily? These questions may well paint too dark a picture of the problems facing the principal. All school districts may not suffer the curtailment of resources as did the one in the example. However, the five reported sources of frustration can be found in all educational organi-zations. Each principal must be ready to deal with them.

The first step to be taken deals with the self-management of the principal. He or she cannot provide adequate supervision until first dealing with himself or herself. The facilitative principal must first (and continuously) assess his or her view of the role. He or she may accomplish a self-assessment consistent with the principles of a facilitative role through responding to such questions as

1. Do I place the implications for the instructional program first when treating problems?
2. Does my routine behavior make the teaching assignments of the faculty easier to accomplish?
3. Am I able to respect the individuality of *each* member of the faculty? And does my behavior reflect that respect?

---

[13]David L. Duke and Adrienne M. Meckel, "The Slow Death of a Public High School," *Phi Delta Kappan*, Vol. 62, no. 10 (June 1980), 674–677.

4. Do I hold the purposes and goals that direct our work clearly in mind? And am I able to clarify objectives for the teachers and resolve conflicts between and among them and students in accordance with those purposes and goals?

The answers that one gives to these questions suggests the direction a principal's supervisory activities should follow. If, for example, his or her routine behaviors tend to take attention away from the instructional responsibilities of the teachers by stressing instrumental procedures (e.g., distributing announcements and maintaining certain records), then he or she has information about how to improve instruction in a simple and direct way. The "improvement" will follow from a modification of the administrative procedures utilized within the school, procedures that the facilitative principal will find ways to manage himself or herself. The first step in a sound instructional supervision program, one that is facilitative, is one that removes institutional and organizational obstacles that are too frequently imposed without careful analyses by the administrative hierarchy.

After the successful introduction of a self-management activity, the facilitative principal will find that the second set of supervisory activities follows quite naturally. They include reviewing teaching styles and instructional strategies with individual teachers and with faculty committees. Facilitative supervision is characterized by a problem rather than a personal focus, by collaborative actions, high levels of mutual confidence, and consensual actions. Roe and Drake report eight characteristics of good instructional supervision, characteristics that also describe what we have identified as facilitative supervision.

Instructional supervision is at its best when[14]

1. The teacher can openly share concerns with the principal, when there is free communication, and each can react and disagree without fear of hurt feelings or reprisal.
2. There is a genuine feeling that the teacher and principal are solving professional problems as colleagues.
3. There is realization that expertise is a function of knowledge and experience and the administrative position does not by itself make the principal an expert.
4. The teacher recognizes that the principal values his or her worth as a person and is concerned about both personal and professional growth.
5. There is recognition of the teachers' professional competence by the helpfulness of feedback and the supportive way it is given.
6. There is recognition that the infinite variability in human beings makes universal applications in teaching and learning questionable. Teaching can be

[14]Roe and Drake, op. cit., pp. 279–280.

risk taking and failure in some experiment or new venture is not a sign of incompetence.

7. The teacher feels professional freedom in that he or she may experiment with teaching procedures and seek help in many different directions without being made to feel inadequate.
8. There is an understanding that teaching is both rational and emotional and that discussions of feelings and interpersonal relations may be as important as talking about the teaching process itself.

Within the second set of supervisory activities, characterized by the conditions described, the facilitative principal develops a regular planning and review agency (committee or council) that deals with all facets of the school operation in a collaborative way. Through this technique, the impact of routine events or operational imperatives on the instructional program is anticipated and managed through decisions reached by consensus. The identification of potential problems can occur before serious situations develop, thereby averting unnecessary negative impacts on instructional activities. The facilitative principal finds more time available for working with department- or grade-level committees as well as individual teachers by virtue of the collaborative activities concluded through the regular planning and review committee.

It is through these two general categories of activities, those dealing with self-management and those that relate to specific interactions with members of the faculty, that the facilitative principal contributes to a clarification of teaching styles and instructional strategies. The key is the development of a "climate" within the school that encourages the professional performance of the principal and the teachers. Within such an environment, true colleagueship can develop, and supervision, in the traditional sense, is no longer appropriate.

The Principal, Instruction, and Students

Instructional supervision, directed as it is toward enhancing the learning environment, must attend to the learners as well as to the instructors. Too often, we fear, the supervisory function of the principal in matters of instruction focuses only on the teaching staff. The next several paragraphs are intended to remind administrators, the principal especially, that all activities and special services organized to serve students directly belong properly within the instructional category. Schools routinely operate counseling services and student activity programs that lie outside the regularly scheduled program of instruction. We view these two as comprising the student personnel services of the school. It is our contention that all components of each category must be organized intentionally to contribute consciously to achieving the objectives that guide the school. The principal has the responsibility of providing the leadership that enables such intentionality to be widely recognized throughout the school and its community.

The counseling program available within a given school ranges in scope from being an informal function of the principal and those members of the faculty who are interested to a formally structured operation staffed by several highly trained and licensed guidance counselors. The variations are attributable to the level and size of the school unit as well as to the professional commitments and local traditions that prevail. The activities involved and services provided students seldom go beyond providing information about the educational status and vocational prospects of the student. Cumulative records are frequently maintained to permit the development of recommendations for placement in special programs for qualified pupils; standardized testing programs are developed, administered, and interpreted; and referrals to youth-serving community agencies are made when students require their services. The facilitative principal is the enabler, the interpreter, and often the arbiter for many of these activities when he or she is blessed with a staff of professional counselors. In their absence, the principal provides these services directly. In both instances, the principal is involved with students in tension-laden situations that provide not only opportunities to intervene constructively in the life of a student but also opportunities to interpret objectives and demonstrate humane problem-solving behavior. No such set of opportunities should be allowed to pass unrecognized and unanswered.

The second general component through which services are provided to the students of the school, services that fall outside the regular instructional program, includes those activities that have traditionally been called extra- or co-curricular. We prefer the more contemporary identification: Student Activities Program. In general, the following types of activities are included:

a student government program
student publications
school assembly program
athletics (interscholastic and intramural)
student productions (dramatic and musical)
student clubs (social, departmental, vocational)

The principal is responsible for providing supervision for these activities. Of course, he or she has help in discharging this instructional leadership responsibility. In larger school units, it may be necessary to establish an activities coordinating council through which the objectives and their derivative operational policies might be routinely examined, reaffirmed, and/or modified. The principal should ensure that the activities themselves produce observable educational value, that they are in fact nondiscriminatory, that they are managed with little or modest cost to students, and that they satisfy recognized and accepted student needs. Wood, Nicholson, and Findley suggest a set of guidelines for student activity programs that all people involved with them would find helpful. Key elements are the following:[15]

1. Student activities should be developed as a result of genuine interest by students.
2. The student activities program should provide for balance between the various kinds of activities.
3. Student activities should have educational values that students can draw upon throughout their life.
4. The student activities program should reflect democratic values.
5. Student activities should be scheduled so that maximum opportunity is available for participation by all.
6. Procedures should be established which insure that a few students don't monopolize the student activities that are available.
7. Adequate faculty supervision should be provided.
8. Each organized group should submit their charter to the student governing body for approval.
9. Student participation in student activities should not involve excessive cost to the individual or the school.
10. Financial accounting systems for student activities should be established in accordance with good bookkeeping procedures.
11. Careful consideration must be given to the establishment of criteria for membership in each activity.
12. The student activity program should be evaluated periodically.

The most direct involvement of the principal in this set of activities occurs in the interscholastic realm and in the financial accounting aspects of the organization's activities. Both present unique opportunities to demonstrate facilitative leadership. The interscholastic activities make possible collaborative planning and consensual decision making of a very different order than do activities that are limited to the school unit itself. In large school systems especially, they involve relationships not only with representatives of other school units but also with central office staff who have coordination responsibilities. The management of internal (activity) accounts enables the principal to demonstrate clearly a facilitative rather than a control orientation simply by the accounting procedures that he or she requires and the efficiency with which they are operated. For example, a proposed expenditure request that falls within system guidelines should be cleared by the principal routinely and with dispatch. It should never be delayed without cause.

[15]Charles L. Wood, Everett W. Nicholson, and Dale G. Findley, *The Secondary School Principal* (Boston: Allyn & Bacon, 1979), pp. 218–219.

The readiness with which students approach the learning opportunities afforded through the regular program of instruction frequently is a reflection of the quality of the program of student personnel services. And, just as frequently, the most significant learning experiences for specific students occur through these activities. It is reasonable to expect the principal to invest a significant portion of his or her time and energy in this important phase of instructional supervision.

UNOBTRUSIVE OPERATION OF SUPPORTING SERVICES

Supporting services in the school unit are defined to include all activities, professional or otherwise, that are necessary to the unit's operation but are outside the actual operation of the program of instruction. Such essential services as the following are included within this definition: supplemental instructional services (visiting guidance personnel, media personnel, instructional consultants, etc.), maintenance and supply services, custodial services, pupil and faculty records maintenance, financial services, health services, transportation, food services, and the school office itself. It is clear that the principal has direct management or supervisory responsibility for few of these services. In most schools his or her responsibility does not extend beyond the management of the school office. All other services are directed customarily from a systemwide or central office organizational unit. The principal is not relieved of some measure of responsibility by such arrangements. Rather than directing and/or supervising the work of the individuals who provide these services, the principal's responsibility is a coordinative one. He or she must ensure that the services needed by the faculty are in fact provided properly and in a timely manner. In short, the principal's task regarding supporting services is to see that the work is being done.

To discharge his or her responsibility, the principal must be fully aware of the systemwide services that are available. It is both necessary and appropriate that he or she maintain a close liaison with the offices that supervise the several services. Further, it is advisable that this liaison activity be organized informally by the principal to establish a network consisting of the individuals who provide the services to his or her building. Information flow in both directions, from the principal to the service unit as well as the reverse, is enhanced by such activity. And the result is the best possible supporting services for the school and friends among the support staff. Such performance by the principal provides hard evidence of his or her commitment to facilitative leadership.

There is some difference of opinion regarding the degree of involvement a principal should allow himself or herself in activities involved in the management of supporting services. One position holds that most of these activities should be delegated to subordinates.[16] Strong support for this argument comes from the reports of those who have observed that an inordinate amount of time and energy is sometimes invested by principals in such exciting and ennobling activities as counting milk money, supervising the bus drivers and routes, and checking attendance records. Of course, if such activities do indeed represent the bulk of the work of a given principal, something needs to be done. We would hold, however, that internal accounting, attendance records, and transportation supervision do not represent the whole of supporting services. Neither are they unimportant to the successful achievement of the objectives that guide the activities of the school. More than one principal has failed because of sloppy record keeping, and more than one school has been engulfed in controversy as a result of transportation problems. The answer is not found in assigning the coordination of these activities to a subordinate, even if that were possible within the school. Rather, the implementation of a facilitative pattern based on collaborative decisions and collegial actions is to be preferred. It is not unreasonable to assume that the best way for a principal to enable the faculty to conduct successful programs of instruction is to develop and maintain the strongest supporting services that are possible. And a facilitative principal can accomplish that without becoming merely an organizational housekeeper.

One of the first responsibilities of the principal in the area of supporting services is the management of the school office. The office is the communications center of the school. It is the first place most parents and other representatives of the community see when calling at the school. It is vital to understanding the school as well as to the work environment of the school that the office be operated effectively and efficiently and in a friendly and open manner. It should communicate such values by its physical conditions and the behavior of its personnel. The layout should locate work stations conveniently and in accordance with the regular flow of work required by the routines of the office. Provision should be made to segregate noisy office machines from the rest of the space, especially the area intended for the greeting of visitors. There should also be security areas for the handling and storing of cash. It is wise to consider the effective impact of the physical environment of the school office on both those who work in it regularly and those who either are visitors or use it infrequently. It does not seem consistent with the "communications center" identity of the office to use it also as a detention hall. Other arrangements ought to be made for students awaiting disciplinary action.

The key to successful office management is found most frequently in the person of the secretary. In larger school offices, this individual may be known

---

[16]Roe and Drake, op. cit., p. 337.

as the office manager. The secretary contributes significantly to the success the school achieves. He or she is frequently the voice of the school, for the secretary is customarily the first contact one has either via the telephone or in person. A pleasant greeting, one that communicates warmth, confidence, integrity, and willingness to be of service, is an important step in creating a positive attitude toward the school. If the school is large enough to have a clerical staff in addition to the secretary, its supervision becomes part of his or her assignment also. The principal, working with and through the secretary, develops assignments for each individual, assigns priorities to various tasks, and reviews office procedures regularly with the whole office staff. The organization and operational policies of the school office should be presented to the teachers so that they know which workers have which responsibilities.

The role of the principal in the management of supporting services does not differ significantly from his or her role in supervising instructional programs. The successful teaching by teachers and learning by students remains the principal's primary objective. The importance of the supporting services is not in dispute. Their significance is assured by the facilitative principal. They remain unobtrusive, as does the performance of the principal. That means simply that they are noticed only when they are absent or when they are inadequate. It is the norm that they are present and in appropriate supply. Therein lies the challenge for the facilitative principal.

THE QUESTION OF EVALUATION

The principal cannot escape the responsibilities involved in the matter of evaluation. It is necessary to discriminate among the teachers on bases that go well beyond personal preference. The principal is a key person in decisions of great importance in the careers of the faculty and staff, and his or her decisions must be well founded. We hold that these decisions and others of an evaluative nature are central to the success of the principal. Further, we suggest that the facilitative mode can accommodate the evaluation imperative in a growth-enhancing manner. To that end, the purpose of this section is to sketch the perspective regarding evaluation that is appropriate to the facilitative principal.

The Meaning and Function of Evaluation

The concern in these pages is with evaluation in the school unit. We understand evaluation to refer to the placing of value on a process, an object, a product, or a person. Educational usage suggests that evaluation is ''the process of ascertaining or judging the value or amount of something by use of a standard of appraisal.''[17] The process or methodology of evaluation includes four elements: the collection, organization, analysis, and reporting of information. Evaluation, then, is a process designed intentionally to improve the rationality of decisions made about the value or worth of an individual's performance. It can be understood as an information process, a decision-making process, or a management process. But its uniqueness derives from its value-assigning characteristic, which is especially sensitive when the performance of people is involved. In the school unit, the evaluation includes the assessing of student achievement, program success, and teacher performance. Although the principal must be vitally concerned with the effectiveness of instructional programs as well as the assessment of student achievement and the system through which those assessments are reported, the present comments focus attention on personnel performance evaluation. Evaluation, in that context, refers to making judgments about the value of the contribution of individual teachers and staff to the success of the educational programs of the school.

Evaluation or assessment activities serve several purposes within the school unit. The accountability movement of recent years is a reflection of the concern of both the public and the profession with quality, the quality of the "output" of educational institutions. Consequently, one purpose of a regular evaluation program is to provide information for the public's review concerning selected quality factors. A second purpose is administrative. The fact that teachers differ in their abilities, and consequently their performance, requires that different responses be made to questions about the promotion and reward of individuals. It is quite simply necessary to evaluate performance when making decisions about the employment, placement, salary, promotion, or tenure of a teacher. But evaluation ought to serve a third purpose also. All evaluation activities must be designed and operated in ways that enable the teacher to improve his or her personal and professional performance. The consequence of an evaluation exercise should not be limited to helpful information for the public or to administrative assistance in personnel matters. It must help the individual to become a better teacher. It must enable the teacher to grow on the job. Evaluation that fulfills this purpose contributes not only to the development of the individual teacher but also to the improvement of the school. The purpose of evaluation within a school unit, then, provides indicators of movement toward successful achievement of objectives.

The nature of the evaluation activity is determined largely by the needs of the school as perceived by the principal. The facilitative principal understands evaluation to be primarily a developmental rather than a "terminal" exercise. That is, an evaluation contributes to the ongoing activities by reporting its findings first to those who are involved in the school. If the activity being evaluated is

---

[17]Carter V. Good, ed., *Dictionary of Education* (New York: McGraw-Hill, 1973), p. 220.

the performance of a teacher (or other staff person), the findings are reported to that individual rather than to a superior administrator or a personnel file. If the activity being evaluated is an experimental instructional program, the findings are reported first to the staff responsible for operating the program. This type is called *formative evaluation* for it is intended to assist the developer or operator of a program. Evaluations that are intended to estimate the impact of a program or an activity are called *summative evaluations*.[18] Although the principal will be called upon to be familiar with each, facilitative behavior requires the formative point of view to predominate even when impact evaluations are required by the circumstances. It is in the operation of evaluation exercises that the understandings and skills of the facilitative principal will be demonstrated.

An Evaluation Process

The principal, involved in both formal and informal evaluation exercises routinely, must first develop an evaluation process or system that can be useful to him or her. A suggested pattern is presented in Figure 13-1. The six-step evaluation process starts with an identification exercise and concludes with a reporting exercise. It is a process that can service both the formative and summative modes. The first step is the identification of the practice or activity to be evaluated as well as the standards by which the evaluation will be made. It will result in a clear and precise statement describing that which is to be evaluated and the criteria to be used. The second step simply requires that the observation be made. It will produce a thorough description of the activity being evaluated. The third step requires that a comparison between the observation(s) and the criteria be made. The report of the observations should be organized in a format that facilitates direct comparison. The nature of the display is dependent on the sophistication of the exercise and the data. The comparison might be accomplished through verbal anecdotes or by statistical techniques. The fourth step identifies and reports any and all discrepancies between the criteria and the observations. A descriptive and clear report form should be developed to aid in completing this step. It should fit the nature of the evaluation and be easily understood by the recipients of the report. The fifth step is the judgment phase of the process. Meaning is assigned to the identified discrepancy. The judgment—from "good" to "bad" or equivalent terms—is sometimes implied by the criteria, or a specific evaluation may require an additional standard. And, finally, the sixth step requires that the "meaning" of the findings as well as the findings themselves be reported to the appropriate individual(s) or agencies. The nature of the evaluation exercise influences heavily the nature of the reporting

---

[18]Scarvia B. Anderson, Samuel Ball, R. T. Murphy, and associates, *Encyclopedia of Educational Evaluation* (San Francisco: Jossey-Bass, 1975), pp. 175–178 and 406–408.

Figure 13-1. A Six-Step Evaluation Process

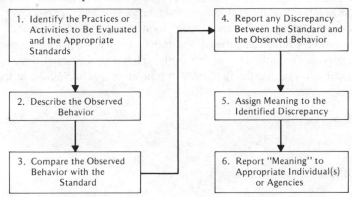

device and technique. For example, if a formative evaluation is being reported, the affected individual has probably been involved in several of the steps of the process and is ready to understand the "meaning" as well as the range of meanings that are pertinent to the exercise.

The utilization of this or some other rational model enables the principal to both practice facilitative leadership and to assess his or her performance concurrently. It is a recommended activity.

SUMMARY

The principalship has been discussed as the administrative leadership position at the front line of educational activity, the local school unit. The occupant of the position is required to deal with a variety of issues, the common denominator of which is their focus on people. The issues that vie for the principal's attention revolve around the people with whom he or she interacts on a daily basis—students, teachers, and parents. The birth and development of this administrative role has paralleled closely the growth of American education. It is proposed that the contemporary principalship should be characterized by its facilitative nature. The facilitative principal demonstrates respect for individuals, is skilled in goal clarification and conflict resolution, and places top priority on his or her instructional leadership responsibilities. Those responsibilities involve stimulating the development and/or maintenance of an institutional climate that encourages open, collaborative, informal, and flexible behaviors that are people oriented and goal directed. This is a difficult challenge. It can be met successfully by a facilitative principal through supervisory relationships with those that are collegial rather than controlling, through supporting strong student services that are broadly defined, through developing a truly service-oriented perspective within the supporting services staffs, and through focusing on the developmental values of the formative evaluation patterns and processes. Through these approaches, supplemented by a continuing program of personal professional development, the principal can become the facilitator of educational achievement at the front line.

EXERCISES

1. As the new principal of a large high school, you become convinced that the quality of instruction is better than its reputation, but you were appointed with the explicit charge to provide "instructional leadership." It is obvious that many—perhaps most—of the faculty do not accept the idea that a principal should adopt such a leadership posture because to do so imposes on teachers' professional rights. Knowing these things, what is your plan of action?

2. As the principal of an urban junior high school, you are convinced that effectiveness requires more diversification of staff than is currently possible; thus, you want to move toward some variant of differentiated staffing. You like the model that calls for master teachers, associate teachers, aides, and some technical help. But this has been criticized by the teachers' union because it tends to look too much like a seniority system. What are your chances of getting it?

3. As assistant superintendent for instruction, you have learned that there is a growing controversy over the plan to mainstream handicapped students in all schools and that the council of principals is asking for this as an agenda item. You are convinced there is still misunderstanding about the concept of "least restrictive environment." How, do you think, can teachers accept this idea if principals do not understand it? How can you develop an attitude of strong support and readiness among principals?

4. As a principal, you are having some difficulty resolving the apparent anomalies between your role as a supervisor and the necessity that you also must evaluate those you supervise. Can you separate these functions, and how can you justify the amount of time that productive supervision demands? Is this also a time management and staffing issue?

5. In one school system, a student fainted and tumbled down several steps and was still unconscious when you arrived. Whether you are a teacher or a

principal, what are you going to do? Determine also what emergency procedures are appropriate for other situations and circumstances.

6. Pregnancy among high school girls is much greater in contemporary society, and there is more tolerance of this condition. What is a good and effective policy for dealing with this problem?

7. Consider that you are a stranger to a local school. What would your impressions be? Go to a school other than one with which you are familiar and record your impressions of the way in which you are received and treated. What was good and not so good about the "environment" there?

SUGGESTED REFERENCES

Bean, Reynold, and Clemes, Harris. *Elementary Principal's Handbook: New Approaches to Administrative Action.* West Nyack, N.Y.: Parker, 1978.

Blumberg, Arthur, and Greenfield, William. *The Effective Principal.* Boston: Allyn & Bacon, 1980.

Erickson, Donald A., and Reller, Theodore L., eds. *The Principal in Metropolitan Schools.* Berkeley, Calif.: McCutchan, 1978.

Hall, Brian P. *Values Clarification as a Learning Process.* New York: Paulist Press, 1973.

Lipham, J. M., and Hoeh, J. A., Jr. *The Principalship: Foundations and Functions.* New York: Harper & Row, 1974.

Mintzberg, Henry. *The Nature of Managerial Work.* New York: Harper & Row, 1973.

National Association of Secondary School Principals. *Job Descriptions for Principals and Assistant Principals.* Reston, Va.: NASSP, 1976.

Roe, William H., and Drake, Thelbert L. *The Principalship,* 2nd ed. New York: Macmillan, 1980.

Simon, Sidney B., and Kirschenbaum, Howard, eds. *Readings in Values Clarification.* Minneapolis, Minn.: Winton Press, 1973.

Wood, Charles L.; Nicholson, Everett W.; and Findley, Dale G. *The Secondary School Principal.* Boston: Allyn & Bacon, 1979.

Chapter 14

Epilogue: Administration as a Continuous Beginning

Mintzberg has noted that managerial work—the activities that occupy the attention of the administrator daily—is characterized by a variety of brief, fragmented activities that occur at an "unrelenting pace."[1] Educational administrators, those who serve at the building level as well as those who work in central offices, are inundated by daily detail; great quantities of detail! The "in" basket is seldom empty. Indeed, it more often overflows. The telephone regularly imposes on conferences and consciousness alike with its jangling imperative. People wait upon the director of the building and upon the service department routinely with issues requiring if not demanding nearly instant treatment and solution. The educational administrator cannot escape these demands, for they supply the raw material of leadership.

Whereas repeating a simple activity frequently carries with it little excitement or interest for the individual who has mastered it, again, using specific skills in varying combinations can produce something new or novel. We think, for example, of the composer who applies a knowledge of the specific sounds and timbers of different instruments repeatedly in great variation; or we think of the successful football coach who demands that the players go through specific "quickness" drills over and over again until the patterns are firmly implanted in the response mechanisms of each individual. In each instance, the consequence of repetitions is socially valued, although individuals may well debate the relative merits of the two examples. Of course, the situation of the administrator differs significantly from that of either the composer or the coach. For

---

[1]Henry Mintzberg, *The Nature of Managerial Work* (New York: Harper & Row, 1973), pp. 28–35.

316

example, the administrator does not initiate the set of circumstances that involve the repetitions. Consequently, both their purpose and their control lie essentially outside his or her realm of action. It is not the administrator's purpose that is being served when several staff members bring the same request, nor does he or she control the timing or the nature of the requests, and thus a certain sense of being unnecessarily imposed upon may well creep into one's self-consciousness. It should also be noted that in each accumulated and apparent repetition, the initiator of, for example, the question, may well be having a new and a first-time experience. It may well not be a "repetitious" incident for that individual, and neither will it be purposeless. The disaffected administrator has been blinded to these facts by the sheer frequency of confrontations with the same inquiry and consequently despairs the condition of always being at the beginning.

In addition to facing relatively minor issues repeatedly, administrators can also become frustrated by the open-endedness of their work. It is not unusual (indeed it may even be the norm) for a principal or a superintendent to be uninformed about the consequences of a specific recommendation or decision. Especially is this consequence characteristic of the issues of lesser scope that are crowded into the administrator's day. And in the case of major actions, the administrator is seldom aware of the host of consequences that result, in ripple-like fashion, from the decision. It seems, then, that neither the passive (reactive) administrator nor the one whose style is more active can be protected from the incompleteness to which we refer as open-endedness. The administrator in educational institutions simply does not have the luxury of seeing the consequences of his or her work in concrete form. It is necessary to see the results of administrative initiatives through the performance of others, often beyond the observation of the administrator. Furthermore, other activities that may have been initiated may obscure the opportunity to follow any single activity through to its conclusion.

So it is that the repetitiousness and open-endedness of much of the work of the school administrator may jaundice the view of an individual occupant of that position. Certainly, if one is unaware of the characteristics that tend to keep the administrator in a state of "continuous beginnings," one is in danger of disappointment at best. The impact of failing to achieve results that are observably "satisfactory" can well be of serious dimensions both for the individual and for the unit being administered. In the case of the individual administrator, such an impact soon produces disenchantment and perhaps a gnawing sense of failure in one's chosen work.

The neophyte administrator must recognize the "continuous beginning" character of the daily work if he or she is to be effective. Awareness is the first step. Students, faculty, and staff should be able to expect their administrators to be aware of and ready to manage the myriad details with some degree of good sense and good nature. As a crusty old athletic director once told a group of high school principals, "They didn't give you that big desk and soft swivel chair for nothin', you know. You're supposed to handle the traffic!!'' ''Handling the traffic'' requires, it seems to us, that the individual be guided by a set of values, values that hold people in high esteem, values that refuse to permit the demeaning and manipulation of individuals simply because they ask ''stupid'' questions or make impossible demands and do so repetitiously. Rather, such values permit, indeed encourage, the understanding of such actions as the material of growth, growth by the individuals posing the seemingly pointless questions, growth of the school itself, and not the least, growth for the administrator who is involved. The ''continuous beginning'' quality of administrative work does, then, have a virtue, a unique virtue.

One of the attractive characteristics of beginnings is the excitement they often engender. Another characteristic of beginnings bears responsibility for that circumstance. Beginnings, in a larger sense, are themselves culminations of a series of activities, of activities that might well be called preparatory.

These characteristics suggest the dimensions of the unique virtue the educational administrator can find in the continuous beginnings aspect of the responsibility he or she assumes. The responsibility cannot be assigned to another; indeed, it is doubtful if it can even be shared. It must be grasped forthrightly and humanely. The problem seems not to reside in the ''beginnings'' nature of much of the work, for it has been demonstrated that beginnings can be fresh and exciting. Rather, the problem seems to be related to the repetitious and open-ended nature in which the beginnings present themselves. The educational administrator's problem is to deal with such issues while not losing the benefits of beginnings for himself or herself and the organization.

SOME BEHAVIORAL REQUISITES

In terms of the behavior of the educational administrator, in place of frustration, he or she needs to see opportunity. Instead of managing a series of unrelated, repetitious trivialities, he or she needs to see opportunities to create a recognizable coherence. The events that comprise the ''unrelenting pace'' at which the administrator works position him or her as the key stone. Links between individuals who were unaware of their common or related interest can be established; links between an individual and resources that will produce achievement can be identified; and links between a specific task or responsibility and an educational objective can be drawn. Seemingly mundane issues also provide the administrator with opportunities to impact on both rigid bureaucratic structures and temporary systems alike with a humane and rational touch that stimulates the growth of understanding and, consequently, of coherence.

Let us consider administrative responses of a principal who receives within a thirty-minute period inquiries from ten students, seven teachers, four patrons, and a board member about a new transportation schedule that had been widely publicized and was developed with broadly based participation and wide-ranging consultation to treat a problem that had caused relatively severe inconvenience for a large number of students the previous year. The inquiries in our example came by telephone and in person during the morning of the first day of school. After the first ten inquiries, one might understand if the responses became short if not curt. Not only should the questioners have known about the change, they should also have been involved in the development of the new pattern. Or so the principal might have reasoned. But to respond in that manner would have denied the proper context of each of the questions as well as the role of the principal. It would have been treating each question as a separate incident related to each other question only by its content. Opportunities to link the content with the commendable process utilized in making the change would have been foregone, as would opportunities to link safe transportation with achieving educational objectives. Also, a principal who would treat the situation in that manner would clearly fail to recognize the multiple and personal objectives at work. The concerns being expressed by students, teachers, parents, and board members could safely be assumed to be different, and the wise administrator should be prepared to seek out those differences before framing a response, however trivial one may believe the inquiry to be. It is necessary to *hear* the speaker as well as the words if the administrator is to establish links that encourage understanding; that is, its seriousness to the questioner must be accounted for by the administrator. Each event, in this example each question, must be understood as a new experience for the questioner, and one that caused some measure of concern. Overcoming the repetitiousness of the work, then, becomes a matter of listening to each person as a unique individual, assigning value to that individual and the inquiry or request, and placing the request in the appropriate context in a way that enables both the individual and the school (or program) to be enhanced. The administrator who is able to develop this skill will find more success and more satisfaction in administrative work, but will not find any less work! Thus, coherence is contextual.

But can open-endedness be managed with equal facility? This condition is most clearly seen at the chief executive level in organizational hierarchies, in the office of the superintendent, but it also is characteristic of all administrative roles. Ambiguity is seen in the necessity to take action, to make decisions, regularly with incomplete information. We are reminded of the veteran superintendent of an explosively growing school system in suburban Washington, D.C. who complained that he could no longer know the whole of the system he led because of its size and complexity. It was necessary "to see the problems and the possibilities through the eyes of my assistants," as he reported his solution to the emerging ambiguity of his role. The farther away from the seat of action an administrator is located in the organizational structure, the greater the chance that an event, proposal, or problem will be reported in vague and imprecise terms or with more than one distinct "meaning." Hence, the condition of open-endedness is compounded by the unavoidable ambiguity that inheres in the very nature of the organization itself.

The primary controls needed in treating the issue of ambiguity reside in the person of the administrator and can be developed as can other skills. For example, an inventory of personal needs and objectives can provide a beginning. Recognition of one's own needs permits one to ameliorate stress-producing differences between the self and the demands of the organization, and movement toward the facilitative mode suggested in Chapter 13 has been initiated. The superintendent can then develop his or her sensitivity to the people in the system to deal with the continuingly unresolved issues that produce ambiguity. A set of five characteristics will mark the behavior of the administrator whose personal development is moving in this direction.[2] Such an administrator is, in the first instance, a self-activating *action-oriented* individual. He or she takes initiatives that produce the information needed to support given actions. Further, the action-oriented administrator assumes that the members of the faculty and staff are also action oriented, at least in regard to their own personal needs. The action-oriented principal or superintendent is characterized by high levels of energy and a willingness to do things. This administrator also is a *decision maker,* one who does not back away from hard choices. Choosing is unavoidable for all administrators, and tough decisions frequently cause anxiety. But the behavior of the growth-oriented superintendent or principal evidences the willingness and the ability to make difficult, but informed, decisions in a manner that respects all people involved. The third characteristic of the ambiguity-reducing administrator is *objectivity*. We do not speak of objectivity as it is used in management, that is, as an impersonal rationalism. Objectivity for the principal or the superintendent means having a clear understanding of the consequences of his or her behavior, both positive and negative. To be truly objective, then, the administrator would be called upon to estimate the whole range of possible consequences of each alternative under consideration and be prepared to deal with the consequences of the action taken. The fourth characteristic of our growing administrator is *authenticity*. We have dealt with this characteristic at some length in Chapter 11, but its significance urges us to comment on it again in this context. The administrator who confronts "continuous beginnings" with constructive results is an authentic person. Such an administrator is one who behaves honestly, as he or she really is. Finally is the characteristic of *tolerance*. The tolerant

---

[2]Adapted from Anders Richter, "The Existentialist Executive," *Public Administration Review,* Vol. 20, no. 4. (July–August 1970), pp. 69–73.

administrator recognizes and insists upon the freedom of other people in the system and its community and recognizes that such freedom imposes no constraints on his or her own. Behavior that characterizes this kind of tolerance is far from passive. For example, an administrator practicing this kind of tolerance does not assist in the resolution of conflict through relying on compromise alone, but rather insists on enlarging the range of options to include new bases for potential solution. This is an active tolerance.

And so, confronting "continuous beginnings" and their frustrations involves administrative behaviors that are oriented toward action, decision making, objectivity, authenticity, and tolerance. It is through such behaviors that the administrator practices a rich contextualism.

Index of Names

Index of Subjects